Paris on the Brink

Paris on the Brink

*The 1930s Paris of Jean Renoir, Salvador Dalí,
Simone de Beauvoir, André Gide, Sylvia Beach,
Léon Blum, and Their Friends*

Mary McAuliffe

ROWMAN & LITTLEFIELD
Lanham • Boulder • New York • London

Published by Rowman & Littlefield
An imprint of The Rowman & Littlefield Publishing Group, Inc.
4501 Forbes Boulevard, Suite 200, Lanham, Maryland 20706
www.rowman.com

Unit A, Whitacre Mews, 26-34 Stannary Street, London SE11 4AB, United Kingdom

Distributed by NATIONAL BOOK NETWORK

Unless otherwise noted, all translations are by the author.

The map of Paris is by Mapping Specialists.

British Library Cataloguing in Publication Information Available

Library of Congress Cataloging-in-Publication Data Available

ISBN 978-1-5381-1237-3 (cloth : alk. paper)
ISBN 978-1-5381-1238-0 (electronic)

∞™ The paper used in this publication meets the minimum requirements of American National Standard for Information Sciences—Permanence of Paper for Printed Library Materials, ANSI/NISO Z39.48-1992.

Printed in the United States of America

3 4633 00330 2716

For Jack

~

Contents

	List of Illustrations	ix
	Acknowledgments	xi
	Introduction	1
	Map of Paris	3
Chapter 1	End of an Era (1929)	5
Chapter 2	Rags and Riches (1929)	21
Chapter 3	It Could Never Happen Here (1930)	43
Chapter 4	The Ooh La La Factor (1930)	63
Chapter 5	Navigating a Dangerous World (1931–1932)	81
Chapter 6	Taking Sides (1933)	107
Chapter 7	Bloody Tuesday (1934)	127
Chapter 8	Sailing, Sailing (1935)	149
Chapter 9	Coming Apart (1936)	169
Chapter 10	War in Spain (1936)	181
Chapter 11	End of the Dream (1937)	197
Chapter 12	In War's Shadow (1938)	221

Chapter 13   Dancing on a Volcano (1939)   241

Chapter 14   Closing the Circle (1940)   263

              Epilogue   283

              Notes   299

              Bibliography   335

              Index   345

              About the Author   359

~

Illustrations

Map of Paris, 1929–1940   3

Sylvia Beach in front of Shakespeare and Company   4

Léon Blum   10

Salvador Dalí with sea urchin   19

Elsa Schiaparelli, in costume   20

André Gide   31

Simone de Beauvoir   38

Palais Brongniart, historic home of the Paris Bourse, or
    stock exchange   42

Le Corbusier's Villa Savoye   47

The *deux magots*, from the Café Les Deux Magots   57

Josephine Baker   62

Fountain from the 1931 Paris Colonial Exposition   80

Jean Renoir during the filming of *La Chienne*, 1931   89

Le Corbusier's Fondation Suisse, at the Cité Internationale
    Universitaire de Paris   98

André Malraux   106

Léon Blum and 1934 protests   126

S.S. *Normandie* arriving in New York Harbor   148

Striking workers at gates of Renault plant, 1936   168

Spanish refugees crossing Pyrenees into France, Spanish Civil War   180

Crowd listening to speech by Léon Blum, 1936   196

Palais de Chaillot, from the 1937 Paris International Exposition   200

Gare Saint-Lazare, where Jean Renoir filmed *La Bête humaine*   220

The Rules of the Game set, with Jean Renoir   240

Eve Curie   257

French fleeing before German advance, 1940   262

Memorial, former internment camp at Drancy   280

General Charles de Gaulle on BBC to France, 1941   282

James Joyce, tomb (Zurich)   287

Jean Renoir's residence, Avenue Frochot, Paris   289

~

Acknowledgments

For many years, my delight in probing the cultural, social, and political dimensions of a vibrant yet relatively small and well-defined geographical area has found a perfect subject in the City of Paris. Encouraged by Mark Eversman, longtime publisher and editor of *Paris Notes*, I long ago moved my focus from American to French history, most especially the history of Paris, and have never regretted it. Now, many years, articles, and books later, I am immensely in his debt for providing the impetus for what amounted to a major career change.

I am also greatly indebted to Susan McEachern, my editor at Rowman & Littlefield, who has provided ongoing support for my explorations, beginning with the earliest years of the Belle Epoque and continuing, book by book, through the tumultuous and dazzling history of the Third Republic. Throughout, I have been the fortunate beneficiary of Susan's experience, taste, and judgment, and I deeply value her guidance through obstacles both large and small.

My thanks as well to Jehanne Schweitzer, who, as production editor for all of my books with Rowman & Littlefield, has seen my manuscripts through to publication, smoothing any bumps along the way. I trust her with my manuscripts, which is the ultimate compliment.

I am also deeply grateful to the New York Public Library, which has provided me, as a resident scholar, with a place in its Wertheim Study Room. Without this, my research in the NYPL's vast resources would have been far more difficult.

Last, my deepest thanks to my supportive family, especially to my husband, Jack, who has been with me on this journey from the beginning. He has walked with me every step of the way, and this book, as with its predecessors, would have been impossible without him.

~

Introduction

Emerging from the madcap romp of the 1920s (or *les Années folles*, as these years were known in Paris), denizens of the 1930s aspired to elegance and glamour. But as the Depression spread from America and Britain to the Continent, fewer and fewer could aspire to much beyond getting bread on the table, even though—prompted by cinematic fantasylands—they could and did continue to dream.

Dream, and agitate. For this was a decade of strife, between the shrinking number of haves and the ever-growing masses of have-nots. This decade, beginning with the Wall Street Crash of 1929 and ending with war and German Occupation, was a dangerous and turbulent one in Paris, in which workers began to flex their economic muscle, and those who opposed them struck back with increasing violence. The Popular Front itself, greeted by the masses as the answer to their prayers, was viewed by their bosses as well as by the well-to-do and conservatives of all stripes as a moral as well as political and economic disaster. The fact that the Popular Front's leader, Léon Blum, was Jewish added a dangerous anti-Semitic element to the mix.

Readers of my previous books on Paris—*Dawn of the Belle Epoque, Twilight of the Belle Epoque*, and *When Paris Sizzled*—will recognize many of the major figures here, including Ernest Hemingway, Gertrude Stein, Picasso, Stravinsky, Coco Chanel, and Marie Curie, in addition to Jean Renoir, Sylvia Beach, James Joyce, André Gide, Jean Cocteau, Man Ray, Le Corbusier, and Josephine Baker. But others now make their appearance, most notably Salvador Dalí, Elsa Schiaparelli, Simone de Beauvoir, Jean-Paul Sartre, Henry Miller, and France's first Socialist prime minister, Léon Blum.

1

Without question, life in Paris became increasingly difficult during the 1930s, as the economy and the job market shrank. No longer were foreign workers welcomed in France, as during the 1920s, when they had replaced the millions of French workers lost or wounded during World War I. Jewish refugees from Hitler's Germany, often left wing in their politics, also encountered increasing hostility. The addition of large numbers of impoverished Spanish refugees, fleeing into France during Spain's deadly civil war, only added to the instability of the times, in which workers and the middle class alike were hit by rising taxes and a falling franc. And women workers, welcomed to the workplace during and immediately after World War I, were now being shooed back into their homes, to bear children for a nation that had suffered a huge loss of population and whose numbers were not rising fast enough to compete with Germany.

Overall, there was the threat of Hitler's Germany and Stalin's Soviet Union, as well as Mussolini's Italy—although a number of French conservatives were quite taken with Mussolini, and as the decade progressed, more and more French were looking with longing at Germany, where Hitler dazzled with his Nuremberg rallies and seemed to offer the kind of authority figure, replete with tradition and order, that they yearned for. As the divide between the haves and the have-nots increased, so did the political split between left and right, with animosities growing to supersaturation and exploding in brutal clashes, intensified by the blistering paramilitary leagues of the extreme right.

Yet throughout the decade, Paris remained at the center of cultural creativity, with photography and cinema the new vehicles for artistic expression, alongside an explosion of untraditional expression among a new flock of artists, especially Salvador Dalí and the Surrealists. Coco Chanel may have held tight to her streamlined elegance, but Surrealism had a ripple effect on Parisian fashion, especially the designs of Elsa Schiaparelli, who—along with Dalí—delighted, and profited, in shocking.

Throughout, France regarded its Maginot Line as a sufficient defense against a renewed and rearmed Germany. Much to the dismay of an arrogant but clear-sighted officer by the name of Charles de Gaulle, most French, including the nation's General Staff, were content to remain passively behind this enormous fortification, without considering the developments that warfare under Hitler were taking. France may have limped out of World War I, but it had in fact been victorious, and its citizens now took comfort in that victory. How could Germany, which they had defeated in 1918, return to haunt them now?

It was a question that Germany would answer decisively in 1940.

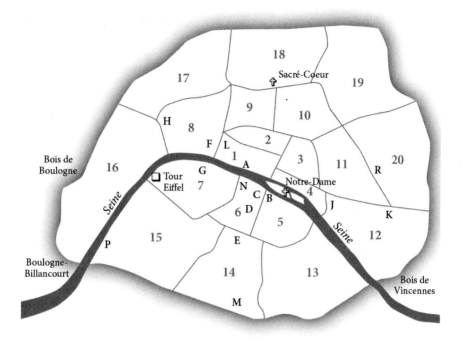

PARIS, 1929–1940

Key

A. Musée du Louvre
B. Sorbonne and Latin Quarter
C. Shakespeare and Company (12 Rue de l'Odéon)
D. 27 Rue de Fleurus (Gertrude Stein)
E. Café du Dôme, Café de la Rotonde, and La Coupole (Montparnasse)
F. Place de la Concorde
G. National Assembly
H. Arc de Triomphe and Place de l'Etoile
J. Place de la Bastille
K. Place de la Nation
L. Place Vendôme
M. Cité Internationale Universitaire de Paris
N. Café de Flore, Café Les Deux Magots
P. Citroën factory, Quai de Javel (now Parc André-Citroën, Quai André-Citroën)
R. Père-Lachaise Cemetery

Paris's twenty arrondissements are indicated by number.

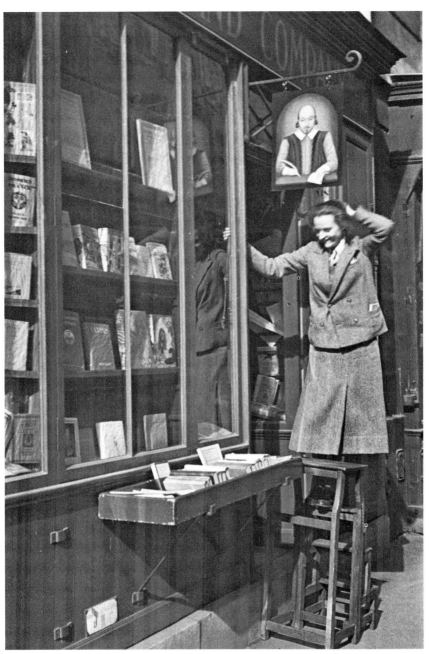

Sylvia Beach bumping her head on the shop sign of her bookstore, Shakespeare and Company, 1936. © Gisèle Freund / IMEC, Fonds MCC, Dist. RMN-Grand Palais / Art Resource, NY

CHAPTER ONE

~

End of an Era

(1929)

On the morning of October 19, 1929, as waves of alarm were beginning to sweep through the New York stock exchange, Sylvia Beach placed a newly published copy of Ernest Hemingway's latest novel, A *Farewell to Arms*, in the window of her Left Bank bookshop, Shakespeare and Company. Hemingway detested the cover, but he had little else to complain about: the first printing of thirty thousand copies had sold out within days, and two more printings of ten thousand each were underway. Its closest competitor that autumn was another unflinching novel from the Great War, *All Quiet on the Western Front*.

Hemingway had first arrived in Paris in 1921 as a young newlywed, eager to partake of the renowned joys of life in the City of Light and to become a famous—and rich—writer. His wife, Hadley, had been just as eager to join the literary life in Montparnasse and the Latin Quarter, which meant getting acquainted with Sylvia Beach, the American owner of the bookshop on Rue de l'Odéon. Ever since its establishment in 1919, Beach's bookstore had been an essential hub for the Left Bank's English-speaking expats, where they could keep up with the latest gossip as well as the latest publications. Beach also served cheerfully as an informal (and free) post office: members of the community regularly left her with messages as well as forwarding addresses for one another, prompting her sympathetic friend, the poet Bryher, to order a post office case for her, complete with cubbyholes.

Shakespeare and Company operated as a lending library as well as a bookstore, but Beach also lent money to her tribe of frequently broke patrons, leading her to observe that she "used to call the shop 'The Left Bank.'"[1] The journalist Wambly Bald took due note of Beach's generosity, and in an October 1929 column for the Paris edition of the *Chicago Tribune* (informally known as the *Paris Tribune*), he wrote that the Left Banker's Trust, located in Sylvia Beach's Rue de l'Odéon bookshop, "is not incorporated and does not extend its favors to everyone. . . . Men of letters have become so attached to the place that they usually call there for their mail, cash checks and borrow money. They usually return the money."[2]

Early in her career as doyenne of Shakespeare and Company, Sylvia Beach established her place in literary history by volunteering to publish James Joyce's *Ulysses* when no other press would touch it. The daughter of a prominent Presbyterian minister, she had lived in Paris during her father's ministry at the American Church there and had returned during the war years. Given Beach's passion for France and for books, a Paris bookstore was a logical if not financially obvious solution to her need to make her own way, free from her parents' oversolicitousness for her health as well as the strain caused by their rapidly disintegrating marriage. Shakespeare and Company began on a small side street, where Beach lived on a daybed in the back room. Aiding her was Adrienne Monnier, owner of the nearby La Maison des Amis des Livres, a bookshop and lending library of French books. Just as the two bookshops complemented one another, so did Beach and Monnier, who soon became partners.

By 1929, Beach had become something of a legend in Left Bank Paris and throughout the literary world. But James Joyce, whose *Ulysses* was the primary source of her fame, was becoming far more of a problem than she was willing to admit.

The poet Bryher (pen name of the English poet and novelist Annie Winifred Ellerman) had by the 1920s become a welcome member of Sylvia Beach's crowd, where she enjoyed a privileged perspective on some of the quarter's leading literary lights, including James Joyce. "He was a naturalist of cities," she observed. "Not a thing escaped his observation, not even the fact that a packet of rice was on another shelf or that the delivery boy's cycle had been moved a few yards up the street."[3]

Joyce's attention to detail frequently astounded those who knew him, as did the oddball nature of his research methods. That summer of 1929, as he continued to write his *Work in Progress* (which would eventually become *Finnegans Wake*), he made a point of visiting the prehistoric site of Kents Cavern, near Torquay. According to Sylvia Beach, Joyce had first been interested in giants, then in rivers. "I think that as his sight diminished," she mused, "his hearing developed so that he lived more and more in a world of sounds."[4] But despite Joyce's severe eye problems, his reading continued, and he regularly dipped into a wide range of newspapers and magazines, which that summer included *The Baker and Confectioner*, *Boy's Cinema*, *The Furniture Record*, *Poppy's Paper*, *The Schoolgirls' Own*, *Woman*, *Woman's Friend*, *Justice of the Peace*, and *The Hairdressers' Weekly*. Also, because of his poor eyesight, he relied on friends, such as young Samuel Beckett, "to look up all kinds of strange data."[5]

Joyce wrote his father that his new book would be about the night, much as *Ulysses* had been about a day, and he similarly told Sylvia Beach that the meaning of *Finnegans Wake* was obscure because it was a "nightpiece."[6] He also insisted that the book's structure was mathematical, and he told Beach that his method of writing was "working in layers" rather than the flat method that others employed. In particular, she noted, "Joyce was for having all the fun you wanted with the word game," and she was as willing as anyone to enter into his Amazonian jungle of language, "so that by the time the whole book appeared I was at home in it and inured to his way of writing."[7]

But friendship with Joyce came at a price—an especially steep one for Beach, who from the outset had taken it upon herself to champion the author and his work, serving as publisher, agent, financial representative (she had his power of attorney), and personal errand runner, all uncompensated. There was no detail in Joyce's life that was too large or small for him to ask Sylvia Beach to handle: he regularly assumed that she should and would drop everything to assist him, and for the most part, she did her best. "I was almost swamped with my one author," she ruefully recalled.[8] Not only were there innumerable errands, but there were also his insatiable demands for money.

At first Beach sympathized with Joyce's steady complaints about the "dreadful struggle" he was having "to make ends meet."[9] But his financial difficulties did not stem from poverty, as she at first so sympathetically supposed. Joyce "spent money like a drunken sailor," one visiting publisher noted, and Ernest Hemingway agreed, caustically noting that "the report is that he and all his family are starving but you can find the whole celtic [sic] crew of them every night in Michaud's," an expensive restaurant on Rue des Saints-Pères.[10] Over time, Beach came to conclude that, while "Adrienne and I just managed to make ends meet by living in the simplest style . . . Joyce liked to live among the well to do." Indeed, Joyce and his family lived in surprisingly high style, occupying a series of large apartments, eating at the best restaurants, and always traveling first class. Beach conceded that, "when you think of Joyce's labors, he was certainly underpaid"—a sentiment with which Joyce wholeheartedly agreed. "But then," she added reasonably, "he should have been a different kind of author."[11]

It never seems to have occurred to Joyce to moderate his style of living, and by the late 1920s, the strain of tending to Joyce as well as looking out for a whole community of expats while running her own bookstore was becoming too much for Beach. She was exhausted, and yet she continued to work on Joyce's behalf—although she was finding it increasingly difficult to give him the total devotion he demanded, especially as her own business eroded.

"Late 1929 was not the best time to be living abroad," Beach recalled. Even though the effects of the "Wall Street killapse" (as she called it) were slow to reach Paris, by early December she could see that businesses involved in the tourist trade were beginning to feel the crunch.[12]

Beach sensed what was coming, but Joyce remained untroubled. He published a segment from his ongoing *Work in Progress* in the literary magazine *transition*, which then suspended publication for financial reasons, not to reappear until 1931. In the meantime, Joyce did not write; instead, he threw his energies into boosting the career of an Irish tenor whose voice he admired, and with whom he shared a common bond: according to Beach, they "both suffered from what they fancied was persecution."[13]

On that day in October when Sylvia Beach placed Hemingway's *A Farewell to Arms* in the front window of Shakespeare and Company, few in Paris anticipated the impact that the U.S. stock market collapse was about to have on their lives. Wall Street's Great Crash, when it came—on Tuesday, October 29—struck quickly and brutally in America, then rapidly spread to Great Britain, but its effects were slower to reach France. Unlike other nations, France in late 1929 was at the peak of its postwar prosperity.

Two weeks after the Great Crash, France's incoming prime minister, André Tardieu, was predicting sunny skies and clear sailing ahead. Based on France's preceding three years of financial prosperity, he announced a five-year program of public spending financed by the huge treasury surpluses that had been piling up. By now, France's budget surplus was nearly four billion francs, and the stock of gold in the Banque de France was growing rapidly. Industrial production held steady, bolstered by orders through the end of 1930, while exports remained high, benefiting from France's 1928 devaluation, which made French exports nicely competitive in the world market. Despite the economic trauma hitting America and Great Britain in late 1929, the French believed they were in no danger. Neither they nor their new prime minister thought that steps were needed to stave off the spreading economic crisis.

As it happened, France seems to have escaped immediate economic devastation because it was somewhat insulated from the global economy, being less invested in the stock market and having a solid banking system—one with control on credit as well as an impressive accumulation of gold. In addition, and not insignificantly, France had lost so many men during the Great War that, as joblessness rapidly spread elsewhere, unemployment in France remained a distant concern. Yet, from the French point of view, it was sensible hard work and thrift that had brought them through the difficult years of postwar reconstruction, and they were confident that, given continued expression of the same solid virtues, only good years lay ahead.

Tardieu came to power shortly after Edouard Daladier, of the moderate-to-left-leaning Radical party, had been called on to form a new government and tried to entice the Socialist party (the French Section of the Workers' International, or SFIO)[14] into a center-left coalition. Daladier offered the Socialists tempting bait, including several ministries and a left-leaning program (reductions in military spending, a lowering of sales taxes, and paid vacations for some workers). Daladier even offered the position of deputy prime minister to Léon Blum, the head of France's Socialist party.

It was tempting. But the Socialists had been there and done that during the mid-1920s and were disinclined to venture that way again. Daladier's shot at forming a government failed, and the conservative Tardieu stepped into the breach. Blum, who had swayed the outcome, found himself widely criticized, not only within his party but across large sections of public opinion, but he was having none of it. Entering the government, Blum argued, would lead the SFIO into the risk of "confusion" with the Radical party. The SFIO, he insisted, should not accept power when that power was shared, nor even when unshared power lacked the backing of a solid parliamentary majority.

As for Tardieu's program, which surprisingly (for a conservative) included public works, social insurance,[15] and free secondary education, Blum summarily dismissed the entire exercise as "militantly reactionary."[16]

Léon Blum, born in 1872 on Rue Saint-Denis to a prosperous Paris dealer of silks and velvets, was raised in a loving and mildly observant Jewish family. An outstanding student, he nevertheless did not do well at the prestigious Ecole Normale and instead headed to law school at the Sorbonne. But what he most wanted to do was write, and soon he was seeing his articles appear with those of other talented young men such as André Gide and Paul Valéry. By the mid-1890s, he was a prominent contributor to the avant-garde *La Revue blanche*, where his aesthetic concerns mingled with an awakening political consciousness.

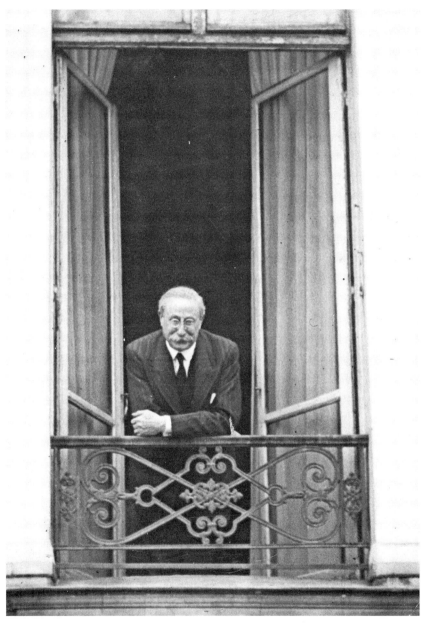

Léon Blum, at the window of his apartment on the Quai Bourbon, 1938. © SZ Photo / Scheri / Bridgeman Images

Social injustice had always roused Blum's deepest passions, and although by his twenties he had become primarily a literary critic, he continued with the law as his profession and was already emerging as a political thinker. Joining France's Conseil d'Etat (Council of State)[17] after an arduous exam, he now earned a comfortable living, and could support his new bride, in the law.

One of the intellectuals whom Blum (and so many other young writers) most admired was Maurice Barrès—at least until the Dreyfus Affair of the late 1890s, when Barrès emerged as leader of the extreme nationalists and anti-Semites who condemned Captain Dreyfus, falsely, of treason.[18] Blum himself came late to the Dreyfus cause,[19] but as a passionate advocate for justice, he became a fervent Dreyfus supporter. Georges Clemenceau, who began his career as the fiery mayor of Montmartre and advocate for the oppressed, drew Blum's admiration for his spirited defense of Dreyfus and Dreyfus's defender, Emile Zola. But it was the great socialist leader Jean Jaurès who truly became Blum's hero and mentor, bolstering the devastated Dreyfus supporters at critical moments and fighting in defense of the Republic. It was no accident when, in 1899, Blum joined the French socialist movement, headed by Jaurès. Soon thereafter, he helped the charismatic leader to found what then was a socialist newspaper, L'Humanité.[20]

At that time, socialism in France was splintered into many factions that roughly gravitated either to Marxist authoritarianism or to what one historian has termed the humanism of Jaurès.[21] During these roiling years, Blum became a staunch advocate of socialist unity, and in 1905 he saw some semblance of unity hammered together into the party called the SFIO, which prospered, both in terms of membership and parliamentary representation. Jaurès soon became the head of this unified socialist movement in France; but Blum resisted the lure of politics and continued to serve the party chiefly as a lawyer and journalist, while continuing his career in literary and dramatic criticism—and enjoying life as a husband and father.[22] His social life, in addition to concerts and the theater, included musical evenings at home with stars such as Alfred Cortot, Pablo Casals, Gabriel Fauré, and Reynaldo Hahn, while he and his wife mingled easily with the cream of the avant-garde artistic set surrounding Misia and Thadée Natanson.[23]

It was a comfortable and happy life, one in which Blum continued his legal and literary career while remaining close personally to Jaurès but aloof from Socialist party politics. Party prospects in fact looked good by the spring of 1914, when success in the spring elections even led to the passage of a top Socialist objective, an income tax law.[24] But the drums of war had begun to roll, and Jaurès's assassination, removing the most powerful French advocate for peace, provided yet one more element that allowed France to stumble directly into a war that would bring unimaginable horror and destruction.

～

Once France was at war, French Socialists backed the war effort and the war government in the name of the *Union sacrée* for national defense. Blum himself, while exempt from military service because of his age (forty-two) and eyesight, served for two years as assistant to the minister of public works. By the war's end, he had emerged as a major figure within the Socialist party and was at the center of a growing rift within the SFIO, which had intensified following the Bolshevik Revolution of 1917. Despite Blum's frantic efforts, the SFIO split in late 1920, with three-quarters of the organization going with the Communists (which now became the PCF, or French Communist party). In the Paris area, the Socialists were almost completely defeated. Even the SFIO's newspaper, *L'Humanité*, went with the winners. Henceforward, the much smaller *Le Populaire* would become the official organ of the French Socialist party.

Not until 1924 did the SFIO claw back some electoral success, leading to an invitation to join the Cartel des gauches (Left-Wing Alliance) in Parliament, along with several centrist and left-of-center groups. During the two years in which Blum and the other members of the SFIO participated in the Cartel des gauches, they found comfort in some of the government's actions, especially the transfer of Jean Jaurès's remains, in high ceremony, to the Panthéon. But they were alarmed by the regime's colonial campaigns and found that they could make little headway on much-desired Socialist goals. When the SFIO broke with the Cartel in 1926, Blum declared that from then on, the SFIO should only assume governmental responsibility if it were in charge—a guideline that, a decade later, would serve as the basis for the Popular Front.

In the following years, Blum—now clearly the leader of the SFIO—endured a drumbeat of attacks from the Communist left and the antirepublican right. Charles Maurras, intellectual leader of France's extreme nationalist, royalist, and antirepublican crowd, wrote that Blum was "a man who should be shot, but in the back," while another right-winger recommended that Blum be sent "with the dregs of the European population streaming into our country to concentration camps in Madagascar." Blum calmly replied that "a piece of filth . . . whether it comes from *L'Humanité* or the fascist press, doesn't count."[25] But this torrent of hatred was difficult to dismiss, especially for a man of Blum's inherent kindness and courtesy.

As 1929 drew to a close, the center-left tried to tempt Blum and the Socialists to join in yet another coalition government, using an offer of several ministries and the deputy prime ministership as bait. But Blum had taken that course before and was tired of having to compromise endlessly with those who had little interest in the Socialists' program. Instead, he was willing to hold out for a government in which the Socialists were in charge.

It seemed an impossible dream at the time, but Blum had always been a dreamer.

⟋⟍

By the late 1920s, another form of dream had taken hold among some of the most avant-garde writers and artists in Paris. It began with the nihilistic Dada movement, formed in the detritus of the Great War, and soon grew into the dream-obsessed movement called Surrealism. Its basic premise was that art arises from the subconscious, and since (according to its leader, André Breton) Surrealism freed the spirit from the chains of reason, this led the Surrealists into the realms of dream narratives, automatic writing, and explorations of the unconscious. Breton took his disciples a significant step further by relentlessly attacking reason-based Western literary culture, which he considered sufficiently dangerous that extreme actions were justified in opposing it. Perhaps it wasn't surprising when, toward the end of the 1920s, Surrealism under Breton's leadership acquired a stridently political dimension, lurching into the camp of the Communists and expelling those Surrealists who were disinclined to obediently march in step.

Breton's publication, *La Révolution surréaliste*, reflected his uncompromising views, especially its December 1929 issue, in which his *Second Manifesto of Surrealism* appeared. Here, with barely suppressed fury, he denounced those who broke with him for their preoccupation with literary and artistic activities. At the same time, he condemned the Communists for their exclusively political concept of revolution.

It was enough to decimate the strongest of movements, but Surrealism continued to survive and even thrive. In large part this was due to the star quality of some of the movement's newest recruits, chief among them being that strange young Spaniard, Salvador Dalí.

Dalí, a talented and perhaps brilliant painter, and one of the greatest, if not the greatest, self-promoter in the contemporary art world, had been quite consciously at the business of self-promotion from the beginning. Perhaps he was eccentric, perhaps even mad; but then again, perhaps it was all a charade. To this day, no one truly knows. What we do know is that he was born in 1904 in Figueres, Catalonia, the second son of a comfortably well-off notary. The notary's first son seems to have been all-important: he died young, and Dalí's parents believed that somehow their first son was reborn in the second, who arrived scarcely nine months after the death of the first. This eerie situation was exacerbated by young Salvador's likeness to his brother.

A sensitive and precocious child, Dalí quickly concluded that he was not loved for himself. He just as quickly learned to manipulate his parents and sister, who worshiped him and were desperate that he not die, like the unfortunate older sibling. With this as a lever, it was easy enough for young Salvador to get what he wanted, and to rage when he didn't. Later he declared, in an attention-getting opening to his memoirs, that from the age of seven "I wanted to be Napoleon. And my ambition has been growing steadily ever since."[26]

In his brief—and unsuccessful—attempt at elementary school, Dalí spent his time fabricating what he later called "false memories," noting that "the difference between false memories and true ones is the same as for jewels: it is always the false ones that look the most real, the most brilliant." It was at this time, between the ages of seven and eight, "that the growing and all-powerful sway of revery [sic] and myth began to mingle in such a continuous and imperious way . . . that later it has often become impossible for me to know where reality begins and the imaginary ends."[27]

By now, as one biographer has concluded, Dalí was "a monstrously spoiled precocious infant who had to be amused, placated, petted, humored, and protected from life."[28] Everything had to be done for him, from tying his shoes to turning the handle on a door. His dependency was tyrannical, and as a result, he could not so much as cross a street by himself. Painfully shy as well as dictatorial, he took refuge in exhibitionism, whether in unusual costumes or by hurling himself down the stairs. But he managed to educate himself by reading, widely, in his father's well-stocked library, and at some point took up painting. Despite his unfortunate early experience with school, he successfully navigated a secondary school run by Marist friars and joined a municipal school of drawing, whose teacher's draftsmanship Dalí admired. By his mid-teens Dalí was exhibiting his work in public to considerable acclaim. He also wrote poetry, art criticism, and short stories, publishing them in a magazine he founded at the age of fifteen.

Despite his continued helplessness in everyday life, Dalí entered the San Fernando Academy of Fine Arts in Madrid, where he met up with the future filmmaker Luis Buñuel and poet Federico García Lorca, who quickly discovered that this strange young man was an outstanding artist. Even at this age, Dalí was still unable to navigate the real world on his own; Buñuel later recalled a time when he and Lorca asked Dalí to go across the street to buy some theater tickets and later learned that he had been unable to figure out how to do it. Still, Buñuel and Lorca introduced Dalí to Madrid's literary cafés and to admirers of Dada, as well as to adherents of a variety of leftist political persuasions, with which Dalí (like his father) sympathized. Dalí's strong political beliefs in turn led to an episode where he took an action (innocently, he later claimed) that led to a student uprising and to his expulsion for a year. Trouble continued back in Figueres, where he was arrested and sent to jail for political sedition—this during a time of dictatorship in Catalonia. After that, he seemed to have learned to keep his mouth shut.

Returning to Madrid, he renewed his friendship with Buñuel and Lorca, and the three were inseparable during several long summers together—until Dalí discovered Lorca's homosexuality and abruptly cut him out of his life (perhaps a defensive stance, given Dalí's repeated efforts throughout childhood to look like a girl, and his frank admission later that he had wanted to be "like a beautiful woman"). But by 1925, Dalí was focused on his painting, and he had his first one-man show at the finest gallery in Barcelona. His paintings were praised, although some complained that they lacked feeling. "He is as cold as ice," his teachers said, and Dalí was pleased to agree.[29]

Revenge seems to have been on his mind when he deliberately failed to take or pass his final exams as a way of punishing his father, who had carried on an affair with Salvador's aunt during the final illness of Salvador's mother. Much to the young man's satisfaction, his father was devastated; this failure meant that Salvador no longer had a safe teaching career before him. Even better, as far as young Dalí was concerned, was that by slamming shut this professional door, he now could pursue a painting career in Paris. Soon after his inevitable school expulsion, he got his way, and in the spring of 1926 he made his first trip to Paris, accompanied by his aunt (now his stepmother) and eighteen-year-old sister. Dalí, now twenty-two, still needed babysitters.

Despite his social infantilism, the young man was adept in professional matters: he had connections to Joan Miró and Pablo Picasso through the Barcelona gallery that had displayed his work, and it was Miró who convinced Dalí's father to let the young man spend some time in Paris. When at last in the City of Light, Dalí looked up Picasso. "I have come to see you," Dalí told him, "before visiting the Louvre." "You're quite right," Picasso replied. Feeling as if he were having an audience with the pope, Dalí felt Picasso's famous eyes drill right through him, and afterward he recalled that each glance that Picasso gave him was "filled with a vivacity and an intelligence so violent that it made me tremble." The great man looked for a long time at a small painting Dalí brought him, then spent two hours showing his own paintings. Throughout the entire time, Dalí was uncharacteristically silent. He left without saying a word, but "just as I was about to leave we exchanged a glance which meant exactly, 'You get the idea?'" And of course, Dalí did indeed get it.[30]

Picasso may have been asserting his kingship, but Dalí was not about to back off. After returning to Figueres, he toiled at his painting, fluctuating between literal representation and semiabstraction. Soon he moved decisively toward Surrealism, painting the grotesque visions that sprang into his imagination. For three years (including his nine months of compulsory military service) he painted, preparing himself for his next trip to Paris. He returned in the spring of 1929, during which Miró paved the way by introducing him as a brilliant young talent.

Dalí was at first completely lost in Paris, where he was without parents or family to help him with every move. His wild laughter, a sign of nervous embarrassment, drew odd looks, but despite these drawbacks, he found himself in exalted company and learned to navigate the social swim. André Breton distrusted him, and rightly so—Dalí had already evaluated the Surrealist movement and decided that it was the "sole one offering me an adequate outlet for my activity . . . [where] I was going to make a bid for power"[31]—but others were quite taken with the young Spaniard. Even his fits of laughter began to serve a purpose as he learned to feign madness, which made him distinctive—a definite plus in the world he was entering. Among Dalí's earliest conquests were the Vicomte and Vicomtesse Charles de Noailles, all-important patrons of the most avant of the avant-garde.

It was Charles and Marie-Laure de Noailles who provided important backing for a joint film following Luis Buñuel and Dalí's *succès de scandale* of that year, *Un Chien Andalou* (*An Andalusian Dog*). Famously, or infamously, *Andalusian Dog* contained one of the most shocking scenes in a movie—a razor slicing through an eyeball (the scene used an ox's eye and was shot in a slaughterhouse, but nevertheless Buñuel was ill for several days after shooting the sequence). Buñuel and Dalí's basic rule in making the film was that "no idea or image that might lend itself to a rational explanation of any kind would be accepted." Buñuel filmed the whole thing in two weeks, and according to him, "there were only five or six of us involved, and most of the time no one quite knew what he was doing."[32]

At the film's October showing, members of the extreme-right Jeunesses Patriotes and Camelots du Roi burst into the theater and trashed the place, creating the kind of publicity that led to a nine-month run. It also led to the offer by Charles and Marie-Laure de Noailles for another Dalí-Buñuel film, *L'Age d'Or*, which the two planned to begin later in the year.

But before the October debut of *Andalusian Dog*, Dalí had returned home for the summer, where he signed a contract with Camille Goemans to act as his agent and to mount Dalí's all-important Paris debut exhibit in November. That summer, Goemans visited the Dalí family at their beach place in Cadaqués, accompanied by Luis Buñuel, the painter René Magritte, and Magritte's wife. Soon the poet Paul Eluard, Eluard's wife Gala, and their daughter Cécile joined them. Despite Dalí's claims in his memoirs to youthful brothel visits and steamy street encounters, he had until then shown little interest in women. That is, until he met Gala.

Gala Gradiva, the muse of the Surrealists, had been married to Philip Eluard for more than a decade when she and Dalí met that summer on the beach of Cadaqués. Russian, with a mysterious background that may have included illegitimacy and certainly included mental illness, Gala was a small, dark-haired dynamo who inspired some of the biggest names in the Surrealist movement. Eluard was devoted to her but serially unfaithful, with a taste for threesomes that Gala for a time accommodated—Max Ernst being the third member of the trio. But by the time Dalí met Gala in 1929, this particular threesome had disintegrated, and her marriage to Eluard was on the rocks. Far from graciously conceding Gala to Dalí, as legend has it, Eluard by this time was chasing after Nusch, a beautiful German whom he married after he and Gala divorced. There would be no break between Eluard and Dalí over Gala.

Gala stunned Dalí, and after some hideous attempts at presenting himself in the most grotesque manner possible, he appeared in a cleaned-up version, sitting speechless (once the laughing fits were over) at her feet. As for Gala, she was in some ways as crazy, or as calculatedly crazy, as Dalí. When he pulled back her head by the hair and shouted, "Now tell me what you want me to do to you! But tell it to me slowly . . . with the crudest, the most ferociously obscene words," she quietly replied that she wanted him to kill her.[33] After considering this, they both cooled down sufficiently that her death wish evaporated and their life together began.

Or something like that. It never was possible to know what was really going on in Dalí's mind, or in Gala's either, even—or especially—when Dalí was presenting himself with apparent candor, whether in conversation, interviews, or his memoirs. Was Dalí a borderline nutcase, or was he a calculating fraud—or somewhere in between? Was Gala truly as smitten by him as she claimed to be, or was she a predatory opportunist? Some likened her to a panther on the prowl, and rumor had it that she chose Dalí because she immediately realized that he would make money.

According to Dalí's analyst, Dr. Pierre Roumeguère, Gala "realized that Dalí was a genius and that this would be her great work. . . . She found this sorry-looking invalid; she was going to mother one of the great men of his epoch."[34] As if confirming this, Gala exclaimed, "My little boy!" when she and Dalí first reached out to one another, adding, "We shall never leave each other." According to Dalí, she saved him from madness. She "cured my madness," he wrote. "My hysterical symptoms disappeared one by one, as by enchantment."[35]

By late autumn 1929, back in Paris, Dalí had reached a new peak in his career: his November show was a big hit (all his paintings sold, at high prices); *Andalusian Dog* continued to do well; and Charles de Noailles had underwritten *L'Age d'Or*, to be longer than *Andalusian Dog* and a "talkie." At that time, it would be only the third movie with a soundtrack to be made in France. Dalí headed for home that Christmas, prepared to meet with Buñuel to collaborate on the screenplay.

As it happened, they met in Cadaqués rather than at Dalí's home in Figueres, since Dalí's father had thrown him out of the house. Dalí later claimed that his father had erupted over Gala, on the grounds that she was entirely unsuitable for Salvador as a wife; but the real cause seems to have been a chromolithograph of the Sacred Heart that Salvador had exhibited the month before in Paris. Across the Sacred Heart he had scrawled in black letters, "Parfois je crache par plaisir sur le portrait de ma mere" (Sometimes I spit with pleasure on my mother's portrait). Dalí senior had read about this in a newspaper article and was livid. Salvador claimed that he merely intended to attack the Church, but his father saw it more literally—as an attack on Salvador's mother. Behind the entire episode reared the secret affair of Dalí's father and his second wife, Dalí's aunt.

Dalí retreated with Buñuel to Cadaqués, where a second fight erupted. Dalí had one vision of their next film and Buñuel another. Buñuel left in anger. Dalí later claimed that Buñuel betrayed him, but Buñuel felt quite differently, especially after Dalí later described Buñuel as "the messenger of [my] fame"[36] and took credit for being the lone genius behind *Andalusian Dog*—a claim with which Buñuel strongly disagreed. Because of their break, little of Dalí remained in *L'Age d'Or* by the time it appeared in 1930. And the rupture between the two remained, exacerbated by Dalí's future politics.

Yet this did not seem to bother Dalí, who felt no need for Buñuel or for anyone other than Gala. "That I had reached fame I felt and knew the moment I landed at the Gare d'Orsay in Paris," he later wrote of that head-spinning autumn. "From then on I regarded most of the people I met solely and exclusively as creatures I could use as porters in my voyages of ambition."[37]

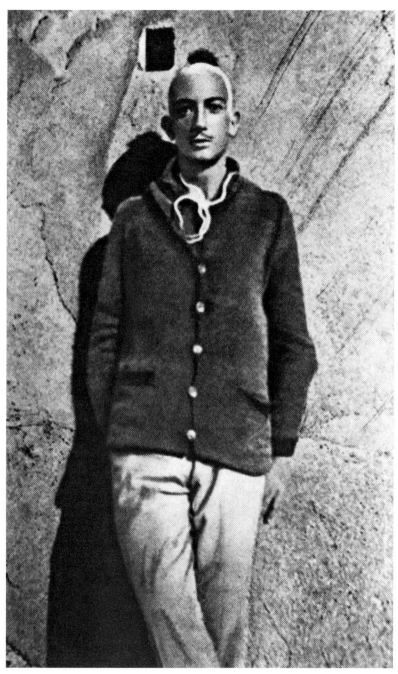

Salvador Dalí in Cadaqués, late 1929, after his father kicked him out of the house. Dalí later recalled that, while in Cadaqués, "I observed the shadow of my profile that fell on a white-washed wall. I took a sea-urchin, placed it on my head, and stood at attention before my shadow—William Tell" (Dalí, Secret Life of Salvador Dalí, *254). © PVDE / Bridgeman Images*

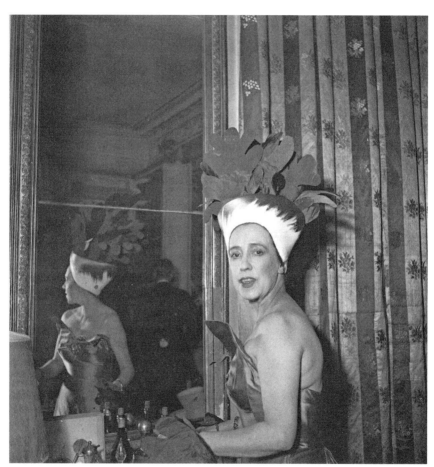

Elsa Schiaparelli, dressed as a radish for a costume ball, the Bal des Quatre Saisons, 1949.
© AGIP / Bridgeman Images

CHAPTER TWO

~

Rags and Riches

(1929)

Barely two weeks after the Wall Street Crash, an ambitious Italian with Paris credentials and a taste for the spotlight arrived from Paris on a short visit to New York. Elsa Schiaparelli, small and dark haired, had once lived in New York, and in fact she had been stone broke with a shaky future when she left Manhattan in 1922. But now, only seven years later, she had become a chic Parisian couturiere who hobnobbed with the celebrities of Montparnasse and would soon find common ground with those edgy members of the avant-garde, Salvador Dalí and Jean Cocteau.

It was quite a story—and Schiaparelli loved stories. A cosmopolitan practically from her birth (1890), she was born in Rome into a family of prominent and well-to-do scholars on her father's side and adventurous aristocrats on her mother's. Unlike her sisters, who were beauties, Schiaparelli was often described as "interesting looking" and spent her childhood in a retreat into books—the more romantic, the better. Much like Salvador Dalí, who would become a friend and collaborator, she performed any number of harebrained stunts to attract attention and early on perfected the art of getting noticed. With a self-described "ardent" temperament, she was a handful from the outset, and even an enforced stay in a Swiss convent school did little to tame her: she went on a hunger strike until they sent her home.

Still, during adolescence she managed to learn English, French, and German and showed some aptitude for cooking, sewing, and writing poetry. Only when her parents proposed to marry her off to an unattractive gentleman of means did she bolt for good, leaving for London but stopping off in

Paris en route. There, she made a sensation at a ball, wearing an impossible dress she had created for herself. Once in London, she met up with William de Wendt de Kerlor, a theosophist, who completely enchanted her. Before her parents could put a stop to it, the two were married. Scarcely a week later, World War I began.

Schiaparelli's new husband was handsome, but he had a sideline of palm reading, which was illegal in Britain; after a series of cautions, he was sentenced to prison and deportation. Evacuating London, the two stayed for a time in Nice, where Schiaparelli took to gambling (without much luck) in nearby Monte Carlo. Her husband then decided that they should try their fortunes in America, and they sailed for New York in April 1916, surviving the threat of German U-boats en route. There, he courted the press with a series of schemes and stunts and did his utmost to find willing patrons; but his fortunes continued to slide, even as Schiaparelli's dowry disappeared. By 1918, they were on the skids—as well as self-described Bolshevik sympathizers—when they took off for Boston, the FBI on their heels.

The FBI soon concluded that they were harmless, but by this time, Schiaparelli had come to the realization that her handsome husband was a fraud. Their marriage was foundering, and at this worst possible moment, she discovered that she was pregnant. In 1920, soon after she had given birth to a daughter (Maria Luisa, nicknamed Gogo), her husband disappeared. Desperate for work and a place to stay, Schiaparelli took to leaving Gogo on the fire escape while she scoured for jobs. Gogo soon contracted polio. Yet even now, with little money, no job, and a very sick child, Schiaparelli refused to return to Rome and to her family: home meant retrenchment. About all she had left was a contact she had made on the Atlantic crossing—Gabrielle Picabia, wife of the French-Cuban painter Francis Picabia, a pioneer in the Dada movement.

Gabrielle, who was well connected with the Paris and New York avant-garde, was now back in New York, her own marriage in disarray. Gabrielle introduced Schiaparelli to some of her artistic New York colleagues, and soon Schiaparelli was involved in their ventures. Tireless, skillful, and organized, as well as keenly sympathetic to her new friends' wildly nihilistic ideas, Schiaparelli did all the bothersome things and soon was put in charge of an exhibition. By 1922, as the emerging Surrealist movement was beginning to take Dada's place (Francis Picabia had already broken with Dada), Gabrielle Picabia concluded that there was a real market in America for Paris fashions, and she decided that Schiaparelli could help with the sales. Accompanied by a friend, Schiaparelli and little Gogo sailed for Paris.

Gabrielle's scheme, which involved the couturiere sister of the great couturier Paul Poiret, never came to anything. But Schiaparelli—who by this time had filed for a legal separation from her husband and had returned to her maiden name—was enchanted with 1920s Paris and decided to stay. Schiaparelli, known to her friends as Schiap, never again suffered from poverty or even the inconvenience of a sick daughter: Gabrielle Picabia, now in Paris, found a doctor who took Gogo into his family, and Schiaparelli moved with a wealthy friend into a large furnished apartment in the fashionable seventh arrondissement. Daytime, she ran the household (with a cook and maid), and evenings, using her ever-growing circle of connections, she hung out in Montparnasse with the in crowd. Moving in the same circles as Man Ray, Francis Picabia, and Tristan Tzara, as well as shipping heiress Nancy Cunard and sewing-machine heiress Daisy Fellowes, she made contacts who would become her collaborators or customers in the years to come.

It was Gabrielle Picabia who helped launch Schiaparelli's fashion career that summer in 1922, when Gabrielle wore a gown that Schiaparelli had created to one of Paul Poiret's glittering open-air events. Poiret noticed and told Gabrielle to convey his compliments. And thus Schiaparelli entered the world of fashion, with little more than creativity, daring, and a mouth full of pins.

Poiret was already on his way down and out in the fashion world, although he would put up a fight throughout the decade; the problem was that his fashions were too intricate and outmoded for modern tastes. Schiaparelli, on the other hand, picked up the prevailing winds of change, contouring her creations for the modern woman, one (preferably with a significant bank account) who preferred a casual, unfussy look, even for evening wear. Schiaparelli's first break came when she completely remodeled that much-derided garment, the sweater, into a knockout fashion statement, knitting together two colors to give an unusual flecked pattern and adding a trompe l'oeil bowknot at the neck. With her unerring instinct for self-promotion, she wore this creation to a luncheon attended not only by rich and fashionable women, but also by some American buyers. She was a sensation, and the buyer from Abraham & Straus placed a large order for skirts as well as sweaters. By late 1927, *Vogue* was calling the Schiaparelli sweater "an artistic masterpiece," and she had already added hand-knitted wool jackets to the pullovers and wool skirts. Late that same year, in partnership with the wealthy businessman Charles Kahn, Schiaparelli formally launched the firm of Schiaparelli and established her first *maison de couture* on Paris's Rue de la Paix—in the building's attic, but nonetheless only a stone's throw from the Hotel Ritz and smack in the center of the universe of the ultrarich.

Already Schiaparelli was branching out into scarves, handbags, and a variety of accessories. And she was incorporating bold and even outrageous elements of Surrealism into her designs, including a sweater flaunting a tattoo-like design of snakes and pierced hearts on the biceps, and another with white skeletal lines outlining the rib cage. Already she was making a sizeable splash in Paris, but Americans were her biggest market—the slimmer, more athletic American figure seemed more suited to her styles. And so, on November 18, 1929, Schiaparelli returned to New York in triumph, with trunks full of clothes and an elegant friend to model them. She also arrived unfettered—her husband had died the year before in a barroom brawl, thus removing any possibility that he could create complications.

Yet her timing was not the best, arriving only a couple of weeks after the Great Crash. Sensing the mood, Schiaparelli had already begun to move away from her predominantly neutral beiges, grays, and blacks into a palette of brighter colors to combat the gloom. She was also moving away from hand-knit sweaters and skirts and toward a new look, one with an accentuated waist and lowered hemline—a look that would define the glamour of the thirties. As she instinctively realized, the Roaring Twenties were over.

Schiaparelli of course was well aware of Coco Chanel, even if Chanel as yet barely recognized Schiaparelli's existence. Chanel, who had scaled the heights of fashion during the 1920s, was rich, admired, and at the center of an international set that boasted some of the biggest names in the artistic world. The Wall Street stock market may have crashed, but despite a decline in wealthy customers, Paris would continue to lead the world in fashion throughout the 1930s, and Chanel would continue to lead the world of fashion.

Her good friend Pablo Picasso was similarly insulated from the economic tidal wave. Even though the Crash left the modern art market "in shambles," as Picasso's biographer puts it,[1] forcing Picasso's agent, Paul Rosenberg, to back off from a major Picasso show for the coming spring, the artist could wait it out, as could his former collaborator, Georges Braque. Henri Matisse was also among this select company, although by the following year, prices even for Matisse canvases had plummeted. By 1934, Matisse would write to his son Pierre that "business isn't going well. I sense a general feeling of apathy."[2]

Nobody was buying modern art now, and collectors were selling off their collections, further depressing the market. Even Picasso's agent, Paul Rosenberg, wasn't buying modern art, restricting his purchases to the Impressionists and post-Impressionists, who seemed a safer bet.[3] Rosenberg would not buy another major Picasso work until 1934. But Picasso suffered little from the Crash, having by now amassed a significant fortune. Some of this went toward conspicuous consumption, such as his luxurious Hispano-Suiza automobile. But on the side, he hoarded gold coins, and he kept a towering stash of banknotes, wrapped in newspaper, in his vaults in the Banque de France. Picasso vastly preferred piles of cash to investments, even if those piles earned no interest.

The Crash found another of Chanel's friends, Igor Stravinsky, strapped for cash (as usual) and anguished about publishers he felt were taking advantage of the fact that, for copyright purposes, he was effectively stateless. After all, he had left behind the Russia of his birth, which in turn had disappeared into the maws of the Bolsheviks. Perhaps, he wondered, he should take out Swiss citizenship, or possibly French? His French courtesy passport was coming up for renewal, and family affairs were pressing. In addition to a sick wife and four children, not to mention an expensive mistress, Stravinsky was saddled with a large and impecunious set of relations, whose tribulations since escaping Revolutionary Russia had put him at wit's end. The Wall Street Crash proved the final straw for one particularly desperate branch of the family, and within several months they owed Stravinsky the sum of fifty thousand French francs. This amounted to about what Stravinsky could earn with several concerts, and as a result of his financial fears, he spent much of the coming year on the road (with his mistress), earning income from playing and conducting, which he viewed as a hedge against the terrible times that he feared were coming.

Chanel herself had little fear in the Crash's aftermath, and indeed spent much of her time in late 1929 dealing with the disintegration of her storied relationship with the Duke of Westminster. Bendor—as he was known to his friends, and to those who breathlessly followed the exploits of the rich and famous—was indeed rich and was well accustomed to the spotlight. An outdoor man and playboy with a history of two unsuccessful marriages and any number of mistresses, Bendor entertained and courted Chanel lavishly during their years together, from cruises on his magnificent yacht, *The Flying Cloud* (with a crew of forty), to house parties at his numerous estates and hunting lodges (Chanel later recalled seventeen Rolls Royces in his Eaton Hall garage alone).

Rumors of their impending marriage circulated and recirculated, but there were insurmountable obstacles, especially Chanel's age (forty-one in 1924, when their affair began) and her apparent inability to bear the heir that Bendor so desperately wanted. In addition, Chanel was a career woman and proud of it; she hesitated to give up that hard-won success and the financial independence that came with it. But perhaps most critical of all was the fact that Chanel, whose hardscrabble background and status as a tradeswoman, albeit a glamorous and successful one, was not the sort of woman that a high-ranking aristocrat such as Bendor could or would marry.

That summer of 1929, their friends noted that Bendor spent little time with Chanel at her own fabulous Mediterranean retreat, La Pausa, and noticed that even when he was there they bickered and fought, especially as Bendor's attentions wandered. He and Chanel continued to cruise together on *The Flying Cloud*, but even there, trouble erupted, most notably on one occasion when Chanel discovered an attractive young woman whom Bendor had brought aboard. Chanel made quick work of her rival, dispatching her ashore, but it was clear that the end was near. By Christmas, Bendor was engaged to an English noblewoman half his age. Despite a reluctant leave-taking of Chanel, to whom he presented his young bride, it was clear that he was determined to find a wife who could bear him a son. As it happened, she did not.[4]

Chanel later told her trusted friend, the writer, socialite, and diplomat Paul Morand, that she had "insisted" that Bendor get married. After all, she mused, "it would be very difficult for a man, unless he were strong, to live with me. And it would be impossible for me, were he stronger than me, to live with him."[5] Probably true, but more to the point, she added, "I grew bored." It may not have been the entire truth, but it sounds about right for this remarkable woman, for whom her trade was her first love.

As she succinctly put it, "Fishing for salmon is not life."[6]

Chanel and her friends, including that adroit and charming hanger-on Jean Cocteau, regularly summered on the Mediterranean and relaxed in numerous other luxury spots. Dwellers of the Left Bank, especially those who were Anglo-American and living off of modest trust funds and their wits, made themselves at home in restored cottages in Normandy or—if they were in Hemingway's crowd—skied in remote villages in Austria, fished in the Pyrenees, and ran with the bulls in Pamplona. But Montparnasse itself was like a small town, complete with small-town bickering—a "very small, backbiting, gossipy little neighborhood," as the young Canadian writer Morley Callaghan put it.[7] Feuds erupted between Ernest Hemingway and Robert McAlmon (who had once been friends with Hemingway and had published Hemingway's stories in his small press, Contact Editions), between McAlmon and F. Scott Fitzgerald, and between Hemingway and Ford Madox

Ford. There were feuds big and small, but the most notable that autumn of 1929 was the one that erupted between Hemingway and Fitzgerald.

Hemingway was notoriously prickly, with a deep need to establish his chest-thumping masculinity, while Fitzgerald was insecure and inclined to self-pity and alcoholism. But the two had been friends ever since they first met in Paris in 1925. At that time, Hemingway had managed to establish himself as a literary person of promise, even without much in the way of publication, but he was on the defensive; Fitzgerald, still in his twenties, was the lauded author of *This Side of Paradise* and *The Beautiful and Damned*, with a new book, *The Great Gatsby*, getting rave reviews. Fitzgerald helped edit Hemingway's first novel, *The Sun Also Rises* (chopping off an overlong beginning), and introduced him to the famed editor Maxwell Perkins of Scribner's. He also had a hand in editing Hemingway's second novel, *A Farewell to Arms*, which was running serially in *Scribner's Magazine* throughout the summer of 1929, where it drew considerable praise.

Hemingway owed Fitzgerald a lot, but when they met again in Paris that summer, their relationship had changed. Sylvia Beach sensed that something was amiss when Hemingway, newly returned from America, asked Beach not to reveal his address to any inquirers, especially not to Fitzgerald, who was coming to Paris to work on his next novel, *Tender Is the Night*. The reason, Hemingway told Beach, was that Fitzgerald's drunken behavior on an earlier occasion had gotten Hemingway evicted from an apartment. Beach obliged, but the situation became awkward when Scott and Zelda Fitzgerald arrived and took an apartment on Rue Palatine, near Saint-Sulpice (6th), just around the corner from the Hemingways, who were located on Rue Férou.[8]

By this time, Ernest was married to Pauline Pfeiffer, had converted to Catholicism (as Pauline required), and had fathered a second son (Ernest's first son, nicknamed Bumby, was from his first marriage, to Hadley Richardson). The Fitzgerald-Hemingway reunion, when it finally occurred, went badly, under the shadow of their book sales: Hemingway's latest, *A Farewell to Arms*, was prominently appearing in serial form, while Fitzgerald was suffering from writer's block. But Hemingway nonetheless agreed that Fitzgerald could accompany him and Morley Callaghan for one of their occasional boxing matches. Callaghan, who later described Hemingway as a "a big rough tough clumsy unscientific man" who could have broken Callaghan's back in a rough-and-tumble brawl, had some experience with "good fast college boxers" and had drawn blood from Hemingway in an earlier match. Hemingway had retaliated by spitting blood at him—a shocking experience, and all the more bewildering when Hemingway smiled and informed Callaghan that this was "what the bullfighters do when they're wounded. It's a way of showing contempt."[9]

Yet Callaghan was still under the influence of Hemingway's charm, which could be considerable, when the Canadian proposed that Fitzgerald, "my friend and Ernest's admirer," be allowed to "come with us some afternoon and be part of our common friendship." Soon after, Hemingway and Fitzgerald appeared together to pick up Callaghan for an afternoon boxing match, with Fitzgerald as timekeeper. All went well until Hemingway became careless, Callaghan drew blood, and Fitzgerald became fascinated. Just then, Callaghan caught Hemingway off guard and sent him sprawling. Perhaps the moment would have passed, except Fitzgerald suddenly cried out, "Oh, my God!" He had let the round go too long. "'All right, Scott,' Ernest said savagely, 'If you want to see me getting the shit knocked out of me, just say so. Only don't say you made a mistake,' and he stomped off to the shower."[10]

Fitzgerald, "his face ashen," whispered, "My God, he thinks I did it on purpose. Why would I do it on purpose?"[11] Callaghan advised Fitzgerald to forget the whole thing; Hemingway would soon forget it, he told him. But Hemingway did not forget, and that autumn the incident took on uncomfortable proportions when a columnist in the *New York Herald Tribune* wrote a gossipy piece about Callaghan knocking out Hemingway in one round. Callaghan, appalled, wrote the columnist what he called "an elegant gloss of the events in question" and then sent a copy to Hemingway's editor, Max Perkins. The columnist agreed to print the correction, and Perkins sent words of comfort, but before the correction was printed, both Fitzgerald and Hemingway weighed in. Bad words were exchanged all around, and Max Perkins tried to calm his authors; but there would be fallout—even though no one in the end blamed Callaghan for putting out the story (Hemingway traced it to Pierre Loving, who then worked on the Paris staff of the *New York Herald Tribune*).[12]

Before the boxing story hit the headlines, Hemingway—who rarely was in one place for very long—continued to write encouraging letters to Fitzgerald. "You could write such a damn fine book," he assured him in September from Madrid. Fitzgerald's problem, as Hemingway saw it, was a review by Gilbert Seldes in *The Dial*, after which "you became self conscious . . . and knew you must write a masterpiece." Later, he wrote, "You surely know by now, I've written it often enough how much I admire your work," but Fitzgerald's continued anxieties annoyed him. "You damned fool," he wrote from Hendaye, France. "Go on and write the novel."[13]

Fitzgerald became especially trying after an encounter with Gertrude Stein, with whom Hemingway had broken three years earlier.[14] Gertrude and her partner, Alice B. Toklas, had been godmothers to Hemingway's first son; but Alice never liked Hemingway, whom she found crude and vulgar, and Gertrude didn't care for his treatment of his old mentor and Gertrude's friend, Sherwood Anderson. Nor, for that matter, did Gertrude approve of Hemingway's treatment of Hadley. And so when Gertrude and Ernest encountered one another in Paris that autumn, they were merely polite. Still, soon after this chance meeting, Gertrude decided to invite Hemingway once again to one of her soirées, and included Fitzgerald and Allen Tate in the invitation. Hemingway decided that numbers offered his best protection and brought a crowd, including his own wife, the Fitzgeralds, Ford Madox Ford, and several others.

Gertrude, as was her custom, dominated the proceedings, during which she lit into Hemingway's work but praised Fitzgerald's. Unfortunately, Fitzgerald misunderstood her and was deeply hurt. Hemingway, in his heavy-handed way, tried to reassure him: Gertrude, he told Fitzgerald, was "only saying that you had a hell of a roaring furnace of talent and I had a small one—implying I had to work a damn sight harder for results obtained." He added, "You're getting touchy because you haven't finished your novel—that's all."[15]

Still, by this time *A Farewell to Arms* had been published, and praise was pouring in. Already, Hemingway's future was assured. As one biographer put it, "Never again will [Hemingway] lack an audience; never again will he read a rejection letter."[16] By contrast, Fitzgerald was making little progress on *Tender Is the Night*. Despite Hemingway's concerns about the effect of the stock market crash on book sales, *A Farewell to Arms* was doing well, and he was pulling in lucrative writing deals, including $1,000 for 2,500 words on bullfighting for *Fortune*, Henry Luce's expensive new business magazine making its February 1930 debut.

Change was coming, and Hemingway read the signs correctly. He may have been wrong about the market "slump," thinking, like most Americans, that it would only be momentary. But his style and subject matter were what the new decade's reading public wanted. Fitzgerald's probe of the 1920s zeitgeist was good for the 1920s, but in the coming decade, it would be left in the dust behind Hemingway's rough-and-ready populism of the foot soldier and the bull ring.

"And who, writing in France today, do you admire the most?" asked Marc Allégret, who at the time was a French tutor but would soon become a noted film director.

"Gide," the poet Bryher replied, firmly and enthusiastically.

"Gide! But he is my uncle. . . . I must arrange for you to meet him at once."[17]

As it happened, Allégret's relationship to André Gide was far more complicated than the young man let on. Rather than "uncle," the more accurate term would have been "lover." But in one sense the young man was right: there was a somewhat incestuous element to the relationship, which began when Gide's mother hired Marc's father, Elie, to tutor young Gide, who was failing in his lessons. Pastor Elie Allégret, a Protestant missionary and family friend, became sufficiently close to Gide that in time he served as best man at Gide's wedding. Gide, who remained close to the family, became "Uncle André" to the Allégret children, who liked and trusted him. Later, during the war, Gide assumed the role of unofficial guardian of the Allégret family while the pastor continued his missionary work in far-off Cameroon. It was now that Gide, at the age of forty-seven, became enchanted with Elie's handsome and rebellious sixteen-year-old son, Marc, and schemed persistently until the two became lovers.

From the outset, Gide's life had been filled with tension and complications. Born in Paris in 1869, his father—a professor of law at the University of Paris—hailed from the south of France, while his mother came from Rouen. Both parents were Protestant, but the softer and more relaxed personality of the father reflected the genial climate of his upbringing, while the mother was a northerner and of far sterner stuff. Gide, according to one biographer, may have insisted "perhaps too strongly on the difference between the two families and the two regions,"[18] but the impact of that difference was one that Gide suffered from throughout his life, as he continued to rebel against his mother's stern Protestantism, even long after her death.

Unfortunately, as far as Gide was concerned, it was his father who died first, leaving the youngster in the hands of his intensely austere mother. A sickly child, Gide spent his boyhood in what he remembered as the chill gloom of Normandy under his mother's puritanical constraints. His emerging sexuality only complicated things, sometimes unbearably. Expelled from school for onanism, he threw himself into a guilt-ridden effort at self-purification and found religious-infused solace with his cousin, Madeleine Rondeaux, who in turn had secrets (her mother's infidelity) that left her horrified of sexuality. Together, they planned a life of piety, and early on, Gide determined to marry Madeleine, whom he would call Emmanuèle in his autobiographical *Si le grain ne meurt* (*If It Die*).

Gide did indeed marry Madeleine (in 1895), but the marriage remained unconsummated to the end of Madeleine's life in 1938—a stark reminder of Gide's crushing failure to reconcile his sexual nature with his puritanical

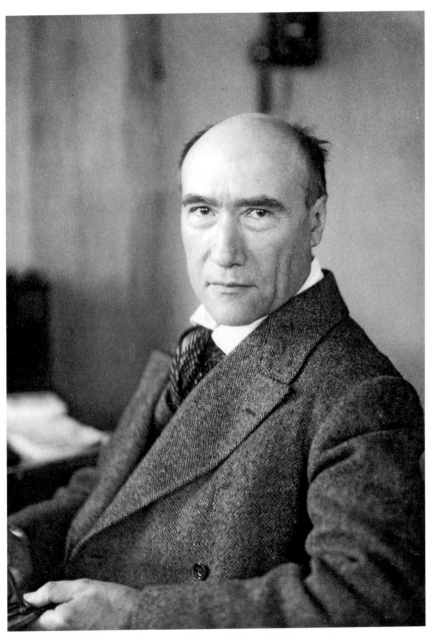

André Gide, 1928. © SZ Photo / Scheri / Bridgeman Images

upbringing. For by this time Gide had discovered and embraced his homosexuality—in Algeria, where a native boy provided Gide's first homosexual experience. On a subsequent trip to Algeria in 1895, he encountered Oscar Wilde (accompanied by Lord Alfred Douglas), who encouraged him to acknowledge his homosexual desires (specifically, as he later clarified, for young boys). Would Gide like the little musician? Wilde asked, after the two watched a "marvelous youth" who played a reed flute for them. "What a dreadful effort of courage it needed to answer: 'Yes,'" Gide later wrote, "and with what a choking voice!"[19]

A few months later, Gide's mother died, and he went ahead and married Madeleine, whom he appeared to love, although the marriage would be a bizarre one. By this time Gide—blessed with an independent income—had begun to circulate with the avant-garde Parisian literary crowd, including Stéphane Mallarmé's Tuesday evenings and Thadée Natanson's *Revue blanche*, where he became friends with Léon Blum. He supported Dreyfus, attacked Barrès, and above all championed liberal individualism and personal freedom in the face of conservative ethics. By 1909, when he took the lead in founding *La Nouvelle Revue Française* (NRF), his prose style, especially his lyrical prose-poem, *Les Nourritures terrestres* (*Fruits of the Earth*), had attracted praise in discerning literary circles. The *NRF*, with its publishing house, Gallimard, soon featured some of the greatest writers of the time, and by the 1920s it would become the leading literary journal in France, and perhaps in Western Europe.

Gide's deep inner conflicts fueled his writing, although not at first overtly. His novel *L'Immoraliste* (*The Immoralist*), published in 1902, broached the topic of pederasty, presenting it as a liberating and ennobling force for the protagonist, whose actions Gide portrayed as consonant with those of the ancient Greeks. But it was not until the publication in 1924 of *Corydon*, a Socratic dialogue on homosexuality, and the 1924 publication of *Si le grain ne meurt* (*If It Die*), an autobiography of his early years, that Gide publicly came out of the closet. In the meantime, he had become romantically involved with Pastor Allégret's handsome young son, Marc, and the two traveled together for months at a time, with Gide taking the precaution of calling Marc his adopted nephew.

Meanwhile, Gide had formed a close intellectual friendship with Maria van Rysselberghe—wife of the Belgian painter Théo van Rysselberghe—whom Gide called "the Petite Dame." They lived in adjoining apartments in Paris (at 1 bis Rue Vaneau), and it was the Petite Dame's daughter, Elisabeth, who in 1923 became the mother of Gide's sole offspring, Catherine—a brief interlude in Gide's otherwise homosexual life that he undertook in the sole interest of providing an heir.[20] (He did not legally recognize Catherine until after his wife's death.) In the meantime as well, Marc Allégret discovered women and broke off his sexual relationship with Gide, although they would remain friends. Marc's photographs and film of their government-sponsored trip to West Africa in 1925–1926 led to his career as a film director.

By 1929, Gide's literary reputation was secure: *Les Nourritures terrestres* had been reissued and became a best seller, *Les Caves du Vatican* (1914) continued to be popular, and *Les Faux-Monnayeurs* (*The Counterfeiters*, 1925), although off-putting to some because of its numerous bisexual or homosexual characters, turned out to be what many considered Gide's masterpiece. But his trip to the Congo had left him horrified by the exploitation and virtual slavery he found there. On earlier trips to North Africa he had observed abuses but had not felt that it was his concern. Now he felt differently. "I know things to which I cannot remain indifferent," he wrote. "I have to speak out."[21]

He was not yet opposed to colonialism or to capitalism, but he tried to do something about the abuses he had seen, through his writing and by speaking with the minister of colonies. But in the end, little changed—except perhaps within Gide himself. Troubled by a sense of unmerited privilege, he now questioned the corrective impact that an individual, any individual, could make.

It could have come straight out of Gide's *The Counterfeiters*: in the preface to a 1929 catalog of first editions, André Malraux wrote, "What is the difference between a good fake and a bad original? Hoax is eminently creative."[22]

Malraux had been eminently creative for years. Born in 1901 on the backside of the Butte of Montmartre, his father—a womanizer and fast-talking but unsuccessful dabbler in any number of professions—soon deserted the family, leaving young Malraux and his mother to live with his maternal grandmother and aunt in nearby Bondy. The small boy suffered from Tourette syndrome, which caused twitches, starts, and blinks, but this didn't detract from the effortless influence he exerted over his friends. From the outset he exercised a magnetism and assurance that drew others to him—characteristics that only grew as he matured, and his remarkable voice with him.

From the age of fourteen, young Malraux traveled to Paris regularly to attend school, and he took the opportunity to explore the city, attend the theater and cinema, and steep himself in books he found there. Hugo, Dumas, and Michelet were his favorite authors, but especially Hugo, who evoked mystical pictures of historical events and believed that "history and legend, each has its own truth."[23] As it happened, Malraux's own truth pointed in a direction other than school, and after the Lycée Condorcet refused him admission, the precocious sixteen-year-old dropped out of school forever, balking at the prospect of office work or shop hours and thinking lyrical thoughts as he wandered the streets of Paris.

Riffling through secondhand books in Paris's multitude of bookstores and bouquinistes, Malraux quickly learned how to spot works of value, which he then resold to book dealers. He learned about paper, typography, engravings, and lithographs, and by the age of eighteen he was supporting himself from finding and reselling first editions and rare books. He then began to create his own editions, mixing literary fragments into composites that specialists disdained but others did not. He also started to write literary criticism, attracting notice by his adroit attacks on fashionable authors. Yet by now art had become his passion, and in its pursuit he explored museums and galleries, read extensively, made contacts, and trained his eye, supplementing his growing expertise with a fine-tuned memory. Soon this self-taught wunderkind was working as an art editor, employing Georges Braque and André Derain to illustrate works by Max Jacob, Raymond Radiguet, and Pierre Reverdy. In addition, after battering at the door of Gide's NRF, he managed to get his foot in as a critic, a step that considerably enhanced his reputation in literary circles.

Women had not played a large role in his life before now, but at the age of twenty Malraux at last met his soul mate, the cultivated and fiery Clara Goldschmidt, with whom he traveled before the two married. Clara was German and Jewish—a fact that appalled Malraux's family but didn't bother Malraux, who proceeded to invest Clara's considerable dowry in some Mexican mining shares that his father (now a stockbroker) was peddling. The two traveled extensively and expensively, winding up in Cambodia after the Mexican shares tanked. There, the adventurers tried a get-rich scheme involving the pillaging and sale of ancient Khmer temple art, a caper that ended with Malraux in jail. It was all a misunderstanding, he insisted—a misunderstanding over a blameless attempt to preserve priceless works of art for posterity. "Many French intellectuals feel moved by my plight," he told an interviewer,[24] and indeed, André Gide, among others, signed a petition on his behalf. When at last released on a technicality (confusion over which temple was involved), Malraux headed home, confident that he had been declared innocent.[25] But not all agreed. As the disillusioned archeologist Georges Groslier wrote to the head of the scholarly organization that had sponsored Malraux (supposedly in studies in Khmer archeology), "I was counting on finding out a great deal about Malraux in Paris. But . . . his friends know nothing about him. . . . Oh, the charm of Paris! . . . A well-cut suit, a pair of deep eyes, and anything goes."[26]

All this before he was twenty-three. Next came an attempt to establish a newspaper in Indochina, one that would expose the injustices of colonialism while enabling Malraux to settle some scores. This did not turn out well, but the experience aroused Malraux's social and political conscience. It also provided material for a series of books, the first being *La Tentation de l'Occident* (*The Temptation of the West*), which was not a best seller but established him as a young writer with a future—a writer, as the publisher Gaston Gallimard realized, who knew his way around the printer's trade. Over the objections of some of the *NRF* staff, Gallimard made Malraux artistic director of the *NRF*'s Gallimard publishing house, where he shepherded through the complete edition of Gide's works, a writer he greatly admired. In time, Gide would return the compliment.

Malraux's first novel, *Les Conquérants* (*The Conquerors*), appeared in 1928, published (according to an earlier agreement) by Bernard Grasset, with the violent politics of mid-1920s China at its heart. Two years later, Grasset published Malraux's second novel, *La Voie royale* (*The Royal Way*), which transposed Malraux and Clara's adventures in Cambodia into a thriller. In the process, Malraux came to be seen as the barely disguised protagonist of his stories, one who occupied an important role in the Kuomintang—a fiction that he let others invent and repeat. He enjoyed cultivating a heroic image, but even more important was the recognition he now received as a major literary figure, complete with laudatory reviews, foreign translations, and large sales. Talk of the Goncourt Prize circulated for both novels, although (much to his disappointment) it passed them by.

Still, by the end of the decade, Malraux had emerged as a literary figure to reckon with, all the while managing to steer clear of the major literary tribes, including the Dadaists and their progeny, the Surrealists (thus antagonizing André Breton and Louis Aragon), and the French Communist party. It was a delicate balancing act, and one that would become increasingly difficult as the 1930s evolved.

But for the moment, Malraux had other things to occupy him. The Middle East now pulled him, and he had what he called some "speculative art trading" in mind. And so, in April 1929, he and Clara boarded a cargo ship bound for Persia.

⌐∽

Not long after Malraux and Clara departed for the Middle East, Major Charles de Gaulle and his family left for his new assignment in Beirut. It wasn't what de Gaulle wanted: he had hoped for a teaching post at the Ecole de Guerre, and he angled for it with his mentor, Marshal Philippe Pétain. The two had previously enjoyed excellent relations, but a rift had developed over a book that de Gaulle was ghostwriting for the marshal,[27] and Pétain—who may not have been anxious to have de Gaulle at close quarters again—urged him to serve in Syria. "You are being given a chance," Pétain advised him. "Do not neglect it."[28] Rumor had it that de Gaulle's appointment at the Ecole de Guerre had been blocked by a coterie of professors who threatened to leave if de Gaulle—known for his arrogance and nonconformity as well as his brilliance—joined their ranks. Instead, Syria was offered, and de Gaulle reluctantly accepted.

About the same time that the de Gaulle family was departing France for Syria, Josephine Baker was returning to France from Latin America. She had toured there throughout the autumn, after deciding that she was through with Paris. She had not left Paris, she told one and all; Paris had left *her*. Her spectacular career, which had begun only three years earlier, was already fading. How long, after all, could a raunchy banana dance look fresh and appealing?

But somewhere on the long Atlantic crossing home, and perhaps buoyed by the unexpected companionship of the owlish architect Le Corbusier, she decided to try her luck again in Paris. Her manager and longtime lover, Pepito, agreed but thought it was time for a change. The public was fickle, he told her, and she needed to remake her image. No more bouncing banana skirts; instead, it was time for "sensitivity, songs, feeling." She could be a sophisticated lady, he told Josephine. And, he reassured her, "I think you're ready."[29]

But how to start all over again? And where?

During those late October days of 1929, they met for breakfast in the Luxembourg Gardens and only parted, reluctantly, at night. They refused external limitations, decided never to lie to one another, called their relationship a "morganatic marriage,"[30] and read prodigiously. Simone de Beauvoir's English was better than Sartre's, and already she had read all of Virginia Woolf and a good deal of Henry James as well as Sinclair Lewis, Theodore Dreiser, and Sherwood Anderson—taking out books from Adrienne Monnier's lending library–bookstore and then venturing across the street to Sylvia Beach's Shakespeare and Company.[31] Sartre, on the other hand, ranked films as high as books and discovered the "fundamental necessity of art" in a movie house.[32] "Even then," Beauvoir recalled, "we still cared very little about what was going on in the world."[33] Although they were becoming more and more sympathetic to the Communists, Sartre did not vote for them, or for anyone else (Beauvoir didn't either, although she would not have been able to: women were still disenfranchised in France). What interested Jean-Paul Sartre was subjective humanism and the application of reason to the problems of existence.

They had met at the Sorbonne, both of them brilliant, both of them iconoclastic. Beauvoir, or Beaver (as Sartre and her other friends called her), came from a rigidly proper bourgeois Parisian family, whose desperate measures to keep up appearances had only intensified as their income dwindled. Repelled by this stultifying propriety (intensified by her mother's devout Catholicism), Beauvoir found refuge in books. In 1924, passage of a law enabling girls' secondary schools to include curricula leading to a baccalaureate made it possible for her to pursue her dream of admission to the Sorbonne, where she studied philosophy and planned to teach.

Jean-Paul Sartre, also born in Paris, was raised in the home of his tyrannical grandfather, to which his mother, a young widow, had to retreat with her infant son. The grandfather bullied the women in his household but spoiled his grandson, who recalled that "an audience of willing admirers surrounded me in my childhood, and encouraged my words."[34] He felt betrayed when his mother eventually remarried, and early on decided against ever marrying or settling down; but unlike Beauvoir, he intended to be a writer. Personal freedom was essential to them both, as was openness to new ideas and experiences. Neither was attractive physically, and Sartre was downright ugly, but they both proved desirable to others, and from the start they maintained an open relationship.[35]

Beauvoir met Sartre while preparing for her postgraduate *agrégation* (the difficult and competitive exam for university and *lycée* teaching positions). Sartre received first place, but she came in a close second—at the age of twenty-one she was the youngest person ever to pass the exam. By this time she had also learned about the delights of café life in Montparnasse and had become a regular at certain bars and clubs. Sartre had learned about life from a budding actress in Toulouse, and soon thereafter he became briefly engaged to a young woman he met while vacationing in the Massif Central (as a grocer's daughter, she was unacceptable to Sartre's formidable grandfather).

Early in 1929, Sartre wrote a lengthy letter to the editor of *Les Nouvelles littéraires* in response to its "Survey of Today's Students." The editors were impressed with his observations, in which he proclaimed that the effort to improve mankind was a farce. "All things carry the seed of their own death," he wrote, and concluded with this biting comparison between his own gen-

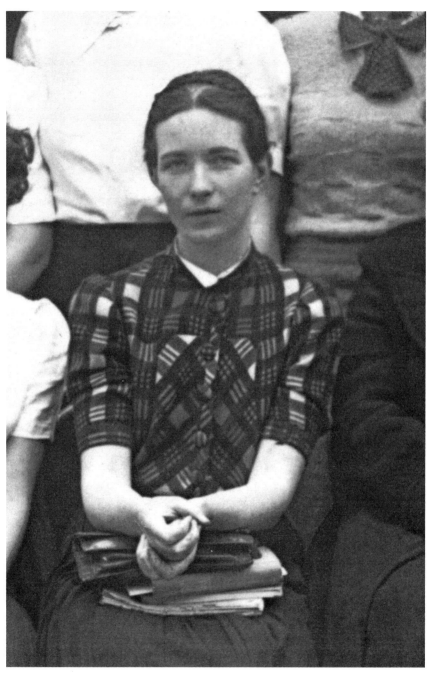

Simone de Beauvoir, at the Lycée Molière, where she was a philosophy teacher, 1938.
© CCI / Bridgeman Images

eration and its predecessor: "We are more unhappy," he wrote, "but nicer to get along with."[36]

That summer, he joined Beauvoir in a rendezvous in the vicinity of her family's summer place in Meyrignac, where they walked and talked—until her parents objected. People were gossiping, they said. That autumn, back in Paris, Sartre and Beauvoir spent their days together and, for the time being, returned at night to their parental (or grandparental) abodes. One night, instead of marriage, Sartre proposed a "two-year lease," complete with theoretical freedoms—an open relationship—for them both: "We would never become strangers to one another . . . but it must not be allowed to degenerate into mere duty or habit."[37] He was about to leave for his eighteen months of military service, and he hoped to be doing some of it near Paris. He encouraged her to find a teaching job nearby.

Beauvoir readily agreed. This "two-year lease" would form the basis for their relationship for many years to come.

That November, as Sartre was setting off for his eighteen months of military service, a nineteen-year-old aspiring Canadian writer by the name of John Glassco noticed the changes that already were appearing in Montparnasse. "Winter was coming on," he later recollected, "and my money was giving out. The number of Americans in Paris was dropping as steadily as the stock-exchange averages, and I saw fewer familiar faces in the quarter."[38] Far fewer tourists were coming to Paris, and the American expats were fleeing home or to cheaper locales. "Slowly but surely the depression was making itself felt among us," wrote Samuel Putnam, who was still employed in translating into English the memoirs of Kiki, who had exuberantly reigned over 1920s Montparnasse. "The great homeward trek had begun."[39]

Those who did not return to America went to smaller and cheaper outposts such as Majorca, Cagnes-sur-Mer on the Mediterranean, or the charming hillside village of Mirmande in southeastern France. There they would not find the perfect lives they sought—as Archibald MacLeish put it in the poem "Tourist Death: For Sylvia Beach," in which he described some of Beach's patrons as those who "lived their lives as tourists, asking to travel forever" in search of a new and better Rive Gauche.[40] Instead, they would experience the same squabbles and backbiting as they had in Paris.

Life in Paris had never been a Camelot, the writer Kay Boyle later pointed out, noting that "all kinds of agonies" were commonplace during the supposedly glorious 1920s.[41] Still, in late 1929, "there was a prevalent feeling that twilight was falling," Samuel Putnam recollected (he even wrote a book titled *Night Falls in Europe*, but he recalled it from the publisher because he felt too close to it). Suicides, especially that in December of young Harry Crosby—publisher, with his wife, Caresse, of the tiny Black Sun Press that published James Joyce's *Tales Told of Shem and Shaun*—"threw a gloom over those terraces [of Montparnasse] from which they were never fully to recover."[42] Even though most of the Montparnasse regulars never knew Crosby personally, they were still all part of the same circle. As Putnam pointed out, they all, like Crosby, "were never very far from the fluctuations of the stock-ticker—he, too, had lost money in that autumn of 1929."[43]

Panic was hitting Left Bank artists and their dealers, who were "feverishly trying to dispose of their wares."[44] But the impact was spreading beyond the Left Bank. "The Wall Street crash has had its effect here," Janet Flanner wrote in the *New Yorker* in late 1929. "In the Rue de la Paix the jewelers are reported to be losing fortunes in sudden cancellations of orders . . . . In real-estate circles certain advertisements have been illuminating: 'For Sale, Cheap, Nice Old Château, . . . Must Have IMMEDIATE CASH; Will Sacrifice.'"[45]

Christmas was not a happy affair for many that year, although Sylvia Beach and Adrienne Monnier joined the journalist Sisley Huddleston and his wife, Jeanne, for a cozy celebration in the Huddlestons' Normandy mill house. Less festive by far was the group that gathered in Switzerland at the Palace Hotel for consumptives in Montana-Vermala. Ernest and Pauline Hemingway, Scott and Zelda Fitzgerald, John and Katy Dos Passos, and Dorothy Parker and her fellow Algonquin Round Table member, the screenwriter Donald Ogden Stewart, tried to buoy the spirits of their good friends, the beautiful American couple, Gerald and Sara Murphy, but it was tough. The Murphys, beloved among their wide circle of friends, had lived what appeared to be a charmed life; but now their son, Patrick, ensconced in the Palace Hotel, was dying of tuberculosis.

Celebrations among other members of the artistic and literary set proceeded as usual that holiday season, although not without strain. On the last day of the year, Victor Hugo's great-grandson, the writer and painter Jean Hugo, joined his friends Charles and Marie-Laure de Noailles at their extravagant modernist château on the Riviera. There he found the renowned art historian Bernard Berenson, who was a guest of the Noailles' nearby neighbor, Edith Wharton. Also present were Marc Allégret, the composer Georges Auric, museum innovator Georges-Henri Rivière, and the poet Jean Cocteau with his young lover, Jean Desbordes. One never quite knew what Cocteau would get up to, which was an essential element of his charm, and true to his devil-may-care reputation (which included a well-known addiction to opium), he announced that he had prepared "a mystification." That is, he had nailed a piece of fabric on a canvas and signed it by Picasso. Presenting it to Berenson as Marie-Laure's latest acquisition, he asked Berenson's opinion of the piece. Berenson hemmed and hawed, and Cocteau pounced, attacking him on his "blindness regarding modern art." It was a fake, and everyone laughed. But Hugo was uneasy, fearing that Cocteau had "glorified himself in his too easy triumph."[46]

It was an uneasy time for many, although those in the know took comfort in the fact that, only several days before, the first funds had been authorized for a new defense system. Charles de Gaulle had been in a distinct (and unpopular) minority by arguing vociferously for the need to invest in what he termed the weapons of the future, tanks and aircraft; far more popular was the idea of something solid—a wall. And so, as Christmas of 1929 approached, Parliament approved funds to build a line of fortifications along the German border, to be named after the minister of war who had backed the scheme, André Maginot.

Due to budget as well as diplomatic considerations, the Maginot Line would not make it past the Luxembourg border. But that, according to the experts, posed no problem: after that point, the Ardennes would provide a natural barrier.

No one seemed to consider, or want to consider, the possibility that the Ardennes were not impenetrable, nor that a German army could simply bypass the fortifications altogether, invading through the Low Countries, as it had done only a few years before.

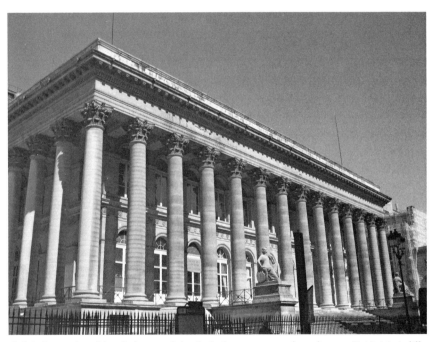

Palais Brongniart, historic home of the Paris Bourse, or stock exchange. © M. McAuliffe

CHAPTER THREE

~

It Could Never Happen Here

(1930)

Youki, wife of the acclaimed Japanese artist Foujita, was appalled. Youki (originally Lucie Badoul, but renamed by her husband) had just returned with Foujita from New York to Le Havre, where a gaggle of reporters met them at the dock. In New York, the two had enjoyed a Broadway show and other delights, but Youki was shocked at the sight of correctly dressed people on the streets selling apples, and unsettled by the prevailing mood of gloom. The bleak atmosphere even pervaded their trip home, on the luxury liner *Ile-de-France*, where Youki discovered a room with a ticker tape showing minute-by-minute developments on the stock market. She couldn't help but notice that people left the room "a little pale." Despite the boat's comfort, she pointed out, "the trip was not very gay, you understand."[1]

Yet despite *"la crise économique de 1930,"* the reporters meeting Foujita and Youki at Le Havre were only interested in what New Yorkers thought about the Affaire Mestorino. What was that? she wanted to know (it turned out to be a sensational murder trial that neither she nor Foujita had heard of).[2] When she tried to turn the French reporters' attention to more serious matters—the horrible economic crisis in America, "which is coming our way"—they simply laughed and went on to ask about the future of the "talkies."[3]

Youki's Cassandra warnings would indeed prove true, and among the first to suffer from the spreading Depression would be the painters, as collectors disappeared and dealers sold off their own stock at bargain prices. At the great auction house for fine art, the Hôtel Drouot, prices would soon be "catastrophic," as Youki put it. Even those dealers who retained confidence in their artists and maintained their canvases (and prices) would not be able to buy any more.[4]

Yet Paris's daily newspaper of record, *Le Temps*, was still able in 1930 to declare, "Whatever the cause of world depression, France can face it with relative serenity."[5]

～

In the midst of the global economic meltdown, France remained content to trust in its gold reserves, its budget surplus, and its determination—generated by the distressing history of the unstable 1920s franc—to keep France's currency steady and secure. Shielded from economic disasters abroad and confident in the government's affirmation of a "policy of prosperity" at home, life continued undisturbed as the French economy chugged along.

Unruffled by dire events abroad, Parisian hostesses in 1930 raised the bar for extravagance. It was a grand season for parties and costume balls, with all the usual luminaries vying to create the wittiest and most dazzling events. The Art Deco artist and designer Etienne Drian gave an exquisite masquerade at his country house, where guests arrived as Louis XV–style shepherds and shepherdesses—with the exception of one lone guest attired as a wolf in sheep's clothing. Elsa Maxwell, the dumpy American whizbang who specialized in entertaining the wealthy on their own dime (or franc), joined with the Honorable Mrs. Reginald Fellowes (better known as Daisy) in giving a masquerade in which everyone had to come dressed as someone else—an invitation that deluged Chanel with orders from young men taking the opportunity to dress as some of Paris's reigning beauties.

Elsa Maxwell also had a hand in the party given by Señora Alvaro Guevara, the former Meraud Guinness of the Guinness family fortune, whose marriage may have been on the rocks but whose splash and dash were not. According to instructions, guests arrived suitably unattired to her "As-You-Were-When-the-Autobus-Called" party: ladies appeared in various states of *déshabillée*, while one gentleman, still in shaving soap, made his entrance attired only in a towel.

Of course the Rothschilds and the Beaumonts could always be counted on to entertain lavishly—a Beaumont invitation determined one's social rank by whether and with what frequency one was included. But it was that season's series of over-the-top costume balls that created the most buzz. The Vicomte and Vicomtesse Charles de Noailles, who specialized in whatever was unusual and avant-garde, gave a sparkling Materials Ball, whose theme was paper (Paul Morand showed up wearing a dinner jacket made of book covers). The couturier Jean Patou encased his entire garden in silver for his Silver Ball, suspending huge stuffed parrots in giant silver cages from silver-encrusted branches. The wealthy American actress, interior decorator, and social doyenne Elsie de Wolfe (aka Lady Mendl) took up the challenge by giving a Gold-and-Silver Ball, transforming the ballroom of the Ritz with cloth-of-gold curtains, gold tablecloths, gold place cards, gold menus, and flowers of gold, silver, and mica, not to mention gold champagne.

But perhaps the most stunning of all was the White Ball given by the Count and Countess Pecci-Blunt (the count being an American who owed his money to his Italian wife and his title to his wife's great-uncle, Pope Leo XIII). The decorations were white, the garden was white, and everyone, according to instructions, was dressed in white, making a striking if possibly monotonous tableau. But the hosts, aware of the dangers of their color scheme, invited the by-now well-known American photographer Man Ray to bring his movie projector, which he placed on an upper window overlooking the garden. From there, he projected hand-colored as well as black-and-white film footage onto the moving couples so that they became a moving screen.

It seems to have been utterly fabulous.

〜

A craze for white satin swept Paris as the decade opened—white satin and lengthening hemlines. Chanel's little black dress did not disappear, but she now led the way with white. "I have said that black had everything," she later told Paul Morand. "White too. . . . Dress women in white or black at a ball: they are the only ones you see."[6]

Continuing her conversation with Morand, Chanel added, "Fashion roams around the streets, unaware that it exists, up to the moment that I, in my own way, may have expressed it." And then what? She readily answered: "The genius is in anticipating. . . . Something I made at the beginning of the collection," she added, "I may find outdated before the end."[7]

Unfortunately, not all fashion designers in Paris remained as attuned as Chanel to change. One whose name no longer was on everyone's lips was Paul Poiret, who had been as explosive a presence on the prewar fashion scene as Chanel was after the war. Poiret, too, had freed women from the corset and had banished the protruding bust and derriere, which he thought "made the lady look as if she were hauling a trailer."[8] Poiret had ventured into new territory by draping his designs in a manner reminiscent of classical Greece, and had looked to the Arabian Nights for exotic allure. His parties were the stuff of legends, and those who remembered them thought that nothing in the present times could top them.

And yet by 1930 Paul Poiret was forgotten. He had ruined himself financially on a variety of ill-conceived and expensive ventures, and he had lost customers when he stayed with the styles that had made him famous, which were too elaborate for the 1920s woman. One of his luxuries was a villa in nearby Mézy, designed by the modernist French architect Robert Mallet-Stevens. It was stunning, and it was expensive—so expensive that Poiret never occupied the main residence, which he could not afford to complete, and instead lived in the caretaker's cottage. To pay his crushing debts, he sold his extensive collection of modern art, but even this was not enough. In 1929, Poiret's shop on the Rond-Point des Champs-Elysées closed, the remaining designs sold as scrap, and in 1930 he sold his villa in Mézy. Unable to afford his palatial town house, he sold most of the furniture and paintings and moved into an apartment above the Salle Pleyel concert hall.

He was not entirely destitute, but as one journal noted, "by 1930, it was all over for Poiret. He had wagered that twentieth-century women would want to turn themselves into sumptuous art objects and fantastical divas, but he bet on the wrong horse."[9]

Another stunning modernist villa on the outskirts of Paris, Le Corbusier's Villa Savoye, was completed in 1930.[10] Considered to be one of his masterpieces, it "liberated the idea of home," according to one biographer, "much as Coco Chanel had freed women by letting them wear pants."[11] Created as a country house for Pierre and Emilie Savoye in Poissy, the Villa Savoye embodied the culmination of Le Corbusier's 1920s concepts for private housing—most especially his five points, or principles, for the new architecture: a free, non-load-bearing façade; horizontal bands of windows; an open interior plan; attractive roof gardens; and *pilotis*, or posts, rising up and supporting the whole, with reinforced concrete at the structure's heart.

This concept, which Le Corbusier had been developing since the war, "opened the door to freedom, paving the way for contemporary architecture," as one of his associates put it.[12] Although Frank Lloyd Wright dismissed the Villa Savoye as "a box on stilts," Le Corbusier certainly did not see it that way. Above all, he aimed at creating a habitation that was, in his words, "open to all four horizons," a country retreat from which to savor the surrounding landscape as well as the villa's own rooftop gardens.[13] As he moved into the 1930s, Le Corbusier's architectural vocabulary would evolve—his

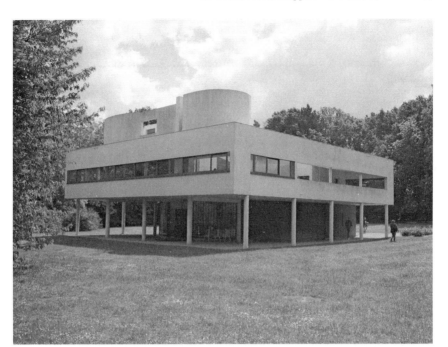

Le Corbusier's Villa Savoye, Poissy, France. © J. McAuliffe

next private house, a country retreat for Hélène de Mandrot in the south of France (1931), would be quite different from the Villa Savoye or his other 1920s structures. But the role that nature and the surrounding landscape played in his architectural concept would become even more pronounced.

Fortunately for Le Corbusier and his cousin and partner Pierre Jeanneret, they and most of their wealthy clients were, for the time being, immune to the effects of the Wall Street Crash. "The crash doesn't affect us," Le Corbusier wrote his mother that April of 1930. "Work comes in from all sides, increasingly interesting."[14] Commissions flooded the office, and he was also lecturing and publishing (in 1930, his *Details Concerning the Present State of Architecture and of Urbanism*). The commissions varied in size, from villas for wealthy clients to his first major building, the Centrosoyus in Moscow (completed in 1930), housing the headquarters of the Central Union of Soviet Cooperatives. He also continued to work on the Salvation Army's huge homeless shelter, the Cité de Refuge in Paris's impoverished thirteenth arrondissement, as well as on another Paris shelter, the Asile Flottant, creatively located on a reconverted barge in the Seine. Both of these projects

were funded by the American (but thoroughly Parisian) arts patron and phi-
lanthropist Princesse Edmond de Polignac (née Winnaretta Singer), whose
fortune—invested in a Canadian trust and managed in Paris—most happily
continued to thrive, even after the Crash.[15]

Aiding Le Corbusier and Pierre Jeanneret was an intriguing young woman
by the name of Charlotte Perriand, who had entered their office and lives
in 1927. Perriand was intent on creating modernist furnishings and living
spaces, and she was equally intent on working for Le Corbusier. But their
first encounter was not propitious: "We don't embroider cushions here," he
told her and showed her the door.[16] Before exiting, she managed to inform
him of her current exhibit at the Salon d'Automne—a nickel-plated cocktail
bar with an anodized aluminum countertop—that caught his attention. Soon
she entered the firm, as the only woman, and would remain until 1937.

"This was a heroic, pioneering age," she recalled, "with no money and
very few resources"—a time when "enthusiastic young men, recent gradu-
ates from the best schools, came from all over the world, not just to design,
but for Corbu [as Le Corbusier was informally known]." These enthusiastic
youngsters, like Perriand herself, were not products of the stodgy Ecole des
Beaux-Arts, with which Le Corbusier fundamentally differed, but instead
were intent on "building, or rather conceiving, the future." Happily working
long hours in the service of this vision ("It was worse than giving birth—we
needed to convalesce"), Perriand memorably created a number of striking
modernist designs, including sling-back chairs and her famous tubular chaise
longue. "We made up a little family," she recalled.[17]

Still, working for Corbu was not always pleasant. On one occasion (sometime in 1930, as she recalled), he asked her to design a project during his
absence. Excited by the results, she presented the finished product to him,
expecting that "he couldn't be anything other than pleased." Indeed, he was
not, and he promptly rearranged everything, lecturing her all the while. She
had to start all over again, and she "didn't accept this meekly." She walked
out and anguished for three days before she finally returned. Corbu's response? "What are you dithering for?" he barked, when he saw her. "Go and
sit down." And she did, staying another seven years.[18]

Le Corbusier's mood swings were becoming more frequent, sometimes fluctuating rapidly between exuberance and depression. His April 1930 letter to
his mother juxtaposed a buoyant "The crash doesn't affect us. . . . Life is en-
thralling" with "Terrible events are occurring and hard times are coming!"[19]

Fortunately for him, activity was an antidote to depression, and there was plenty of work for him that year. Others were not so fortunate.

Marc Chagall, whose fortunes had been on the upswing ever since returning to Paris from Russia after the war, was caught by the Wall Street Crash just as he committed to purchasing and renovating a large house for his family in an expensive quarter of Paris, the sixteenth arrondissement. At the whiff of economic troubles, his dealer, Bernheim-Jeune, canceled Chagall's contract, leaving him in the lurch even before he and his family could move in. Having what they saw as little alternative, they moved in anyway, but the financial pressures on Chagall would now be enormous.

By the end of 1930, Maurice Goudeket, the current lover and future husband of France's acclaimed writer Colette, was bankrupt. Goudeket, the son of a Dutch diamond merchant and himself a pearl seller, had ignored the American financial crisis, and his already-failing business—financed with borrowed money—could not take the additional strain. The couple lived expensively ("We're luxurious creatures," Colette noted),[20] and even the success of her autobiographical *Sido*, which appeared shortly before the Crash, was not enough to offset their financial difficulties. "The reception accorded *Sido*," Janet Flanner wrote in the *New Yorker*, "has been exceptional even for a writer to whom exceptional receptions have become a commonplace."[21] But despite reverential reviews, it was not a very happy time for either Colette or Goudeket. Forced to sell their house, the two had to move out in a hurry to make way for their impatient buyer—Coco Chanel.

As ripples from the Great Crash began to spread, others were affected—in a few cases, to their benefit. The cosmetics queen Helena Rubinstein had sold off the American portion of her business to Lehman Brothers the year before and did quite nicely in the transaction; but then the Lehman Brothers' sales strategy fell apart, pummeled by the Wall Street Crash. Rubinstein was ill, she was bored, and she was more than frustrated with Lehman Brothers, who had "tried to go mass; to sell my products in every grocery store." Her husband, the Left Bank publisher Edward Titus, urged her to retire, but she wasn't ready for that yet. Instead, with shares in Helena Rubinstein Inc. at an all-time low, she decided to buy back control. Not a good idea, Titus told her. The only things that really mattered now were "the children's life [they had two sons], your life and mine, the combined life of the four of us. Everything else are only things, just things."[22] But Rubinstein was adamant, and she immediately began the tricky business of secretly courting her shareholders while buying whatever shares became available. She would indeed win back her beloved company, but her marriage would be another matter.

While Rubinstein ultimately benefited from the Crash, the well-regarded Michelin family firm did not. With an important American market and a tire plant in the United States, Michelin was hit hard by the Crash and had to close its Milltown, New Jersey, plant. Even in the heart of Michelin's French manufacturing country, in Clermont-Ferrand, massive firings began in 1930 and would continue through 1935, creating a legacy of bitterness. In defense, Edouard Michelin, grandson of the founder and head of the company during the 1930s, emphasized that "we were on the edge of bankruptcy in 1930."[23] Yet even in that difficult year, Edouard found the cash to bolster automaker André Citroën when Citroën regained control from his banking partners, Lazard Frères. It would prove a brilliant move for Michelin, but not for Citroën—although he did not yet realize it.

In 1930, French auto production was falling, from approximately 250,000 vehicles to 225,000, and Citroën—who had occupied a prime perch in the French auto market—suffered accordingly. His great rival, Louis Renault, was more diversified in his offerings and for years had dominated the French market for trucks and commercial vehicles and had built airplane engines and tanks as well (although the market for tanks suffered when the victorious nations scrapped their tanks after World War I). As the 1930s opened, Renault began to extend his Billancourt works, just outside of Paris, onto the Ile Seguin, connecting the two with a bridge—and ignoring the warning that the government might make him tear it down. Soon his Billancourt assembly line would have thirty-two thousand workers operating fifteen thousand machines, in what amounted to the greatest industrial concentration in France.

André Citroën, in the meantime, headed his own magnificent industrial spread just across the river, along the Quai de Javel (now Quai André-Citroën), at the edge of Paris's fifteenth arrondissement.[24] The rivalry between Renault and Citroën dated from the early postwar years, when Citroën, who had made his name and prewar fortune with an invention for gears, fearlessly entered the postwar auto market with a car and market strategy that was more attuned to the average buyer than anything his competitors had ever dreamed of.

Some, looking at the backgrounds of these two men—both of whom were the same age, had been raised in bourgeois homes in central Paris, and had even attended the same school (Lycée Condorcet)—imagined a rivalry that went back to boyhood. Although Renault and Citroën might well have known one another during their school days, there is no evidence of much more than this. What mattered was that, by the 1920s, a real rivalry had emerged, and the one who felt it most deeply was the dour industrialist, Renault. Citroën, by contrast, was an affable personality, who socialized at all the best nightspots and (unlike Renault) got along well with his workers. In addition, Citroën thought up promotional gimmicks that appalled the far more conservative Renault. Putting one's name in lights on the Eiffel Tower, as Citroën did in 1925, simply disgusted Renault.[25] Sending one's automobiles on cross-Sahara treks was even more annoying, because it demanded a countermove from Renault.

But what especially bothered Renault—and many others—was Citroën's propensity to gamble. It was a recreational form of gambling, and Citroën made a point of never gambling with his company's funds. Yet despite Citroën's insistence on keeping his private indulgences separate from his business, this was in fact impossible: Automobiles Citroën was an owner-managed company, with all the dangers of exposure that this involved. As a consequence, in 1928, when Citroën's personal financial difficulties became sufficiently dire, he had to accept a takeover by Banque Lazard, a French banking syndicate that reorganized the finances of Automobiles Citroën and placed managerial control in the hands of a board of directors.

This arrangement did not last. In November 1930, with the financial assistance of Michelin and the approval of Citroën shareholders, André Citroën once again took control of his company. The bankers had done well by Automobiles Citroën during the two years of their management, and despite a growth of labor disputes and strikes there—hitherto unheard of under Citroën's paternal management—the company was in sound shape when Citroën once again took the helm.

The wild card, of course, was the spreading economic crisis. Yet Citroën did not see that year's drop in sales as anything but a temporary setback. After all, his French market was holding strong, even if his foreign sales were sagging. Ever the optimist, he envisioned boundless opportunities, provided that he could hold down his prices by continually increasing production. Looking beyond France and Europe, he pictured his market expanding into Africa, India, and Asia.

Citroën based his strategy on his continued use and improvement of the Taylor method of assembly-line mass production that Henry Ford had pioneered. But not only did Citroën keep the price of his automobiles down;

he also insisted on improving the quality of design and performance, providing advances well ahead of his competitors every step of the way. It was in this spirit that, once again in control of his company, Citroën embarked on a three-year period of intense activity and unlimited spending, during which he completely modernized and rebuilt his Quai de Javel factory and developed the revolutionary Traction Avant automobile—one that included front-wheel drive, automatic transmission, independent front suspension, hydraulic brakes, and (eventually) rack-and-pinion steering. Citroën set a high bar for his new automotive baby: it had to be beautiful to look at (long, low slung, all steel), "rapid and responsive to drive, spacious and comfortable to ride in and affordable to own and run." Not only that, but the Traction Avant needed to be "an outstandingly reliable and economical vehicle," and reasonably priced as well.[26]

It was a huge demand to make on Automobiles Citroën, especially since to get the Traction Avant out the door as quickly as possible, Citroën concentrated solely on this one, unproven design. It was an enormous risk, but Citroën was accustomed to risk—although in business, his risks were calculated to keep him at the forefront of the ever-more-competitive race for market share. But daring was not enough. What differentiated Citroën from his competitors was vision: virtually every part in Citroën's new automobile would be new and different from anything he had made before. Other automakers, for example, including Renault and Peugeot, considered front-wheel drive not only technically unfeasible but also potentially dangerous. Citroën disagreed and was willing to place his entire future, and the future of his company, on the line in order to prove it.

Edward Titus, husband of Helena Rubinstein, was for the first time in his life enjoying some professional success. A journalist, he had left New York for Paris during the 1920s to establish (with his wife's considerable financial support) a Montparnasse shop for rare books called At the Sign of the Black Manikin. Soon, Titus's endeavors expanded to include the tiny Black Manikin Press, which struggled along until, in 1929, Titus unexpectedly landed a best seller with D. H. Lawrence's *Lady Chatterley's Lover* (after Sylvia Beach turned down the opportunity).[27] Then in 1930, Titus published another best seller, the English translation of Kiki's *Memoirs*, for which Titus persuaded Hemingway to write an introduction (for the record, Hemingway protested that "it is a crime to translate it").[28]

That June, Bennett Cerf, chief editor of Random House, was in Paris, and Titus took the opportunity to show him the first unbound pages of Kiki's

Memoirs. Cerf promptly ordered a large number of copies, which Titus just as promptly shipped. Unfortunately, this first lot fell into the hands of the censors at U.S. Customs, who confiscated them. Wambly Bald interviewed Kiki when he heard of the disaster. "Laconically and with a characteristic shrug, she remarked: 'I am not losing any weight over it.'"[29] Nor did Titus, who after that mailed smaller shipments to various Random House editors and employees, which arrived unimpeded.

In addition to running his bookshop and publishing enterprise, Titus published a literary magazine, *This Quarter*, with the help of Samuel Putnam, who had arrived in Montparnasse with his wife during the early 1920s. They then spent most of the decade on the outskirts of Paris until their return to Montparnasse in 1930, when Putnam became associate editor of *This Quarter* and translated Kiki's *Memoirs* into English. Putnam understood the difficulty of translating those memoirs: "The problem," he wrote, "is not to translate Kiki's text, but to translate Kiki." To do this, he added, "one must have the *feel* of Kiki, the feel of the café du Dome at five o'clock on a rainy, bleary, alcoholic morning." But even this was not enough. Hemingway may have criticized any attempt to translate Kiki, but Putnam hoped to be faithful to her true nature. "May God and Kiki forgive me," he concluded, "and then, perhaps, Mr. Hemingway will!"[30]

Putnam never really liked Montparnasse. "Why did the 'exiles' tend to gather here in this garish environment," he later recalled, "with so much that was palpably false about it, to associate almost exclusively with other Americans?"[31] It was a rhetorical question, a broadside against the area and the era. Yet Paris still exercised a pull on him, and he was willing to concede that there were some serious writers there. After quarreling with Titus (over the merits of James T. Farrell's fiction, which Putnam liked and Titus did not), Putnam left *This Quarter* to found his own literary magazine, the *New Review*, which published writers he approved of—including Farrell and a tough new writer on the Paris scene, Henry Miller.

It often seemed as if there were almost as many literary reviews and small presses in Montparnasse as there were writers. Opinions were strongly held, and groups formed around commonly held opinions, with each having its own particular vehicle for expression. One of the most notable of these "little magazines" was Eugene Jolas's *transition* (intentionally not capitalized), which emerged in the mid-1920s with the declaration, "The writer expresses. He does not communicate." Jolas intended *transition* to be revolutionary, "An International Quarterly for Creative Experiment," and in its first issue he printed his "Manifesto: The Revolution of the Word." It was *transition* that first published portions of James Joyce's *Finnegans Wake* (originally called *Work in Progress*), which already was puzzling and even irritating those of his friends who attempted to read it. These included Ezra Pound, who wrote Joyce, "Nothing so far as I can make out, nothing short of divine vision or a new cure for the clap can possibly be worth all the circumambient peripherization."[32]

Intentionally cutting edge, *transition* published a broad spectrum of experimental and linguistically challenging writing, including works by Surrealists and several pieces by Gertrude Stein—most notably "An Elucidation," which the befuddled typesetter set in the wrong order. Unfortunately, *transition* ceased publication in 1930, but only for a brief hiatus. Meanwhile, Titus's less experimental *This Quarter*—which, in the words of journalist Sisley Huddleston, "chose to lead the reaction against the cult of unintelligibility"[33]—continued to publish established writers such as D. H. Lawrence, Ernest Hemingway, Robert Penn Warren, Allen Tate, Samuel Beckett, and E. E. Cummings. All the while Samuel Putnam's *New Review*, aided by Ezra Pound on the masthead and considerable publicity from Putnam's good friend Wambly Bald, attempted to go its own way in fighting *transition*, leaning heavily toward literary realism and taking on the "corpse-raisers, pretenders and cheap miracle men of the past decade."[34]

Only Titus had the money to continue publishing if and when he wanted, while most of the others led perilous and fragmentary existences, including Putnam's *New Review*, which he took with him after the third issue when he left Paris for Provence (the fifth issue would be the review's last). Equally perilous were the prospects for small presses in Paris, except for those run by publishers with (or with access to) significant funding. Titus's Black Manikin Press certainly had reliable funding as well as a proven track record, and the wealthy American expatriate Caresse Crosby continued with the couple's Black Sun Press after her husband's suicide in late 1929, publishing beautiful and exclusive editions of modernist writers such as Hart Crane's 1930 epic, *The Bridge*. Robert McAlmon no longer carried on the notable work of his famed Contact Editions, but in 1930, the English shipping heiress Nancy Cunard moved her Hours Press from a Norman farmhouse into Paris, where she set up her antique printing press at 15 Rue Guénégaud, across from the Hôtel des Monnaies.

Nancy Cunard, daughter of a San Francisco socialite and an English baronet, and a direct descendant of the founder of the Cunard shipping line, held strong objections to the English aristocracy and everything it stood for. Early in life, her mother's admirer, the Irish poet and novelist George Moore, had introduced Nancy to fine literature, French painting, and English poetry (Moore, who played the role of Nancy's often-missing father, was suspected, probably falsely, of being her actual father). This informal education, plus studies in music and literature in France and Germany, prompted her to write her own poetry (her first six poems appeared in an Edith Sitwell anthology). At the war's end, after a failed marriage and life at the tantalizing periphery of London's literary circles, she finally made her break, at the age of twenty-four, for Paris.

There, Nancy Cunard became an astonishingly unconventional figure in the avant-garde social scene, easily spotted by her tall, rail-thin body, which she loaded with African-inspired necklaces and ivory bracelets rather than with the gold and jewels that she could well afford but despised. She was painted by Oskar Kokoschka, photographed by Man Ray, and sculpted by Brancusi; Aldous Huxley found inspiration from her for a leading character in *Point Counter Point*, while William Carlos Williams said that "Nancy was to me as constant as the heavens in her complete and passionate inconstancy."[35]

"Stunning . . . is the word most often used to describe her appearance," wrote a longtime Montparnasse resident, the writer Morrill Cody. "She always seemed to be leading others, always out in front a step or two." Her friend and collaborator, Hugh Ford, highlighted "ardor and passion . . . action and industry" as Cunard's prominent characteristics.[36] She hung out with Dadaists and Surrealists, and she would have been regarded merely as an eccentric heiress if it hadn't been for the publication of several well-regarded volumes of her own poetry during these years. Taking an interest in political activism that would remain with her for the rest of her life, Cunard lived for two years with the Surrealist poet Louis Aragon, who joined the Communist party in 1927 and would become its leading French spokesman in the 1930s. "I have never seen anyone with such concentration as Aragon," she later recalled. "He once wrote in front of me a long analytical essay, *Philosophie des Paratonnerres*, which he began one evening before dinner and finished some thirty-six hours later, with hardly any time off for sleep or meals."[37]

While still with Aragon, Cunard decided to learn hand printing and moved with him into a charming but quite rustic farmhouse in Normandy. There, she set up the Hours Press, buying up a two-hundred-year-old Belgian handpress and a supply of Caslon Old Face type from Bill Bird, owner of the much-admired but now defunct Three Mountains Press, which in its heyday had published Hemingway, William Carlos Williams, and Ezra Pound. The

Hours Press thus had, in Cunard's words, "a distinguished, even illustrious lineage," and after a remarkably quick learning curve, aided by Bill Bird and a printer blessedly proficient in the old ways, she soon published an edition of *Peronnik the Fool* by her "first friend," George Moore, who insisted on heading her list of publications. "I want to start your press off with a good bang!" he told her.[38]

Cunard's two hundred copies of *Peronnik* sold out on publication day. More successes followed, even before she moved her press to Paris in January 1930. That year she published ten volumes, including Ezra Pound's *XXX Cantos*, and she also published Samuel Beckett, then young and unknown, who won a poetry contest she sponsored—sliding his entry, *Whoroscope*, under the door at 3:00 a.m. on the contest's final day.[39]

By this time, Cunard had met, and was living with, "an enchanting aide and companion," the Afro-American jazz musician Henry Crowder. It was Crowder who introduced Cunard to "the astonishing complexities and agonies of the Negroes in the United States," to which she listened "with growing indignation."[40] Soon, Crowder's teaching would lead to the compilation and publication of Cunard's masterwork, her *Negro Anthology*.

But for now, Cunard was in the midst of running her press and its adjacent bookshop, which became such a neighborhood gathering place that she sometimes had to lock the doors when interruptions became too numerous. The best spots to meet with friends, she noted, were the well-known Left Bank literary and artistic centers, the Café de Flore and the Café Les Deux Magots.

～

The Deux Magots, located on the Place Saint-Germain-des-Prés, had an unusual origins story going back to the early 1800s, when it began as a lingerie shop under the same name. Moving around the corner to its present location, it was eventually replaced by a café but kept the name, which it seems to have owed to a popular play called *Les Deux Magots de Chine*—a "magot" being a Chinese mandarin.

Somewhere along the way, the Deux Magots acquired the two large figurines of mandarins that still gaze placidly from their perch on the room's central pillar. The café also acquired the reputation, especially between the wars, as *the* place for artists and writers to meet over drinks. The Surrealists made it one of their favorite watering holes, and the nearby publishing houses of Grasset and Gallimard, as well as the theater, Le Vieux-Colombier, drew their own crowds, including Gide and Malraux and eventually Sartre, Camus, and Simone de Beauvoir.

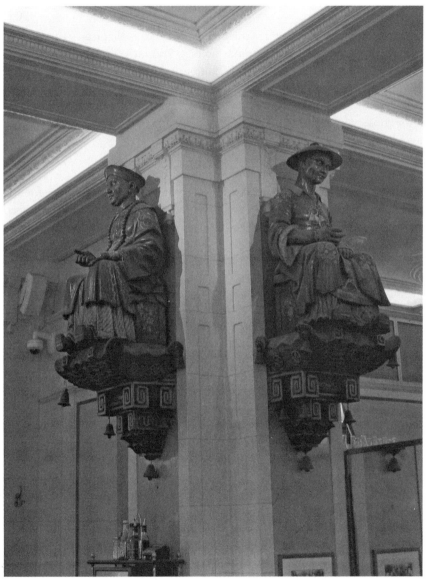

The deux magots *(two Chinese mandarins), from the Café Les Deux Magots, Paris.* ©
M. McAuliffe

The Flore, located only a few steps from the Deux Magots, did not enjoy quite as long or complicated a history, dating only from 1870 and having been a café from the start. Existing for many years in the Deux Magots' shadow, the Flore was beginning to emerge into its own by the 1930s, although it still labored under the stigma of Charles Maurras—the leading thinker of the monarchist, ultranationalist, and far-right Catholic organization, Action Française—who had famously held court there. During the height of the Dreyfus Affair, Maurras's deeply anti-Semitic publication, *Action Française*, was born at the Café de Flore, and for some time thereafter those who abhorred Maurras and Action Française made a point of avoiding the Flore.

Cafés, although supremely popular, were not the only meeting place for artists and writers in postwar Paris. After Ford Madox Ford and Stella Bowen went their separate ways, Ford started his Thursday afternoons and "much-talked-of sonnet-writing evenings," while Bowen opened her studio to an eclectic mix of British and American painters, writers, and others.[41] The *transition* crowd and a number of Surrealists gravitated to the Montparnasse apartment of the wealthy American expats, Mary and Bill Widney, while the Russian-born sculptor Ossip Zadkine, who spoke English beautifully, often invited Anglo-Americans to his garden-surrounded home on the Rue d'Assas, where they could chat with his French and Russian colleagues. Closer to the Seine, on the Rue Jacob, Natalie Clifford Barney continued to hold her salon as she had for years, in the eighteenth-century tradition, where grace and wit prevailed. Barney had once entertained Proust and, true to her literary pedigree, still attracted leading literary figures such as Paul Valéry and André Gide.

Gertrude Stein (who insisted on being called by her full name, or by "Miss Stein") was still holding forth regularly at her famous salon at 27 Rue de Fleurus, as she had for the past twenty-five years. There, she predictably ran the show and relegated wives and other females to the supervision of her partner, Alice B. Toklas. The American writer Kay Boyle, who thought highly of Gertrude Stein in professional terms, added that she was "difficult to celebrate. She had a monopoly on reverence for herself."[42] But then again, Gertrude Stein had not treated Kay Boyle very well. The English poet Cedric Harris (pen name, Archibald Craig) brought Boyle one evening to 27 Rue de Fleurus, where she had made the best of being cordoned off with Alice, having a pleasant chat with her about cooking and recipes. But afterward, Gertrude Stein told Craig not to bring Boyle again, on the grounds that she was "as incurably middle-class as Ernest Hemingway."[43]

By this time, a number of people had broken with or simply had enough of Gertrude Stein. Hemingway, who had been Stein's good friend and loyal supporter during his early years in Paris, had offended her deeply with his novel *The Torrents of Spring*, in which he satirized her almost as much as he had his mentor and her friend, Sherwood Anderson.[44] But there seems to have been more to their estrangement than this. Hemingway later circulated several accounts of their break, the one silly and another, as told in *A Moveable Feast*, far less laughable. There, he claimed to have overheard an unsettling exchange between Gertrude and Alice that graphically reinforced Alice's reputation as manipulative and domineering. He also became contemptuous of what he came to view as Stein's fundamental laziness—"a very great writer who stopped writing because she was too lazy to write for other people because writing for other people is very hard."[45]

Gertrude would in time have the opportunity to take "big patches of skin off Hemingway," as Sherwood Anderson put it, in her 1934 *The Autobiography of Alice B. Toklas*,[46] but she seems to have genuinely believed that Hemingway had lost touch with his true genius and was wasting his talent with a growing obsession with sex and violent death. At the same time, she continued to suffer greatly from the fame that continued to elude her while bestowing its blessings on other writers such as Hemingway and James Joyce. Gertrude Stein had always preferred those writers who were struggling.

Gertrude and Man Ray fell out the old-fashioned way, over money. On February 12, 1930, Man Ray decided that it was about time that Gertrude pay for the portraits he had made of her and her dog, Basket, and sent her a bill for 500 francs. She immediately wrote back (on the same sheet of paper), refusing to pay and dismissing his effrontery: "My dear Man Ray, we are all hard up but don't be silly about it." Gertrude had always been cheap, rarely paying for what she insisted she should receive for free; but in addition, Man Ray's success seemed to rankle her. As he put it, "her bitterness really showed up when others [Hemingway, Joyce, the Dadaists, the Surrealists] got universal attention before she did." On the other hand, Man Ray resented the fact that Gertrude Stein only seemed to value him as a photographer, not for his "real work" as a painter.[47]

Yet another with a grudge, or at least every right to hold a grudge, against Gertrude Stein was Fernande Olivier, Picasso's mistress from his Bateau-

Lavoir days on Montmartre. Since that time in 1912 when Picasso had abruptly parted with Olivier in favor of another mistress, Olivier had cast about for the means to support herself—as a movie extra, as a salesperson, as a nanny, as a cashier in a butcher shop, and as manager of a cabaret. Then in 1928 she hit on the scheme of publishing memoirs about her life with Picasso and brought her manuscript to Gertrude Stein, who had once been a close friend—although until then Stein had ignored Olivier's pleas for help.

Stein was greatly interested in Olivier's manuscript and promised to find a translator and an American publisher for her; but as it turns out, Stein merely wanted to use Olivier's material in her own forthcoming book, *The Autobiography of Alice B. Toklas*. Naturally, Stein was not eager to see Olivier publish before her, and no translator or American publisher ever appeared. But Olivier found a ready buyer on her own—the popular evening newspaper, *Le Soir*, where her memoirs appeared in installments in September 1930. The revelations of opium use, multiple mistresses, and involvement in thefts from the Louvre (all mostly true) titillated the public and embarrassed Picasso's wife, Olga, who put a stop to publication—although in later years Picasso would remark that it was the only account that captured what life in the Bateau-Lavoir had really been like. In any case, the editor of the prestigious *Mercure de France* liked what he had seen, both of the *Le Soir* excerpts and of the still-beautiful Olivier, and arranged for further publication.[48]

As for James Joyce, Gertrude Stein had never much cared for him, his writing, or especially the esteem in which he was held. Her touchiness about Joyce may have stemmed, at least in part, from her irritation at being linked with him as a modernist writer, despite her conviction of their fundamental differences. But at the core she seethed because she had been first, and because she had the unshakable conviction that she was better. Joyce "is a *good* writer," she remarked condescendingly on one occasion, "but who came first, Gertrude Stein or James Joyce? Do not forget that my first great book, *Three Lives*, was published in 1908. That was long before *Ulysses*."[49]

"If you brought up Joyce twice, you would not be invited back," Hemingway wrote. "It was like mentioning one general favorably to another general. You learned not to do it the first time you made the mistake." Gertrude (with Alice) marched into Shakespeare and Company soon after *Ulysses* appeared to announce to Sylvia Beach that, as a consequence of Beach's role in publishing the offending book, they had transferred their membership from Shakespeare and Company to the American Library, then located across the

Seine. Beach seems to have recovered nicely from the blow: "In the Rue de l'Odéon, I must admit, we kept low company," she added with a twinkle after recounting the event.[50]

And Kay Boyle recalled a memorable occasion when, at a party given by the editors of *transition*, Gertrude Stein and Alice B. Toklas entered like a "ceremonial cortege" across the room from James Joyce, who seemed not to notice.

As Joyce later remarked, "I hate intellectual women."[51]

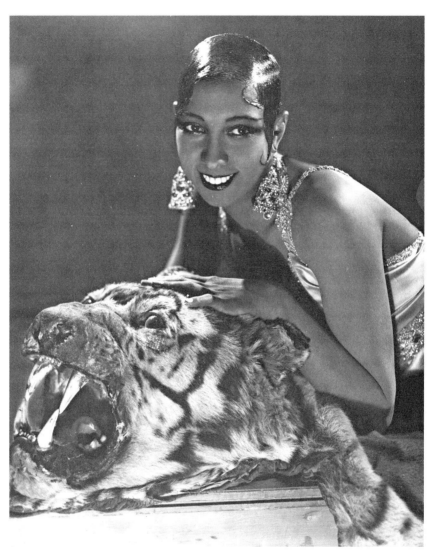

Josephine Baker in 1931. © Spaarnestad / Bridgeman Images

CHAPTER FOUR

~

The Ooh La La Factor

(1930)

Josephine Baker was remaking herself—from a sexy banana-skirted jungle girl into a sexy grown-up vamp. Dancing would be out, or at least it would be more subdued, and singing would be in. Her manager and lover, known as Pepito, had declared that this was the right direction, now that Josephine's original act had gone a little stale—especially with talking pictures posing a threat to live entertainment. The public wanted something else? Right. Josephine would deliver.

She got her chance with a new music review at the Casino de Paris music hall, on the outskirts of Montmartre. The review, *Paris Qui Remue* (*Bustling Paris*), which opened in October 1930, took as its theme France's upcoming Exposition Coloniale, celebrating the French empire. Josephine acquired the job of representing, in a showbiz sense, the empire's African colonies as well as French Vietnam. In her first act, as a bird pursued by hunters, she floated down a steep staircase, adorned in two enormous white-feathered wings. In the second, as the Vietnamese mistress of a Frenchman, she slinked in gold lamé and sang "J'ai Deux Amours," the show's most famous song, and one that she would make her own. In her last act, she emerged from an African forest to entrance her audience, if not her leading man, Pierre Meyer—who may have been as much of a draw as Josephine, but mortally offended her by refusing to sleep with her. So she had him fired. In any case, she regarded the cheetah, Chiquita, as her real costar.

Josephine may not have been a hit with Meyer, but she certainly was with her audiences. "She left us a *négresse*, droll and primitive, she comes back a great artist," wrote one critic. Another effused, "The beautiful savage has learned to discipline her instincts. Her singing . . . transported the crowd."[1] Janet Flanner was in the minority when she mourned that Josephine Baker "has, alas, almost become a little lady," one that "has become thinned, trained, almost civilized."[2] But Flanner was not alone in noting Josephine's much whiter skin. The critics managed to attribute Josephine's lighter appearance as well as her newfound elegance to France's colonizing power, which they praised for having civilized the erstwhile savage. But for several years Josephine had been whitening her skin, bathing in a mix of goat's milk, bleach, lemon, honey, and water, just as she had been exercising her body and training her voice. With Pepito's help and numerous lessons, Josephine Baker had taken an active role in creating her new image.

This new image did not extend to Baker's lifestyle, which she refused to moderate. Despite pleas from the Casino's anguished producers, she led her life as she wished, in full public view, including the naughty pleasure of having sex with a handsome stage manager right in the wings. "She had a lot of time off in the last act," as one of her colleagues put it. Nor did Baker's new sophistication lessen her ferocity in dealing with rivals, who were ferocious in turn. Mistinguett, long the darling of the Paris music-hall scene, had responded like a panther to this threat to her stardom. Mistinguett's legs may have been insured by Lloyds of London for five hundred thousand francs, but she was now in her fifties and had lost the bloom of youth. Backstage tensions escalated as she called Josephine "La Négresse," and Josephine dismissed her as "the Old One"; but in time, Mistinguett would become a role model for the younger woman. Twenty years later, Baker would say that "when I am . . . on the point of dropping . . . I think about Mistinguett. And I . . . accept that one must go on, work hard . . . survive."[3]

Hard work—uncomplaining hard work—was the virtual motto of Marie Curie. Ever since she was young, she had worked—at her schoolwork in Warsaw; at her doctoral studies at the Sorbonne; at the grueling physical and mental labor leading to the discovery, with her husband, Pierre, of radium; and in all the laborious research thereafter. All done in circumstances, at least in her early Paris years, of grinding poverty, during which she successfully combined the duties and privileges of raising two daughters with the obligations and joys of her work. Throughout, Marie Curie calmly refused to be intimidated by the men (and women) who denigrated her scholarship and research and who tried to deprive her of recognition and reward. Even long after winning her first Nobel Prize, the French Academy of Sciences denied her membership, and disbelief that a woman had accomplished what she had indeed accomplished almost prevented her from receiving her due recognition, with Pierre, for that first Nobel Prize in 1903.

Marie Curie certainly did not fit the model of the French feminine ideal, and the very fact that, in addition to her professional achievements, she managed to maintain a beautiful (if tragically brief) marriage to Pierre Curie, as well as raise two healthy and intelligent daughters, aroused considerable ire among her new countrymen. Her achievements, coupled with her disinterest in financial gain or fame, seemed to many to be unbelievable. The press attacked her as a foreigner and as a woman who did not know her place, but she nonetheless quietly persisted in the work she believed essential. In the process, she exposed herself to poisoning from the very substance she and Pierre had discovered, and by 1930 she was far more ill than she was willing to let on. Her health was rapidly declining, especially her eyesight, which required numerous cataract operations—the last, in 1930, leaving her with renewed, although severely impaired, sight.

Marie Curie would not admit that she was ill, or that she was working too hard. And she fiercely protected her privacy, letting few know of her troubles. "Tell them as little as possible, darling!" she enjoined her youngest daughter, Eve, in a typical refrain. Yet occasionally her resolution wavered: "Sometimes my courage fails me and I think I ought to stop working, live in the country, and devote myself to gardening," she wrote her older sister, Bronya. Although, she added, she did not know how this would be possible, or how she could arrange it. "Nor do I know" she confessed, "whether . . . I could live without the laboratory."[4]

The laboratory was, in a real sense, Curie's life; and so it was fortunate that the gift of radium, or the fifty thousand dollars necessary to buy it (which her women supporters in America raised in 1929 for a radium institute in Curie's Polish homeland), managed to survive the Wall Street stock market crash. Indeed, Curie received the cash presentation from President Hoover on October 30, 1929, the day after the Crash. Most fortunately, despite the widespread losses that must have impacted Curie's donors, the presentation proceeded as planned.

All the Curie women were remarkable. Marie's eldest daughter, Irène, was a brilliant scientist in her mother's footsteps and often collaborated with her mother at the Radium Institute as she came of age in the 1920s. In 1925 she earned her doctorate with a remarkable thesis on the emission of alpha rays from polonium—an element that her parents had discovered. It was the sort of subject, especially from the daughter of a dual Nobel Prize winner, that attracted attention, and soon predictions began to spread that Irène would be the next woman to win a Nobel Prize.

At about the same time, Marie put Irène in charge of teaching complex laboratory techniques to a young man, Frédéric Joliot, who had come highly recommended by Marie's former lover and still close friend, the prominent French physicist Paul Langevin.[5] Frédéric, who was three years younger than Irène, was handsome as well as talented, and he eventually caught the attention of the workaholic and usually aloof Irène. The two combined their research on the study of atomic nuclei, and soon they combined their lives, wedding in 1926 and hyphenating their surnames to Joliot-Curie. Although the two possessed quite contrasting personalities, they were complementary, with Frédéric's charm and sunniness balancing Irène's seriousness. "I discovered in this young woman," he later said, "an extraordinary, poetic and sensitive being who, in a number of ways, was a living representation of her father."[6] In addition, the two shared a passion for their work, as well as an increasing ardor for antifascist and pacifist politics and humanitarian causes, Irène easily assimilating the activism that had been an important part of Frédéric's upbringing.

Eve Curie, the younger daughter, could not have been more different from Irène, nor, for that matter, from their mother. Eve, who was beautiful, fashionable, and outgoing, had no interest whatever in science. Her inclinations and abilities leaned toward music, and her abilities as a pianist became evident at quite a young age. She yearned to become a concert pianist, and Marie readily provided her with lessons and a grand piano; but by 1930, after playing recitals in France and Belgium, Eve decided that she would not be able to make a living at it. Casting about for her role in life, she became a music as well as film and theater critic, under an assumed name. Her true calling still lay in the future, but in the meantime, she felt dismissed by some (although not by her family) for not being a scientist like her mother and sister.

By 1930, Irène and Frédéric had a three-year-old daughter, Hélène, and that spring, Frédéric successfully defended his own doctoral thesis, "A Study of the Electrochemistry of Radioactive Elements," on the strength of which he received a substantial government grant, allowing him to focus on his research. But that summer Irène, who had never fully regained her health after the birth of Hélène, was diagnosed with tuberculosis. At length, after putting up quite a resistance, she agreed to go for a rest cure in the French Alps. Now it would be up to Frédéric to manage household, daughter, and laboratory work—at least until the end of summer, when Irène returned, claiming to be much better. She ignored her mother's pleas to stop work, just as she would ignore her doctor's warning not to risk another pregnancy.

～

After a wrecked marriage to a Frenchman, an affair with the poet Ernest Walsh (ending only with his premature death), and the birth of an illegitimate daughter by Walsh, the American writer Kay Boyle was back in Paris, drawn into the artistic and social circles of the Left Bank. There, in the late 1920s, she reestablished her friendship with numerous notables, including William Carlos Williams, Constantin Brancusi, and Robert McAlmon. Despite McAlmon's revulsion at Eugene Jolas's *transition* and all it stood for, Boyle became close to Jolas as well; her work began to appear in *transition*, and she headed the list of literary figures signing *transition*'s manifesto, "Revolution of the Word."

She also met Raymond Duncan. Raymond, brother of the famed dancer Isadora Duncan, had long been a familiar figure in Paris, striding along the streets in his long tunic and sandals. Affecting a Grecian style, à la Isadora, he developed a cult whose members gathered in a commune around him, living largely on goat cheese and yogurt and supporting themselves through the sale of articles that Raymond claimed they made themselves. Boyle decided to join them, in part because "my social conscience was in such a bad way,"[7] but also because it offered child care for her daughter, who joined the mob of other colony children while Boyle worked at the colony's gift shops and wrote in her spare time.

It was a disillusioning experience from the outset ("the filth, the disorder, the cold," as Boyle later described it in her autobiographical novel, *My Next Bride*).[8] And it rapidly became worse after the colony members traipsed off to Nice for the summer, taking Boyle's sixteen-month-old daughter with them. Boyle, left to mind the shops and abysmally lonely, "tripped and reeled and stumbled" in and out of what she termed "every bar in Montparnasse." Her misadventures left her deeply depressed, ill, and pregnant. At length, not even knowing who the father might be, she decided to have an abortion. Her good friend Caresse Crosby (of Black Sun Press) helped her "find the place and the time, and Harry (who had no part in it) paid the enormous bill."[9]

Traumatized and ill, Boyle now completely collapsed with an attack of cerebral meningitis that her doctors attributed to the filth in the commune's living quarters. When she finally returned from the hospital to the colony, Duncan reproached her for her absence, calling it a breach of loyalty. In addition, Boyle was having severe doubts about the ethics of selling items supposedly handcrafted in the colony, which indeed were not—especially when she learned that one especially large sale of twenty-five thousand dollars was destined for a Raymond Duncan wing in a Kentucky museum. Duncan himself saw no problem with this and even, according to Boyle's fictionalized version of the event in My Next Bride, scolded her for not extracting more money from the gullible buyers than she already had done. He then went and bought himself a large, luxurious automobile with the proceeds. This was too much, and Boyle realized she had to leave—but how, with her daughter virtually held hostage?

At length, with the help of friends, Boyle managed to retrieve her daughter, and the two hid for a time in Caresse and Harry Crosby's Norman cottage, Le Moulin. Soon Boyle would begin her life anew with Laurence Vail, a poet and artist previously married to Peggy Guggenheim. By the spring, the two were expecting a child (Apple-Joan would be born in late 1929), and more children would follow. Boyle and Vail married in 1932, and despite Vail's rancorous breakup with Guggenheim (over child custody), she and her current lover, John Holms, attended the wedding. "We did not want to go," Guggenheim later wrote, "but we had to, so as not to offend the children." In any case, she had to admit, "Kay [Boyle] was a very good stepmother."[10]

⁓

Abortions, like Kay Boyle's, occurred in 1930s France, but they were illegal, expensive, and risky (and would continue to be so until they were legalized in 1975). Even contraception was discouraged under the influence of the Catholic Church and France's ardent nationalists, who feared that their nation's low birth rate put them at a disadvantage with Germany's booming population. France had lost one and a half million men in the Great War, with three million more wounded—many so severely that they would not be able to work or function normally again. More children were needed to make up the deficit, and the natalists backed a strong family policy, one with home-based social services and benefits going to mothers (which was considered a more reliable way of providing child benefits than to the fathers).

Until late in the 1930s, French employers' organizations (usually organized industry by industry, although sometimes across industries) bore the burden of providing family allowances, calculated as a percentage of a worker's wage (a certain percentage for one child, and exponentially more for each additional child). This provided a way to redistribute income from childless workers to those with children, especially to those with large families, and it significantly altered the wages for large families dependent on a single earner. Family allowances certainly appealed to wage earners, but they had their appeal for employers as well. Not only were the benefits directed to mothers, thus countering the influence of the heavily male and (more to the point) heavily Communist Paris unions, but these ostensibly benevolent family allowance funds were entirely under the control of the employers, who used them to contain—and during the Depression, to drive down—wages and combat unions.

The state would not become involved in French family policy until late in the decade, when the German threat became inescapable. At this time, a comprehensive Family Code was established, now including employers, agricultural workers, and the self-employed, which continued to link family allowances to wages and family needs. The system remained a form of reapportionment of national income from the childless to those with children, and—with an eye toward its birth rate—included even stricter penalties for abortions. Not surprisingly, French feminists, who still were few in number and without the vote, were not thrilled.

As for social insurance, the legislation introduced in 1928 and put into practice in 1930 provided all employed persons below a certain wage level with medical insurance, maternity benefits, modest pensions, and disability benefits. Significantly, unemployment insurance was not included, and when the Depression started to have its impact, it was the women, the elderly, and foreigners who were the first to lose their jobs.[11]

~

There were feminists in France during this decade, but there was no strong feminist movement. The Napoleonic heritage of male supremacy was still deep seated, and throughout the 1930s, French women, as one historian has put it, were "politically marginal"[12] and did not receive the vote until 1944. Although the Chamber voted three times in favor of female suffrage during the 1930s, this was a sham; everyone knew the Senate would never pass it.

Paris in the 1930s, including literary Paris, was filled with men who, if not outright misogynists, were at least disparaging of women. Not surprisingly, Gide, as a gay man in a strange marriage, as well as one who had close female friends, was ambivalent on the subject. Pondering what he termed the "very eloquent" antifeminism of contemporary French writer Henry de Montherlant, Gide wrote in his journal that he believed "that the error consists in looking upon woman merely as an instrument of pleasure." Yet, Gide added, "I come to wonder if there is not still more danger in allowing more than the flesh to be involved, and if he who escapes love's trap most cheaply is not precisely the one who risks only the slightest and least valuable part of himself."[13]

While Gide was troubled by his relationship with women, James Joyce's outright dislike of women was becoming ever more strident. Joyce owed much to the women in his life, and his resentment against them—and against women in general—grew as his dependence on them increased. Despite his substantial income, Joyce by 1930 was spending more recklessly than ever and was borrowing ever more heavily from Sylvia Beach as well as from his other devoted supporter, the Englishwoman Harriet Weaver. Neither of these women was wealthy, and when in late 1930 Miss Weaver's solicitors strongly suggested that Joyce try to live within his income, Joyce clearly felt persecuted and dramatically canceled plans for his upcoming birthday celebration, accompanying his sacrifice with self-pity and grumbles.

Yet Joyce believed himself to be an expert on women and proudly displayed a 1932 letter from Carl Jung praising him for his psychological insight. Jung, like so many others, was especially taken with Molly Bloom's long soliloquy at the end of *Ulysses*, which he termed "a string of veritable psychological peaches." But Nora, Joyce's common-law wife, emphatically disagreed: James "knows nothing at all about women," she said flatly.[14]

As it happened, in late 1930, after many long years of refusing to marry Nora (Joyce thought little of the institution of marriage), he decided that the wedding bells should ring—solely because he wished to ensure his children's inheritance, whose rights would be better protected if the two were legally wed.[15] His son's upcoming marriage as well as his daughter's increasing mental instability may have prompted the move, and probably had a bearing on another development as well: late in 1930, Joyce suddenly insisted that he and Sylvia Beach sign a contract for the world rights to *Ulysses*. Until then, despite Beach's suggestion, Joyce had found such a contract unnecessary and bothersome; but now, with an expensive lawsuit against the U.S. publisher of a pirated edition underway—a lawsuit in which Joyce had officially claimed that *Ulysses* was Beach's property rather than his own—he decided to put her ownership and responsibility for *Ulysses* into writing. It was, as Beach's friend Janet Flanner called it, a "strange Jesuitical document,"[16] which contained an important section that allowed Beach's rights to be purchased at a price set by herself, if both she and Joyce deemed such a sale to be in the author's interests.[17]

Joyce himself would breach this contract.

In March 1930, Henry Miller arrived in Paris. He had visited there two years before with his wife, June, but had not stayed. When he next appeared in Paris, he was alone.

June was Henry's second wife, whom he had met in a New York dance hall. She was a "taxi dancer," paid by the dance, and Henry fell desperately in love with her. His journalist friend Alfred Perlès, who was wary of June, described her as "one of those dark *femme fatale* types one comes across in certain French novels—beautiful, temperamental and eccentric." Perlès knew that June "was bad for Henry and he probably knew it himself. She put him through the tortures of hell." Still, Perlès remarked philosophically, Henry was in love with her, and added, "I dare say he still loves her."[18]

As Miller's biographer, Robert Ferguson, has pointed out, the question of Henry Miller's relationship with June is central to understanding Miller as a person as well as to understanding Miller's writing, in which he used the torments that June heaped on him as fodder for his autobiographical fiction. It made for quite a story, but one that raised the question of whether Miller was dismally abused by his wife, or whether he in fact was the abuser. That is, how much of his story was invented? Perlès and others of Miller's (mostly male) friends and admirers were of one mind in viewing June as the oppressor, "worse for him than alcohol and opium combined."[19] They tended to view Miller as a literary outlaw in search of wisdom, whom June tried to destroy. But others (especially female) have taken June's side, declaring Miller a misogynist, a literary fraud, and little more than an unabashed pornographer; Miller, from this point of view, used June simply as a device to prod and shape his writing.[20]

Henry Miller, born in 1891 in Manhattan and raised in Brooklyn, was perhaps born to write fiction: he was an exaggerator, a fable teller, and a liar from the start. "He believed with all his heart that he owned himself," writes Ferguson, "and that owning himself gave him the right to invent himself too."[21] This does not seem to have been the product either of genetics or environment: Miller came from solid, unfanciful German-American stock and spent his boyhood in Brooklyn trying to avoid following his father's footsteps into the tailoring business. As an only son, with a mentally and physically incapacitated younger sister, he was doted on but also had to make his way in a tough immigrant world. Bright, gregarious, and musically inclined, he received a reasonable although unmemorable education, which he abruptly terminated after one dull semester at City College (Latin, German, physics, chemistry, and gym).

By then he was clearly floundering, with no idea of what or where he wanted to be. Wandering westward, he ended up in California, where, among other jobs, he worked on a cattle ranch, and where he had his first encounters with socialism, anarchism, and Nietzsche. Deciding that he was not a cowboy after all, he returned home, broke off relations with a mistress fifteen years his senior, and entered his first marriage, where in due course he fathered a daughter. He was beginning to read (Henri Bergson and Herbert Spencer; Walt Whitman and probably Emma Goldman; Theodore Dreiser, Jack London, and Frank Norris), and to write. But nothing so far indicated that he would ever make anything of himself, although his lengthy stint at Western Union, in charge of the company's extensive messenger service, was for him unprecedented—and would inspire his brutalizing "Cosmodemonic Telegraph Company" in *Tropic of Capricorn*.

Miller's first wife, Beatrice, played the piano and was respectable. His next wife, June, was not. After Beatrice gave up on him and left, Miller, now in his thirties, started to write and to collect rejection letters. He also embarked on what he described as a life of promiscuity and hung out at a variety of nightspots, including the dance hall where he met June Edith Smith, the woman who would alternately blast apart and fill his life and his writing for decades.

June was precocious, romantic, and sufficiently able to keep up with Miller in conversations about Strindberg and Dostoevsky. She was also bold and daring, the most powerful and provocative sexual being he had ever encountered. He had to have her, and for her part, June shamelessly led him on, flirting with other men—and women. She was intellectually out of her depth, but fully in charge in matters sexual, to the point of taking a female lover and temporarily turning her marriage with Miller into a bohemian and nightmarish ménage à trois. June and her lover even went to Paris together for two months, without him. In the meantime, Miller learned to survive by using to advantage his friendly, outgoing nature, coupled with his general air of incompetence and helplessness—much like an exasperating but engaging puppy. From now on, he would rely heavily and shamelessly on the generosity of anyone who would support him. As Alfred Perlès put it, Miller was "good at getting money from people, and knowing which ones and where."[22]

Miller arrived in Paris in March 1930, intending to return to New York, but by November he had decided to stay—allowing June, who joined him briefly—to return without him. Miller quickly found friends, lived contentedly in utter squalor, and fell in love with Paris. Unlike the Americans who had preceded him, he was not part of the Lost Generation and did not hang out with the Anglo-American Left Bank crowd. He avoided Shakespeare and Company, Gertrude Stein's salon, and the writers or would-be writers who congregated around Hemingway, Fitzgerald, and Joyce.

His French improved, and many of his friends were French and European, such as the Viennese-born journalist Alfred Perlès and the Hungarian photographer Brassaï, although he had some American friends. These mostly were characters who operated on the periphery of Left Bank literary society, such as the journalist Wambly Bald, the bohemian lawyer Richard Osborn, and the Lithuanian-American writer and publisher Michael Fraenkel. Like Perlès and Bald, many of Miller's friends were journalists. He sponged off them and camped out with them, often at length. In return, he offered these lonely and often strange people the gift of friendship, one permeated with his unfailing delight in his fetterless condition—to do as he chose, and to do so in this most wonderful of all cities. As he later wrote in the opening sentence of *Tropic of Cancer*, "I have no money, no resources, no hopes. I am the happiest man alive."[23]

Miller had already discovered Proust and was intrigued by Proust's (and Proust's narrator's) obsession with his fictional character, Albertine. This gave Miller the idea of writing in a somewhat similar manner about June, only not in a Belle Epoque setting, but one with working-class characters and surroundings. He also discovered that writing about June, and about her magnetic pull on him—as well as about the horrors, or his perceived horrors, of their life together—was therapeutic. In particular, it allowed him to get back at, and even dominate, the woman who had refused to be dominated.

That April in Paris, while spring heralded flowers and young love, Zelda Fitzgerald had her first mental breakdown. Scott Fitzgerald, wracked by a deadly cocktail of anguish and guilt, placed her in a clinic just outside Paris, then moved her to another in Geneva. Perhaps he already realized, or at least feared, that he would spend the rest of their married life in a state of virtual suspension, vacillating between Zelda's temporary periods of recovery and the breakdowns that inevitably followed. He feared for her health, but he also blamed himself for the part that his alcoholism had played in her breakdown. For fifteen months he would live near her in Switzerland, while visiting their young daughter, Scottie, for several days each month in Paris. Added to his woes, he wondered how he could ever earn enough money to pay for her expensive treatments.

Hemingway sent his condolences from Key West the following year, explaining that he had been laid up with a broken arm and unable to write. It was the result of a bad car accident in Montana, but despite his complaints of going crazy in the hospital and of having to cancel his plans for an African safari, his life was going well: *A Farewell to Arms* was receiving fine reviews and soaring book sales and was being translated into French and German. In addition, a lucrative film deal with Paramount Pictures was underway. But Hemingway's enthusiasm for Paris was waning. He had returned to the States in early 1930 with some sports fishing in Key West in mind. A year of travel, including hunting in Wyoming and that bad car accident, took up the rest of his year.

With the exception of his broken arm, Hemingway was doing well, very well indeed, but his second wife, Pauline, was worried. Her husband was showing some of the same restiveness he had shown when he was finishing his first novel, *The Sun Also Rises*, at the time when he was leaving Hadley for Pauline. Although, or perhaps because, he had found fame and fortune, Hemingway suffered increasingly from bouts of anxiety and depression, especially after he had typed that last page. There was no other woman as yet, but there would be, and Pauline was worried.

Hemingway was not alone in his bevy of women, although few other men felt the necessity of marrying them all. Picasso, in particular, went through numerous mistresses as well as wives in the course of his colorful career, and in 1930 he was in the midst of a lengthy affair with Marie-Thérèse Walter while maintaining at least a modicum of decorum with his Russian wife, Olga. Marie-Thérèse was young and delectable, while Olga, now ill and aging, was not. That June, Picasso—obviously feeling no financial pain—purchased the Château de Boisgeloup, near Paris, a country retreat where he could paint and sculpt in relative seclusion while Olga presided over an array of houseguests. This lifestyle was to Olga's taste, and she was pleased with the château; but she would not have been pleased to know that whenever she returned to Paris, Marie-Thérèse quietly appeared. In addition, Picasso and Marie-Thérèse had a place of their own in Paris, on the Left Bank, and later they had a separate apartment on Rue La Boétie, the street where Picasso and Olga lived. There was no end to Picasso's inventiveness when it came to meeting his mistress.

Did Olga know what was going on? According to the stories going around, she had no idea until Picasso's 1932 retrospective exhibit at the Georges Petit galleries, when the multiplicity of paintings of Marie-Thérèse, even in the form that Picasso presented her, alerted Olga to the presence of a rival. Others insist that Olga was not stupid and must have known. In any case, whenever she found out, it did not add to the Picassos' marital bliss.

Gertrude Stein, in the meantime, while not maintaining a lifestyle even remotely resembling that of her friend Picasso's, had a similar interest in real estate, and one summer she and Alice found the summer house of their dreams in Bilignin in the Haute-Savoie. They had spotted it in 1926 as they drove around the countryside, and Gertrude told Alice, "I will drive you up there and you can go and tell them that we will take their house."[24] This lord of the manor approach did not impress the occupant, an army officer in the French regiment stationed nearby, who had no intention of leaving. But Gertrude was undaunted.

She soon learned that if this officer was promoted to captain, he would have to be transferred, since there already were too many captains in his battalion. Gertrude then went to work on influential friends in Paris to have him promoted, which meant his transfer to another garrison. It took many months, but eventually the man was transferred to Africa, his family decamped, and Gertrude and Alice became the delighted tenants of a house that would remain in their hands for years. Their means of getting it does not seem to have in any way diminished their delight.

By 1930, a favorite guest was Bernard Faÿ, whom Gertrude later described as "one of the four permanent friendships in Gertrude Stein's life."[25] Faÿ—a professor of Franco-American relations, with a master's degree in modern languages from Harvard and a doctorate from the Sorbonne—came from an *haute bourgeoisie* family of Catholic royalists and frequently referred to Gertrude as "our lady."[26] He first met Gertrude during the mid-1920s, introduced by another of Gertrude's favorites, Virgil Thomson (who had written the as-yet unperformed *Four Saints in Three Acts* with Gertrude's libretto). By 1930, Faÿ had entered Gertrude's inner circle, having proved the depth of his devotion by praising Gertrude in print as "the most powerful American writer today."[27] Already he was engaged in translating into French *The Making of Americans*, whose force he feared no translation could convey.

Still, Faÿ's praise was not always as unqualified as Gertrude would have liked. In the *Autobiography of Alice B. Toklas*, she has Alice recall hearing Bernard Faÿ say "that the three people of first rate importance that he had met in his life were Picasso, Gertrude Stein and André Gide and Gertrude Stein inquired quite simply, that is quite right but why include Gide."[28]

⌒

Gertrude Stein was not the only one of Paris's literary and artistic set who was surviving the Depression in comfort, even though she had to sell one of her beloved Picasso paintings (*Girl with a Fan*) to self-publish when she could not find a publisher for her books. This undertaking became what she and Alice named the Plain Edition press—its first book, in 1930, being *Lucy Church Amiably*.

Other writers, artists, and musicians in and around Paris were managing to keep their heads above water, but those doing the best were those who had already made their reputations, such as Picasso, Stravinsky, Maurice Ravel, Fernand Léger, and the sculptor Aristide Maillol. Among the younger artists,

Salvador Dalí was doing remarkably well, with Gala's shrewd assistance—causing a certain amount of jealousy and wisecracks: André Breton came up with a nasty anagram for Dalí, "Avida Dollars," and called Gala the Cash Register.

Despite the catcalls, Dalí was emerging as a star of the Surrealist movement, and nothing seemed to stop him. When his dealer went bankrupt, the Noailles introduced him to a new dealer, and Gala negotiated with them to pay for a painting in advance. Despite Dalí's timorous response to everyday life, he dived with enthusiasm into the most repugnant subjects and found a market for his depictions of the dark and dangerously morbid. From a technical standpoint, no one questioned his extraordinary abilities, although some Surrealists worried that instead of pushing the boundaries in the name of Surrealism, Dalí was simply expressing personal phobias. Still, his startling subject matter brought him the attention—and, eventually, the buyers—that he and Gala craved. Some suspected that this was what it was all about.

Dalí certainly was garnering attention. Although he—like Duchamp, Picabia, Max Ernst, and so many others—was in revolt against Abstractionism and Cubism, he had attracted Picasso's interest. Picasso (according to his biographer, John Richardson) had noticed the young Spaniard, visited his 1929 exhibition, and looked carefully at Dalí's scandalous drawing, *The Sacred Heart*, in preparation for his *Crucifixion* painting of early 1930. The difference between them, though, as Richardson sees it, was that although Dalí blamed his "blasphemous attack" on the "dictates of his subconscious," it was a calculated shock tactic: "Dalí played to the public; Picasso to the demons within him."[29]

Jean Cocteau was also having a good year, creating the kind of rumpus he liked best. His opera, *La Voix humaine*—a monologue with one singer desperately telephoning a lover who has abandoned her—had its opening in February at the Comédie-Française. Not only did it reap critical and lasting praise, but it also incited a riot. The Surrealists, with whom Cocteau had long been at odds, were once again intent on disruption, and ten minutes into the production a voice began yelling from the balcony, "Obscene! Enough! Enough! It's Desbordes [Cocteau's lover] on the other end of the line!"[30]

Some thought the intruder was the Surrealist leader André Breton, but it turned out to be Breton's henchman, Paul Eluard. Scandal! In the darkness, pandemonium broke out. Women screamed, and voices shouted for Eluard's arrest. People grabbed him, tore his jacket, and even stubbed out a cigarette on his neck, but when Cocteau rescued him, Eluard merely growled, "I will end up killing you, you disgust me." Yet Cocteau was far from upset, tele-graphing his good friend Marie-Laure de Noailles that he had had "a great triumph with the public, but some bad temper from some intellectuals." And as his erstwhile best friend, Valentine Hugo (now living her life as a Surreal-ist), put it, "Jean is enchanted. He has had his scandal."[31]

Cocteau raised the stakes with his next venture, the film *Le Sang d'un poète* (*Blood of a Poet*), funded by the ever-daring Charles and Marie-Laure de Noailles. Cocteau (despite his denials) almost certainly had seen Buñuel and Dalí's sensational 1929 *Un Chien Andalou*, complete with its slashed eyeball and ant-infested hand, when in early 1930 he hatched an idea for a film that the Noailles agreed to finance. Cocteau's aim was to film poetry, and he called his picture "a realistic documentary of unreal happenings."[32] That sounded promising, but when his sponsors saw the results that autumn, they were horrified—especially by their role in it, in which they found them-selves playing members of a theater audience who were laughing at a suicide. The need to remake this scene, as well as a surge of right-wing furor at the Noailles, delayed the release of *Le Sang d'un poète* until early 1932.

The immediate uproar was caused by another film commissioned by the Noailles, *L'Age d'Or*, which was the second one by Buñuel and Dalí (mostly by Buñuel, after his break with Dalí). Its credentials as a Surrealist master-piece have since been established, but its savage anticlericalism and graphic attacks on bourgeois sexual repression caused riots when it was shown that December. Far-right hooligans assaulted viewers, threw ink at the screen, and slashed Surrealist works in the lobby. Soon Paris's prefect of police, Jean Chiappe, weighed in, and the Board of Censors banned the film. There was talk of the Noailles being excommunicated from the Catholic Church, and the couple certainly suffered a kind of social excommunication: Charles was even expelled from the famous Jockey Club, which reportedly was a difficult blow to bear.[33] In any case, there was no question for the moment of a license to show *Blood of a Poet* in public.

The year 1930 marked the onset of a decade of agitation in Paris, on the left and on the right. Even while experts continued to obsess about the dangers of inflation, clung to the gold standard, and complained about the injustices of German reparations payments, activism at both ends of the political spec-trum grew rapidly as unmistakable signs of the Depression multiplied.

Heavy-duty rhetoric led to outright violence among the Surrealists, as when André Breton and his adversaries fought it out over Breton's uncom-promising and abusive *Second Manifesto*, during which the poet René Char was knifed. Matters escalated after Louis Aragon visited Russia that autumn and returned an ardent Communist, having agreed to reject Breton's *Second Manifesto* and follow party directives in literary as well as political matters.

Communists and Nazis were both showing greater strength in Germany, where the cosmopolitan Count Harry Kessler, a frequenter of artistic high society in Paris, noted in his diary for September 15, 1930: "A black day for Germany. The Nazis have increased the number of their seats almost tenfold." That, plus the more than seventy Communists and forty-one supporters of the right-wing nationalist Alfred Hugenberg totaled "some 220 deputies who are radical opponents of the German state . . . and want to do away with it by revolutionary means."[34]

Closer to home, the treaty-mandated Allied occupation of the Rhineland ended that October, thus erasing a buffer zone, however small (by that time, merely the area around Mainz), that had existed since the end of World War I. Britain endorsed this move, and France agreed, with its Parliament approving the evacuation by large majorities. But this development set off alarms within the French right, especially the Catholic royalist and ultranationalist Action Française, which, figuratively speaking, had been at the barricades ever since the Dreyfus Affair.

Deeply anti-Semitic as well as fervently anti-Germany, Action Française had been in decline ever since its unsuccessful confrontation with the Vatican in the late 1920s. The Vatican had found Action Française's belligerent nationalism off-putting—especially when served up by the unapologetically unreligious Charles Maurras—and placed its publications on the Index of Prohibited Books. When Action Française leader Léon Daudet was pardoned in late 1929 and allowed to return from Belgian exile after escaping from a Paris prison, he found the organization in disarray.[35] Still, with its Camelots du Roi—widely feared bully boys formed to provide protection for Action Française and its activities—the organization retained its abilities to quickly mobilize for (usually violent) action. In addition, a small group within the parent organization, working in secret with like-minded individuals in the army and a variety of antiparliamentary leagues, would soon form the clandestine and dangerous fascist organization, the Cagoule.

Along with ultranationalism, its cronies—nativism and anti-Semitism—were also on the rise. Immigration had soared during the 1920s (nearly 7 percent of the French population by 1931), to replace the millions of French workers killed and maimed during the war. By 1930, *L'Ami du Peuple*, the newspaper of the right-wing perfume and cosmetics millionaire François Coty, was serving up large quantities of chauvinism daily to its three million readers—a hostility that would only increase as jobs became scarce. The Jewish population in France had also grown—more than doubled by 1930. But although remaining a small part of the total population, it exercised an economic, social, and intellectual influence out of proportion to its numbers and suffered from the barely concealed contempt of those who steadfastly viewed Jews as "foreign." As historian Eugen Weber notes, this anti-Semitism was "latent and mostly dormant when not challenged. But it took little to stir the embers."[36]

Amid this unsettling environment, a number of religious or semireligious musical works began to appear, including Stravinsky's 1930 Symphony of Psalms, first performed in Paris that December. Stravinsky's biographer observes that this symphony, commissioned as a secular work, emerged as "not merely choral, but severely, ritualistically sacred," and dedicated "to the glory of God."[37]

"We are about to have another war," the poet Bryher wrote around this time after visiting a German school and noting the hours each day devoted to gliding and aerodynamics.[38] Especially after France's evacuation of the Rhineland, unease in Paris swelled with the talk of war. Julien Green, the conservative American Catholic writer born and raised in Paris, may have been especially sensitive to these undercurrents when he entered the following in his journal for October 16: "How can I work on a novel when peace is threatened?" A few days later, he noted that he was far from alone in his anxieties: "everywhere," he wrote, "it is only a question of the next war. In salons, in cafés, that is all one hears talk of, with the same tone of horror."[39]

Despite France's complacency as the decade began, even the sparkling charms of a Josephine Baker could not completely distract Parisians from an unsettled feeling that all was not well, and that danger lay ahead.

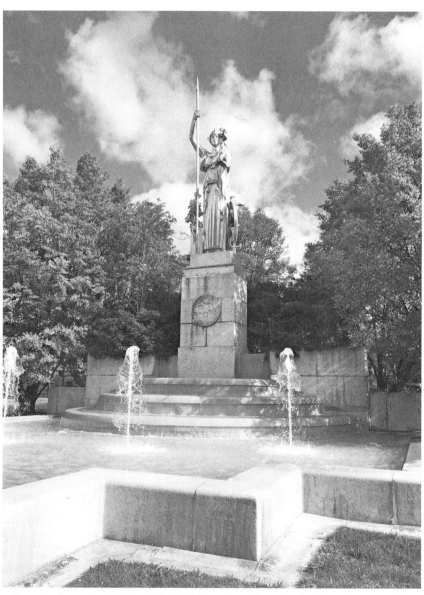

Fountain from the 1931 Paris Colonial Exposition, Porte Dorée, Paris. © J. McAuliffe

CHAPTER FIVE

~

Navigating a Dangerous World

(1931–1932)

"In 1931," Charlotte Perriand wrote in her memoirs, "I set out to fulfill my dreams." Her dream was to visit the Soviet Union, and although her boss, Le Corbusier, warned her that she might well be disappointed, she firmly held to her vision of a Soviet-created promised land. Stopping off en route in Berlin, she was appalled by the sight of "a clean, anonymous, starving crowd" staring hungrily at brightly lit shop windows filled with food. But in Moscow, much to her dismay, the sight was even more unnerving: "a population fantasizing about food in front of empty shops." This brutally opened her eyes to what, as she put it, was "simmering beneath the world's surface"—the "shadow of Hitlerism on the one hand, and the aftermath of the Communist Revolution in the Soviet Union on the other."[1]

That same year, travel-addicted André and Clara Malraux left for Persia and Afghanistan and then decided to go around the world. They had returned to Paris in late 1930 from their first trip to the Middle East, bringing their loot with them, and then promptly turned around to pick up more. Their precious objects found a receptive audience in Gaston Gallimard's new NRF Gallery, which opened in early 1931 as an adjunct to the prestigious *NRF* literary magazine. Its inaugural exhibit starred Malraux's Afghan sculptures—curiously, all heads, and even more curiously, heads that were severed from their torsos at exactly the same angle. How could this be? a curious journalist asked. "They were separated by the wind," Malraux unhesitatingly explained.[2]

Learned archeologists were suspicious. To begin with, forty-two carved heads, not to mention ones of this quality, were quite a lot for an amateur archeologist to have discovered, especially in three and a half months. Even Malraux's description was suspect; he described his finds as "Gothic-Buddhist," a term that baffled and even amused the experts. If Malraux had not personally sawed off the heads, or supervised their decapitations, it was clear that someone had. But even though bereft of their exact provenance, the heads nonetheless were pleasing, and a number of them found buyers, despite the Depression.

Wasn't the hunt dangerous? Malraux was asked. Well, for anyone else, he replied, but not for him: "I was a commissar in Canton," he elaborated, and "the armed nomads of the Pamir recognize a man who can handle a revolver or a machine gun."[3] He never was a commissar in Canton, and neither he nor his wife spent any time in the Pamirs, but there were few at the time who could debunk him. As Paul Valéry later remarked, Malraux was "a Byzantine barfly. Very curious, and very shady."[4]

But Malraux, that purveyor of myth and charm, was expert at a tale smoothly told, and he swept away objections with ease. And so in late 1931, he and Clara returned to the Middle East (all expenses paid by Gallimard), stopping off in Moscow and Tashkent en route. But now India and the Far East beckoned, and they followed.

There was treasure to be had.

As the decade opened, Marie Curie and her daughter Eve decided to visit Spain together. It was a propitious moment, soon after that nation had replaced its centuries-old monarchy with a republic. While Eve described the trip as a "dazzling, never-to-be-forgotten journey," Marie wrote to her other daughter, Irène, that she found it "very moving to see what confidence in the future exists among the young and among many of their elders. . . . May they succeed!"[5]

Marie Curie's interests extended well beyond her laboratory, although that beloved laboratory was always the center of her attention—and her existence. Yet after a typical day of twelve to fourteen hours of work, she would pause at dinner with Eve and ask, "Now darling . . . tell me something. Give me some news of the world!"[6]

She remained, as Eve described her, a progressive in her political and social views. "That France should be lacking in hospitals and schools, that thousands of families lived in unhealthy lodgings, that the rights of women should be precarious—all these," according to Eve, "were thoughts that tortured her." Marie Curie was equally vehement about dictatorships, although she spoke gently. "I have lived under a regime of oppression," she would answer anyone within her hearing who praised a dictator. "You have not. You don't understand your own good fortune in living in a free country." Yet she never sanctioned violent revolution, whatever the provocation. "You can never convince me," she once commented, "that it was useful to guillotine Lavoisier."[7]

Marie Curie also journeyed to her Polish homeland, where she took part in the celebrations surrounding the 1932 opening of the Warsaw Radium Institute. It was a family affair, as the institute was the product of her sister Bronya's dreams and labors, and Marie herself had traveled to America to obtain that all-important gram of radium for it. Much to her satisfaction, the president of the Polish republic attended the dedication.

Meanwhile, the Joliot-Curies were busy navigating new frontiers of their own, as Irène—despite ill health and her doctor's warnings—gave birth in 1932 to a second child, named Pierre, after her father. Embarked on a partnership to discover what would eventually be identified as the neutron, she and Frédéric spent long hours in the laboratory and incorrectly attributed a strange phenomenon she had noted to an elusive type of gamma ray. Knowing that others were also hot on the trail, they raced to publish their findings in early 1932, shortly before Pierre was born. Two British physicists, Ernest Rutherford and his student James Chadwick, disagreed with their findings, and Chadwick beat them to the correct interpretation, identifying the cause of the mysterious phenomenon as a particle with no electrical charge—the neutron. Chadwick won the 1935 Nobel Prize for Physics for his discovery.

Particularly painful for the Joliot-Curies was the realization that they had misinterpreted their own data, in effect discovering the neutron without knowing it. Equally devastating was their close loss to another physicist in the discovery of the positron (giving him the 1936 Nobel Prize). But that was the nature of scientific experimentation and discovery at the farthest edges of knowledge.

They simply would have to keep on. And as Marie Curie herself put it one evening in a conversation with Eve, "I think that we must seek for spiritual strength in an idealism which, without making us prideful, would oblige us to place our aspirations and our dreams very high."[8] They, and their entire family, had placed their aspirations and dreams very high indeed.

⌒

France's colonies, from Africa to the Far East, figured large in Parisians' imaginations when a blowout Exposition Coloniale Internationale went up in 1931 on the eastern edge of the city in the Bois de Vincennes. The idea was to glorify France's imperial mission by highlighting the cultures of her various colonies, and almost eight million people came to gawk at native huts and Buddhist temples, including a pagoda representing Togo and Cameroon, and a magnificent replica of Angkor Wat.[9]

Josephine Baker was elected Queen of the Colonial Exposition, but she never managed to be crowned. She wasn't even French, protesters complained, let alone a French colonial. Perhaps her show at the Casino de Paris had confused those who voted for her, because she portrayed several showbiz versions of France's colonized women. In any case, Josephine was consolable, with more shows at the Casino, more lovers, and more jewelry. "It was well known," recalled a businessman who bought the Belgian franchise for Josephine's popular hair oil, Bakerfix, "that a night with Josephine cost thirty-three thousand Belgian francs, and the waiting list was long.[10]

But according to one friend, there was another side to Josephine that few knew about. According to this woman, Josephine regularly visited the poor quarters of Paris, bringing medicine, clothing, food, and toys. "We arrived at this six-story walk-up," the friend recalled, and Josephine honked her horn. All of a sudden faces appeared, and children and their mothers came running. "The sight of Josephine picking up the little ones, stroking their heads, made tears come to my eyes. This was not done for effect," the friend added. "Or for an audience."[11]

Late in 1931, Major Charles de Gaulle returned from his Levant posting to Paris, where his former mentor, Marshal Philippe Pétain, had once again evaded de Gaulle's request to teach at the Ecole de Guerre. Instead, Pétain recommended him for a position in the Secretariat-General of the Supreme National Defense Council (SGDN), which de Gaulle joined in 1932 as a drafting officer.

De Gaulle now had experience in Germany, Poland, and the Levant and had collected glowing recommendations along the way. The SGDN, as de Gaulle explained, was "a permanent body at the disposal of the prime minister for the preparation of war." In his memoirs, he wrote that for the next five years, under fourteen administrations, "I was concerned on the planning level with every aspect of political, technical and administrative activity that had to do with the country's defense."[12]

At a time when, in de Gaulle's words, "Germany was bursting with menace" and "Hitler was drawing nearer to power,"[13] France's military establishment (with the prominent exception of Marshals Joffre and Foch, both recently deceased) had come to support the principle of a continuous fortified line—in other words, an entirely defensive policy. The only question under consideration was whether France should protect its entire northeastern frontier or, as Pétain advocated, merely its eastern border. Pétain's position (by far the less expensive option) won out, and at this point the SGDN shortened the line of defenses to protect only Alsace and Lorraine. Adding to de Gaulle's anxiety, France was little concerned with alliances, and pacifism was rapidly winning converts.

By 1932, de Gaulle had published his *Le Fil de l'épée* (*The Edge of the Sword*), in which he wrote that "wishes and hopes turn towards the leader as iron towards the magnet. When the crisis comes, it is he who is followed. . . . A kind of tidal wave sweeps the man of character to the forefront."[14] Those who read these words may well have wondered whether de Gaulle was thinking of Pétain, in his World War I days of glory, or of himself.

∽

In March 1931, André Citroën sent a publicity-reaping expedition of Citroën vehicles across the Asian continent. Soon after, he traveled in the opposite direction, to America, where he addressed a conference at Columbia University and met at the White House with President Hoover (at the same time, it turned out, that members of Citroën's adventurous Central Asian Expedition were temporarily being held prisoner by a Chinese warlord). His tour ended with an obligatory visit to curmudgeonly Henry Ford in Detroit, who had famously driven the Taylor method of mass production to startling success.

Throughout, Citroën's message of free trade as the key to reviving demand was not greeted with any enthusiasm, although this was predictable; nor was his visit with Ford especially warm. This, too, was predictable, not only because Citroën was a rival, but also because he was Jewish. By this time, Ford's deep anti-Semitism was blatantly on view, chronicled in his own newspaper (the *Dearborn Independent*) and in a multivolume diatribe called *The International Jew: The World's Foremost Problem*.

Still, the trip had its benefits: en route back to New York, Citroën once again visited the Philadelphia corporation that, years before, had provided him with an all-steel auto-body-building technique that he had immediately licensed. This occasion proved similarly rewarding: much to his delight, Citroën observed a front-wheel-drive prototype that was a revelation. Now he could see the way clear to making his dream of a front-wheel-drive automobile practical.[15]

Upon his return, an obviously buoyant Citroën announced (via that new-fangled invention, the radio) that he would follow in the steps of the Americans and raise quality while reducing prices—but (unlike the Americans) without lowering salaries. And then, in a typically expansive mode, he introduced the Citroën Orchestra, made up of one hundred musicians who were employees at his Quai de Javel factory.

Yet another Parisian headed west in 1931, although not in Citroën's footsteps. Coco Chanel set sail that spring for New York, bringing her good friend Misia Sert with her. Samuel Goldwyn, convinced that unemployed Americans wanted escapism, and that American women in particular would flock to see the latest Paris fashions, had offered Chanel a huge sum (rumored to be one million dollars) to outfit his leading ladies in Hollywood. At a time when rich Americans were an endangered species and sales of luxury goods in Paris were plummeting, the offer was tempting. After a lengthy consideration (Goldwyn claimed that he had first made the proposition three years earlier), Chanel graciously agreed to give Hollywood a look. "I will see what the pictures have to offer me and what I have to offer the pictures," she told the *New York Times* after landing in New York, adding, "I have not brought my scissors with me."[16] It wasn't something she yearned for, but it was an interesting move from a business standpoint: films might make a lucrative way to introduce her fashions, worn by movie stars in glamorous settings.

Her visit was top drawer all the way, including an all-white luxury express train to California, which Chanel and Misia shared with that disreputable but entertaining young writer, Maurice Sachs. Once there, she stayed long enough to create the wardrobes for the first of three films, but she quickly became disenchanted. "Their comforts are killing them," she reportedly said of Hollywood's royalty.[17] In any case, her name rather than her actual presence was what was wanted, and she soon returned to Paris, where she could design the clothes based on what she had learned of filmmaking, and fit stars like Gloria Swanson when they came to Paris.

Rumors always flew in Hollywood, and the rumor quickly spread that Chanel's costumes had not been sufficiently eye catching on screen to warrant all the press buildup or the money. Hollywood, and Goldwyn in particular, wanted dazzle, not chic. Whether or not that was the case, this episode ended Chanel's involvement with Hollywood. Another, far more flamboyant Paris designer—Elsa Schiaparelli—would soon take her place.

That December, Lee Miller—the astonishingly beautiful American who had come to Paris in 1929 with the express purpose of studying photography with Man Ray—finally left Paris. After three years as Man Ray's lover, model, collaborator, and muse, Lee Miller left Man Ray and Paris to establish her own photography studio in New York.

She had quickly risen from Man Ray's assistant to partner and ally, and together they had worked on new projects and methods, including the process of solarization, in which the image on a developed print is surrounded by a kind of dark halo or aura (although Man Ray characteristically took credit for the discovery, which Miller discovered first). Together, they had been significant figures in the Surrealist movement, with Miller (much to Man Ray's jealousy) attracting the attention of Jean Cocteau—who in any case had no sexual interest in women, but who cast Miller as a beautiful Greek statue in his *Blood of a Poet*. Later, Man Ray mused that their relationship never recovered afterward.

Unwilling to be bound to Man Ray, Miller moved into her own Montparnasse apartment and set up her own studio, working for *Vogue* and important couturiers such as Patou, Schiaparelli, and Chanel. She slipped away from him again and again, leaving him in anguish. Finally, she slipped away for good, and Man Ray used Edward Titus's *This Quarter* magazine to express his dismay, publishing a drawing of a metronome with a cutout photo of Miller's eye attached to its stem. Its caption began, "Cut out the eye from a photograph of one who has been loved but is seen no more," and finished brutally: "With a hammer well-aimed, try to destroy the whole at a single blow."[18] He also placed a photo of her eye in a paperweight shaped like a glass ball filled with water; when shaken, the eye disappeared in a flurry of white flakes.

Miller had fallen in love with Aziz Eloui Bey, a wealthy—and married—Egyptian businessman many years her senior. She did not marry him—not at first. Instead, she left for New York, and on the night that she left, Man Ray posed at midnight with a pistol held to his head. His terrified friend, one of his former models, did not know whether or not the gun was loaded.

By this time Luis Buñuel, creator (with Salvador Dalí) of the daring Surrealistic films *Un Chien Andalou* and *L'Age d'Or*, had made his way to Moscow after an uninspiring stint in Hollywood. Before leaving Paris for Russia, he told Wambly Bald that "Hollywood is quite hopeless." As for the Soviet Union, he wanted Bald to know that "there is great hope for free film in Soviet Russia, despite the burden of propaganda."[19]

Film was the new art form as well as the newest form of entertainment, and while Hollywood led the way in unabashed commercialization, film as something more serious flourished in Europe. This did not mean that film-makers such as René Clair, who had already established his reputation with *The Italian Straw Hat* and *Under the Roofs of Paris*, did not hope for commercial as well as artistic success. Clair achieved both with films such as *A nous la liberté*, his brilliant 1931 comic diatribe against modern mechanization, and *Le Million*, his madcap musical comedy from the same year, involving a frantic chase after a lost lottery ticket.

By 1931, Marc Allégret, André Gide's former lover, was also beginning to make a name for himself in the film world by directing his first feature films (*L'Amour à l'américaine*, *Mam'zelle Nitouche*, and *La Petite Chocolatière*), and he would hit it big the following year with his film *Fanny*. Josephine Baker's favorite starring role, in *Zou Zou*, would follow.

But Jean Renoir was still struggling. The middle son of France's renowned painter Pierre-Auguste Renoir, Jean had spent a lot of time in Paris watching movies after recuperating from a bad leg wound received during the Great War. At the war's end, after initially following his father's preference for him to become a potter, Jean found himself at loose ends—financially independent, thanks to the father's bequests to each of his three sons, and undecided about his future.[20] By now he was married—to his father's last model, the beautiful Andrée Heuschling, known as Dédée. Soon the two became as enamored with films as they were with each other, and Jean found himself interested in filmmaking, with the sole purpose of making his wife a star.[21]

This led to a fascination with filmmaking itself: "The bug of film-directing had now taken root in me, and there was no resisting it," as he later put it.[22] But despite his aspirations, Jean Renoir's reputation as a playboy preceded him, preventing producers and investors from taking him seriously. Some of his work, especially his photographic techniques, caught the attention of avant-garde film aficionados, but Jean found that he was having to sell off his treasured Renoir paintings to underwrite his ventures. As the decade ended, his professional hopes were foundering, even as his marriage was falling apart.

In 1929, Jean joined up for the first time with the actor Michel Simon in a silent comedy, *Tire-au-flanc* (*Goof-Off*), which François Truffaut later

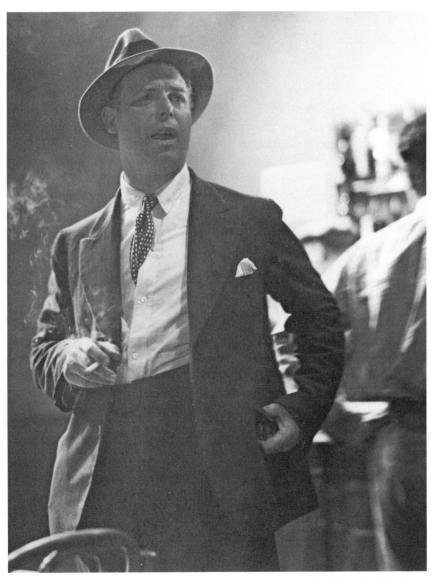

Jean Renoir during the filming of La Chienne, *1931. © Ministère de la Culture / Médiathèque du Patrimoine, Dist. RMN-Grand Palais / Raymond Voinquel / Art Resource, NY*

called "one of the funniest films ever made in France, and one of the greatest silent comedies." Truffaut also praised Renoir's camera work here as "a *tour de force*."[23] But audiences weren't as enthusiastic, and it, too, failed at the box office.

"Unlike René Clair," the film critic André Bazin later wrote, "Renoir is decidedly a sound director." As the talkies entered French filmmaking and theaters in the 1930s, Renoir "welcomed technological advance because it helped him achieve the realism he had sought since . . . the silent era."[24] But it was uphill work, with the French middle class sunk "in intellectual torpor," as one critical history puts it,[25] while small theater owners continued to show silent films because of the expense of sound equipment.

To prove himself in commercial terms—a necessary qualification to get the financial backing for the harshly realistic film he badly wanted to do (*La Chienne*)—Jean Renoir made a quick sound film with Michel Simon and Fernandel called *On purge bébé* (*Baby Takes a Laxative*). This unlikely subject provided Renoir with a comedy about a babied boy refusing to take a laxative, setting off fireworks between his parents and involving a hapless luncheon guest. Obviously enjoying his rousing challenge to bourgeois decorum, Renoir even has the father engage the luncheon guest in a bowling sequence using porcelain chamber pots. "It was the age of bad sound," Renoir later recalled. "To show how dissatisfied I was, I decided to record the flushing of a toilet. It was a kind of revolutionary act."[26]

On purge bébé was a hit, and although other filmmakers, such as Cocteau, Buñuel, and Dalí, were making more important films, Renoir was delighted to be working with this particular cast, especially Michel Simon and Fernandel (in his first film role, a small but key part). He was even more delighted by the opportunity that followed, to make *La Chienne*—although the producer turned down Renoir's wife (who had adopted the stage name Catherine Hessling) for the lead in favor of an actress under contract with his studio. By this time, Jean Renoir was more interested in making the film than he was in Catherine's role in it, but Catherine regarded it as a betrayal. This, according to Renoir, "marked the end of our life together."[27]

La Chienne (*The Bitch*), which Renoir made in 1931, would be a turning point in his career. "I believe," he later said, "that in it I came near to the style that I call poetic realism." No longer was filmmaking a kind of diversion or game for him. With his break from Catherine, Renoir expressed more "drive, freedom, and originality," as one biographer puts it, and with *La Chienne* in particular, he began—considerably before other filmmakers—to experiment with depth of field as well as with sound, including street sounds, which were recorded live. As he later put it, "a sigh, the creak of a door, the sound of footsteps on the pavement, things such as these can say as much as the spoken word."[28]

Unfortunately, Renoir's producer had expected a musical comedy, which *La Chienne* definitely was not, and he erupted when he saw the final product. Renoir had been less than forthcoming about the film he wanted to make ("I made the film as I wanted . . . without the slightest regard for the wishes of the producer"), and his irate producer went so far as to bar him from the studio, at one point even calling in the police.[29] Finally giving up, the producer released the film as it was but sent it to a much smaller metropolis, where he attempted to attract an audience by billing it as a comedy. Soon after this disaster, a courageous distributor in Biarritz gave the film the kind of advance publicity it deserved, and it did well, leading to a run in Paris.

Because of Renoir's innate distaste for the great producers of his day, for whom the director was "only a cog," as well as his fear that he would have a hard time finding work after the *La Chienne* altercation, his next films were financed by his friends.[30] These ventures most notably included *Boudu Saved from Drowning* (1932), a classic comedy starring Michel Simon as the incorrigible tramp, and the shadow-filled *La Nuit du carrefour* (*Night at the Crossroads*), the first screen adaptation of a work by Georges Simenon, and one of the first Simenon novels in which Inspector Maigret appears. Much like *Boudu*, which Michel Simon financed, *Night at the Crossroads* (1932) was made with as well as financed by Renoir's friends and family, with his older brother, Pierre (a well-known stage actor), playing Inspector Maigret, and Jean Renoir's good friend Georges Simenon present for much of the shooting. It was the first talking picture that Renoir made without the supervision or intrusion of a producer, and he gloried in the opportunity, creating the light-and-shadows atmosphere that Simenon so effectively described. There wasn't enough money, but it didn't matter: they all were friends and were devoted to their project. "When I go through that intersection," Renoir later recalled, "I see myself in that hot, wet fog: it was wet because the rain never stopped falling, and hot from our passion for our craft, which we longed to extricate from the marketplace."[31]

Although not at first a success, due to some double exposure at the film's end, *Night at the Crossroads* would become a favorite of the French New Wave. Jean-Luc Godard called it "the only great French detective movie—in fact, the greatest of all *adventure* movies."[32]

⁓

Jean Renoir had never taken much interest in politics, but as his marriage disintegrated, he now had a mistress, Marguerite Houllé—a young film editor from a family of trade unionists and activists—who held strong political opinions of her own. Renoir, his male friends noted with interest, found it natural to listen to a woman's point of view, possibly because he had been raised in a household of women (Pierre-Auguste's former models always seemed to hang around, in one capacity or another, once their modeling careers had ended). He listened to Marguerite and became interested in politics, although thus far he was unwilling to get involved.

The Depression had now begun to have its impact on France. As unemployment increased, so did the campaign to return working mothers to the home, led by a Catholic women's organization (the Union Féminine Civique et Sociale, or UFCS), which quickly grew to over ten thousand women. Even though unemployment in France had not yet reached epidemic proportions, the very idea of women filling jobs that men could occupy had become highly contentious. This, despite the fact that in 1931, of the almost four million married women in the workforce, most worked with their husbands on farms or in shops, while fully one-half of the working-women in France were single, widowed, or divorced. For years, during and after the war, women's work had been essential to take the place of those men whose positions were otherwise vacant. But now, although a small group of feminists rallied to the defense of married women's right to work, they faced an irate opposition, typified by the French physiologist Charles Richet, who in 1931 wrote to the Parisian daily *Le Matin* to call for a legal prohibition on work by married women.

By the early 1930s, movements of all kinds were rapidly gaining adherents, especially the peace movement. Postwar reconstruction had officially ended, including a monument to the fallen in virtually every town in France—most dramatically, the Tomb of the Unknown Soldier in Paris. In the wake of the Great War, the French (as minister of war André Maginot put it) had a horror of war, while another observer believed that her fellow French in the 1930s suffered from "a sort of national exhaustion."[33]

Large numbers of French yearned for peace, especially as events to the east—whether in the Soviet Union or in Germany—unnerved them. In July 1932, Hitler's National Socialist party won 13.7 million votes (some 37 percent of the total), while Bolshevism continued to thrive under Stalin. The question of international peace and disarmament outweighed even the growing economic crisis, and the May 1932 elections brought together a comfortable majority for the pacifist left-of-center—although neither the centrist Radicals nor the Socialist leader Léon Blum wanted Socialist participation in the government, which led to yet another parliamentary turnover in just a few months.

Political instability was the rule (there would be eleven different ministries in France between May 1932 and May 1936), due in large part to the fragmented nature of the French party system. On the left, the French Communist party (PCF) was at low ebb, while the Socialist party (SFIO) had become the dominant left-wing party, but the two continued to snipe and snarl at one another. They were hardly alone in their combativeness: the so-called Radicals were fractured on almost every issue, maintaining a façade of leftist idealism but leaning conservative on economic questions, while a multiplicity of other groupings added to the political volatility.

Underlying the roiling political waters loomed a mounting economic catastrophe that defied all the usual solutions. In the summer of 1931, Austria and Germany went off the gold standard after suffering banking panics; that autumn, Britain was next, abandoning the gold standard after experiencing its own banking crisis. In 1932, more countries followed, with the United States finally going off the gold standard in 1933. Meanwhile, France, determined to protect the franc, held on to the gold standard until 1936. Even while economic downturn and unemployment were seeping across French borders, hitting the Paris region the hardest, the Bank of France continued to sit on its pile of gold (by now, about a quarter of the world's gold supply). The French franc remained one of the strongest currencies in the world, and even while France's economy declined, budget deficits and fear of inflation continued to obsess decision makers and the man in the street alike.[34]

Despite the uncompetitive French franc and the attendant fall in industrial production, including French auto production, André Citroën in late 1931 inaugurated a bus company to operate in the Paris and Lyon regions and added yet another stunning Citroën showroom in Paris, at the Place de l'Europe, that included a cinema, library, café-bar, and restaurant.

Credit had collapsed in central Europe, and the Hoover moratorium had effectively ended any prospect of further reparations payments from Germany. America had erected steep tariff walls, and the British had devalued the pound, but Citroën remained optimistic. In late 1931 or early 1932 he gave the go-ahead to his Traction Avant front-wheel-drive project, recruiting a top-level design and development team to work in total secrecy, separate from Citroën's factory on the Quai de Javel. As for his Quai de Javel plant, Citroën had grand schemes as well, undertaking a major modernization project to be completed in record time. Later, Louis Renault claimed that he had incited Citroën to embark on this huge project, having invited his rival to view the enormous new Renault factory on the Ile Seguin, across from Renault's original Billancourt works. Citroën, Renault claimed, tried to do "in three months what had taken me thirty years."[35]

⁓

"God knows I wanted love," Coco Chanel once remarked. "But the moment I had to choose between the man I love and my dresses, I chose dresses."[36]

Early in 1930, the Duke of Westminster—Chanel's "Bendor"—married the daughter of the First Baron Sysonby, thus definitively ending his long relationship with Chanel. Yet despite her storied independence as well as her devotion to her profession, Chanel soon found another lover—Paul Iribe, the French artist and designer who had famously illustrated the prewar fashions of Paul Poiret before moving on to create opulent Art Deco sets and costumes for Cecil B. DeMille's 1920s Hollywood productions. Iribe's Hollywood career ended unpleasantly after a disastrous stint at directing—although his enemies, of whom he had many, pointed to his nasty temper and predilection for fights as the underlying cause. In any case, by the late 1920s, Iribe had returned to Paris, where he maintained his role as one of the leaders of the Art Deco decorative arts movement, assisted by his wealthy American wife, Maybelle, who sought out well-to-do clients and provided him with an interior design studio for home furnishings and jewelry.

According to one story, among these clients was Chanel—although her path must already have crossed Iribe's, as they shared some of the same friends, including Jean Cocteau and Misia Sert. In some ways, Chanel and Iribe were made for one another, as both were witty, sophisticated, and attractive to the opposite sex, sharing similar tastes in politics as well as in fashion and design. Both were deeply nativist and anti-Semitic, as were so many in their crowd, with a bent for right-wing movements. Neither bothered with sympathy for the poor or downtrodden, and so it perhaps was no surprise when, in late 1932, Iribe was working with Chanel when she announced the showing of a lavish diamond jewelry collection that she had designed for the De Beers diamond merchants.

It was an odd as well as extraordinarily insensitive move to make at a time of economic duress, especially given Chanel's well-known disdain for expensive jewelry: after all, she spent her career designing costume jewelry and mocking the real stuff. "Why allow yourself to become obsessed with the beautiful stone?" she asked her good friend Paul Morand near the end of her career. "You might as well wear a cheque around your neck."[37] But De Beers had wanted some publicity to counteract its sinking profits, and it signed on Chanel for the job. Charity had something to do with this gaudy exhibition, but no one paid much attention to that angle. People oohed and aahed over the fifty million francs' worth of brilliants, as they were supposed to, and De Beers was well satisfied: two days after the show opened, Janet Flanner noted that "De Beers stock was reported to have jumped some twenty points on the London exchange."[38]

Out of all this came a new love affair for Chanel, one permeated with Iribe's ultranationalism and racism, which corroborated and intensified Chanel's own increasingly hard-right views.

Action Française and its shock troops, the Camelots du Roi, found fresh life in the economic and political troubles of the 1930s, as did a burgeoning number of extreme right-wing leagues with paramilitary contingents, ready at a moment's notice to break heads and shed a little blood for their cause. In addition to Action Française and its Camelots du Roi, there was cosmetics millionaire François Coty's xenophobic, anti-Semitic, and ultranationalist Solidarité Française, as well as champagne czar Pierre Taittinger's Jeunesses Patriotes, whose military wing was inspired by Mussolini's Blackshirts. Several organizations of right-wing veterans from the Great War were also jostling their way to prominence, believing themselves more than qualified by their heroism on the field of battle to defend their country in the fields of culture and politics. Most notable among these was the Ligue des Croix-de-Feu, subsidized by Coty and led by Colonel François de La Rocque, who personally may not have embraced fascism or anti-Semitism but whose followers—and chief bankroller— supported a volatile mix of extreme nationalist, anti-Communist, and authoritarian convictions.

While the right-wing Cercle Fustel de Coulanges (under Henri Boegner) appealed to teachers and professors vacillating between the siren calls of communism and the far right, Action Française was recruiting with increasing success among France's small local industrialists and landowners, as well as among the nation's physicians and military officers—the latter being especially responsive to Action Française's uncompromising elitism and undisguised monarchism ("If the Republic will not or cannot reform itself, we shall have to let it die, and we shall cry, Long Live the King," announced one supporter, quoted in a May 1931 issue of the organization's journal, *Action Française*).[39]

Any number of issues could arouse the far right's furor, whether a play sympathetic to Captain Dreyfus or the savage anticlericalism and antimilitarism of Buñuel and Dalí's film *L'Age d'Or*. Conspiracy theories, such as the myth of the so-called two hundred (largely Jewish and Protestant) families who supposedly dominated France's economy, policy, and the press, now gained widespread traction, appealing to the anti-oligarchic Communist and trade unionist left as well as to the anti-Semitic and anti-Freemason right.[40] But it was the peace movement that set off the real fireworks. Action Française was especially alarmed by reports of German rearmament in violation of the Versailles Treaty, and in late 1931, a coalition of the Camelots du Roi, the Croix-de-Feu, and the Jeunesses Patriotes broke up a major pacifist meeting at the Trocadéro by assaulting and driving away the speakers, breaking the microphone (set up for radio listeners), and pummeling the police. No prosecution followed, and when Parliament discussed the affair soon after, the prime minister—the increasingly reactionary Pierre Laval—shrugged off the left's protests.

As French pacifism rose, Action Française became ever more agitated. Although small businessmen in the throes of the economic downturn seemed more concerned about their own prospects than they were about Hitler, by and large it was the pacifists and internationalists of the left, as well as America's continued demand for repayment of France's war debt, that drew the far right's ire. The Camelots and their associates broke up pacifist lectures and meetings at every opportunity, while students responded to Action Française's summons in late 1932 and rioted impressively until the Chamber of Deputies voted down any question of payments of France's war debt to America—an unpopular measure in any case in light of Hoover's halt of German reparations payments.

One of the most concrete examples of the postwar international peace movement was the Cité Internationale Universitaire de Paris. This experiment in international living got its start when the wealthy French industrialist Emile Deutsch de la Meurthe decided that he wanted to create some sort of tangible legacy and contacted the rector of the University of

Paris, who at that moment was despairing over the postwar dearth of student housing. Together with the minister of public instruction, they came up with the idea of a *cité universitaire*, or campus of residence halls—not a novel idea in itself, except that this particular group of residence halls would have a unique and heartfelt purpose: true to the spirit of the times, the Cité Internationale Universitaire de Paris would be dedicated to promoting international peace.

The idea was that if enough students from the four corners of the world lived together in close quarters, they would form friendships and learn to understand and appreciate one another. Walls of bigotry and misunderstanding would crumble, and wars like the terrible one from which they had just emerged would never again engulf the world. In this spirit, the first buildings of the experiment were opened in 1925 on an eighty-five-acre strip of land on the far edge of the fourteenth arrondissement that became available at the end of the Great War, when the last outmoded fortifications surrounding Paris (the Thiers fortifications) were torn down.

Other buildings on this international residential campus quickly followed, thanks to generous support from numerous governments, corporations, and private individuals, including John D. Rockefeller Jr., who was a major donor. Oddly, given the original purpose of the place, most of the residences were set up as national houses, with students of a particular nation residing in that nation's building (Americans, for example, in the Fondation des Etats-Unis, and Japanese in the Maison du Japon). Nations responded to the call with architecture that either reflected their national identity or represented the latest and best of what their architects could do, creating a kind of world's fair of architecture. Among these, a federation of Swiss universities decided to bestow their nation's commission on Le Corbusier—now a French citizen, but born Swiss. Their likely intent was to mollify the architect's deeply wounded feelings after his controversial rejection by the competition judges for the League of Nations headquarters in Geneva.[41]

Le Corbusier's Swiss Pavilion (Fondation Suisse), completed in 1932, is clean lined and airborne, resting its weight on elongated *pilotis* or pillars—"a veritable laboratory of modern architecture," as he put it, even though the effort was hampered by a severely constrained budget.[42] Charlotte Perriand worked on the project after her return from the Soviet Union and was almost as disappointed as Le Corbusier by the critical reception it received. It seemed that almost everyone, especially the Swiss, had expected something more like a Swiss chalet. According to Le Corbusier, the inauguration ceremony was like a funeral.

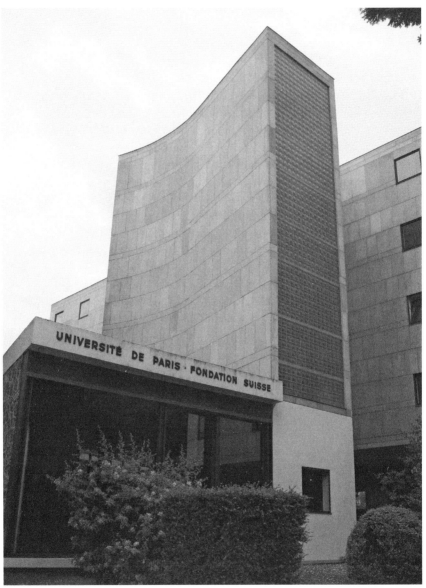

Le Corbusier's Fondation Suisse, at the Cité Internationale Universitaire de Paris. ©
J. McAuliffe

⁓

The site of Paris's last wall, the Thiers fortifications, offered a huge land grab once the fortifications came down—a process that was not completed until 1932, but when finished offered up a chunk of land equal to one-quarter of Paris.[43] The fortifications themselves belonged to the military, but the land around them—a barren military sector called the Zone—belonged to a hodgepodge of private and public owners, including the villages and communes outside the wall. The Zone itself had been for decades a dismal no-man's-land, a dangerous dead end inhabited by tramps, thieves, ragpickers, and the outcasts of society. The idea that this last reserve of unoccupied land in the city could become something better had for decades attracted interest, and when France passed its first national planning law in 1919, there were already optimists with dreams of new housing as well as hospitals, schools, and parks for this insalubrious ring around Paris.[44]

One plan was to create attractive open spaces by constructing a ring of landscaped parks. These in turn would be linked by an irregular boulevard that incorporated gardens and courtyards in the spaces between buildings and streets. But contrary to hopes and expectations, the land was developed piecemeal, with some worthy projects, such as the Cité Internationale Universitaire de Paris and Parc Kellermann (in the thirteenth and fourteenth arrondissements), receiving sizeable allotments, but so much else built up helter-skelter by private developers. Hammered by real estate interests and hampered by the cost of expropriation proceedings and clearance operations, the government seemed paralyzed. Soon it became evident, as architectural historian Norma Evenson has noted, that "what many had anticipated as a well-planned residential district, embodying abundant greenery and reflecting enlightened design concepts, had evolved into a dense wall of mediocrity encircling the city." As Le Corbusier put it, "Profit prevailed. Nothing, absolutely nothing was done in the public interest."[45]

Paris by this time had a population of almost three million, with a proliferation of automobiles that intensified the congestion. Of this population, approximately forty thousand unfortunates eked out an existence in the Zone. Efforts to help them with inexpensive housing had begun during the late 1920s, but these could accommodate only a fraction of those being relocated. More low-cost housing went up throughout the decade, mostly in the form of unattractive seven-story apartment buildings ringing the outer edges of the city.

Le Corbusier had his own solution, which he tried out with his Cité de Refuge, a large multistoried homeless shelter erected in the thirteenth arrondissement, and his Asile Flottant, or Floating Refuge, a dormitory located on a reconstructed barge in the Seine—both efforts underwritten by the Princesse de Polignac for the Salvation Army and completed between 1930 and 1933.[46] Charlotte Perriand worked on the Cité de Refuge and made sure that it included special accommodations for single mothers and their children as well as dormitory lodgings for the homeless. The Asile Flottant also accommodated families with children, who were reported to enjoy the trips it took up the river during the summer. According to Henry Miller's friend Alfred Perlès, the boat was permanently anchored at the Pont du Carrousel, "where they gave you a plate of gruel and a hammock for the night provided you could sing a few hymns in praise of the Lord."[47]

Outside Paris proper there were two million more people living in the *banlieue*, or suburbs, where poverty was endemic, especially to the north and northeast. A plan for rationally developing the region outside Paris city limits emerged in 1932 but was sapped by the onset of the Depression as well as by the municipality's fear of the so-called Red Belt—the tough working-class area that sprawled both inside and outside of the northern and northeastern city borders, a region notorious for its overwhelming support of the Communist left.

Le Corbusier's high-rise solution to such insalubrious areas, which he proposed as early as his 1925 scandal-creating City of Three Million, would have low-budget imitators by mid-century, and even as early as 1931 would have an unhappy imitation in the Cité de la Muette in Drancy, which was not yet completed when in 1942 the Germans turned it into a horrific internment camp for Jews en route to Auschwitz.[48]

Henry Miller did not mind poverty, especially not in Paris. "God knows," he later wrote, "when spring comes to Paris the humblest mortal alive must feel that he dwells in Paradise." He certainly preferred to be poor in Paris rather than return to America. "The streets were my refuge,"[49] he wrote, and some of his most evocative descriptions are of the streets of Paris by night. According to his good friend Brassaï, Miller's description of Rue de Lourmel in the fog is "perhaps the most beautiful that has ever been written about a Parisian street."[50]

When the American lawyer Richard Osborn offered to let Miller share his apartment without payment, Miller jumped at the chance. Osborn was lonely, like so many others Miller encountered, and enjoyed Miller's good humor and friendship. Osborn (who would appear in *Tropic of Cancer* as Fillmore) left his flatmate with pocket money each morning, and in return Miller kept house and cooked dinner—surprisingly well, all things considered, striking Osborn and others with the "methodical German nature" that underlay Miller's bohemianism. While there, Miller wrote the first two articles that he published in Paris, which appeared in Samuel Putnam's *New Review*.

Miller and Osborn split up after Osborn brought home an eccentric Russian refugee whose lack of hygiene appalled Miller. He then lived for a time at 18 Villa Seurat with Michael Fraenkel—another, like Osborn, who would appear in barely disguised form as Boris in *Tropic of Cancer*. Other major figures in *Tropic* were Perlès (Carl) and Wambly Bald (Van Norden), who soon formed a kind of Three Musketeers with Miller. Only the arrival of Miller's wife that autumn of 1931 disrupted his easygoing life—although less so than before. Late that year, while June was still trying to get Miller to come back with her, he described himself to a friend in New York as one of the few Americans in Paris who had actually embraced French culture rather than simply using Paris as a backdrop for their very American lives. Writing this friend, he said, "I am fixed, resolved, happy. I turn slowly with the wheel because I am at the hub."[51]

And then he met Anaïs Nin. Nin, raised in Europe and New York, with artistic parents of Spanish and Danish descent (her father was a concert pianist and composer, her mother a singer), was the ultimate cosmopolitan. Beautiful, with exotic good looks, she projected an engaging if misleading aura of frailty that appealed to Miller. Married to a wealthy banker who had suffered from the Crash, Nin nonetheless managed to maintain a freewheeling lifestyle. She was a reader and a writer—of a critical evaluation of D. H. Lawrence as well as of an obsessively maintained diary (in its forty-second volume when Miller met her)—and could discuss in depth an impressive number and variety of writers, from Dostoevsky to Proust. Still reasonably well-to-do, and emphatically bored with life, especially with her husband, Nin was also neurotic and deeply into psychoanalysis. Miller found her enchanting.

Miller, and his working-class background, also appealed to Nin, but the immediate problem was that Nin also found June enchanting. This led to some tense weeks of flirtation between the two women (both maintained that it was nothing more) and a veiled fight between them over Miller. In the end, June returned to New York without Henry, but the next autumn, she returned to Paris and tried again to retrieve him and revive their marriage. In the meantime, Henry took a disastrous teaching job in Dijon, during which he concluded that June would be the great subject of his writing, much as Albertine (or Albertine's real-life counterpart) had been for Proust.[52]

He and Nin became lovers in March 1932, but June remained a fixation for them both. By this time Miller was living in Clichy with his friend Alfred Perlès, who found a job for him as a proofreader at the *Paris Tribune*. This lasted only six weeks, after which Miller worked full time on *Tropic of Cancer* while Nin supported him. He began the practice of writing down his current literary project on giant sheets of wrapping paper taped to the wall, telling his friends "how much he needed these wall murals at eye level in order to see graphically, and in a certain order, the enormous mass of material he had in his head or in his notebooks."[53]

As for those friends who—after reading Miller's barely fictionalized account of their lives—took him to task for his lack of truth in storytelling, Miller firmly believed (as Brassaï put it) that reality was only real to the extent that it was "ruled absolutely by the mind and by the imagination, which transform reality freely, re-creating it, destroying it, turning it into myth and legend."[54]

Miller finished his first draft of *Tropic of Cancer* during the summer of 1932, and connected with a literary agent who appreciated it and the small Obelisk Press that agreed to publish it. Jack Kahane of Obelisk Press was notorious for publishing dirty books, but he published serious works as well, when he could afford to, and had little fear of *Tropic of Cancer*'s sexually explicit passages and language. As Alfred Perlès put it, "this was not a book that could be bowdlerized, it was a question of all or nothing."[55] Still, it was overlong, and perhaps at Kahane's suggestion, Miller began to revise the book to about one-third its original size. This put off publication until 1934.

Meanwhile, June—"the queen mother of all the slippery Babylonian whores," as Miller put it[56]—once again appeared, arriving that October and creating a major storm. Henry was frantic, complaining that June's presence made it impossible for him to work; but by this time Nin, the third member of their trio, was bored with June and doing her part to break up the two for good. "Feel free to do with her as you will," Henry finally wrote Nin, "that's my gift to you."[57] He tried to escape to London but, with virtually no money in his pockets, was jailed as a potential vagrant and shipped back to France. There he remained in hiding with Nin until June finally departed.

June's parting shot, written on a piece of toilet paper, was "Will you get a divorce as soon as possible."[58] At long last, their marriage was over.

⁓

Sylvia Beach recalled that Henry Miller and Anaïs Nin approached her, too, in the effort to find a publisher for *Tropic of Cancer*. She took one look at it and suggested that they show the manuscript to Jack Kahane, who she thought would appreciate "something that combined literary and sex value. Kahane," she added, "was fond of a certain forthright sexiness."[59]

In the meantime, Beach's troubles with James Joyce had only accelerated. Joyce, still upset about suggestions from his benefactors that he try to live within his means, had sulked alone through his February 1931 birthday. To make amends, Beach soon after arranged a "grand meal with champagne" at his favorite restaurant, to which all who attended ordered in advance and contributed to allay the expense. When Joyce's plate arrived, it appeared that he had ordered only a dish of lentils—a gesture of "pure cussedness," as one of the guests put it.[60]

It was the little things like this that rankled—such as when Beach held her first poetry reading, with Edith Sitwell, and Sitwell's friends Gertrude Stein and Alice B. Toklas were given seats in the front row. Joyce came in late, sat in the back row, and—as everyone could not help but notice—ostentatiously slept through the whole thing. But it was the bigger picture, the ongoing and escalating demands, that exhausted Sylvia. Even while Joyce sojourned with Nora in England for several months in 1931 to establish an English domicile ("for the sake of marriage and inheritance"), he kept Beach busy with a barrage of requests and continued to spend wildly. In addition, Joyce was beginning to sound out American publishers about publishing *Ulysses*, and—given the inquiries that Beach was receiving—clearly was misrepresenting her decadelong role, characterizing her merely as his representative rather than as his publisher, with no mention of her rights as publisher.

Finally Beach's devoted partner, Adrienne Monnier, had enough. If Beach would not give Joyce a piece of her mind, then Monnier would. Monnier had stood by for years as Joyce had imposed on Sylvia, contributing to her declining health and straining her financial resources. In May 1931, Joyce had written Sylvia about royalties ("in my case, one must always go to the limit"). Monnier now wrote back, opening with a dismissal of André Gide's remark that Joyce's indifference to success or money had something saintly about it: "What Gide doesn't know," she wrote, "[because] we put a veil over it—is that you are, on the contrary, very concerned about success and money. . . . Rumor has it that you are spoiled, that we have ruined you with overwhelming praise and that you no longer know what you are doing. . . . My personal opinion is that you know perfectly well what you are doing." And then she added, "Times are hard, and the worst isn't over."[61]

Joyce ignored the letter, but it undoubtedly contributed to his sense of martyrdom.[62] Beach meanwhile (after encouragement from Hemingway) decided to reply to publisher inquiries as Joyce's publisher, as the one who by contract had "exclusive right of printing and selling" *Ulysses*. In this capacity she asked twenty-five thousand dollars for the American rights plus at least a 20 percent royalty for Joyce and a five-thousand-dollar advance to Joyce upon signing a contract. As she wrote to Joyce's London agent, "Considering that much time, expense and influence have been used in developing the sales during all these years, this is a modest estimate of the value that *Ulysses* represents to me."[63] The publishers simply thought this ludicrous, while Joyce and his family were convinced that Sylvia had made a fortune from *Ulysses*, which they believed she was keeping from them.

In the meantime, offers kept coming in to Joyce for publication of his upcoming *Work in Progress* (ultimately titled *Finnegans Wake*). Despite Beach's option to publish it, she told Joyce that it would be to his advantage to sign with a big publishing house, and he signed with Viking. But *Work in Progress* was far easier to relinquish than the publication rights to *Ulysses*. As the economic crisis deepened, sales at Shakespeare and Company were rapidly declining. Beach cut all unnecessary expenses, dismissed her assistant, sold their car, and canceled their vacation, but still financial difficulties beset her. Her only real potential source of profit was her rights as publisher of *Ulysses*. As it happened, she now had (at Joyce's behest) a contract stating that "the right to publish said Work shall be purchased from the Publisher at the price set by herself."[64]

Unknown to Beach, Joyce—irritated by her unwillingness to give up claims to her publishing rights—was negotiating secretly with Random House and had recruited a friend in Paris to badger Beach daily to discuss the need for an American edition of *Ulysses*. "I never saw such a man for secret maneuverings," Beach later wrote of Joyce in an unpublished section of her memoirs. "It seemed only a harmless little amusement when I was aware of his manipulations of others, but when I began to get some of it myself, I didn't find it so funny." When Joyce's envoy urged her to give up her imaginary claims, Beach demanded, "But what about our contract? Is that imaginary?" He retorted, "It doesn't exist, your contract." When she produced the contract in question, he simply said, "You're standing in the way of Joyce's interests."[65]

Dumbfounded, Beach angrily called Joyce and released all claims to *Ulysses*. Early in 1932, on the occasion of Joyce's fiftieth birthday, she resigned as his publisher, giving him full control of *Ulysses*. It was a birthday gift—much as the first printed copy of *Ulysses* had been, exactly ten years before.[66] She did not air her grievances in public, even in her published memoirs, but it was clear that, even though there was no open breach between them, their friendship was over.

Joyce—who after the American edition of *Ulysses* came out told Beach that he had already received forty-five thousand dollars from Random House—had never felt any financial obligation to Beach. For her part, she had come to realize that "working with or for James Joyce, the pleasure was mine—an infinite pleasure; the profits were for him."[67]

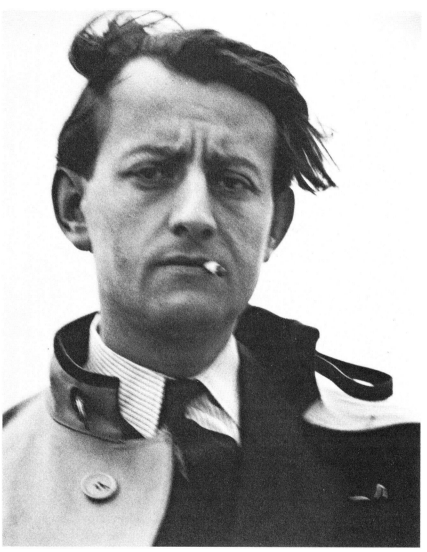

André Malraux, photographed by Gisèle Freund. © Gisèle Freund / BnF, Dist. RMN-Grand-Palais / Art Resource, NY

CHAPTER SIX

~

Taking Sides

(1933)

Sometime in the early 1930s, André Malraux met at a restaurant with André Gide, along with the writers Jean Giono and Pierre Drieu La Rochelle. Malraux and Drieu began to argue. And argue. It was "extraordinarily intelligent," Jean Giono later remarked, but the talk went on for six hours, after which Giono told Gide that he had not understood a single word. Gide replied wearily, "I, too, understood nothing." And then he added, "I don't think they did, either."[1]

There was a lot of intense talk going on in Paris at this time, largely in cafés and restaurants, as intellectuals argued about almost everything—but most especially about politics. Hitler's rise to the chancellorship of Germany in early 1933 set off a storm of controversy, especially among the political left. The far right was less inclined to argue and instead favored using muscle to end all the nattering and simply overthrow the Republic, replacing it with strong one-man rule or (as Action Française hoped) a restored monarchy.

Less than a month after Hitler became chancellor of the German Reich, the Reichstag fire—which Hitler blamed on the Communists—gave him the pretext to liquidate the powerful German Communist party and consolidate his power.[2] That autumn, Hitler dissolved the Reichstag and withdrew Germany from the League of Nations and the Geneva Disarmament Conference; Japan had already broken with the League after it condemned Japan's invasion of Manchuria. As the failure of that summer's world economic conference in London plainly showed, none of the participating nations seemed able to cooperate in order to deal with the Depression, let alone anything else.

Strikes began to break out throughout France—first the textile workers, then the miners, followed by violent agrarian demonstrations. The extreme-right leagues, with their membership growing daily, were primed for battle as crises multiplied on all fronts. In Paris, the far right battled in the streets, largely with Communist members of the left, while the police, led by prefect of police Jean Chiappe, cracked skulls, mostly of left-wing agitators, whom Chiappe was known to despise.

In the midst of this furor, the peace movement gained increasing traction. Only days after Hitler came to power, the Oxford Union, the prestigious students' debating society, voted that under no circumstances would any of them take up arms to fight for king and country. Newspapers in Paris heartily endorsed this sentiment.

And still the Hitler juggernaut roared on, while in the Far East, Japan had already swallowed Manchuria and was rumbling into northern China.

Soon after Hitler's rise to power, the poet Bryher visited Berlin for the last time. She saw "savage faces and clenched fists" and was appalled to hear of the schoolgirl daughter of a friend who "lay for twenty minutes on the pavement near where I was staying while two political groups shot it out over her head." Bryher and some friends had their own terrifying encounter one night with Hitler's Brownshirts: "Who were we? Where were we going?" they demanded. Fortunately, the bus arrived before there could be any trouble, but the uncertainty was as terrifying as the actuality of violence—especially as "people were beginning to whisper about each other." On which side did a friend or acquaintance stand?[3]

Bryher's analyst, who was Jewish, was decamping to Boston. "It meant a severance from the language and literature that formed the core of his life," she noted sadly, but there was nothing she could say. It was a judicious move under these fraught circumstances. And he was hardly alone: "The station was filled with the more fortunate refugees," she wrote. These were not necessarily rich, she added, nor were they all Jewish, but they shared a common desire to get out of Germany, "to end their days in peace."[4]

The German aristocrat Count Harry Kessler entered in his diary for April 1, 1933, that "the abominable Jewish boycott [in Germany] has begun." Referring to "this criminal piece of lunacy," he wrote on May 5, "This is the most horrible suicide a great nation has ever committed." Kessler, who had become a pacifist and a strong supporter of the League of Nations after serving as a German officer in World War I, was appalled by the details of refugee escapes as he heard them. "Clearly sadism, a hysterical pleasure at [the] flow of blood and suffering, plays an important part" in the Nazi mind-set, Kessler concluded after hearing these accounts. It amounted to "a pathological feeling of power in the imposition of torture . . . suddenly active among hundreds of thousands."[5]

Kessler himself had become a refugee that March after learning that his socialist sympathies had placed him in the crosshairs of Hitler's SS, and he quickly fled Berlin for Paris. Stopping off en route at his home in Weimar, he talked with a terrified old porter at the railway station, who told him that "things were terrible in Weimar . . . with 'auxiliary police' (SA) [Storm Troopers or Brownshirts] everywhere and nobody daring to speak a word." After arriving in Paris, Kessler learned that there was no chance that he could safely return to Germany: his manservant had betrayed him, stealing Kessler's belongings and supplying the Nazis "with the wildest information" about him.[6]

"And so they arrived," Kessler's biographer writes of that spring's flood of refugees into Paris, "some by first-class coach with steamer trunks, others by the skin of their teeth having lost nearly everything."[7] They included bankers, publishers, journalists, writers, philosophers, pacifists, politicians (Socialists, Communists, and liberals), and especially Jews. Even the most eminent nonpolitical figures were in danger simply by being Jewish: under threats of violence, the famed conductor Bruno Walter was shut out from conducting in Leipzig, Frankfurt, and Berlin, while no less a personage than Albert Einstein lost his position at the Berlin Academy of Sciences (Gide tried to get Paris to offer Einstein a chair at the Collège de France, but Princeton got its invitation in first).

"Lack of intellectuality is the most terrible thing about the Hitler regime," Kessler noted that October. "For the time being, though, there is nothing to be done about it other than creating a haven where the intellectuals can take refuge."[8]

Paris at first looked like such a haven. By late 1933, more than twenty thousand Germans had left Germany for France, and by the end of the decade, more than fifty thousand had passed through en route for other lands. From 1933 on, around eight thousand per year settled in Paris, of those about one-third being Jewish—at least until 1938, when the numbers grew.[9]

Comparatively, these were not large numbers, but their impact was great, politically as well as culturally. Most of the books published by German Jewish émigrés in Paris between 1933 and 1939 (some three hundred books and scores of articles) embraced left-wing views, whether socialist or communist, and as the first wave of sympathy for the victims of Nazism began to wane, conservatives in particular began to take umbrage, summoning up anti-Semitic images of an "invasion." Not only were most of these Jewish refugees German in origin, but they were largely pacifist to boot. None of this endeared them to a broad spectrum of French conservatives. Einstein, as a leading pacifist and embracer of left-wing causes, in addition to being Jewish, might not have found Paris especially compatible during these years.

~

As a Jew, as a leading Socialist, and as a pacifist, Léon Blum was not finding life easy. Despite his long years of endorsing pacifism, he was now being attacked by the right as a Jew who, as an antifascist, must obviously want war. At the same time, elements from within his own Socialist party (the SFIO) were openly opposed to his continued resistance to power sharing with a government that was far too conservative for his taste. Although he managed to beat back the proponents of government participation, the opposition was steadily growing. By summer of 1933, it led to a split within the SFIO, with Blum's opponents, led by Marcel Déat, calling themselves the Neo-Socialists.

Blum thought he saw a kind of fascism in Déat's brand of activism. Déat advocated a strong state—one, of course, that acted on behalf of the workers, even while its authority trumped social democracy. Déat's supporters noted that authoritarian states were currently popular for a reason: after all, as one put it, "the strength of fascism comes from the necessity . . . for a strong state, for a powerful state, for an ordered state." From this point of view, what fell by the wayside with such a government was of little importance: as another Déat supporter put it, "Must we base the organization of the world on freedom and justice?"[10]

As Blum listened, aghast, he heard his opponents attack him with anti-Semitic slurs that might have come directly from the right-wing press. Not surprisingly, he saw the SFIO's reason for being as well as the future of French socialism at stake. In the midst of one especially brutal tirade, he broke in: "I am listening to you with an attentiveness you can imagine," he said, in what one witness said was heart-rending tones. "But I confess to you that I am appalled!"[11]

At length, after a two-hour fight from the platform, Blum managed to obtain a censure of the Neo-Socialists on disciplinary grounds, after which they promptly seceded. Represented by several senators and deputies in Parliament, this breakaway group was not without power on the national political scene but still represented only a splinter of about twenty thousand members. They would play no significant role until Vichy.

For Blum was right: Déat and many of his followers found it easy to embrace fascism and would become collaborators during the German Occupation of France.

Something powerful was going on in French society as economic depression was creeping in and Hitler's Germany was on the rise. Germany under Hitler was rearming and, under its authoritarian ruler, looked increasingly muscular, while France's own government remained chronically weak and divided. Hitler seemed to be doing all the right things, and although the French had not yet experienced defeat in war or enormous unemployment, there were many—especially among the middle classes—who were looking with a certain amount of envy at their German neighbors.

Fascism appealed not only to the French middle classes but also to intellectuals, especially to those such as Pierre Drieu La Rochelle, who once had been enamored of the now-decrepit French Communist party (the PCF). Germany's Communists had taken it on the chin from Hitler following the Reichstag fire, and France's party had atrophied during the 1920s, having experienced the difficulties of following a party line directed from Moscow, which at best seemed clueless and at worst disinterested in what was actually going on in France.

French Communists during the early 1930s were for the most part fiercely antifascist and just as fiercely pacifist—positions that would increasingly be at cross-purposes. Most of that handful of Surrealists who had tied themselves in knots in order to accommodate themselves to the party followed André Breton and Paul Eluard as they exited the Communist-controlled Association of Revolutionary Writers and Artists in 1933, after the two had committed the unforgiveable sin of calling (in print) the party's antiwar movement a betrayal of class warfare. Breton in particular would now become a staunch and especially incorrigible foe.

But even as Stalin was starting to exercise his iron control over the party apparatus by expelling, imprisoning, and soon physically eliminating great masses of members, a growing group of French intellectuals were beginning to gravitate leftward. Even while Pierre Drieu La Rochelle was vaulting over the political center to abandon communism for fascism, his colleague and Surrealist leader, the poet Louis Aragon, was confirming his status as an increasingly staunch and fanatical party member. Aragon's commitment solidified during his 1932 visit to the Soviet Union, after which he published an incendiary poem, "Front rouge" (Red Front), containing the lines "Kill the cops / comrades / Kill the cops," which got him into serious trouble with French authorities.[12] Only the active support of his Surrealist friends helped Aragon avoid prosecution, but the Communist party proceeded to muddy the waters, precipitating a final break between Aragon and Breton and confirming Aragon's departure from Surrealism. After that, Aragon began to write for the Communist newspaper L'Humanité, and at the same time worked assiduously on behalf of the Association of Revolutionary Writers and Artists.

André Gide's growing sympathies with the Soviet Union were a good indication of what was happening. Although in May 1933 Gide wrote in his journal, "Excellent speech by Hitler in the Reichstag. If Hitlerism had never made itself known otherwise, it would be more than merely acceptable," for some time he had been looking with interest, then with fervor, toward Russia. In 1931, he wrote in his journal, "My whole heart applauds that gigantic and yet entirely human undertaking."[13]

Following his 1925–1926 trip to the Congo, Gide had begun to question how much any individual could accomplish in changing the vast ills he had witnessed, and as the 1930s opened, his journal entries showed an increasing joy in what he hoped, and believed, to be the solution. "I should like to cry aloud my affection for Russia," he wrote in July 1931, and enthused about the Soviet Five-Year Plan. He yearned to see "what can be produced by a state without religion, a society without the family," adding (in a reflection of his own personal experience) that "religion and the family are the two worst enemies of progress." In late 1932, he wrote, "I have declared as loud and clear as I could my sympathy . . . for the U.S.S.R. and for all it represents in our eyes, in our hearts, despite all the imperfections that are still held up to us." As for those who accused him of being fooled by a mirage, he had this reply: "Mirage, as you say. . . . It is enough for me to glimpse it in order to wish, as fervently as I am able, for it to become reality."[14]

Yet Gide's burgeoning political interest had its downside, as he clearly realized: it "distracts me frightfully from literature," he confided to his journal. He found himself weary of writing, even in his beloved journal, believing at times that it was "as if everything I had to say was said." But he also realized that "the too keen interest I take in events under way and particularly in the situation of Russia turns my mind away from literary preoccupations."[15] Nor was his interest one sided: Moscow, as well as the French Communist party, was keenly aware of the big catch that Gide represented and had taken due note of his receptivity. How best to reel him in?

The party chose Louis Aragon, by now a devout party member, to do the job. What about making a film of Gide's book, *Les Caves du Vatican*? Aragon asked him, suggesting certain changes that should be made to increase its anti-Catholicism. Gide, appalled at the idea, turned him down. The party was undeterred: *L'Humanité* next tried to persuade Gide to run *Les Caves* in its pages in a serialized form but announced the great event—in print and with a large photograph—before Gide had the opportunity to consider, let alone accept. In any case, as *L'Humanité* told him, it was already too late to refuse: the issue starting the serialization had already gone to press.

In the meantime, Gide turned down the opportunity to chair a large meeting of the Association of Revolutionary Writers and Artists on the grounds that it would keep him "from ever writing anything again." To no avail: he was told that it was too late to object—all the posters had been printed, and it would look like desertion, if not outright treachery, to back out. He gave in. Next, much to his surprise and annoyance, he learned (by reading about it in *Le Temps*), that he was going to be one of France's representatives to the European Anti-Fascist Congress. "I am eager to point out," he wrote testily in his journal for June 6, 1933, "that my acceptance of that congress was taken from me by surprise. My categorical *refusal* having 'come in too late.'" Worse, he realized that there would be even more trouble in trying to correct the error than simply to give in and accept: "I should then seem to be *withdrawing* from a congress to which I merely did not want to belong."[16]

Soon he was roped into a stage production of *Les Caves du Vatican* for a Communist amateur theater group (the group's organizer "was so insistent that in the end, I gave in"),[17] and in addition he found himself billed as one of five honorary presidents of an upcoming World Conference of Youth against War and Fascism. If it wasn't one conference or meeting it was another, and Gide found himself bewailing in his journal, "How can I recover that serenity of mind indispensable to work? I really believe I have lost it forever."[18]

Despite his protests to his diary that June ("I know nothing about politics. If they interest me, they do so as a Balzac novel does"), Gide was now regarded by the literary world as a thoroughgoing Communist. "What leads me to Communism is not Marx, it is the Gospel," he protested,[19] but this made little difference to the firm anti-Bolsheviks of his acquaintance, including the Royal Society of Literature, which abruptly terminated his membership that November. There was no point in asking why.

At about the same time as Gide, Malraux, too, was being drawn toward—and pulled into—the Communist camp, even though he remained reluctant to become a card-carrying member. Having left the Far East as it was erupting in flames, he returned to Paris, where his novel *La Condition humaine* (translated as *Man's Fate*)—about individuals caught in the tumult of a failed Communist insurrection in Shanghai—at last won him the coveted Goncourt Prize. Whether or not Malraux had actually spent time in China and experienced these events was of no matter; he vividly imagined the chaotic world his characters inhabited, and his book's success was enough to raise him out of relative obscurity to become a literary star—one that the Soviet Union found worth courting.

Malraux was quite willing to be courted, although less willing to commit himself. His wife Clara, being Jewish, made him sensitive to the dangers of German Nazism and inclined to side with those who opposed it. Nazis were already burning books, boycotting Jewish shops, and arresting opponents by the thousands, and in March they opened Germany's first concentration camp for political prisoners at Dachau. Not yet an extermination camp, the place nonetheless served as a portent of what was to come.

According to one biographer, Malraux was involved in persuading Gide to change his mind about chairing that spring's meeting of the Association of Revolutionary Writers and Artists that Gide had tried to turn down. Despite this bumpy prelude, Gide seems to have chaired the huge meeting with distinction. But perhaps the occasion's most memorable moment came when Malraux, master of the dramatic gesture, raised his fist and shouted, "If there is to be a war, our place is in the ranks of the Red Army!"[20]

"Between 18 and 20," Malraux once remarked, "life is like a market where one buys values not with cash but with acts. Most men buy nothing."[21] Already Malraux was establishing his public reputation as a man of action. Behind the scenes, his marriage with Clara was falling apart, despite the birth of their daughter (named Florence, in honor of their first romantic trip to Italy). Clara, who had been faithful to him, in her fashion, through numerous crises, had become less and less enamored of the man she had married. But this seems to have mattered less to Malraux than his sudden literary success and the possibilities it created to emerge in the image he most admired, as an adventurer and a hero.

Charlotte Perriand had joined the Association of Revolutionary Writers and Artists in 1932, soon after it was founded. "It brought together writers, visual artists, and musicians," she wrote, "as well as people in the movie and theater business, all with different political opinions, yet united in their determination to defend and enrich France's culture." With characteristic enthusiasm, she added, "the golden age was there, within arm's reach, and that spurred us on. The French Communist Party (PCF) was to be the driving force; it urged us not only to fight for progress, but also to resist war and fascism."[22]

Others were more ambivalent in their response to Hitler. Jean-Paul Sartre and Simone de Beauvoir were decidedly leftist in their sympathies but disinclined to get involved. "We took no more than a moderate interest in the Stavisky Affair," Beauvoir recalled, and "more than once during these years, Sartre was vaguely tempted to join the Communist Party." But the two decided that "we had our own tasks to fulfill, and they were not compatible with joining the Party."[23] Later, Sartre insisted that until 1939 he regarded himself as "the 'solitary man' who opposes society because he doesn't owe society anything and, most important, because society has no hold over him." He told one biographer that he "didn't manage to escape [this idea] until the walls came tumbling down in 1939."[24] For her part, Beauvoir wrote (from a postwar perspective) that "today it astounds me to think how we could have stood by and watched all this so calmly. We were indignant enough it is true. . . . But we refused to face the threat which Hitler's behavior constituted to the world." Or, as she also put it, "We would not set our own shoulders to the wheel of history, but we wanted to believe that it was turning in the right direction."[25]

At this point, Malraux's writing appealed to Sartre, especially *La Condition humaine*, which Sartre thought encapsulated his ideal of the engaged yet solitary individual, one who forges himself through his own actions—or inactions—in an irrational and random world. While pursuing his writing, Sartre and Beauvoir continued their lives together and apart, traveling with and seeing one another regularly, since they were now teaching at schools that were fairly close to one another as well as to Paris. But this was not to continue. Sartre had applied for a research scholarship at the French Institute in Berlin to study phenomenology and was accepted for the 1933–1934 school year. Before he left, they spent the summer traveling in Italy, where Mussolini's Blackshirts were everywhere, causing the two a bit of annoyance in Rome.

Once in Berlin, Sartre's fellow French students were derisive of Nazism and Hitler—despite the exodus of German scholars and artists, despite the blatant Nazi anti-Semitism, and despite the recent Nuremberg rally, where some three hundred thousand Brownshirts marched before a victorious Hitler. They, like the bulk of the French left, were all convinced (as Beauvoir put it) that "Hitlerism was liable to collapse at any moment" and that the Nuremberg congress was "due to a temporary fit of collective hysteria."[26] This, despite Hitler's own belief that "the year 1933 was nothing other than the renewal of the millennial condition. The concept of the Reich . . . has victoriously asserted itself with us and in the world."[27] The real threat, Sartre and Beauvoir agreed, was not Hitler: it was panic among France's right wing.

In the meantime, Sartre believed strongly that his "job was to write and that writing was in no way a social activity."[28]

In 1933, the Bauhaus—that notable postwar German school of modernist art, design, and architecture founded by Walter Gropius and, since 1930, run by the equally celebrated Mies van der Rohe—closed under Nazi pressure. It was a fist in the face of modernism.

Hitler's acolytes had not appreciated either the Bauhaus style (its faculty included Paul Klee and Wassily Kandinsky) or its politics, which the Nazis equated with "cultural Bolshevism." Despite Mies's efforts to protect the Bauhaus by privatizing it, Hitler's regime brooked no left-wing modernist nonsense, which it condemned as un-German, and closed the school. Mies fled Germany for America in 1937; Gropius would arrive that same year, after a stopover in Britain.

Le Corbusier, being in France, did not have to deal with the same immediate threats as his German colleagues, and his politics vacillated according to how others treated him. While refusing a 1933 invitation to join the Legion of Honor, on the grounds that he did not wish "to enter the rank of certain people [from the Académie des Beaux Arts] with whom I am in acute disagreement," he remained intensely aware that he was being pummeled by the left as well as by the right. "Here in Paris, and in Moscow as well," he wrote a friend, "*L'Humanité* accuses me of being vulgar bourgeois. *Le Figaro* and Hitler denounce me as a Bolshevist."

By this time Le Corbusier bore grudges not only against the Beaux Arts traditionalists, whom he believed had conspired to do him out of his League of Nations commission, but also against the Soviets, following his 1932 failure to make even the short list for the commission to build Moscow's Soviet Palace of the People. Once somewhat enamored of the Soviet Union—following his success with a design for Moscow's central office of cooperatives—Le Corbusier was now bitterly anti-Soviet and had wired his outrage directly to Stalin. "I am and desire to remain an architect and an urbanist," he remarked, "with all the consequences which that may involve."[29]

Le Corbusier was not imagining his enemies, although those on the right were by far his most virulent. Among these was Chanel's lover, Paul Iribe. Whether or not rumors of Chanel's engagement to Iribe were correct, it certainly was true that by mid-1933, he and Chanel had embarked on an affair, Iribe's wife had left him, and Chanel had agreed to back a resurrection of Iribe's journal, *Le Témoin*, which premiered in December 1933. This weekly, which ran for two years, served as a megaphone for Iribe's increasingly ultranationalist elitism, anti-Semitism, and anti-Bolshevism, all of which he managed to serve up in a stew of alarm over what was happening to French art, fashion, and design. Foreigners, in Iribe's view, were to blame for the rise of modernism, and he found a convenient target in Le Corbusier, Picasso, Gropius, and many others, attacking them for conspiring against France's very identity and calling for a movement to "make France French again."[30]

Colette called Iribe "demonic,"[31] and others found him equally unattractive, but Chanel embraced not only her lover but her lover's caustic worldview, which in many ways complemented and intensified her own. What was uncharacteristic was Chanel's brief capitulation to Iribe's need to dominate her, allowing him for a time to manage her business. Iribe had never run a business and knew nothing about it, although he seemed to think that he did. Not surprisingly, this led to an unfortunate mess during a complicated time when Chanel was trying to win back more control over her perfume empire.[32] Soon, a majority of the board of Les Parfums Chanel voted Iribe off the board, and in 1934 it removed Chanel as president.

Iribe would unexpectedly die of a heart attack a year later, leaving Chanel in shock but once again in control of her life. As she later told Paul Morand, "I had a great affection for Paul and was very fond of him," but "he was the most complicated man I ever knew." She added, "He loved me with the secret hope of destroying me."[33] Fortunately for Chanel, it never came to that.

Following Hitler's rise to power, Salvador Dalí dismayed the Surrealists by insisting that the Führer was some sort of enchanting new addition to Dalí's pantheon of oddities—a view with which Breton in particular could not agree. Eluard insisted that at heart Dalí was not and could not be a Hitlerite, but at the same time he recognized the "almost insurmountable difficulties which this Hitlerian-paranoiac attitude of Dalí, if it persists, will entail."[34]

Paranoia appealed to Dalí, who at about this time came up with his "paranoiac-critical method" of creation. Roughly speaking, this amounted to putting down an obsessional idea churned up by the unconscious, then elaborating on it by the paranoiac association of ideas that it suggested. Dalí was exploring some of the same territory as the Surrealists, who had tried to navigate the unconscious via free association and dream symbolism, but Dalí calculatedly added the role of the conscious, applied at the right moment. Their paths were diverging, and he and Breton would soon part company, acrimoniously. Dalí's aims were far too bent on commercial success for Breton, who disdained the kind of success Dalí sought.

Dalí's drive for moneymaking acclaim now seemed within reach. From the small beginnings of the Zodiac group (twelve patrons who shared in his support and drew lots each month for their choice among his work), he was rapidly expanding his horizons. His 1931 painting, *The Persistence of Memory*—that enigmatic and disturbing composition with the limp watches, which may have been inspired by his late-night encounter with a small, round, and very soft Camembert cheese—was bringing a satisfying degree of attention, as did several other works, including *The Dream*. Dalí's one-man show in late 1933 at Julien Levy's New York gallery brought favorable reviews, most notably from Lewis Mumford, even as more opportunity in America beckoned.

Dalí did not attend this first New York exhibit. He may or may not have intentionally made a fetish of his continued fear of crossing the street, let alone the ocean, but by now he was definitely courting attention with his moustache, which he was beginning to curl at its long, waxed ends. By late 1933 it was clear that Salvador Dalí, whatever his political leanings, was as adept at self-promotion as he was with a paintbrush.

Henry Miller did not think much of, or about, politics. Nor did he think much of so-called normality, which he considered a state of existence inimical to the truly interesting people in life. Whether it was a one-legged prostitute or the paranoid schizophrenic lawyer from Connecticut with whom he briefly roomed, Miller found oddness fascinating and even, to some extent, endearing. But he didn't think much of Salvador Dalí, who for four years lived just down the street from him.[35]

The two seem to have avoided one another, with the exception of one unfortunate occasion in 1940 when both were staying at Caresse Crosby's recently acquired Virginia mansion. According to some accounts, Anaïs Nin accompanied Miller, but it seems that her encounter with Dalí was on another and probably earlier occasion, when she was not with Miller. By then, Dalí was a long-term and pampered resident at Caresse's estate, and Nin got along well enough with him, although she took to her diary to wonder whether he was truly mad, or was it a pose?[36] Gala she found imperious and insufferable. When Miller arrived, he was traveling by car across America, accompanied not by Nin, but by the artist Abe Rattner. Miller was taking a look at America for his book *The Air-Conditioned Nightmare*. Whether or not there was a shouting match between Miller and Dalí, as rumor has it (Caresse diplomatically omits Miller's visit and emphasizes Dalí's charm), the evening definitely was not a success. Miller promptly left.

In any case, he had already made up his mind. As far as Miller was concerned, Dalí was a complete fraud—although he put it a little more colorfully.

"Have you become a Communist?" Hemingway asked Fitzgerald in April 1931, writing from Key West. "In 1919–20–21 when we were all paid up Communists . . . all those guys thot [*sic*] it was all tripe—as indeed it proved to be—but [I] suppose everybody has to go through some political or religious faith sooner or later." As for him, he "personally would rather go through things sooner and get your disillusions behind you instead of ahead of you."[37]

Hemingway's life had changed in many ways since that not-so-distant past. He now was writing for mainstream American publications such as *Esquire*. His best-selling novel, *A Farewell to Arms*, had been made into a Hollywood movie starring Gary Cooper and Helen Hayes. And he now lived (and deep-sea fished) in Key West, but traveled extensively, from game hunting in Montana and Wyoming to big-game hunting in Africa, with time spent in Spain and Paris in between.

Money was no problem for him, as it was by now for Fitzgerald, but Hemingway had his own set of difficulties. His book of short stories, *Winner Take Nothing* (1933), had received unfavorable reviews, including one in the *New Yorker* that urged him to move on from his focus on sport and sudden death, which he had developed "to the saturation point." But it was the response to Hemingway's book on bullfighting, *Death in the Afternoon* (1932)—especially the scorching review by Max Eastman in the *New Republic*—that gave Hemingway apoplexy. Not only had Eastman's review, titled "Bull in the Afternoon," disparaged Hemingway for "juvenile romanticism" and a literary style of "wearing false hair on the chest," but it declared that the reason behind Hemingway's macho swagger was his lack of confidence that he was "a full-sized man."[38]

At this, Hemingway exploded. His good friend Archibald MacLeish (still a friend despite a Hemingway outburst the year before) sent a letter of protest to the *New Republic* at what he condemned as a slur on Hemingway's sexual potency. Eastman claimed to be flabbergasted at this implication and sent a letter of apology, but Hemingway did not calm down. In a letter to his own publisher, Maxwell Perkins, Hemingway threatened that "if [Eastman] ever gets a solvent publisher to publish that libel between covers it will cost the publisher plenty of money and Eastman will go to jail." What his so-called friends in New York couldn't get over, Hemingway concluded, was that "I can write." Even if they didn't like it, "Papa will make them like it."[39]

As if the Eastman imbroglio wasn't enough, Hemingway had Gertrude Stein to contend with. Much to everyone's surprise, Stein's 1933 *The Autobiography of Alice B. Toklas* landed on the best-seller list. At long last, weary of being ignored, Gertrude Stein had decided (with Alice's prompting) to write a popular book, one that was not only readable but fun. For many years the famous and the about-to-be-famous had beaten a path to her door. Why not write about it? Unfortunately, from her perspective, to write such a memoir would be demeaning. Yet the idea of something that would readily find a publisher and make a lot of money had its attractions.

It was when Stein got the idea of writing just such a memoir, under the thin disguise of an autobiography by Alice, that it all began to come together. She soon found an agent (William Bradley, who was representing Henry Miller), a publisher (Harcourt, Brace), and an opportunity for *Autobiography* to appear, in an abridged version, in the *Atlantic Monthly*, where Stein had long and unsuccessfully attempted to get her work published. Soon she even made the cover of *Time* magazine. Wambly Bald expressed the general amazement: "Gertrude Stein has crashed (of all things) the *Atlantic Monthly*, and her autobiography is accepted for publication by the Book-of-the-Month Club."[40]

It was a dream come true for Gertrude Stein: "I love being rich," she exulted, "it makes me all cheery inside." There were no downsides that she could see to having money: "First I bought myself a new eight cylinder Ford car," she reported, and then an expensive coat for her dog, made to order by Hermès. She loved having her own greatness corroborated, and she enjoyed being a celebrity: "I never imagined that would happen to me to be a celebrity like that but it did and when it did I liked it."[41]

But for many of those whom Stein mentioned in the course of her gossipy reminiscences, it was closer to a nightmare. Picasso (and his wife) was dismayed to read embarrassing stories about his past personal relationships and broke with Stein—an estrangement that lasted for two years. Worse were Stein's self-flattering accounts that distorted or turned reality topsy-turvy. Eugene Jolas, editor of *transition*, was irritated by Stein's claims to have been the inspiration for his beloved literary review: "There is a unanimity of opinion," he wrote, "that she had no understanding of what really was happening around her." In response to the *Autobiography*, he and others, including Henri Matisse and Georges Braque, joined to point out Stein's factual errors and distortions (including her unflattering description of Matisse's wife), and agreed (in Jolas's words) that Stein had presented the epoch "without taste and without relation to reality." Her brother Leo, from whom she had been estranged for years, summed up the appalled Left Bank response: "God," he exclaimed, "what a liar she is!"[42]

Of all those that Gertrude Stein offended, though, it was Ernest Hemingway who was the most infuriated. Not only did Gertrude claim that she and Sherwood Anderson had "formed" Hemingway and that "they were both a little proud and a little ashamed of the work of their minds," but she asserted that Hemingway had learned the basics of how to write from correcting the proofs in 1924 for her *The Making of Americans*. Worst, though, at least from Hemingway's point of view, was her avowal that Hemingway was "yellow."[43]

Hemingway was furious. He told the editor of *Esquire* that Gertrude "was a fine woman until she went professionally goofy," and he dropped in words like "lesbian" and "menopause." He wrote Janet Flanner that he was very fond of Gertrude, "and god knows I was loyal too until she had pushed my face in a dozen times." He wrote his editor, Maxwell Perkins, with more comments about "poor old Gertrude Stein," and wasn't it a shame about menopause: "Suddenly she couldn't tell a good picture from a bad one, a good writer from a bad one, it all went phtt."[44] According to the writer and longtime Montparnasse resident Morrill Cody, Hemingway was "particularly infuriated by [Gertrude's] claim that she had 'discovered him' and had helped him find a publisher: 'It is we who tried like hell to find a publisher for *her*.'"[45]

Public payback began with Hemingway's opportunity to write an introduction to the book by everyone's favorite Montparnasse bartender, Jimmie Charters, which Morrill Cody ghosted. Publication was in 1934, and Hemingway filled his introduction with acid comments about certain unnamed women who hold salons, especially those who write their memoirs and use the occasion to denigrate those they have fallen out with. "Surely," he remarked, "Jimmy served more and better drinks than any legendary woman ever did in her salon, [and] certainly Jimmy gave less and better advice."[46]

Of course, like all feuds, this particular one had a long history—one in which Hemingway's treatment of Sherwood Anderson was deeply involved.[47] Gertrude Stein liked Anderson and especially appreciated his compliments. Given this, she did not like the way Hemingway behaved toward Anderson, who, early in Hemingway's career, had served as his mentor. Back in the 1920s, Hemingway had turned on Anderson, trashing his book *Dark Laughter* with a nasty parody called *The Torrents of Spring*. Hemingway's aim had been to break off one book contract and sign on with a more desirable publisher. He succeeded, and his first hit novel, *The Sun Also Rises*, was the outcome. But it was the result of what both Gertrude Stein and Sherwood Anderson regarded as a betrayal, and neither of them forgot it.

The morning after his October arrival in Paris, Hemingway went to see Sylvia Beach. "He and I are good old friends," Beach wrote to her sister the following day, and Hemingway unloaded his woes about Max Eastman and Gertrude Stein. Beach, as always, listened sympathetically, but she had troubles of her own.

It was all very well for Hemingway to talk of Paris in the past tense and to declare that it was a fine place to be young in, but he and Pauline were en route to an expensive three-month safari in Africa, while Beach had tough financial realities to deal with. Her rent had recently tripled, and her business had declined dramatically after the departure of Americans from Paris following the Crash. At the same time, the government was trying to bolster the by now rapidly shrinking treasury by increasing taxes—which desperate shopkeepers, including Beach, protested by closing for a day.

Workers, too, joined with shopkeepers to demonstrate against pay cuts and oppose tax increases—protests which, as not many realized, were organized by right-wing pressure groups such as the National Tax Payers Federation and the Comité de Salut Economique, whose own movers and financers included organizations such as Action Française and individuals such as the perfume tycoon François Coty.

Coty had long been a major subsidizer of extreme-right organizations, including the Croix-de-Feu, which burst into prominence under Colonel de La Rocque's leadership in 1931. Not long after the 1933 tax protests, Coty founded Solidarité Française, a far-right league claiming some 315,000 members by year's end, with a significant following among the lower middle classes. Solidarité Française had its genesis just as Coty was being brought to trial for accusations in his newspapers, *Figaro* and *L'Ami du Peuple*, that the Union of Jewish Ex-Soldiers as well as several Jewish sports organizations were merely revolutionary bodies in disguise. He lost the case in July and that autumn lost both *Figaro* and *L'Ami du Peuple* to his first wife as a result of their long-running and acrimonious divorce case.[48]

But Sylvia Beach had little interest at the moment in what François Coty was up to. Nor was she especially interested in the latest gossip revolving around *The Autobiography of Alice B. Toklas*, although she was surprised to learn that, according to Gertrude Stein, Sylvia Beach was "very enthusiastic about Gertrude Stein." But Beach had larger concerns on her mind. Not only was her beloved bookshop "suffering excruciatingly," as she wrote her sister,[49] but events surrounding James Joyce's *Ulysses* were providing more than the usual headaches.

Ever since *Ulysses* had first appeared, it had been banned in the United States and Great Britain on grounds of obscenity, and throughout the 1920s and early 1930s, copies were regularly seized and burned.[50] But in 1932, Random House offered to assume all the risks of a court battle as part of its publication offer to Joyce. The day after Joyce signed, Random House's publisher, Bennett Cerf, hired the prominent civil liberties lawyer Morris Ernst to take its case to court.

When *Ulysses* came to trial in the autumn of 1933, Nazi book burnings had already begun. Much to the delight and relief of *Ulysses*'s supporters, the judge, who had read it, called *Ulysses* "a very powerful commentary on the inner lives of men and women." His decision—that "in spite of its unusual frankness," *Ulysses* was not pornographic and therefore could be admitted into the United States—was a milestone for civil liberties and artistic freedom.[51] Ten minutes after the verdict was announced, Cerf—who had been doubtful of the trial's outcome—gave the signal for the typesetters to get to work, and Random House soon sold thirty-five thousand copies.

But Sylvia Beach was still dealing with a James Joyce who drank too much, spent too much, and insisted that everyone around him, including and especially Beach, was betraying him. Until the moment came in late 1933 when Joyce knew that Random House could publish *Ulysses*, he prodded Beach to publish a cheap Continental edition of *Ulysses* to keep it available and the royalties flowing until the American drama was resolved. But Beach had checked out the printing prices and decided that this would be too expensive, especially given her own financial difficulties and the prospect that a Random House edition would present disastrous competition. As far as she was concerned, she had handed over *Ulysses* to Random House, and she wanted to be done with it.[52]

It was with uncharacteristic bitterness that Beach described the enormous understatement of Joyce's characterization of her role, which he wrote in his preface to the American edition. The sentence in which Joyce so inadequately summed up Beach's contribution was, "My friend Mr. Ezra Pound and good luck brought me into contact with a very clever and energetic person Miss Sylvia Beach. . . . This brave woman risked what professional publishers did not wish to, she took the manuscript and handed it to the printers." This prompted Beach to write her sister that Joyce "has written a preface to the new edition connecting me up with Ezra Pound [now a defender of fascist Italy] in the first [American] publishing of *Ulysses*. So as you might say, he has not only robbed me but 'taken away my character.'"[53]

Although Sylvia Beach was worried about her bookshop and about her difficulties in dealing with Joyce, she was at this point only intermittently worried about Hitler. France, in her opinion, was becoming overly panicky, with gas masks for sale and officials inspecting shelter locations in case of war. Her partner, Adrianne Monnier, on the other hand, was convinced that Hitler's rise meant that war was inevitable.

Jean Renoir, who was in Berlin at the time of Hitler's election as chancellor, was similarly worried. He never forgot the cruelties he witnessed then, including "something abominable," when a gang of Brownshirts "forced an elderly Jewish lady to go down on her knees and lick the pavement, saying that this was the only work suitable for Jews." He saw women go down on their knees as Hitler's car passed, while men "wept with emotion."[54]

But he also experienced the debauched nightlife of the German capital, whose decadence—despite his familiarity with Berlin in times past—was far more extreme than anything he had seen before. "That evening," he later wrote, "convinced me of something that I already knew, namely that defeat had thrown these people completely off-balance. Wounded pride can be dangerous!" Even though Berliners "hid their resentment under a mask of absolute indifference," he realized that "the face of Berlin in those days, under the display of sardonic ribaldry, concealed a monumental despair."[55]

Disinclined to condemn, Renoir added, "Defeat had corrupted Germany, but no more than so-called victory had corrupted France." He could now understand that, "win or lose, no nation can escape the decadence engendered by war."[56]

∼

War was something that Major Charles de Gaulle understood, and something that he vainly tried to persuade his colleagues, and especially his superiors, to understand more clearly—that is, from his point of view. In his new position at the Supreme National Defense Council, or SGDN, he pushed for a comprehensive plan for France's leaders to have at hand in case of war, one that would avoid the improvisation that he had seen and experienced during the Great War.

De Gaulle was worried about Hitler, and "as no one proposed anything that would deal with the situation [the Nazi ascendency in Germany], I felt myself required to appeal to public opinion."[57] And so in the spring of 1933, despite his military training to the contrary, de Gaulle went over the heads of his superiors by starting to write for magazines—that is, taking his case to the general public. Essential to a successful defensive plan, he argued, was military preparedness. This meant, fundamentally, a professional army (not one of conscripts), one that was thoroughly and intelligently equipped with mobile armored divisions of motorized tanks.

From now on, de Gaulle would not only crusade for a professional army but for the role of autonomous tank units within it. He never claimed to be the first to do so: "I had naturally taken advantage of the lines of thought set in motion all over the world by the appearance of the fighting internal-combustion engine," he later wrote.[58] By 1933, Germany was already working on its panzer divisions, with the first three established in 1934, only a year after Hitler came to power.

By late 1933, the newly promoted Lieutenant Colonel de Gaulle, although a staunchly conservative Catholic who still read *Action Française* (albeit with a mixture of admiration and irritation), was never tempted by the leagues or by a nationalism gone rampant. Nor did he ever consider appeasing Hitler as a means of opposing communism. As he wrote in 1937, "How can one accept that social order is purchased by the loss of liberty?"[59] First and foremost he was a fervent defender of France, who looked with grave concern on Hitler's rise and was eager to do something about it.

Although hardly a perfect democrat, Charles de Gaulle was from the outset consistently opposed to Hitler and fascism.

⌇

As Hitler continued to expand and consolidate his power, pacifism continued to grow in France: "Never again," the SFIO put it, in its effective campaign slogan. At the same time, small shopkeepers, irate taxpayers, and the unemployed were joining with war veterans in their growing fury at the Republic's leaders, who seemed completely unable to address the nation's problems. Soon this swelling discontent would coalesce around a financial scandal that surfaced in late 1933, known as the Stavisky Affair.

As a scandal, this one was not especially noteworthy. A small-time con man named Alexandre Stavisky—a naturalized French citizen of Ukrainian Jewish origins—had managed throughout his slippery career to evade jail while maintaining a convincingly flashy lifestyle. This, combined with a certain cleverness, brought him into contact with ever-more-prominent businessmen and politicians, who willingly protected him. By the early 1930s, Stavisky was managing Bayonne's municipal pawnshops (the Crédit Municipal of Bayonne), where he used his supposed possession of the Spanish crown jewels (allegedly slipped over the border in 1931 with Spain's fleeing monarch) as the basis for issuing a whopping two hundred million francs worth of tax-free but nonetheless counterfeit bonds. These appealed to a variety of unwary targets, who scarfed them up after several government figures, including France's then-minister of labor, endorsed them.

Stavisky came to a bad end in early 1934 after his scam was exposed and he fled. Officially he committed suicide by gunshot, but speculation quickly grew that the police had killed him to prevent him from talking. Conspiracy theories promptly took off. Janet Flanner approached the subject with the irony it seemed to deserve ("Not since the Panama Canal scandal has there been such astonishment at corruption among government bodies"),[60] but the public's dismay and anger were real.

And so, by the end of 1933, Stavisky's last scam was growing into a full-scale Affair, and no one was very happy. As Count Harry Kessler put it on New Year's Eve: "Before midnight in bed. Thus ends this tragic year."[61]

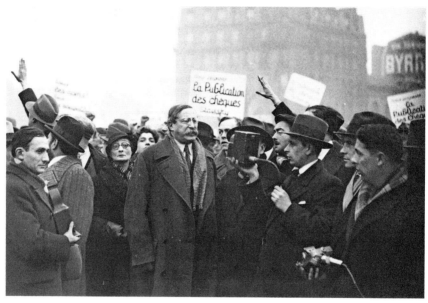

Léon Blum speaking in front of a Socialist and Communist audience during the general strike in Paris, February 12, 1934. © SZ Photo / Scherl / Bridgeman Images

CHAPTER SEVEN

~

Bloody Tuesday

(1934)

As the year opened, Parisians were far more agitated by the speculation and anger that Stavisky roused than they were by the dangers posed by any foreign power, even one as close and alarming as Hitler's Germany. In large part, as numerous historians have pointed out, this was because the Paris press blew the Stavisky Affair into enormous proportions.[1]

Not that there wasn't a crooked Stavisky, or a distressingly large scam played upon a number of innocent, or somewhat innocent, victims. But the Paris press, which in 1934 was rarely known for its objectivity, was determined to make something spectacular out of this particular scandal, which involved a government of Radical (that is, center to left-of-center) politicians. Of course scandal of any sort sold newspapers, but this was a city where a large number of newspapers leaned to the right and took every opportunity to discredit the Republic, especially when a Radical government was in office. According to a survey taken only a couple of years later, some twelve Paris publications of the right and the extreme right had a combined circulation of one and a half million, while those of the left or extreme left sold about seven hundred thousand, with the mass-circulation dailies catering to a many-million crowd of readers who were vaguely centrist but decidedly anti-left.[2] Readership was large and avid, especially with a juicy scandal going on. All it took was for the right-wing press to hawk a particular outrage, and the mass-circulation dailies would come galloping after.

This was especially true as the Depression began to hit advertising revenues, which never had been sufficient to pay the bills—except for the mass-circulation *Paris-Soir* and *Paris-Midi*, which managed to turn a profit. This meant that the rest either had to rely on private fortunes (as with François Coty's *L'Ami du Peuple*) or look elsewhere for subsidies, which could be substantial. Most Paris newspapers sold their news columns to whoever would pay, including banks, industry, or governments, French or foreign. In addition, Paris newspapers commonly refused to cover certain speeches, exhibitions, and sporting events, or even to mention the names of certain individuals, unless money changed hands. In this atmosphere, the reading public had no way of knowing what was factual and true and what was not, let alone what was or was not suppressed.

According to some, the public did not even care. As long as people were entertained, they kept on reading. And since more people now were reading than ever before, anxiety and disorder could, with just an extra push, blow out of control.

The first Paris publication to see the possibilities in the emerging Stavisky mess was the far-right *Action Française*. A terrible rail disaster to the east of Paris on December 23, with its own list of blunders, charges, and counter-charges, had captured the headlines. Economic doldrums hung heavy on the chill winter air, and Parisians were irate, determined to find the real culprits—whether for the rail disaster or for their own falling salaries, which had declined significantly (by one count, by almost one-third since 1929), creating a soaring number of bankruptcies along the way.[3] France was now experiencing the full force of the Depression, and morale slid as pockets emptied.

And then the convoluted story of Stavisky began to come to light. *Action Française* was quick to see the political ramifications, even as the rest of Paris remained preoccupied with the rail disaster and a dismal Christmas. But Stavisky, in *Action Française*'s eyes, was doubly culpable, as a Jew and as a foreigner, and his many connections to the Radical government created some tantalizing political possibilities. *Action Française* persisted in uncovering the scandal's reaches in the hope of bringing down the current government, and soon the rest of the press was hot on the trail. "Down with the Thieves!" *Action Francaise*'s banner headline screamed on January 7, followed by an appeal, "To the People of Paris," calling upon Parisians to "clamor for honesty and justice" and to "take the law into their own hands."[4] To reinforce this point, Action Française's street brawlers, the Camelots du Roi, demonstrated violently on the Left Bank and in the Place de la Concorde, tearing out trees and railings. Already the barricades were going up.

In late January, as rioting accelerated, the current prime minister, Camille Chautemps, was forced to resign, accused by the press of responsibility for Stavisky's murder. "For the first time in the history of the Third Republic," wrote one Socialist, "a parliamentary majority has capitulated and its government has abandoned power under the menace of the streets."[5] But Chautemps's resignation did not bring calm. By early February, the government was in disarray, and violence was escalating, with the police doing little to stop it. The left blamed Paris's powerful police prefect, Jean Chiappe, for this state of affairs: after all, Chiappe had a history of close ties to the far right. Reluctant to stir up this particular hornet's nest, the newly formed government was divided on what to do with Chiappe until left-wing pressure finally led to his transfer to Morocco—a plan that backfired when he refused to go. At that, the prime minister had no choice but to dismiss him, making Chiappe a martyr of the right.

The turmoil now grew, with rowdy crowds shouting the revolutionary "Ça ira, ça ira, ça ira," mixed in with "A bas la République!" The Croix-de-Feu, along with Action Française, the Jeunesses Patriotes, Solidarité Française, and other leagues of the extreme right, called on their followers to protest. Word soon spread of a huge plot against the people: according to this rumor, machine guns, cannons, and even tanks had been brought into the National Assembly, which—according to this appalled gossip—was prepared to spill the blood of its citizens. And then on Tuesday, February 6, the worst street violence since the 1871 Commune uprising broke out in Paris as a mass demonstration of extreme-right leagues and veterans' organizations stormed the barricades erected at the Pont de la Concorde to defend the National Assembly, located just across the bridge. Shots were fired, razors slashed, and buses were burned. In the end, fifteen people were killed and more than one thousand injured.

The right claimed that what had happened was blatant and unprovoked government aggression against its own people, while the left countered that it was an attempted fascist coup. Some of the extreme-right leaders certainly admired Mussolini and Hitler, but at its heart, Bloody Tuesday seems to have been something far simpler and elemental: a massive display of anger against everyone in charge, prodded by extremists and enthusiastically supported by a public fed up with the deteriorating quality of their lives—and the inability of their elected officials to do anything about it.

The clashes continued, with a Communist mobilization on February 9 that left nine dead and hundreds wounded, followed by a general strike on February 12 that roused more than one million Paris workers to rise up in protest. Still, after the rioting stopped and the cleanup began, it turned out that little had changed. The Republic was still standing, but the government (the fifth in twenty months) was now in conservatives' hands, with Marshal Philippe Pétain as minister of war—which reassured some while throwing others into a funk. The streets were quiet. And life, such as it was, went on.

～

"Paris was still breathing," wrote Elliot Paul after his November 1934 return from Spain, "but vultures were wheeling in a lead-colored sky." Paul, an American writer who had been coeditor of the literary journal *transition* during his heady Montparnasse days, had in the early 1930s disappeared quite suddenly from the Paris scene, reportedly after suffering a nervous breakdown. Reminding his readers—in his retrospective, *The Last Time I Saw Paris*—that the Radical party (officially the Radical Socialist party) "was neither radical nor socialist but opportunist-center," he described the chaos of the post–February 6 political scene as differing little from the confusion that had come before: "Political parties," he wrote, "in the interest of clarity, should not have names but numbers, like football players on the field."[6]

Yes, it was confusing, and throughout the bloody days of February, Sylvia Beach and Adrienne Monnier stocked up on candles and groceries and pored over the papers, trying to make sense of what was happening. But what was happening was no mystery to Beach's good friend Janet Flanner, who interpreted it as "everyman" against those who "banditized [them] by state taxes, state politicians, state-protected swindlers." She added that the "French cost of living, compared to French wages, [is] higher by thirty per cent than any other on earth," and mentioned that, not surprisingly, a current play by Edouard Bourdet called *Les Temps difficiles* was selling out, "since it describes [the] *haute bourgeoisie* as either rotted by money-love or else not worth their salt to France as a class."[7]

Anger and fear remained like a dismal fog, even after the riots subsided. On the extreme right, where few but the royalist Action Française were interested in restoring the monarchy, the Jeunesses Patriotes, Solidarité Française, and especially the Croix-de-Feu now rapidly increased in numbers. Some of these leagues were more inclined to hooliganism than others (the Croix-de-Feu under Colonel de La Rocque, who could not abide unruly mobs, prided itself on its relative restraint and had backed off during the height of the February 6 riots). But even hooliganism wasn't sufficient for some of the far right's disaffected members, who would start to drift into La Cagoule, officially the Comité secret d'action révolutionnaire (Secret Committee of Revolutionary Action), which began its violent career after February 6 with the aim of overthrowing the Republic. All of these leagues talked a good game about restoring order and morality, but a common denominator linking all of them was their extreme nationalism, anticommunism, authoritarianism (including paramilitarism), and anti-Semitism, the latter exacerbated by the recent arrival of Jewish refugees from Nazism, who caused alarm by gravitating leftward. In addition, the far-right leagues held in common a mutual antipathy to the Freemasons, whom they feared and despised as a supposedly dark underground brotherhood that secretly ran everything.

For its part, the left was even more divided than the right, since the Communists had fought the Socialists for years, rejecting any and all offers of cooperation. Still, the left was terrified by Bloody Tuesday and what it portended. February 6 may not have been an attempted fascist putsch, but to those on the left, it certainly looked like one. Suddenly the idea of left-wing cooperation seemed not only possible but necessary. When the Socialists called for demonstrations on February 12, backed by a General Confederation of Labor (CGT) strike, the Communist PCF and its CGTU (Unitary General Confederation of Labor) decided to join in. At first the "joining" was a little tentative, with the Communists and the Socialists marching separately to the Place de la Nation, and there was more than a little anxiety over what would happen when all three hundred thousand of them actually met. But what happened, much to the astonishment of many, was a major event of fraternization among the rank and file. Suddenly, as one participant recalled, there were "arms opening, eyes meeting, voices mingling." As Blum himself later put it, "It was not a collision, it was a fraternization. Through a kind of ground swell, the people's instinct and the people's will had imposed the unity of action of the organized workers for the defense of the Republic."[8]

The Socialist and Communist newspapers continued to snipe at one another, but something important, even historic, had happened. In July, the two parties signed a unity pact, but on looking back, many—including Blum—thought that this remarkable February event represented the "true birth of the Popular Front."[9]

Not only did the February riots prompt the beginnings of leftist cooperation, but they lit a spark among intellectuals, including the Surrealist leader André Breton, who promptly called a meeting of leftist intellectuals that ended (after an all-night debate) with a manifesto urging a union of all non-Communist leftists. Soon this and other left-wing prodding led to a watchdog group, the Vigilance Committee of Antifascist Intellectuals, which included scholars and academics such as Paul Langevin and Irène Joliot-Curie—all of whom, in Charlotte Perriand's words, were "fighting for the freedom of democracy."[10] But the real powerhouse in the intellectual community was the Communist-sponsored Association of Revolutionary Writers and Artists (AEAR), which included Gide, Malraux, and other leading intellectuals. Breton's attempts to exclude the Communists from the antifascist fight were stillborn at the outset.

Unlike her mother, Irène Joliot-Curie was staunchly involved in political causes and willing to take a public stand on those issues that deeply moved her. She had long been involved in public protests, having supported Sacco and Vanzetti in the 1920s; but in the 1930s she and her husband became especially active as they worked closely with their good friend and Frédéric's mentor, the prominent physicist Paul Langevin. Langevin, a graduate student of Pierre Curie's and, after Pierre's death, Marie Curie's lover, had forged a brilliant career of his own, and now, as a member of the Academy of Sciences, was in the forefront of those causes in which he deeply believed. He and his son took part in the February 12 joint Socialist-Communist march, and he even managed to persuade Marie Curie to express her displeasure, albeit in private, over the Stavisky Affair. Now, in the aftermath of the February riots, he was keenly involved in fighting the fascist menace. For him, this meant working on behalf of the Soviet Union, which he had come to believe embodied the best hope for mankind. A committed Marxist, Langevin had already visited Russia on three occasions and had invited the Joliot-Curies to go with him on his most recent trip (Frédéric went, but Irène had to beg off, being ill at the time. She would join Frédéric on a future Moscow trip).

By now, despite the time that Irène was spending in the mountains for her health, she and her husband had become leading figures in the world peace movement. Their remarkable scientific achievements certainly qualified them as stars: in January, the Joliot-Curies discovered artificial radioactivity—a startling breakthrough that would win them the joint Nobel Prize for Chemistry the following year. "With the neutron we were too late; with the positron we were too late," Frédéric later commented. "Now we are on time." But he was well aware of the dangerous forces that this particular discovery could unleash. "Scientists," he observed, "building up or shattering elements at will, will be able to bring about transmutations of an explosive type."[11] It seemed especially fitting that the discoverers of this particular breakthrough were heartfelt proponents of world peace.

Happily, Marie Curie lived long enough to witness her daughter and son-in-law's remarkable discovery, although by this time her own health was rapidly declining. She worked to the end, scorning (as Eve put it) "a fatigue which became more evident every day, and the chronic ills that oppressed her." She died on July 4, 1934, and was buried with her husband in Sceaux, just outside Paris, "without a politician or an official present." According to her wishes, Madame Curie "modestly took her place in the realm of the dead . . . in the presence of her relatives, her friends, and the co-workers who loved her."[12]

Years later, in 1995, she would be moved with Pierre into the Panthéon, the first woman to enter that exclusive resting place on her own merits. It had taken more than sixty years, but here too, as in life, Marie Curie continued to be a pioneer.

Gide was in Sicily during Bloody Tuesday, where he was reading John Dos Passos's *Manhattan Transfer* (which "rather irritated" him) and *Othello* (for the sixth time). "I feel a great need to be alone," he had written a friend in late January, as political events were spinning out of control, and he promptly left for Syracuse. It was not the first time that Gide had abruptly taken to the road, and he acknowledged his almost compulsive need for travel: "I am well aware how prejudicial to me can be this wandering and disjointed life I am living," he wrote in his July 1933 journal. "But the only place in which it is permitted me to settle down," he added, "is Cuverville"—where his wife resided, and "where my thought soon becomes numb."[13] Tied to his wife by a bond he was unwilling to sever, he found himself unable to settle for long anywhere else, even in his Paris apartment. Then again, there were other compelling reasons for travel: so many of his journeys, especially to North Africa, were prompted by love affairs—or the search for love affairs—with young men. But on February 6, while Paris was in turmoil, Gide was in search of escape: by his own account he was immersed in reading, writing, and music, while deliberating the diction of French verse.

The turmoil that Gide was escaping was not only political; he had just been exposed to the outcome of a collaboration with Stravinsky that greatly upset him. The work was *Perséphone*, a dance-drama set to Gide's poetry, and Gide had been jolted by the music's jagged accentuations, which he thought made mincemeat of the words. He did not attend any of the rehearsals, nor the preview or the April premiere. Instead of attending the third and last performance, he instead chose to chair a meeting with Malraux to protest the imprisonment of Germany's Communist leader, Ernst Thälmann.

Stravinsky took care to publicize Paul Valéry's praise for *Perséphone*, and he criticized Gide, whom he had known during many years, for "the absence of rapport which emerges so obviously from your attitude"—a dig at Gide's chilly Protestantism and, more recently, his Communist ties.[14] Later, in his memoirs, Stravinsky took a swipe at Gide's knowledge of music, including

Gide's beloved Chopin: "That Gide understood nothing about music in general is apparent to anyone who has read his *Notes on Chopin*." As for Gide's writing, Stravinsky panned it as "very often like *eau distillée*." Gide, Stravinsky added snidely, "was not grand enough as a creator to make us forget the sins of his nature, as Tolstoy makes us forget the sins of *his* nature."[15]

Not surprisingly, after *Perséphone*, Gide and Stravinsky did not meet again.

Stravinsky spent Bloody Tuesday engrossed in *Perséphone*. Soon he would take out French citizenship and lease a fifteen-room apartment (including three salons and four maid's rooms) in an expensive quarter of Paris.

It was unclear whether or not he was still receiving money from Coco Chanel: she had been supporting Stravinsky and his family since 1920, and as recently as 1933 he had written her good friend Misia Sert to complain that "Chanel has not sent us anything since the 1st and so we are without a radish to live on this month; therefore I ask you to be kind enough to mention it to her."[16]

Stravinsky's new abode was near the Place de la Concorde, where all the trouble had broken out, and he was sensitized to trouble—having been recently attacked in Germany by Nazi thugs who thought he was Jewish, which he was not. Stravinsky's nose may have been a joking matter to his friends, but it was not something he found humorous, especially when it prompted anti-Semitic behavior toward him. Perhaps ironically, Stravinsky himself was anti-Semitic; he was also ready to do anything necessary to work in Germany, where in 1933 his name had appeared, as a Jew, on a list of undesirables. But money was money, and Stravinsky regularly went through a lot of it. And so he was quite willing to provide Hitler's minions with a detailed Stravinsky genealogy, including some self-serving diatribes against anyone or anything of which the Nazis might disapprove. He also began to be careful about whom he associated with, especially those Jewish artists who now were unwelcome there.

But despite his efforts, the Germans under Hitler were not welcoming avant-garde musicians such as Stravinsky, and he turned with more enthusiasm—and clear-eyed opportunism—toward Mussolini, with whom he had a private audience in 1933. "He is the savior of Italy," Stravinsky told an Italian music critic that year, "and—let us hope—of Europe."[17]

Simone de Beauvoir, much to her later embarrassment, remained tranquilly removed from February's riots and "only followed the sequence of events from a distance, being convinced that it was no concern of mine."[18] Gertrude Stein, on the other hand, was convinced that Stavisky was the mastermind behind the rise of Blum and what would become the Popular Front. In 1937, she described her views to one of the American soldiers she had befriended during World War I: "You see," she told him, "Stavisky was a real boss and he organized the Radical Socialists to stay and that machinery is still functioning though the real majority are tired of it."[19]

As for Hitler, Gertrude Stein shocked one of her 1934 guests by speaking of him as a great man. "I was stunned," the guest later recalled. "Hitler's persecution of the Jews was well publicized in France by that time."[20] And of course, although her guest did not say it, Stein was Jewish. Yet her praise of Hitler was not an anomaly: that May, she told an interviewer with the *New York Times Magazine* that "Hitler should have received the Nobel Peace Prize . . . because he is removing all elements of contest and struggle from Germany. By driving out the Jews and democratic and left elements, he is driving out everything that conduces to activity. That means peace."[21]

Unquestionably, Gertrude Stein enjoyed shocking people, and these pronouncements have been defended as examples of her irony and dark humor. But there was a disturbing continuity and insistence in her praise of Hitler throughout the decade, and it certainly mirrored that of her right-wing friend Bernard Faÿ, to whom she wrote in the early 1930s, "Of course I see politics but from one angle which is yours."[22]

Nonetheless, other things now were occupying Gertrude Stein far more than politics—in particular, her own success. That February, her opera *Four Saints in Three Acts* (with music by Virgil Thomson) debuted to fine reviews on Broadway, followed only a few months later by her triumphal lecture tour of America (October 1934 to May 1935). Gertrude Stein had always said that she would not go back to America until she was a lion, and now she was delighted to find that she was the lion she had longed to become. America embraced both Gertrude and Alice as appealing eccentrics, who amused and distracted the country during the bleakest years of the Depression. Gertrude and Alice in turn were enchanted with America and Americans, although Gertrude was adamantly opposed to President Roosevelt and the "riffraff" of the Democratic party; instead, she enthused about the Republican party's potential for strong leadership.[23]

Still, some things bothered Gertrude Stein about the nature of her success. Her *Autobiography of Alice B. Toklas* may have been gratifyingly popular, but it was not representative of her writing and she knew it. She anguished about her current creative atrophy and also about the very question of her identity as a writer. Had she become someone who was famous for being Gertrude Stein rather than for the writing she had slaved over all these years?

It was deeply troubling, and Gertrude could only conclude that fame was all very well, but like war, publicity "prevents the process of civilization."[24]

⌒

Like André Gide, Henry Miller wanted only to escape as he walked the streets of Paris during the February bloodshed. Although usually fascinated by the sordid and the ugly, he was little interested in the Stavisky Affair, the rise of fascism, or the economic deterioration that underlay the riots. He had not read a newspaper for a week when he wandered into the middle of things, and just as quickly got out. "Saw the mob pressing me flat against the walls and the bullets mowing us down," he wrote. "Looked frantically about for an exit. Got home just as the thing broke loose." He wrote in *Tropic of Cancer* that "Rome has to burn in order for a guy like me to sing," but he plainly didn't want to be around for the bonfire.[25]

Home, his moving refuge, was about to move once again: after living for two years in Clichy with Alfred Perlès, Miller moved that autumn to 18 Villa Seurat, where he had briefly lived before. Only this time he was not bunking with Max Fraenkel; this time he was a paying renter in an attractive studio apartment high above the Montsouris reservoir, with a skylight, balcony, private bath, and kitchen. The street, in the fourteenth arrondissement, was an up-to-date private cul-de-sac created for painters and sculptors, and Miller happily settled in, secure in the knowledge that someone else—Anaïs Nin—was paying the rent.

On the September day of Miller's arrival, his publisher, Jack Kahane, ceremoniously delivered the first copy of *Tropic of Cancer*. *Tropic* did not bring Miller immediate fame and fortune, but it did bring a complimentary note from T. S. Eliot, plus an appreciative review from the poet Blaise Cendrars, titled "Unto Us an American Writer Is Born," which appeared in the literary review *Orbes*. Even though *Tropic of Cancer* was bound for censorship in the United States, where (despite the recent victory for *Ulysses*) it would be banned until the 1960s, Miller was elated. The move and the book represented a new beginning for him, as did the finalization of his divorce from June that December. "Hooray!" was his response when the divorce papers arrived.

What Miller did not know was that Anaïs Nin's baby girl, stillborn three months prematurely that August, was his child. It was a difficult time for Nin, especially since Miller's biographer, Robert Ferguson, suggests that she may have taken steps to abort the child.[26] In any case, Nin seemed to believe that it was essential to shield Miller from all responsibilities and never communicated any of this to him. And so Henry Miller, happily domiciled at the Villa Seurat, settled down to write more obsessively than ever about June, in what would become *Tropic of Capricorn* (the "June book," as he thought of it),[27] even as Nin, perhaps in revenge, left with her psychiatrist for New York.

⌒

New York that November was kind to Jean Renoir's film *Madame Bovary*—a much-needed boost, since Paris had not been at all receptive. Of course Paris in January 1934 was in the throes of the Stavisky Affair and was not inclined to look attentively at much else. Still, Renoir was disappointed. An unlikely set of circumstances had led to his commission for this film (from Gaston Gallimard's New Films Society), and he had forged ahead with his prize, determined to shoot the film in the most natural surroundings possible—real farms, real cows, and actual houses. Renoir could carry his demands to extremes, such as the time a hare unexpectedly popped up between the hooves of the star's horse, and his cameramen failed to catch this wonderful shot on film. This resulted in an entire day spent trying to coax the hare from its burrow for a reshoot. Unfortunately, Monsieur Lapin was not interested, and so a disappointed Renoir dropped the entire scene.

But shooting a film with Jean Renoir, however aggravating at times, was nonetheless special. As one of his colleagues recalled, "On the set, Renoir was truly great. No one was ever better than he at directing the actors and getting the most out of them."[28] As the theatrical agent Lulu Wattier once remarked, "Renoir could make a wardrobe act."[29] Part of the Renoir magic was the camaraderie he nurtured on his films. Cast and crew alike gathered like a family for raucous dinners after the day's work, which in the middle of the Norman countryside was much like attending a country wedding. Everyone, down to the prop man, felt included in the warmth of Renoir's personality.

As for the film itself, Renoir's friend Bertolt Brecht was enthusiastic about it, but its final version was too long (as well as way over budget), and the version finally shown in public was a mutilated one. Adding to Renoir's woes, his brother Pierre, who had taken a leading role, managed to seduce the leading lady, who unfortunately was the producer's mistress.

By this time, the bloody events of February 6 had engulfed Paris, and Jean Renoir's friends, many of whom were Communists, felt personally threatened. He understood how they felt, and even approved of their sentiments, but he was not yet ready to become involved in their struggle on behalf of the working class. Still, in his next project, *Toni*, he sensitively filmed a story of immigrants and gypsies—wanting to "bring to life men and women who were not usually presented on film," people who, as he put it, were "threatened with expulsion for the slightest lapse." He wanted to portray this rugged story on location, to accomplish his "dream of uncompromising realism." Thanks to Marcel Pagnol, a successful novelist and playwright (known especially for his trilogy, *Marius, Fanny,* and *César*) who had started his own production company in Marseilles, Renoir was able to accomplish his dream. Although he confessed that, instead of filming "a squalid episode based on real life," he ended up "recounting a heart-rending and poetic love-story," albeit one "that really happened."[30]

With this film, on which Renoir's nephew, Claude, was for the first time the chief cameraman, Jean used several panoramic as well as angle shots, in addition to longer-playing shots, to avoid what Renoir called fragmentation. That is, he wanted "to shoot the actors in close-up and then follow their movements," something that "calls for great skill on the part of the operator"—especially given the cumbersome equipment of the time. Renoir was also preoccupied with sound ("I am a passionate believer in authentic sound," even if it is "technically bad") and took pride in sound that was recorded at the same time, rather than dubbed. "In *Toni,*" he pointed out, "the sound of the train arriving at Les Martigues station is not merely the real sound of a train but that of the one which one sees on the screen."[31]

He shot *Toni* on location, in Les Martigues, near Marseilles, "with the people from the place, breathing their air, eating their food, and living in every way the life of these workers." All the actors, even the professionals, came from the region, "and their local accent was genuine."[32]

That summer, while Renoir was shooting *Toni,* Austrian chancellor Engelbert Dollfuss (who had assumed dictatorial powers modeled on Mussolini's) was assassinated by Nazis in Vienna. This occurred shortly after Hitler brutally consolidated his power in a blitz of political murders known as the Night of the Long Knives. Adding to France's jitters, in early October, King Alexander I of Yugoslavia was assassinated in Marseilles while on a state visit to France—killed by Croat assassins who probably were in Mussolini's pay. Louis Barthou, the French minister for foreign affairs (who had pushed for a French treaty with the Soviet Union as well as for the U.S.S.R.'s admission to the League of Nations), also died in the attack and was replaced by Pierre Laval, who promptly signed an agreement with Mussolini that gave Italy a free hand in Ethiopia.

By the time of *Toni*'s first public showing in early 1935, the French had been pummeled by current events, and they were not reassured by the early January news that the coal-rich Saar region between France and Germany (occupied by France and Britain since the war) had overwhelmingly voted to become part of the German Reich. Unfortunately for Renoir, *Toni* was not of interest to the 1935 French cinema-going public, which most certainly did not want to be confronted with social concerns or uncompromising realism when it went to the movies.[33]

～

The response to Bloody Tuesday in the more fashionable parts of town was at first blasé. Comte Jean de Pange was upset because he was unable to find a taxi to take him to dinner. His colleagues shrugged off the riots as merely "a dispute of the left," and they and their friends continued to eat undisturbed at expensive restaurants while wealthy women continued to attend that season's couturier dress shows.[33]

Still, anxiety soon crept in amid the nonchalance, as more and more Parisians began to regard February 6 as an insurrection and attempted coup—either of the left or the right, depending on one's particular political point of view. Unrest continued, especially after a figure in the Stavisky case was found dead on the train tracks and as events outside of Paris continued to rattle Parisians.

Perhaps it was as a distraction in the face of the unknown that upper-class Parisians that summer, and in the summers to come, threw an endless series of fancy dress balls—a Waltz Ball, a Colonial Ball, and other extravaganzas that turned already luxurious settings into fanciful and exotic dreams. The Left Bank's wealthy Caresse Crosby recalled the decadent and expensive glamour of her own crowd that summer: "We always did receive the best everywhere," she wrote, "and we were the gayest, the most lavish, the most envied in Paris that season—1934—the very gizzard of the glamorous years."[34]

Glamour was the keyword, and Chanel was the epitome of Parisian glamour. Despite the tension throughout Paris, her show (positioned on what turned out to be the day before Bloody Tuesday) took place as usual, featuring a hard-edged and smart look, with open-necked white shirts beneath artificial silk dresses. But taxi service was disrupted by strikes, and Janet Flanner noted that the "taxi strike plus riots coming during spring fashion shows [were] estimated to have lost big houses one million francs each."[35]

Chanel was mum over any losses suffered by the tumult, but it certainly did not soften her attitude toward her workers, which had always been a tough one. Increased pay and worker rights? Never. February 6 only hardened Chanel's opinions, especially under Iribe's influence.

She was at the top of the fashion world, but she had competitors on her heels and she knew it. Chief among them was Elsa Schiaparelli, who by 1934 was employing four hundred workers and producing between seven and eight thousand garments a year—quite an achievement for a relative newcomer. Schiaparelli's was not yet among the largest of the couture houses, but given the shrinking Depression markets, she benefited from her house's relatively small size as well as her willingness to work with American manufacturers. Americans loved her clothes, and she caught the attention not only of *Vogue* and *Women's Wear Daily* but also *Time* magazine, which in 1934 called her a genius. Iribe in fact may have had Schiaparelli in mind when he attacked foreigners for conspiring against France's identity in art, fashion, and design. Schiaparelli, despite her Paris residence, was unquestionably Italian.

Iribe need not have worried: the Depression notwithstanding, Chanel (now ensconced in the Ritz) was living well. But Schiaparelli was also experiencing the rewards of success; not only was she now able to send her daughter to expensive schools, but she had expanded her showroom and moved to a chic apartment on Boulevard Saint-Germain, where on one occasion she entertained Chanel, who (according to Schiaparelli) looked around in horror and then shuddered, "as if she were passing a cemetery."[36] Stark white walls with black tables and rubberized orange and green upholstery were definitely not Chanel's idea of style, but no matter: Schiaparelli delighted in shocking.

Schiaparelli also delighted in competition, and soon she would bring out her own line of perfume, in Chanel's footsteps. Yet with Schiaparelli's usual audacity, she completely bypassed the Chanel image of streamlined elegance and modeled her perfume bottle on Mae West's generous curves, naming it "Shocking." It was about this time that Schiaparelli hit on the vibrant pink that she named "Shocking Pink," which became synonymous with her name. Both perfume and color were instant hits.

Salvador Dalí also delighted in shocking, and that year he expanded his audience by a trip to the United States—financed by his good friend Caresse Crosby, who was a member of his patron Zodiac group. Dalí was terrified of travel, but two new one-man shows in America drew him: one at New York's new Museum of Modern Art (MoMA), where Alfred Barr was shaking the foundations of the art establishment, and the other at Hartford's Wadsworth Atheneum Museum, which was entering the modern art world with gusto under its new director, A. Everett "Chick" Austin Jr.[37]

Caresse took Dalí in charge, who was cowering in a corner of the train compartment when she found him, with all his canvases attached by strings to his clothing or fingers. "I am next to the engine," he told her, "so that I'll get there quicker."[38] On shipboard, he tanked up on champagne (to give himself courage), went around in a life jacket, and huddled whenever possible next to Gala—who as of January was his lawful wife, thanks to her divorce from Eluard (who had married Nusch) and Eluard's encouragement that they wed, especially before any trip to the puritanical United States.

Caresse promoted Dalí to the reporters who met them at the dock, his paintings once again attached by strings. He convulsed them, especially when he described the portrait of his wife with lamb chops on her shoulder. Lamb chops? But of course. Dalí liked lamb chops, and he liked his wife. That plus the "melting watches" did it—along with the eight-foot baguette he carried around, and his famous (and possibly apocryphal) quote, that "the difference between himself and a madman was that he was not mad." Dalí made for dream copy, as he instinctively understood. "I thought [the enormous baguette] would be an intriguing object for the reporters," he wrote in his memoirs, and although the reporters were at first too embarrassed to mention the outsized loaf, Dalí basically got the attention he wanted. He was a genius at self-promotion, in a country that fully appreciated this talent, and he reveled in it. "These reporters were unquestionably far superior to European reporters," he observed. "They had an acute sense of 'non-sense,' and one felt, moreover, that they knew their job dreadfully well. They knew in advance exactly the kind of things that would give them a 'story.'"[39]

And Dalí was prepared to give it to them.

Across the Atlantic, Marcel Duchamp—who stunned the artistic world at the 1913 New York Armory Show with his *Nude Descending a Staircase*—had for several years been on the road, in pursuit of the ideal chess tournament. Duchamp was not out to shock audiences or to promote himself. He didn't even care about winning. Winning was not the point, and it could even be distracting: his primary interest was the aesthetics of the game. While on this quest, Duchamp maintained his friendship with his frequent chess partner, Man Ray, and arranged exhibits for other friends, such as Constantin Brancusi. He also worked on *The Green Box* (1934). This painstaking endeavor consisted of exact reproductions of color plates, manuscripts, drawings, photographs, notes, sketches, and studies—the ideas and thought processes behind Duchamp's magnum opus, *The Bride Stripped Bare by Her Bachelors, Even (The Large Glass)*, which he had completed in New York shortly after the war and left with a supporter in Connecticut. The idea was that the viewer should consult the contents of the box, in whatever order he or she chose, when viewing *The Large Glass*.[40]

While Duchamp was painstakingly reproducing each scrap of paper for 320 deluxe editions of *The Green Box*, his friend Man Ray was publishing a collection of his first fifteen years of photographs, subsidized by James Thrall Soby, an American patron of the avant-garde who then was connected with the Wadsworth Atheneum. French critics loved Man Ray's book, but the Americans did not: Lewis Mumford in the *New Yorker* even said that Man Ray was wasting his time on "photographing calla lilies so that they will look like drawings by a second-rate academician."[41] Man Ray had always harbored a resentment toward photography, which earned him his living but did not feed his soul. Dismissed by so much of the art establishment, it was difficult to persevere when he himself did not even know how to value what he did.

Adding to his woes, he had not yet gotten over Lee Miller. When she left him to go to New York, he was devastated, and he had actually threatened to shoot himself—or her. During that first dismal winter without her, he kept to himself and turned to his preferred art form, painting. It was then that he began his huge (eight feet by three feet) Surrealistic painting, *The Lips*. "A pair of lips haunted me like a dream remembered," he later recalled. "The lips, because of their scale, no doubt, suggested two closely joined bodies. Quite Freudian."[42] It would take him two years to complete. During this time he learned that Lee had married Aziz and that the marriage had quickly foundered. And Man Ray kept on painting. Officially, this mammoth work is known as *Observatory Time—The Lovers*, and it quickly became known as the definitive Surrealist painting.

In the meantime, as he meticulously painted, the Brooklyn-born Man Ray was feeling the economic downturn ("the slump is beginning to have its effect on me," he complained to his sister in one of his rare letters home). He had barely communicated with his family for years, but now he wired them for money—even as they were struggling to survive. His wire was to the point: "dear folks: am well can you wire me funds love man."[43]

Perhaps it was fitting that, after fourteen years, Man Ray's wife, Adon, unexpectedly surfaced. They had never officially been divorced, and she claimed that her now-famous husband owed her money.

Soon changes at the fashion magazines led to new commissions for Man Ray, especially from *Harper's Bazaar*, giving him what one biographer has called "the most lucrative and visible fashion assignments of his life."[44] Changes were also occurring in the French automotive world, but these would not favor André Citroën.

Citroën's dream of a front-wheel-drive car came true in 1934, to great applause: his first Traction Avants went on sale in France that May, and despite having been rushed into production—resulting in some glitches in the early models—were a huge success. As *L'Auto Journal* rhapsodized, "the front-wheel-drive Citroën 7 . . . is so up-to-the-minute, so audacious, so rich in original technical solutions, so different to all that had been done before that it truly deserves the epithet 'sensational.'"[45]

Yet this venture seemed to pay off for everyone except Citroën, largely because it did not pay off sufficiently quickly. Since early in the year, the company had been hanging on by its teeth, counting on the Traction Avant to save it. Throughout the year, as Blum and the Socialists demanded nationalization, rumors spread that Citroën was in trouble; and indeed, Citroën was doing his utmost to stave off his creditors. Finally Michelin, his largest creditor, agreed to a short-term loan in addition to the existing debt—on condition that Michelin be given an option to buy the company and that Citroën offer up his own personal shares in Automobiles Citroën as security.

Citroën then went to work to persuade banks and the French government to back his refinancing proposals; but much to his dismay, all refused. Especially galling was the role of the government, now under the conservative leadership of Pierre-Etienne Flandin, which (despite concerns of an American takeover of Citroën) refused to participate. Given Flandin's politics and his friendship with Louis Renault, many heads nodded wisely that old scores were being settled and that perhaps even a touch of anti-Semitism was involved. Indeed, the Flandin government at one point even proposed that Renault take over Citroën. (Apparently Renault replied that he could never do it: "If I did, people would say that I wanted to destroy him.")[46] But more than this, the times were too unstable for Citroën's business colleagues, or even a government of this political stripe, to run to his support. If there had been no world economic crisis during the 1930s, Citroën might have pulled it off. But there was a world economic crisis, and he was stuck.

In the end, it was a small creditor who threw the proverbial monkey wrench in the works, setting affairs in motion that in late December forced Automobiles Citroën to declare bankruptcy. Michelin soon took over, having acquired controlling interest in exchange for assuming responsibility to pay off all the company's debts.

André Citroën's beloved Traction Avant remained in production, but now with the Michelin Man at the wheel.

Another steering wheel, or at least an automobile, played a role that year, although Maurice Ravel did not realize it at the time. Two years earlier, a taxi in which he was riding collided with another taxi in Paris. He suffered a blow to the head that left him in quite a bit of pain; but at the time his condition was not considered serious, and he brushed it off with typically wry humor. As he told his friend, the Spanish composer Manuel de Falla, he had pretty much mended: "there remains only an irrational fear of taxis."[47]

By now, Ravel had recovered from his wartime illness and exhaustion (he had served as a truck driver on the front), but he was less than robust when the taxi accident occurred. Still, he retained his enthusiasm, especially for the young and the new. "I am an admirer of jazz," he told an interviewer in 1932, "and I think it . . . is not just a passing phase, but has come to stay." Similarly upbeat, "our epoch pleases me," he told another interviewer. "This wonderful uneasiness, and sincere research in all directions—aren't these the signs of a fertile period?" He was at the railroad station at the time, having transformed himself (in the words of his interviewer) "into an indefatigable traveler," drawn to the four corners of Europe by the success of his piano concerto.[48]

This was Ravel's Piano Concerto in G Major, as distinct from his Piano Concerto for the Left Hand, which in an admirable feat he wrote at the same time. The Concerto for the Left Hand, a virtuosic explosion in Spanish rhythms, had been commissioned by the Austrian pianist Paul Wittgenstein, who lost his right arm during World War I. Pianists, even those with ten functioning digits, consider it a point of honor to play it with one hand, although Ravel himself (recognizing his limitations as a pianist) preferred to play it with both. But it was his Concerto in G Major that was dear to his heart. It took him several years to compose (Janet Flanner wrote, after the premiere, that it was "worth waiting all these years to hear"),[49] and he told the pianist Marguerite Long, who premiered it, that he composed the exquisite slow movement "'two measures at a time,' with the assistance of Mozart's Clarinet Quintet."[50]

Mozart was his favorite composer—Mozart "remains the most perfect of all," he remarked, repeating this evaluation in one way or another over the years.[51] With Mozartian tranquility, Ravel remained calm and mildly amused throughout the rising furor of the times, although music—especially his own—could arouse his passions (as happened with the famed conductor Arturo Toscanini, whom Ravel sharply criticized for conducting *Boléro* "twice as fast as it should go"). He now lived in the countryside outside Paris, but he loved visiting factories "and seeing vast machinery at work. . . . It was a factory which inspired my *Boléro*," he added. "I would like it always to be played with a vast factory in the background."[52]

But Ravel's basic decency could not accommodate the era's rising fascism. At first he found it "odd that people still talk about races at all!" But in 1933 he became distinctly upset when Madeleine Grey, who was to perform his *Chansons madécasses* at the Florence Festival, was replaced, due to the anti-Semitic policies of fascist Italy.[53]

Unfortunately, Ravel's health was becoming a problem, and he increasingly complained of feeling "washed out" and had to bow out of performances. His letter of August 2, 1933, to his friend Marie Gaudin is, as Ravel authority Arbie Orenstein notes, a poignant document, "as it shows the beginning stages of Ravel's final illness, in which his ability to write deteriorated sharply."[54] Later authorities have concluded that the blow Ravel received to his head during that taxi accident may well have exacerbated an existing condition.

Ravel was not in Paris at all during the February outbreaks, having taken up residence in a Swiss rest home due to his doctor's concerns for his health. In April, he returned to Paris, but to a clinic. Told that he could be cured, he was reassured, yet added, "But it's taking so long!"[55] He continued to stay in touch with friends, but his doctors prescribed complete rest and forbade all work, even his beloved composing.

He bore his difficulties well, but it was tough. There was still so much he wanted to do.

The Depression may have reached France, and political crises may have raged in the streets, but Josephine Baker paid little attention. She was doing well, thank you, starring in the movie *Zou Zou* (the film she liked best) and in the Offenbach operetta *La Créole*—legitimate theater this time, not music hall—where she regularly sold out performances. While starring in *La Créole*, Eddie Cantor visited her backstage and told her it was time for her to tackle New York, but Baker was not interested. "They would make me sing mammy songs," she objected, "and I cannot *feel* mammy songs."[56]

Josephine Baker was well paid and fully employed, but by Christmas 1934, so many others were not. As the year came to a close, her friend Bricktop (aka Ada Smith), the powerhouse jazz singer, dancer, and owner of the Paris nightclub Chez Bricktop, experienced the slowest Christmas Eve in all her years as a club owner. Reportedly, she announced that she had had it, and that nothing would prevent her departure for America "save the complete destruction of all ships and planes."[57]

Josephine had a completely different take on the situation. To a friend who was now in New York City, she wrote, "You mentioned in your letter you were trying to love America. Darling," she advised, "forget it."[58]

As the year ended, Lieutenant Colonel Charles de Gaulle was focused on two fronts: his beloved France and his beloved family. Upon returning from Lebanon, the de Gaulle family took a large apartment on Boulevard Raspail, near the Collège Stanislas—the Catholic school that de Gaulle himself had attended and where their oldest son, Philippe, now went to school. De Gaulle and his wife, Yvonne, also purchased a country house, Colombey, which at the time had neither running water nor central heating. Even without these amenities, Colombey was well beyond their means, but they felt it was necessary for their children, who now included their son and two daughters, Elizabeth and Anne.

Anne, the youngest, was born with Down syndrome and was her father's darling. When it became clear that medical treatment could not help, her parents quickly realized that only love and tenderness would do—and this Yvonne and Charles supplied in abundance, although there always was a special bond between Anne and her father. She remained with her family for the rest of her short life (she lived to the age of twenty), and throughout, her favorite place was on her father's knee.

For his part, Charles de Gaulle was always there for Anne, breaking away from important meetings and even military maneuvers to be with her when she needed him. After her death in 1948, one of the family doctors heard him say that "without Anne, perhaps I should not have done all that I have done. She made me understand so many things. She gave me so much heart and spirit." And in old age, de Gaulle wrote in a copy of his memoirs: "It is by suffering that we learn."[59]

Apart from his family, the other major center for Charles de Gaulle's devotion was his country, his beautiful France. In the aftermath of February 1934, Pétain had become minister of war in a conservative government, and even though Pétain spoke of "making the utmost use of modern machines," de Gaulle was well aware that his former mentor disapproved of de Gaulle's proposals and, especially, his indefatigable efforts to put them into practice.[60] In May, de Gaulle published his *Towards an Army of the Future*, in which he warned that France's geography doomed it to invasion unless it was defended, not by fortifications, but by machines honed into a striking force—these in turn run by a well-trained professional army. Germany had the advantage of numbers; France would have to rely on a far better quality of military training than at present, and the use of a mechanized, motorized armored force.

In addition, and even more controversially, de Gaulle used this book to call for a leader capable of overcoming the unwillingness of the current French military to accept change. De Gaulle stated bluntly that "a master has to make his appearance, a master whose judgment is independent, whose orders cannot be challenged—a man upheld by public opinion." This made for "somewhat uneasy reading," as de Gaulle biographer Jean Lacouture puts it, especially when antidemocratic and totalitarian movements were on the rise.[61] Still, de Gaulle was calling for reform, not overthrow, of France's institutions, especially its military, and given the torpor of the French army and the politicians behind it, he thought it essential, indeed his duty, to light a fuse beneath all those who slept.

As it happened, very few copies of *Towards an Army of the Future* sold, and although it received a smattering of good reviews, those de Gaulle most wanted to influence remained mum. After more than a year of silence, Pétain finally surfaced in an article that ended with an endorsement of the present system and of the need to exercise the utmost caution in reforming France's defenses.

Basically, de Gaulle was ignored.

Count Kessler was despondent over what was happening in Germany. Now ill and virtually homeless, he was in Paris during the performance of Nicolas Nabokov's ballet *La Vie de Polichinelle* at the Paris Opera. Afterward, he joined Nabokov and Misia Sert for vespers at the tiny Left Bank church of St-Julien-le-Pauvre, following which the three walked along the Seine while Kessler talked about "the end of his hopes, his dreams, his efforts." Everything now was gone, he anguished, including his famous pictures and sculptures, and he sympathized with Nabokov as a Russian refugee.

And then, according to Nabokov, Kessler added softly, "This thing in Germany will be long. I will not live to see the end of it."[62]

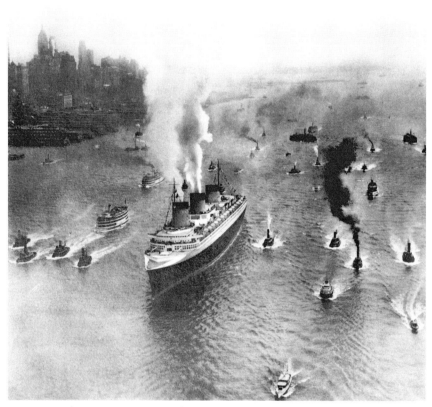

S.S. Normandie, arriving in New York Harbor on June 3, 1935, after its first transatlantic crossing. © *Tallandier / Bridgeman Images*

CHAPTER EIGHT

~

Sailing, Sailing

(1935)

On May 29, 1935, the luxury liner S.S. *Normandie* steamed out of Le Havre harbor on its maiden voyage to New York. The star of the French line Compagnie Générale Transatlantique, she was the largest and, as it turned out, the fastest passenger ship afloat, breaking all Atlantic speed records en route (she would break them again on her trip home). Her size was mind boggling, and the technical feats of her design were similarly impressive; but it was the overwhelming elegance and luxury of her interior that was truly awe inspiring. Likened by some to a Busby Berkeley Hollywood extravaganza, the *Normandie* boasted an Art Deco décor that was nothing short of magnificent. "The ship without peer," one historian has called her, "probably the greatest ship ever built anywhere." The pride of the French, the *Normandie* was the twentieth century's memorial "to perpetuate our civilization," as one proud Frenchman put it, "[much] as the cathedrals perpetuate that of the Middle Ages, the castles of the Loire that of the Renaissance, and Versailles that of the age of Louis XIV."[1]

Its career would be short—the four-year career of the *Normandie* placed it, along with the other grand liners of the decade, in the category of dinosaurs, behemoths that were about to be overtaken by air travel.[2] Yet, for the moment, the *Normandie* represented the epitome of glamour and elegance, delighting its wealthy passengers with grand staircases, a dance floor, a winter garden, and twenty-foot-high bronze doorways leading into an enormous first-class dining hall. This in turn rose three decks in height and was lit by glittering Lalique columns and chandeliers—a space dripping with gold and crystal that could comfortably seat seven hundred. These were attended by an army of stewards, who rode escalators with their heavy trays. Ensconced in this magnificent (and air conditioned) setting, the *Normandie*'s pampered guests could graciously partake of the finest French cuisine, undisturbed either by the hoi polloi or by children, the latter having a sweet dining room of their own. These fortunate passengers could retire at night into individually designed suites, some with their own private dining rooms as well as multiple bedrooms and, of course, private decks.

This, of course, was for the rich; the less well-off were not so comfortably provided for, and indeed represented a distinct minority of the *Normandie*'s passengers. As John Maxtone-Graham puts it, "it is harder to rhapsodize about conditions in tourist class. All the space, all the luxe, and, especially, all the light seemed to have been expended on first class."[3] Indeed, the majority of the *Normandie*'s cabins and public space were reserved for first-class passengers—a fact that soon contributed to the liner's failure to compete, in financial terms, with other liners of the day.

It was an unfortunate reality that the flood of tourists from America had dwindled after the Crash; but even more unfortunate was the reality that, during the heyday of 1920s tourism, a majority of sightseers had been looking for bargain fares, and the Depression only exacerbated this trend. Steamships had generally appealed to this market by refitting their interiors from the steerage-class accommodations given immigrants during the earlier years of the century to something more like the current-day economy airfares offered the general public. But the *Normandie* was disinclined to throw glamour overboard in the competition for paying passengers and as a consequence had to rely on government subsidies throughout the rest of the decade.

Yet for those who could afford it, for a brief and shining moment there was no more luxurious way to travel between France and New York than the S.S. *Normandie*, which boasted a passenger list that included the crème de la crème of the traveling world, including Hollywood and Broadway stars, dukes and duchesses, leading political figures, and a panoply of literary and artistic luminaries. Among these were Colette and Maurice Goudeket (now married in order to stay together in New York, whose hotels would not otherwise permit cohabitation), who were on board as journalists covering the *Normandie*'s maiden voyage—Colette for *Le Journal* and Maurice for *Paris-Soir*.

Colette, now sixty-two, was at the peak of her career, having been freshly named by a poll of French writers as the greatest living master of French prose, in addition to being recently elected to the Belgian Royal Academy of French Language and Literature. (No stranger to honors, Colette had been a member of the Legion of Honor since 1920 and in time would be elected to the Académie Goncourt.) Somehow she managed to carry on with an overwhelming amount of work—as a drama critic, journalist (two weekly front-page columns), promotional writer, and writer of film screenplays, as well as author of a continuing rich flow of fiction and memoirs. Politics did not interest her, whether the rise of fascism or the fall of the franc. Current events only caught her attention when they involved intense human interest, especially crimes of passion. Always, Colette would be a chronicler of the heart, especially the hearts of women, and she directed her delicately pointed scalpel at the critical intersection of love, power, and vulnerability.

Years before, during her marriage to Henry de Jouvenel, editor of *Le Matin*, Colette (then in her forties) had embarked on a lengthy affair with Jouvenel's sixteen-year-old stepson, Bertrand, that led to her divorce. By coincidence, Bertrand de Jouvenel, now in his thirties and a well-known political economist, was a journalist covering the same maiden voyage of the *Normandie* with Colette and Maurice. At the time, Jouvenel was becoming increasingly disillusioned with France's stalemated political system and was moving rightward (in early 1936, in a famous interview with Hitler for *Paris-Midi*, Jouvenel would refrain from challenging the dictator's claim to be a statesman intent on preserving European peace). He was also having an affair with the beautiful and brilliant American journalist and future war correspondent Martha Gellhorn and was en route to meet her in New York.

Bertrand and Colette had remained friends, albeit distantly, and he had once introduced Gellhorn to her in Paris. The two had not hit it off. "She was a terrible woman," Gellhorn recalled. "Absolute utter hell. She hated me on first sight, that was obvious. . . . She was jealous of me. . . . And Bertrand just adored her all his life. He never understood when he was in the presence of evil."[4]

Even though Gellhorn and Colette's paths did not cross again, the four-year romance between Gellhorn and Jouvenel was already coming to a close. Jouvenel's wife would not give him a divorce, and in any case, Gellhorn was about to attract the attention of Ernest Hemingway.

⌒

Josephine Baker, fresh off from filming *Princesse Tam-Tam* in Tunisia, also sailed for New York that year on the *Normandie*, although not on the liner's maiden voyage. Lee Shubert wanted her for his next Ziegfeld Follies, scheduled to open later in the year, and she sailed with Pepito on October 2, leaving time to rehearse and travel before it opened.

Her chief worry was about staying in a hotel: "I don't want to be refused in a hotel," she wrote a friend. But as it turned out, the reception she received from blacks was just as grating as that from whites. To a large extent, this was Baker's own fault: she insisted on playing the sophisticated French lady—even speaking only French when she so chose. Whites did not respond favorably to this ("Does the Countess Pepito Abatino ever pause to dwell in memory on her pickaninny days in America?" a *Vanity Fair* columnist snidely wrote), nor did blacks, who castigated her for being snooty.[5] She compounded her image problems by praising Mussolini in his war against Ethiopia. But not all of her troubles were self-inflicted: much to her discomfort, her husband, Billy Baker, from whom she had never been legally divorced, now surfaced and announced that he expected to renew their marriage as soon as possible (as it turned out, this was merely a stab at notoriety rather than a serious threat).

Josephine was right in one regard: the Hotel St. Moritz welcomed Pepito but left her standing on the street. Several other luxury hotels also refused to admit her, and at length even her chauffeur complained that he didn't want to be seen driving a black woman. At last, a good friend took Josephine to her studio, where she stayed until she found a penthouse apartment at the Bedford, where a diverse group of actors and artists resided. Of course, Josephine could have stayed in Harlem, but the thought of being shunted off there disagreed with her. Even the Bedford was a step down, and she sent her postcards from the St. Moritz, as though she was staying there.

When rehearsals were delayed, she traveled home to St. Louis, where, according to one family friend, "it was like having the queen of England to visit." And then back to New York and the Follies, where she had the number 2 dressing room (Fanny Brice had the number 1), and where she had only three acts to Fanny's seven. No longer able to play the diva, as in Paris, and wounded by the obvious racism among the cast members (the legendary tap dancer Fayard Nicholas, also with the Follies, once found Josephine in tears because her dance partners refused to touch her), Josephine made life difficult for her costars, making sure that everyone knew she "was French now," not "a maid or something."[6]

She had songs to sing by Ira Gershwin, and costumes by young Vincente Minnelli, while George Balanchine, now in New York, choreographed the dance "Five A.M." for her. But she couldn't wear the Paris gowns she wanted, and she spent much of her rehearsal time in isolation. The show opened in Boston in late December with mixed notices for Josephine. It then moved to Philadelphia, where the *Philadelphia Tribune* reported that her voice was "high, thin, reedy" and that she might be "released from the current 'Ziegfeld Follies' because she failed to click." More to the point, as one acquaintance put it, "the audience, mostly white, was unable to accept the public adoration [even in a dance number] of a black woman by four handsome young white men." Most blacks, he added, were uncomfortable with it as well.[7]

When the show finally opened in New York in January 1936, the critics panned Josephine. In addition, gossip quickly spread that she was feuding with Fanny Brice and that Brice threatened to resign if Josephine stayed in the cast. No one denied that Josephine was being difficult—although Brice was no piece of cake, either. But Josephine had far more at stake than the Follies: failure for her in New York was a double failure, for she had hoped—and had every reason to believe—that conquering New York would lead the way to a Hollywood contract. Now this was no longer a possibility.

Fortunately for Josephine, the Folies Bergère now reappeared in her life, offering her a favorable contract. She sailed for Paris on the *Normandie* in May 1936, immediately after the Ziegfeld Follies closed. Officially, the production ended due to Fanny Brice's illness, although gossip blamed the closing on Josephine, who (it was said) had given Brice a nervous breakdown.

Overall, New York had not gone well for Josephine, and during these months her relationship with Pepito had deteriorated. Pepito left for Paris well before Josephine, who according to one close friend refused to pay his hotel bill at the St. Moritz. Pepito, her longtime partner and manager, was critically ill, although she did not yet know it. What was obvious, though, to anyone acquainted with them, was that their long relationship was over.

So, for that matter, was her attempt to win over the country of her birth. Back in Paris, where she had often sung of two loves, "my country and Paris," she now wanted her audience to understand that "my country, it is Paris, and Paris is my country."[8] America was no longer in her heart, even as an aspiration.

Josephine Baker was only one of many luminaries traveling between Paris and New York on the *Normandie*. In October 1935, shortly after Baker's crossing to New York, the architect Le Corbusier took to the high seas on this fairy-tale liner. He was making his first trip to the United States, prompted by the Museum of Modern Art's exhibition of his recent work, which opened on October 24. A packed lecture tour followed, which he scheduled in the expectation of meeting new clients while having a good look at the country he had heard so much about.

But Corbu (as Le Corbusier was informally known) immediately got off to a bad start with the American press by belittling New York's skyscrapers. They were too small, he said, and too close together, creating confusion and manifesting "the selfishness inherent in capitalism." Personal gain, he pronounced, had trumped benefits to humanity, adding (as he wrote in *When the Cathedrals Were White*) that New York was not yet finished and should be "demolished and replaced by structures which are noble, but also efficient." In his view, this would not be difficult: "New York has such courage and enthusiasm," he wrote, "that everything can be begun again . . . and made into something still greater."[9]

Despite his initial disappointment, Le Corbusier had not given up on New York, nor on America: he loved the bridges surrounding Manhattan and applauded the cleanliness of Americans. And he could not forget New York, "now that I have had the happiness of seeing it there, raised up in the sky." But at present, he condemned the city's living quarters as being "uninhabitable." There were many who would have agreed when he wrote that he was "not able to bear the thought of millions of people undergoing the diminution of life imposed by devouring distances, the subways filled with uproar, the wastelands on the edges of the city . . . the blackened brick streets, hard, implacably soulless streets . . . the slums of New York or Chicago." "Hopeless cities," he added, "and cities of hope at the same time."[10]

Le Corbusier undertook a rigorous lecture schedule, hoping to convert his hearers to his idea of the "Radiant City," which as Charlotte Perriand described it "not only addressed the negative side of the machine age, such as pollution, noise, and traffic hazards . . . [but] also considered the development of technology and skills."[11] Yet by and large he was disappointed that his audiences did not embrace his vision, even though they were attentive to his lectures and excited to meet him. He admired the energy of Franklin D. Roosevelt and the Works Progress Administration (WPA), although FDR was too busy to meet him—as was Frank Lloyd Wright. In Philadelphia, Le Corbusier offended Dr. Albert Barnes (which was not difficult), while in Detroit he admired the Ford factory, seeing in it "a perfect convergence of the totality of gestures and ideas."[12] Still, as his biographer put it, overall Le Corbusier saw in America "a neurotic culture of pathetic, defeated people whose lives revolved around the need to earn money." As he concluded, "The country is daring, the Americans are timid. The enterprises are bold, the Americans are afraid."[13]

Back in Paris, and with Manhattan "fixed in my memory," Corbu believed that "the new scale of enterprises which belongs to machine age society need bring no disturbance to the beauty of Paris." The city's innate sense of proportion, he added, "will master the new tasks and establish itself in the city in new and triumphant prisms."[14] One wonders what his response would have been to the Tour Montparnasse, which he did not live to see.

In the meantime, Corbu was continuing to work on his concept for a pavilion for the upcoming 1937 Paris Exposition Internationale des Arts et Techniques dans la Vie Moderne (Paris International Exposition of Arts and Technology in Modern Life), for which he had already drawn up several different schemes—all of which had been rejected. Traditionalists held the upper hand, clearly signaled by the resignation of modernist architect Robert Mallet-Stevens from the exhibition's official committee. Corbu's 1935 submission, a unified housing scheme, or tower, for four thousand occupants—

the product of a joint effort by several enthusiastic organizations joined by a surge of eager young architects—encountered the usual opposition. Corbu and his associates had envisioned this structure as something that could and would remain after the exposition was over, but Paris's city council definitively pulled the plug by adding a demand that all constructions be demolished at the exposition's end—a "detail" that, as a disappointed Charlotte Perriand put it, "was total hypocrisy" and "the project's death sentence."[15]

Yet upon returning to Paris, Le Corbusier's greatest disappointment was the fact that America—much like the Soviet Union—had not embraced him as its architectural leader and master planner. He continued to insist that "thus far I have never had anything to do with politics"; but his disillusioning encounter with what he viewed as the selfishness inherent in American capitalism would, as his biographer put it, help "pave the way for what soon was more than a flirtation with the forces of fascism and repression."[16]

While some Paris residents were traveling to New York, others were returning from New York to Paris. One of the most prominent among these was the now-famous Salvador Dalí, who had capped his six-month stay in America with a New York going-away bash (courtesy of Caresse Crosby) that grabbed headlines. Crosby had invited her guests to come as their most recurrent dream, giving rise to some startling outfits. Even Dalí claims to have been surprised by the macabre nature of some of these creations, which (he gleefully recounted) "brought out the germs of mad fantasy that slumbered in the depths of everyone's brains and desires with the maximum of violence."[17]

While Dalí took the guise of a decayed corpse equipped with tiny breasts, society women "appeared with their heads in bird cages and their bodies practically naked. Others had painted on their bodies frightful wounds and mutilations," while "eyes grew on cheeks, backs, under-arms, like horrible tumors." Dalí was especially enchanted by "a man in a bloody night shirt [who] carried a bedside table balanced on his head."[18] Pierre Matisse, the artist's younger son—who by then was an influential gallery owner in New York—came, as he put it, "as Pierre Matisse," but he described the décor and costumes as "amazing." Not only had one of the guests cut his face "and had pins sticking to it with wax," but "downstairs, there was the carcass of a steer ready to be butchered . . . and in it sat one of the patrons of the exhibition at a table, having tea with her daughter."[19]

Most controversial, though, was Gala's outfit: on her head, Dalí tells us, "she had fastened a very realistic doll representing a child devoured by ants, whose skull was caught between the claws of a phosphorescent lobster." He thought she looked like an "exquisite corpse," but the press was outraged.[20]

This so-called Dream Ball took place soon after the kidnapping and murder trial of the Lindbergh baby, and the press was not alone in concluding that Gala had dressed as the dead child. Dalí claimed that there was no such intent, and Caresse Crosby insisted that the costume and the ball itself had been blown well out of proportion by an overanxious press, eager to show the decadence of American culture. The ball, she insisted, "was enormous fun."[21]

But Pierre Matisse was not persuaded. He had heard the Dalís make comments such as, "You have to boil Americans right down to their bones"—typical of them, he commented, beneath their charm.[22]

Back in Paris, Dalí had to face a different kind of music: the Surrealists called him to account for having denied a Surrealist act. This marked his break with Surrealism, and although he claimed to be delighted, his former colleague, Luis Buñuel, said that none other than André Breton told him that Dalí had gone down on his knees to beg for a reprieve. The press had gotten it wrong, Dalí pleaded, and he claimed that he had never denied that Gala's outfit truly depicted the corpse of the Lindbergh baby.[23]

Whatever the truth of the matter, Caresse Crosby's Dream Ball undoubtedly was a far more dissipated event than she was willing to admit. Nor was it an isolated affair. Whether in New York or Paris, decadence increasingly accompanied glamour, as a certain segment of that endangered species, the fabulously wealthy, searched for distraction from boredom. Fancy dress balls, extravagant parties, and luxurious settings were only a beginning as jaded palates sought experiences that roused them from lethargy and brightened their otherwise dull days, or provided escape, especially from sleepless nights.

Misia Sert and Chanel became users and abusers of opiates, while Jean Cocteau was notoriously addicted (during the 1920s, Chanel had repeatedly paid for his stays in expensive clinics).[24] Although in one sense Chanel may have taken control of her life again following Paul Iribe's sudden death in 1935, she became drug dependent soon after, in search of untroubled sleep. Misia Sert had taken to morphine in the 1920s during the painful breakup of her marriage to José-Maria Sert. "For Chanel," Misia's biographers write, "drugs were harmless sedatives; for Misia their purpose was forgetfulness." One close friend came to believe that Chanel's drug dependency "was her last defense against the night."[25]

By 1935, Chanel employed four thousand workers who were fashioning almost twenty-eight thousand garments a year. Still, the Depression was having its impact on the couture market, and rivals such as Schiaparelli were giving Chanel a run for the declining number of wealthy clients who remained. By now, Schiaparelli was collaborating with Chanel's longtime friend Jean Cocteau, as well as with Salvador Dalí, to create dreamlike, witty, and sometimes outrageously Surrealistic fashions—such as Schiaparelli's famous "lobster" dress (the bright red lobster painted on a white dress), her insect-adorned jewelry, or her monkey fur–draped boots. Chanel at first tried to ignore her (calling her "that Italian woman who makes dresses"),[26] but Schiaparelli was difficult to ignore. In 1935, with upward of six hundred workers now in her employ, she moved her showrooms to the extensive salon and workrooms at 21 Place Vendôme that had been the realm of fabled couturiere Madame Chéruit. Ensconced here, at the center of Paris's luxury trade, Schiaparelli was the hit of Paris fashion from 1935 through the rest of the decade—especially after introducing her popular Schiap Boutique for off-the-rack fashion, which she proudly described as "the first of its kind."[27] Although Chanel remained undeniably important, Schiaparelli now eclipsed her.

Life was glittering and glamorous for the wealthy few who could patronize fashion designers such as Chanel and Schiaparelli—a glamour that by now had an outré overtone, as Caresse Crosby perhaps unwittingly put it when she called mid-decade Paris "the very gizzard of the glamorous years."[28] It was no accident that Schiaparelli, who was considered eccentric but entirely original, labeled her trademark color "Shocking Pink." She meant to shock, and her delighted clients followed her all the way to the cash register.

But what about the couturiers' underpaid workers? After all, Chanel in particular was fierce about keeping her wages low. Or what about all those Parisian women who could barely afford to put food on the table, let alone buy a new dress?

Life became ever more difficult for Parisian women as the Depression wore on, as they were "brutally pushed aside, or expelled" from jobs that they had held when there were not enough men to fill them. "Never has life been the object of more arduous combat," wrote the author of *Femmes au travail* (*Women at Work*), who examined the lives of seventeen professional and working-class French women in 1935. "Never," she added, "has daily bread been so rare or so hard to earn."[29]

Still unable to vote, despite years of effort (as Clemenceau once said, "We already have universal [male] suffrage. No need to aggravate a futility"), women in 1930s France possessed few legal rights, even (if married) over their own earnings. As historians Philippe Bernard and Henri Dubief point out, "the first victims of [French] unemployment came from groups that were considered . . . unimportant," that is, women and immigrants, neither of which had the vote.[30]

Making matters worse, the economy—which by early 1935 had been showing signs of recovery—dived downward following the severe deflationary measures pushed through that summer by Pierre Laval's right-wing government. These imposed a 10 percent cut in all public expenditures (most especially wages), along with a reduction in the price of gas, electricity, and coal—all aimed at deflation and maintaining that economic holy grail, the gold standard. A June 1935 law even permitted Laval's government to operate by decree in order to avoid currency devaluation. This policy was a total failure, and social unrest, already rampant, continued to grow, with widespread demonstrations, strikes, and riots erupting throughout the summer. Huge rival demonstrations took place that July 14, as more than thirty thousand members of the far-right Croix-de-Feu marched up the Champs-Elysées to the Arc de Triomphe, while the newly unified left marched in its part of town, between the Place de la Nation and the Place de la Bastille.

In a quiet but symbolic moment in the midst of all this furor, a private burial took place in Montparnasse. On July 14, assembled members of the left observed a moment of silence as Lieutenant Colonel Alfred Dreyfus was buried in Montparnasse Cemetery. Dreyfus, despite his every intent, had remained a symbol of division: Action Française, which had led the charge against him during the original affair, was still at the forefront of the extreme right, while a direct line could be traced between the pro-Dreyfus League of the Rights of Man and the coming Popular Front. Dreyfus may have believed that he was "only an artillery officer whom a tragic error prevented from following his course."[31] But as Julian Jackson has noted, "It was no coincidence . . . that in 1935 the Socialist leader Léon Blum published his *Memories of the [Dreyfus] Affair*. To the left, the events of February 1934 seemed only too familiar."[32]

By this time, France was encountering daunting difficulties abroad as well as at home. Pierre Laval, France's prime minister from June 1935, was far more concerned about Stalin than he was about Hitler or Mussolini, even while Mussolini invaded Ethiopia and Hitler continued his rise, showing his strength at a massive Nuremberg rally in September and rearming Germany—in effect tearing up the relevant clauses of the Versailles Treaty. Residents of the Saar, a small but vital area on France's border that the Versailles Treaty had placed under French control, had already voted overwhelmingly in January to rejoin Germany.

Laval, as foreign minister following Barthou's assassination, had reluctantly followed up Barthou's spadework and signed a military defense agreement with Stalin in May, in response to saber rattling from Hitler's Germany: as de Gaulle put it, "We do not possess the means to refuse Russian help, however much we may loathe their regime."[33] But Laval ensured the agreement's ineffectiveness by avoiding all military entanglements, while as foreign minister he had already (in January) signed an accord between France and Mussolini, including a verbal agreement that France would not oppose Italy's policy in Ethiopia. Mussolini's invasion of Ethiopia in October set off fireworks, and when the League of Nations set sanctions in place against Italy, France—despite Laval's preference to retain Mussolini as an ally—was left to look to Britain for friendship and tepidly joined it in endorsing sanctions, while Italy and Germany began to draw closer together.

Laval, who had arrived in Paris in the early years of the century to study for his *baccalauréat*, began as a Socialist and drifted rightward as his fortunes improved. The son of an Auvergnat café owner, he stayed in Paris, became a lawyer, and married well—all useful preliminaries for a career in politics. His first elected position was as a Socialist deputy for the Seine, but he edged away from socialism during the postwar years, winning the position of mayor of Aubervilliers under his own colors and beginning his rapid climb in a series of national governments, during which he also accumulated a considerable personal fortune. By 1931 he had become prime minister, but he continued in ministerial positions after his 1932 defeat, becoming minister of foreign affairs in 1934 and, once again, premier in 1935.

That year, Laval's only daughter married Count René de Chambrun, a wealthy and well-connected young man whose impressive family tree prompted Janet Flanner to comment that the marriage "was pyramidal for the granddaughter of a jolly Auvergnat innkeeper."[34] It was reported that on this occasion Laval gave his daughter a dowry of sixteen million francs, and although the family was quick to deny it, no one disagreed that both the bride and the bridegroom were very rich indeed.

None of this went down well with the less fortunate. Especially galling was that summer's surge of activity among the extreme-right leagues, which for the moment Laval did little to curb, while talk of war was once again on the rise. Police and civil authorities were distributing posters and brochures advising on "precautions to be taken against bombs from planes,"[35] while Elliot Paul, back in his working-class neighborhood on the Rue de la Huchette (5th), reported that "from one end of the street to the other, my decent and well-meaning friends were ashamed of what their Government was doing"— that is, blessing Mussolini's Ethiopian campaign. He added that in January of that year, "a Paris newspaper conducted a poll to choose a most likely dictator, and Pétain won hands down." Laval came in second.[36]

The Communists were quick to make use of the growing uproar against Laval and his government, on the foreign as well as on the domestic front. Abandoning for the moment their talk of revolution, they began (under Moscow's directive) to work with their erstwhile rivals, the Socialists, starting with the Paris municipal elections of May 1935, which resulted in gains everywhere for the left, including Paris's fifth arrondissement, where the first candidate on what amounted to a Popular Front ticket won his seat. This forerunner of the Popular Front found its style and its images in that huge and emotional assembly of various leftist contingents during that year's July 14 celebrations, and reached some measure of practical working arrangements that September with an agreement between the SFIO and the PCF.

At the same time, the Communists were actively wooing intellectuals, who then as now played a major role in France's court of public opinion—at least in an influential segment of it. This courtship culminated in June 1935 with the First International Congress of Writers for the Defense of Culture, held at the Palais de la Mutualité in the Latin Quarter—a major attempt to mobilize writers from around the world against fascism. There, in the stifling heat, about two thousand writers from Germany, the U.S.S.R., America, China, and points between joined to listen to literary stars such as Gide, Malraux (included in this pantheon ever since his 1933 Goncourt Prize), Bertolt Brecht, and Boris Pasternak (who at the last minute replaced Maxim Gorky, who by then was quietly under house arrest). Despite Gide's efforts, conservative writers like Paul Valéry, or Catholic intellectuals such as Jacques Maritain, were not invited.

Gide and Malraux were honorary joint chairmen, although Malraux actually ran the sessions. Malraux, who at the age of thirty-four had just published his fourth novel, *Le Temps du mépris* (*Days of Wrath*), had visited Moscow the year before for a writers' congress. Although never a comfortable fit with Stalin's Soviet realism, or for that matter with anything fencing him in, he was willing to praise the Soviet experiment, even while rapping the Stalinist view that writers are the engineers of the soul. "Do not forget," he brashly told his hosts, "that . . . art is not a submission, it is a conquest."[37] Despite this daring affront, the Communists did not drum him out of the fold, nor did he feel it necessary to abstain from their 1935 extravaganza. Antifascism was the key to this event, and it kept a number of potential abstainers from straying.

But there remained vocal opposition, most especially from André Breton, now a supporter of Trotsky, whose fierce hostility to Stalinist communism now equaled the support he had given the party only a few years before. Breton bristled at the knowledge that, despite its antifascist trappings, the congress's primary purpose was to rally this remarkable group of writers in support of the Soviet Union and its policies, whether on culture (Soviet realism) or foreign affairs (specifically, the U.S.S.R.'s mutual assistance treaty with France). Breton badly wanted to express his objections from the podium, and those in charge of the event just as badly wanted to keep him off; Breton even came to blows with the lead organizer over the issue. It was only the dramatic suicide of the poet René Crevel, a former Surrealist who frantically and unsuccessfully tried to reconcile the parties, that finally provided an opening for Breton, when the shocked committee members agreed to let Breton speak, by proxy, with Paul Eluard reading his speech late at night. Otherwise, all dissent—especially that on the fate of dissident writers in the Soviet Union—was quashed.

The Franco-Soviet Pact would prove to be toothless, but the question of intellectuals' potential subservience to Moscow's directives, whether over culture or war, still remained. An intellectual Popular Front had formed, and its dangers would become more apparent as the decade progressed.

～

"France," notes historian Eugen Weber, "was now entering an open power struggle between the Left and the Right."[38] Italy was one dividing point, as Mussolini's invasion of Ethiopia that autumn left only Action Française and the extreme right as full-throated supporters of Italy. Stalin and the Soviet Union were another, as Moscow played the antifascist card, uniting the left around opposition to Hitler's Germany. Peace became a political football in this arena, with everyone wanting it, but most divided over whether it was best gotten by refraining from warlike actions (i.e., building up the military and reintroducing military service) or by preparing to oppose Hitler outright. The latter option smacked of warmongering to many, while others cited Bismarck to warn against the delusion that Hitler could ever be appeased ("He who seeks to buy his enemy's friendship with concessions will never be rich enough").[39] Two-year military service began in October 1935, but the rancorous debates only accelerated.

As the year progressed, the far right and the left solidified, with the Jeunesses Patriotes and Solidarité Française forming a "national front" in May (an entity that would have a postwar incarnation in Jean-Marie Le Pen's Front National), while the various segments of the left drew closer in what would become the Popular Front. Attitudes flipped and flopped as events and the world turned: Italy's invasion of Ethiopia reoriented the politics of France's foreign ministry, while Stalin's signature of the Franco-Soviet pact gave Soviet policy and the corresponding objectives of the French Communist party a new look. As Communists reached out to Socialists, anti-Communists were left with the option of viewing the true enemies of peace as those who wanted to oppose either Germany's Nazis or Italy's fascists. It was confusing. And throughout, under the stress of the deepening Depression, public opinion increasingly polarized, while bloody fights and attacks on rival meetings accelerated, as both right and left sought broader popular support.

Warning that the division of France into two camps had not been so starkly evident since the days of the Dreyfus Affair, the monarchist weekly, the *Courrier royal*, declared, "We are on the eve of a civil war."[40]

⁓

By December, the threat to public safety from armed right-wing paramilitary leagues was sufficient to prod the government into requiring advance notice and permission from local authorities for all parades, demonstrations, and public meetings—an act that at long last conveyed a warning that the leagues, if they continued on their current course, might be dissolved.

But firm in the belief that they and only they could fend off revolution, the leagues thumbed their noses at any and all attempts at constraint, while members of the left continued to agitate for the causes they believed in. Most notably, Irène and Frédéric Joliot-Curie made use of the platform their joint Nobel Prize gave them to call for peace and women's rights. Irène, in a late November interview, spoke extensively on behalf of women, while Frédéric, in his 1936 Nobel lecture (they each had their own opportunity to speak), warned of the probable path that their joint discovery would take: "We may feel entitled to believe that researchers, building up or breaking down elements at will, will be able to bring about nuclear reactions of explosive nature," he told his rapt audience. "Alas," he continued, "we can only look forward with apprehension to the consequences of the unleashing of such a cataclysm."[41]

Jean Renoir was more wary of political ties, especially with the Communist party. The cause he most believed in was his own freedom to make the kind of movies he wanted—something that still was difficult for him, as he had yet to establish his professional credentials with French moviemakers, who continued to regard him as an amateur. The filmgoing public was no more welcoming: *Toni*, like so many of Renoir's other serious endeavors, was not a success. Added to his ongoing professional woes, Renoir's private life had its own share of disappointments, especially his marriage to Catherine. His legal separation from her took place that July, and although now freed from Catherine and her dreamworld, the end of their marriage was not a happy event.[42]

Still, Renoir's mistress, Marguerite Houllé, remained a warm and intelligent companion. It was through Marguerite that Renoir had connections to the Communist left, and although he continued to keep a certain distance from them, he was unable to forget what he had seen of Hitler in Berlin.

Later, he remarked that "the Communists were the people most active in the struggle against Hitler in those days, and I thought I should help them a bit."[43] In any case, he did not find it difficult to embrace their social perspectives: in the film *Le Crime de Monsieur Lange* (*The Crime of Mr. Lange*), which he shot in the autumn of 1935 with the support of a group of left-wing artists, actors, writers, and musicians, Renoir deftly tells the tale of an evil boss, a workers' cooperative, and a murder that seems in the film's context to be entirely justified. A real death is substituted for a false one, and the workers triumph—all with wit and panache. As François Truffaut puts it, "Of all Renoir's films, M. *Lange* is the most spontaneous, the richest in miracles of camera work, the most full of pure beauty and truth."[44]

The film went over well with the critics, even if it was not a great financial success, and it went over even better with the Communists, who soon invited Renoir to show *Toni* at a Moscow film festival. It was a brief and intense visit, during which Renoir had little opportunity to do much except view films, although he saw a number of Soviet ones that he much admired. In addition, the French Communist party asked him to make a propaganda film, which as he later recalled he was "delighted to do." As he put it, "I believed that every honest man owed it to himself to resist Nazism. I am a film-maker, and this was the only way in which I could play a part in the battle." The charming if obviously naïve and politicized *La Vie est à nous* (*Life Belongs to Us*) was the outcome. Thanks to this and another film, *La Marseillaise*, Renoir later wrote that he "breathed the exalted air of the Popular Front. For a short time the French really believed that they could love one another. One felt oneself borne on a wave of warm-heartedness."[45]

By March 1935, André Citroën was gravely ill, and by July he was dead—due, as some said, to a broken heart. Michelin, which had taken over Automobiles Citroën, had introduced a very different management style from the personal approach that Citroën had brought to his company.[46] Michelin supported the high quality in design, engineering, and production on which Citroën insisted, but in personnel matters it was frugal and austere, reducing salaries and unhesitatingly firing those workers it deemed nonessential.

Already ill and depressed, Citroën received the last blow in January, when Pierre Michelin suggested (ordered?) that he no longer come into the office but stay at home to rest. His friends and family believed that this broke his will to live. With depression added to illness, Citroën died in July.

Exactly two weeks after Citroën's funeral, François Lecot began to drive a black standard-production 11CV Traction Avant back and forth from his home near Lyon to Paris, or alternately to Monte Carlo, 715 miles each round trip, for an unbelievable 365 days at eighteen hours a day. Adding up to almost 250,000 miles (the tires were changed every fifteen thousand miles), it was the longest marathon run in motoring history, undertaken to demonstrate the reliability and endurance of the Traction Avant.

The idea had originally been Citroën's, but Michelin was not interested in this kind of publicity stunt. And so Lecot—a fifty-six-year-old hotel keeper and devotee of Citroën and his automobiles—decided to go ahead with the marathon privately, at his own expense, mortgaging his hotel to do it. Allowing himself only half-hour breaks for meals and four hours' sleep at night, Lecot's marathon (monitored by the Automobile Club of France) was an act of devotion, done in homage to one of the greatest automakers in history.

Citroën's death left Louis Renault at the pinnacle of the French auto world, establishing him among the most powerful men in France. For the moment, he remained aloof from the decade's social unrest. But although he did not realize it, he was about to encounter those forces of which he was contemptuous, and whose significance he did not understand.

If he had been less important, Renault might have managed to steer clear of politics, and until 1935—despite his opposition to trade unions and workers' collective agreements—he managed to do so. Unlike Citroën, Renault was deeply contemptuous of what he called "paternalism," which he regarded as the operations of the welfare state. These, in his view, merely made workers slaves, either of the factory owner or the state.

But starting in 1935, Renault increasingly became the target of those who viewed him as an archcapitalist and "bloody war merchant." In the end, Citroën's bankruptcy and death would not be a gift to Renault.

In 1929, the writer Kay Boyle had proclaimed, "The writer expresses. He does not communicate."[47] But now, by the mid-1930s, she had changed, embracing political activism in an ever-more-volatile world.

She was not alone. Writers of the 1930s, especially American writers and playwrights such as John Dos Passos, James T. Farrell, Clifford Odets, and John Steinbeck, were portraying the struggles of everyman and everywoman in the midst of economic disaster, while they themselves were becoming increasingly politicized, for the most part embracing left-wing politics (Ezra Pound, who turned to fascism, was an exception). Social criticism was in; art for art's sake was out, and with it, writers such as F. Scott Fitzgerald. Although Hemingway at first refused to enter the arena of politics, the Spanish Civil War would soon convert him; Fitzgerald, however, was left high and dry in the 1930s, as current literary fashion rushed past.

In the spring of 1934, Fitzgerald had at last published his long-awaited novel, *Tender Is the Night*, a powerful and intensely personal work drawn from his 1920s experiences and friendships, especially those of his Paris-based American friends, Gerald and Sara Murphy, to whom he dedicated the book. But at its heart, *Tender Is the Night* is a deeply felt autobiographical study of the deterioration of a marriage and the onset of madness and alcoholism in its main characters, Dick and Nicole Diver.

The book received praise from the all-important critic Gilbert Seldes and from the equally important *New York Times*, while the Communist *Daily Worker* predictably savaged it for deviating from the party line. But much to Fitzgerald's distress, Ernest Hemingway remained bafflingly silent. At last, a month after publication, Fitzgerald wrote Hemingway to ask, "Did you like the book? For God's sake drop me a line one way or another. You can't hurt my feelings." The last part was palpably untrue, and Fitzgerald was crushed when Hemingway at last replied, "I liked it and I didn't like it." Hemingway then followed with a two-page critique in which he complained that Fitzgerald had made "silly compromises" by taking "liberties with peoples' pasts and futures." He conceded that "there were wonderful places and nobody else . . . can write a good one half as good reading . . . but you cheated too much in this one. And you don't need to." The final crushing blow was, "It's not as good as you can do."[48]

Tender Is the Night did not sell well, whether because people had little money to spend on books or because of its unfashionable subject matter. This, combined with Zelda's third breakdown and frequent suicide attempts, along with Fitzgerald's alcoholism and financial plight, contributed to three notorious articles that he wrote in late 1935 that he called his "Crack-Up" essays (published in *Esquire* in early 1936). According to one Fitzgerald biographer, these black personal revelations, which Fitzgerald called the outpouring of his "dark night of the soul," played a significant role in the development of American literature, "blast[ing] open the reticence that had characterized American literature before World War II and [having] a liberating influence on the writers [such as Truman Capote, Tennessee Williams, and Norman Mailer] who followed Fitzgerald's innovative path."[49]

But Hemingway—who himself was going through a period of insomnia and depression ("Non sleeping is a hell of a damned thing," he told Fitzgerald. "Have been having a big dose of it now lately too")—now belatedly wrote Fitzgerald in late 1935 to tell him that "the more I think back to it the better book Tender Is The Night is."[50] Unfortunately Fitzgerald had already written what Hemingway (writing to Dos Passos) called "a very supercilious letter . . . telling me very pontifically how bad my book was" (the book in question being Hemingway's *The Green Hills of Africa*, a nonfiction account of his and Pauline's African safari, which Fitzgerald was not alone in criticizing). Fitzgerald's

Crack-Up essays recharged Hemingway's antagonism. Writing his publisher, Max Perkins, Hemingway lambasted Fitzgerald for "almost tak[ing] pride in his shamelessness of defeat."[51] And when Hemingway's "The Snows of Kiliman-jaro" came out that summer of 1936 in *Esquire*—written at the height of his success—it contained an astonishing slam at Fitzgerald: the story's dying writer condemns himself for "squandering the talent which never creates the fiction of which it was capable" and thinks on "poor Scott Fitzgerald and his romantic awe" of the very rich. Fitzgerald, as Hemingway has the dying writer reflect, thought the very rich "were a special glamorous race and when he found they weren't it wrecked him."[52]

Fitzgerald, still ill and depressed, wrote Hemingway to ask that he "lay off" him in print and take his name out of the story when it was reprinted. Hemingway retorted "with ill grace," as Fitzgerald put it.[53] Which prompted Fitzgerald to observe that Hemingway was as "nervously broken-down" as he was, only with Hemingway it took a different form: "His inclination is toward megalomania," Fitzgerald commented, "and mine toward melancholy."[54]

Jean-Paul Sartre was depressed. He had just turned thirty and was still only a provincial schoolteacher with a stack of unpublished writings. Having spent his life until this point focused on living for and in the moment, he suddenly realized that he was no longer young and that tomorrow was not necessarily going to be any better than today. Hoping to deal with his aimlessness and depression, he experimented briefly with mescaline, with disastrous results that lasted on and off for many months. He also brought one of Beauvoir's teenaged students into a ménage à trois, which did not please Beauvoir, although in time she learned to accommodate and even initiate such rela-tionships. For the moment, she vastly preferred to see Sartre interested in another woman than be depressed, but it was an unsatisfying situation all around. As Sartre later put it, "the deep cause of my neurotic problems, I think, was the difficulty I had accepting that I was growing up. It was a kind of identity crisis."[55]

James Joyce was also on the brink of despair, but the cause was not so much himself but his daughter, Lucia. True, Joyce was convinced that his American editor, Bennett Cerf, was now neglecting *Ulysses* in favor of Ger-trude Stein's *Autobiography*; he also was upset by the news that Sylvia Beach was selling some of her rare books and Joyce manuscripts in order to keep Shakespeare and Company afloat. Joyce took particular offense at this, be-cause it implied (even if Beach never said such a thing) that Beach, "by her generous sacrifice of all her rights in U[lysses] to me, resigned herself to abject poverty." Irate, Joyce complained that "I threw these MSS at her [Beach] because I did not know what to do between her acts of insane adulation and meaningless rage."[56]

But it was Joyce's daughter who was plummeting him into despair, a despair that deepened as her schizophrenia worsened. According to Joyce, for the past three years Lucia had required twenty-four doctors, twelve nurses, and eight companions and had been in three institutions, at the cost of four thousand pounds. Even sessions with the eminent Swiss psychoanalyst Carl Jung could not effect a permanent improvement.

Later, Jung commented that Lucia and her father "were like two people going to the bottom of a river, one falling and the other diving."[57]

The image of imminent disaster was beginning to haunt those who were carefully watching what was going on in Europe. In early January, Charles de Gaulle, ever more anxious, wrote the center-right politician Paul Reynaud, who was taking a lonely stand in calling for French rearmament and resistance to German aggrandizement. De Gaulle warned Reynaud that the Third Reich had already set up three panzer (tank) divisions, while in France, "their creation had not been seriously begun." De Gaulle was distressed that he had "found a plan of salvation for his country" but instead was seeing that plan "wholly and completely brought into effect by a potential enemy."[58]

But de Gaulle was only a lieutenant colonel, and despite his concerns, France remained dependent on a defensive military strategy, as symbolized and embodied by the Maginot Line. "Who cannot see that the war will depend on tanks and airplanes?" wrote a student at the military academy of Saint-Cyr to his friend, Elliot Paul.[59] Yet as late as 1935, a military review argued that the horse was "the only true cross-country conveyance that obstacles fatal to vehicles will not stop. Besides," it added, "France had plenty of fodder but little oil."[60]

And so it should have been an ominous sign when, as the S.S. *Normandie* made its glorious way across the Atlantic and into the history books, the *Graf Zeppelin*, with a "big new-minted swastika on her fin," floated above her—a veritable "Nazi in the Sky."[61]

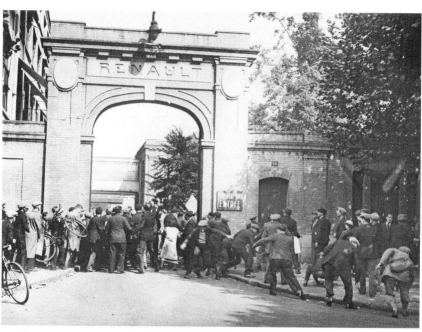

Conflict between striking workers and strike breakers at the gate of the Renault factory in Paris during the 1936 general strike in Paris. © SZ Photo / Scherl / Bridgeman Images

CHAPTER NINE

$\sim$

Coming Apart

(1936)

L ate on the morning of February 13, 1936, a group of paramilitary right-
wingers attacked Léon Blum as he was returning home from the National
Assembly.

The attack began when Blum—driven by his friend Georges Monnet—
had the bad luck to encounter the funeral cortège of Jacques Bainville,
a prominent figure in Action Française. As the last of the long funeral
procession crossed Boulevard Saint-Germain, slowly moving from Rue de
l'Université to the Church of St-Pierre-du-Gros-Caillou, Monnet tried to
move past. Immediately, members of the crowd—heavily populated by young
thugs—surrounded the car. The large black car angered them, the deputy's
sticker on it angered them even more, and when they discovered that Léon
Blum was in the backseat, they erupted.

For years, Action Française leaders such as Charles Maurras and Léon
Daudet had called Blum a "public enemy" and "human garbage who should
be treated as such!" For years, and with increasing urgency, leaders of the
extreme right had encouraged their followers to lynch Blum, to "shoot him
in the back," or to slit his throat "with a kitchen knife." And there he was!
Boiling with hatred, the mob shattered the car's back and side windows, tore
off the doors, and began to pummel Blum. "Kill the Jew!" they roared as
bystanders shouted encouragement.[1]

Blum, who was sixty-four at the time, suffered a savage beating. Rescued
by two policemen and several workmen, he was taken to the Hôtel-Dieu,

where he was stitched up and bandaged (a photo of his bandaged face appeared on the March 9 cover of *Time* magazine). He refused to bring charges (it was not an artery that had been cut, he protested, merely a vein), but when news of the attack reached the National Assembly a short time later, almost the entire Chamber reacted with anger and disbelief, and Premier Albert Sarraut forcefully condemned "the iniquity of such an act."[2] That evening, the cabinet decreed the dissolution of Action Française, the Etudiants d'Action Française, and the Camelots du Roi.[3]

Three days later, on February 16, the left organized a massive tribute to Blum, who was still recuperating (he would remain absent from public affairs until the end of March). For five hours, nearly half a million demonstrators marched from the Panthéon to the Place de la Nation, via the left's traditional rallying point, the Place de la Bastille. But the far-right press, instead of expressing remorse over the incident, lambasted the marchers as supporters of violence and came up with its own account of the beating, claiming that Blum had asked for it—that Monnet's "magnificent car" had driven headlong into the crowd—and that Blum had barely received a scratch, but could have been more severely injured had it not been for members of the Camelots du Roi, who had gallantly intervened. There were even growls among the right that it was a plot, a Bolshevik provocation in revenge for the campaign against Stavisky, while many right-wingers expressed regret that the mob had not permanently finished Blum off. As one member of the extreme right put it, "If ever we take power, this is what will happen: at six o'clock, the Socialist press is suppressed; at 7 o'clock, freemasonry is forbidden, at eight o'clock, Blum is shot."[4]

Action Française, along with its Camelots du Roi and the Etudiants d'Action Française, were now gone for good, but their members, along with their virulent viewpoints, would continue in other forums, especially since the organization's newspaper, *Action Française*, continued on, unaffected by the dissolution. Action Française supporters now carried copies of *Action Française* instead of the badge of the now-forbidden organization. By summer, following the dissolution of the rest of the leagues, these militants would regroup into several organizations—in particular the ultranationalist French Popular Party (PPF), led by former Communist Jacques Doriot, and the French Social Party (PSF), which emerged out of the Croix-de-Feu. All of them were self-described "patriots" and defiantly displayed their tricolor banners. As one dogged supporter of Action Française announced, "Between M. Charles Maurras, an eminent writer and sincere patriot, and Léon Blum, this Hebrew full of hatred . . . our choice is made."[5]

～

In 1936, France had a population of forty-two million, with demographic projections that worried those eyeing Germany's booming crop of babies (German population that year registered at more than sixty-five million). Of France's population, barely half were active, and scarcely one-third were under twenty. Instead, there were many sick and elderly, many invalid war veterans, and a high male mortality rate due to tuberculosis and alcoholism. Few died of old age in 1930s France. As for the working population, more than half were urban, and of these, industrial workers comprised the largest group. Their income had fallen steadily throughout the decade, exacerbated by Laval's deflationist policies, and unemployment was growing—to almost one million at the outset of 1936.[6]

Since the war, Paris had become a major working-class center, with an industrial population that spilled over city borders to the suburbs, or *banlieue*. Most of Paris's workers were employed in factories, where the management method known as "Fordism" regulated their lives. Named after Henry Ford, who had first used the relentless assembly lines advocated by Frederick Winslow Taylor to raise production and lower prices, this form of production was widely abhorred by those it regulated—not only for its strict discipline and relentless adherence to the time clock, but also for the widespread system of management spying that accompanied it.

The filmmaker René Clair mocked this system in his classic 1931 film, *A nous la liberté*, but at the end of the day, not everyone had the option of Clair's heroes—to leave it all behind and hit the open road. More likely, the Parisian industrial worker alternated from oppressive conditions at work to unsanitary and depressing accommodations at home. According to one study, in 1936 more than half of poor young Parisians lived in one room or in a kitchen-bedroom with no toilet, no electricity, no heat, and no running water, requiring the use of slop buckets and chamber pots. These tenements would not receive running water and direct-to-sewer drainage for several more years.[7]

Even many in the middle class were not doing well in the current economy, adding to the social strain, especially as a few in the upper bourgeoisie continued to do well—very well, indeed. The so-called "wall of money," also disparagingly referred to as the "two hundred families"—who were the largest shareholders in the Banque de France—attracted increasing attention and animosity as France grew ever more unequal, with resentment burgeoning among the have-nots as they witnessed the political as well as economic clout of the haves.

⌒

While Blum convalesced, crisis upon crisis continued to mount—not only the social and economic crises at home, but the ongoing rise of Hitler and Mussolini on France's borders. In March, Hitler invaded the demilitarized Rhineland, but France did little but protest. Hamstrung by a deflationary economic policy—which for several years had dictated a drop in military spending—and constrained as well by a widespread pacifism tinged, at least in some quarters, with anti-Semitism (the belief that it was Jewish émigrés who were pushing for a military response to Hitler), the government settled for appeasement rather than tangle with Germany. As for calling upon the Soviet Union for help, this was ruled out, given the strenuous opposition from the right, which held huge meetings to protest against what it called a "Masonic and Soviet war."[8] Not only did the right detest such an alliance on principle, but also on the political grounds that it might give the Popular Front an edge in the coming elections.

These hard-fought elections consumed France during the spring of 1936 as the split between left and right widened. Despite unease at the news of Hitler's military move in the Rhineland, people with property were more concerned with defending it than they were with confronting Germany, while workers were indignant at German aggression but were unwilling to take up arms to oppose it. Overall, the coming elections were all-absorbing, with workers calling loudly for "Bread, Peace, Liberty!" and property owners just as vociferously demanding the defeat of the revolutionary and dangerous proletariat.

Amid the furor, anti-Semitism clothed in the guise of nationalism burgeoned as the right fulminated against "aliens," especially that symbol of the so-called alien, the Jewish Léon Blum. It was now that the bizarre rumor took hold in certain quarters that Blum had been born in Bessarabia with the name of Karfunkelstein.[9] Elliot Paul noted that everyone in his Rue de la Huchette neighborhood took sides, and the resulting ill feeling "transform[ed] the formerly charming and harmonious neighborhood into two hostile camps."[10] And as Eugen Weber bluntly put it, "More than twelve months of unabated civil dissension had left the country gutless and spent, with hatred enough only for fellow-Frenchmen."[11]

Everyone considered the spring elections to be crucial, with both sides contending that a vote for the other would be a vote for war. The elections did indeed result in a virtual revolution, although an internal war was more likely than one with an external foe. In both the first and second ballots, the

Popular Front gained spectacular victories, leaving the moderate center as well as the right in the dust. On the night of May 3, jubilant crowds filled the boulevards of Paris, while sounds of the Internationale wafted on the warm night air.

For the first time, the socialist SFIO received more votes than the Radical party, and Blum became France's first Socialist prime minister. For the first time as well, the Communists now comprised part of the government's parliamentary majority, although—much as the Socialists had done in 1924 and 1929—they refused to participate in the cabinet, even though they had no intention of leaving power to the Socialists. As the Communist writer Paul Vaillant-Couturier put it, "the Communist party will carry on outside the government a sort of 'ministry to the masses,' with the most determined elements of the Popular Front."[12] But this "ministry to the masses," as Vaillant-Couturier put it, left the Popular Front cabinet in a fragile position, buffeted by the Communists on the left and divided between the Socialists and the centrist Radicals.

Dark clouds hovered as Blum prepared to take office. "France under the Jew" screamed the front page of *Action Française*, while the General Council of the Seine considered a proposal to end "Jewish tyranny" by curbing Jews' right to vote and run for office (to be accomplished, at least in part, by voiding all naturalization approved since the war's end). Blum's customary appearance before the Chamber of Deputies upon assumption of office was marred by challenges and invective from the right, including one member who announced that "this peasant nation would be better served by someone whose origins, however modest, reach into the entrails of our soil than by a subtle talmudicist."[13] This resulted in fists flying and a general uproar, which the Speaker had difficulty in restraining.

But even more unsettling were the strikes that erupted during the month between the May 3 election and the June 4 date when Blum and his Popular Front government took office. By the end of May more than seventy thousand industrial workers were on strike in the Paris area alone, and by the time Blum's government took office, Paris—and all of France—was virtually paralyzed by an almost total general strike. Strikers now included employees of everything from chocolate factories, printing works, and insurance companies to hotels, restaurants, and department stores. In addition, strikers were now embracing a new tactic by occupying their factories and places of work to prevent employers from dismissing their workers and hiring the unemployed in their place.

Although angry employers blamed this "social explosion" on the Communists, it seems to have been largely a spontaneous outburst, prompted by exhilaration in an election victory as well as by the dismal nature of salaries and working conditions. Unlike militant revolutionaries, the occupiers seemed to emanate more good-natured camaraderie than class hatred and anger. As the days went on, a general party-like atmosphere prevailed, with food supplies brought in to the occupying workers and the sound of accordions in the air. As Charlotte Perriand recalled, "wives and daughters brought the men plates of food and boosted their morale by joking, flirting, and singing, until the day the money ran out."[14]

During this turbulent month, workers took an almost proprietorial care to prevent destruction in the workplaces they occupied. Contrary to newspaper headlines of revolutionary acts, there was little evidence of disorder in the thousands of occupied plants. Much to his surprise, Louis Renault found that the thirty-two thousand workers at his Billancourt plant had protected his property. Renault's nephew, François Lehideux, corroborated this for the Billancourt works, having been caught inside the factory when it was occupied and told politely but firmly that he could not leave. According to Lehideux, the workers at Billancourt formed committees to arrange for cleaning and upkeep, dormitory accommodations, and feeding the huge crowds of strikers, as well as for providing leisure arrangements to occupy the crowds of men and women who otherwise had nothing to do. To prevent trouble, beer was allowed, but wine and spirits were not. To prevent fire, smoking was forbidden. Duties were shared among the workers, with one day off for every three days of duty. "Although the wheels were not turning, the plant was kept in perfect condition, oiled and polished daily. The floors were swept, [and] improvised beds, mattresses and hammocks were rolled up during the day beside the work-benches."[15]

Although the strikes, and the Popular Front itself, horrified the bourgeoisie, especially devout French Catholics, elements of the Roman Catholic Church now stood behind the workers. The archbishop of Toulouse announced that "we believe that present social conditions . . . are contaminated by the supremacy of money, which is devoid of all Christian spirit," while the archbishop of Paris, Cardinal Verdier, invited Catholics to support the creation of "this new order." Verdier even recommended that good Catholics should subscribe to the first loan that the new government floated. In response, Premier Blum—who unlike previous left-wing political figures showed no signs of anticlericalism—made an early and controversial visit to the Papal Nuncio. But many, including much of the press, were not paying heed to these goodwill gestures, which in fact would not permanently heal the fundamentally chilly climate between this government and the Church. Noting this, the gentle Abbé Mugnier, whose wit and erudition had made him beloved in a conservative literary crowd that included Cocteau and (until his death) Proust, privately mourned the lack of tolerance around him. "Hatred against the Jews, hatred against the Germans, political hatred, social hatred, familial hatred—we are dying of all that," he despairingly wrote in his journal that November.[16]

But it was far more complicated than simple lack of tolerance. Renault, according to his nephew, could not understand how he, "a hard worker [and] a man devoted to his factory, and through it to the welfare of his workers, who had never taken a purely financial or selfish view of his activity, who never mixed in politics . . . he could not imagine that he could be so misunderstood."[17] Angry and humiliated, Renault attempted, unsuccessfully, to take legal action against his workers on grounds of trespassing.

Coco Chanel was equally devastated and lashed out when her Paris staff demanded shorter hours, higher wages, collective contracts, and the abolition of piecework. Enraged, Chanel fired all three hundred employees, who infuriated her further by staging a sit-in. In retaliation, she offered to resign and sell her business to them; they in turn refused the offer, being (as she well knew) in no position to buy her out. Chanel's shop and studios remained closed for three weeks, stalemated; in the end, she grudgingly gave in to some of her employees' demands. But she had just as hard a time as Renault in facing this uprising among her own employees. Later, turning the episode upside down, she told Paul Morand that her employees had been motivated not by demands for more pay but by their desire to see more of her. "It was a strike for love," she insisted, "a strike of the yearning heart."[18]

In contrast, her rival, Schiaparelli, dealt with her own workers by readily negotiating and emerged from the episode on good terms with them. According to one biographer, her "lifelong indignation at oppression and exploitation, her genuine solicitude for her staff, her generous wages and benefits . . . were all well known."[19]

～

On May 24, 1936, a record-breaking crowd of six hundred thousand participated in the left's traditional march to the Mur des Fédérés in Père-Lachaise cemetery. Here, members of the left had gathered year after year to commemorate the demise of the last fighters of the Commune uprising of 1871, shot against this very wall by French government soldiers. On this year, the painter Fernand Léger joined with his good friend Le Corbusier in the hours-long march. "Would you believe it," Léger wrote a friend, "crossing the cemetery took one and a half hours!" Corbu was exasperated and wanted to leave, but Léger convinced him to stay to meet Communist leader Maurice Thorez, who turned out to be an "extremely nice guy." The whole affair was "really quite wonderful," Léger went on, and "bucked us up a little." Rather than a wake, it resembled a "huge local fair." "We sat on the dead," he added, "and shouted out for future life."[20]

Soon after taking power on June 4, Blum and his associates met with representatives of both employers and employees to resolve the strikes. Earlier in the year, the communist CGTU had merged with the socialist CGT, strengthening the entire union movement, and the outcome of these meetings, the Matignon Agreements, gave workers wage increases along with union rights, freedom of opinion, and a guarantee of no reprisals for striking—all this in return for evacuating the factories. Very quickly, Blum presented the Assembly with five proposed laws, including the forty-hour week, two-week paid vacations, and collective bargaining. The last two were easily adopted, and the forty-hour week went into effect by the summer's end (the eight-hour day had gone into effect in 1919). Not surprisingly, union membership soared.

⌢

As Charlotte Perriand rhapsodized, that summer "Parisians learned what it was like to sit on fresh grass, see apple and cherry trees, and gaze on cornflowers and poppies in wheat fields. . . . Children ran after chickens and rolled around in the hay."[21] Blum's new secretary of leisure and sports (derided as the Ministry of Idleness) encouraged popular playhouses, theaters, festivals, and youth hostels. Young people like Simone de Beauvoir, who was an avid hiker and cyclist, took advantage of new cheap railway fares to take to the open road. L'Oréal's Eugène Schueller, always alert to the latest trends, came out with a suntan lotion called "Ambre Solaire." And those on the go could now quench their thirst with a new drink called Orangina.

But sports, like so much else, had by now become politicized. Nazi Germany's glorification of the perfect human body had become a fascist fixation, which grew into an art form with the sculptures of Arno Breker, who celebrated the fascist male ideal, and Leni Riefenstahl's *Olympia*, her memorable documentary film of that summer's Olympic athletes. Riefenstahl's techniques were groundbreaking, and her devotion to the beauty of the perfect athletic body was an artistic triumph, starting with her leisurely perusal of ancient Greek statues before moving to the actualities of the 1936 games. No one questioned Riefenstahl's ability and artistry; it was the politics behind her documentary that made the film controversial.

These were, after all, Hitler's Olympics, held in Berlin during the first half of August to showcase his "new Germany," and it was Hitler that Riefenstahl first and foremost was celebrating. Again and again her camera returns to focus on the Führer's face as he watches events, or as athletes march past him with their salute (for the record, the British and American athletes did not give the Nazi salute; the French did, or may have—they later claimed that they gave the somewhat similar Olympic salute, which has since been dropped from use). The French won gold medals in boxing, cycling, and weight lifting but could not compete with Germany's overall total of eighty-nine medals, which eclipsed them. Most head-shaking, at least for the French, was their complete absence from the medal platform in tennis.

Throughout the 1920s, the French had dominated tennis, with Suzanne Lenglen (dubbed "La Divine") regularly triumphing in women's tennis, and René Lacoste just as regularly triumphing in men's. Both had an impact on more than sports, as Lenglen dressed in chic outfits that inspired couturiers such as Jean Patou and Elsa Schiaparelli to enter the new field of sportswear, while Lacoste would soon enter the clothing business himself. With his two best friends (together the three were known as the Musketeers), Lacoste won the Davis Cup in 1927, and in 1928 the three successfully defended it in the newly inaugurated Roland-Garros stadium outside Paris. He then went on to win again at Wimbledon and at the French Internationals in 1929 before retiring from tennis.

Lacoste, known as "the Crocodile" for his prominent Gallic nose, was already deeply interested in developing a better tennis racket, which he eventually took to new levels with his antivibration string damper and his revolutionary steel racket, which quickly replaced the older wood models. He also perfected a training machine that could launch balls, which he began to manufacture on a large scale in 1930. But it was in the clothing area where he had his biggest impact, again by following his own needs and interests.

In 1927, Lacoste had discovered a British-made shirt constructed of a mesh material that was far more comfortable than the long-sleeved and buttoned men's shirts traditionally worn on the tennis court, which flapped about and did not allow the skin to breathe. He had some made up in England and wore them in subsequent matches, creating something of a sensation. By 1933, he had joined forces with a French manufacturer of knit underwear. Together, they began to mass-produce the short-sleeved Lacoste shirt with the crocodile symbol that a friend had designed for him, using polo shirts as a model. At first produced only in white, the shirt was made from a lightweight knit fabric with a special honeycomb weave that let the fabric breathe. Not surprisingly, it was a hit.

Lacoste, like his colleagues, was known for his sportsmanship, in an era when manners, courtesy, and pleasure in the game still mattered. Unquestionably, even during Lacoste's years of dominance, dedication to one's sport was becoming increasingly important, as sports ceased to be a purely leisure activity and tennis champions vied at Wimbledon, the Davis Cup, and the French Open. But money and fame did not yet matter as much as they soon would, and a defeated player could still celebrate the winner's victory in a spirit of genuine camaraderie. As for patriotism, sports in general had not yet become politicized. It was Hitler's 1936 Summer Olympics that changed all that, from Riefenstahl's *Olympia*, conceived as propaganda and secretly financed by the German government (reportedly for millions of dollars), to the aura of national competition that overhung the entire event.

Peaceful competition and international goodwill were now out in athletic events, and they would remain so.

That year's national celebration on July 14 marked the high point of the Popular Front. With the Matignon Agreements and the legislation that resulted, workers now for the first time were emerging from the dark shadows of industrialism. In addition to paid vacations and the forty-hour week, Blum's Popular Front government soon established a public works program, nationalized the arms industries, seminationalized the Bank of France, and extended the age of required schooling to fourteen. Much to the relief of many, it also disbanded those right-wing leagues that had remained after the dissolution of Action Française earlier in the year. Although the Croix-de-Feu turned itself into a political party (the Parti Social Français, or PSF) that soon grew to eight hundred thousand members, the dissolution of the paramilitary leagues met with applause from workers and unionists, who felt most threatened by them.

Parallel with its efforts to transform the basics of working-class life, the government also undertook unprecedented actions to enrich workers' cultural life, including traveling library buses, numerous popular choruses and orchestras, and a 40 percent reduction on train tickets during paid vacations to encourage workers and their families to travel (this last prompting a cartoon in *Le Canard enchaîné* showing an elderly lady sitting in a bathtub at the ocean's edge and fulminating, "You don't think I'm going to bathe in the same water as those Bolsheviks!").[22]

This year's July 14 Bastille Day was triumphant, as a million Parisians marched through the Place de la Nation beneath an enormous portrait of Jean Jaurès surtitled "Down with war! Long live peace!" That evening, crowds packed into the tenth arrondissement's Théâtre de l'Alhambra for a performance of Romain Rolland's *Le Quatorze juillet*, which received star treatment with a curtain designed by Picasso that featured fascism in the form of a predatory bird supporting the dying body of capitalism, with a star-wreathed young man raising his arm to finish it off. Well-known composers such as Darius Milhaud, Arthur Honegger, and Georges Auric contributed the rousing music.

But three days after that triumphant July 14, 1936, the Spanish Civil War broke out, changing everything.

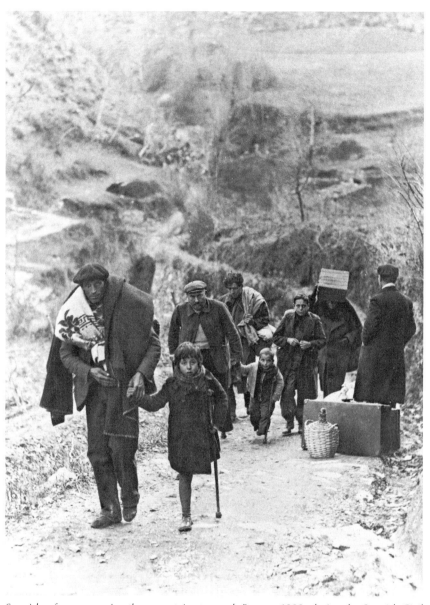

Spanish refugees crossing the mountains to reach France, 1939, during the Spanish Civil War. © Tallandier / Bridgeman Images

CHAPTER TEN

~

War in Spain

(1936)

All the ingredients for conflagration had been building in Spain since early in the decade, when the Spanish replaced their centuries-old monarchy and a military dictatorship with a republic. In February 1936, the narrow political victory of a coalition that included Socialists, Communists, and other left-wing parties under a Popular Front banner created the sparks that ignited a civil war. By now, Spain's centrist parties had all but collapsed, while the right—supported by landowners, the nobility, and the Catholic Church—continued to agitate, leading to a series of assassinations and the growth of Spain's fascist movement. Finally, on July 17, a coup d'état under the command of General Francisco Franco set off a civil war. Unable to seize power quickly as planned, the coup's leaders began a slow and devastating war of attrition against the Republican government in Madrid and the people who supported it.

The outbreak of the war in Spain marked what one historian has called the end of the "springtime of innocence" for France's Popular Front.[1] Blum, who wanted to go to the aid of the beleaguered Spanish Republic, faced a huge campaign against intervention from pro-Franco French nationalists (including many in the French General Staff), as well as opposition from the Radicals in his cabinet. At the same time, despite his efforts to obtain a nonintervention pact, Germany and Italy interceded at once in support of Franco, while France's Communists, dropping their peace platform (in line with Moscow), pressed Blum to go to the aid of Spain's Popular Front government.

But Britain quickly made it clear that it intended to stay out of the fray, and France, as Blum realized, would end up fighting a proxy war in Spain against Italy and Germany without much help from anyone, including Stalin, who at first was disinterested in supporting the Spanish Republic and only got around to sending tanks and planes in late October, well after the Germans and Italians had thrown their support to Franco. At length, yielding to the whiplash of pressures, Blum reluctantly agreed to a policy of nonintervention—prompting bitter Communist attacks and setting off the first breach within his Popular Front coalition. After all, as supporters of the Spanish Republic pointed out, not to aid the Spanish Republic in itself constituted what amounted to an effective intervention in the ongoing civil war.

At the same time, Blum's economic gamble was not paying off. Salaries were rising, but not as fast as prices. In September, despite earlier assurances, Blum's government was forced to deal with the rising cost of living by devaluing the franc, aligning it with the dollar and the pound and, in the process, going off the hitherto sacrosanct gold standard. Critics of the Popular Front argued that the whole mess was the result of social legislation that made people want more pay for less work, while others less antagonistic to progressive politics pointed to the owner class's refusal to create jobs or increase production, although no one knew quite why—possibly out of pique over Popular Front legislation and disgruntlement over higher wages.[2]

By the year's end, Blum would find it necessary to reassure the well-to-do by abandoning some of the Popular Front's social reforms and making it illegal to strike without first submitting to arbitration. This would soon be followed, early in 1937, by an official "pause" in social reforms, along with a cut in public expenditures. This meant abandoning pension schemes for elderly workers, a national employment fund, and other progressive measures.

On November 1, Hitler and Mussolini declared the Berlin-Rome Axis, which soon extended to include Tokyo. France by now was looking for allies and, despite continued cries for peace within and without the Popular Front, was beginning to beef up its armaments. This in turn cost money, which had a negative impact on the faltering economy. Meanwhile, throughout autumn and into winter, the war in Spain continued to unsettle the Popular Front's prospects, both at home and abroad.

Even though some, including the French novelist Roger Martin du Gard (soon to receive the Nobel Prize for Literature), remained adamantly pacifist—writing a friend in September, "Anything rather than war! Anything,

Hitler rather than war!"—others concluded that the time for pacifism was over, and the time for organizing resistance had come.[3]

That certainly was the opinion of André Malraux, who quickly became a passionate supporter of the Spanish Republican government. Reveling in the opportunity for heroic activism in a good cause, he immediately signed on to bring essential planes and pilots to the aid of the Loyalists. Through a complex web of discreet maneuvers involving the finance ministry's customs department, Malraux was able to divert several new aircraft from the French air force to Spanish airfields under the Republic's Loyalist control. This complex arrangement took place under the guise that these aircraft were "in transit" from factory to the French air force. This in turn meant that, under this thin subterfuge, France officially was not intervening. As Malraux well knew, any civil war can use both heroes and con men, and it helps if one is a little of both.

On July 30, he received a standing ovation at Paris's first massive demonstration in support of Republican Spain, in the seventeenth arrondissement's Salle Wagram. By this time Malraux had recruited a growing squadron of professional mercenaries and volunteer pilots as well as ground crews. Malraux's pilots were a mixed lot, but for the most part they brought more daredevil than ideology to their assignments: "This guy could fly a barn door," as one remarked admiringly of another. This was fortunate, since many of these pilots had to fly the equivalent of barn doors after aircraft losses forced them to take to the air in a series of junk heaps, held together with little more than hope.

Early August saw Malraux once again en route to Madrid, this time with both wife (Clara) and mistress (Josette) in tow, as Clara refused to be left behind. There, he indisputably established himself as head of the Spanish squadron, even though he could not fly and was no good with a machine gun. Charisma counted, as did Malraux's political and public relations abilities. Yet despite the warmth and conviviality among Malraux's men, they were worried, and with good cause: airplane and pilot losses were mounting, and the Republic's military was a shambles.

Discipline was badly needed, and by October, a source of iron discipline—the Russians—had arrived. But the outcome was brutal: Malraux was far too popular and independent for the Communists, and by year's end, they had stepped in to move him far from the front line and send his unit into what amounted to extinction. The remains, now under army discipline, were romantically renamed the Squadron André Malraux, but this meant nothing. The dream was over.

Still, despite these grievous disappointments and serious alarms, Malraux firmly believed that the time to fight Stalin was after the war was over. Only Stalin, to his mind, could effectively face both Hitler and Mussolini in Spain.

Meanwhile, Ernest Hemingway was in no great hurry to get to Spain. During the last week in July, as the civil war there was revving up, he wrote a friend that "we ought to have been in Spain all this week." But instead, he headed west for an extended stint at fishing and game hunting. Even as late as December, while men like the journalist Paul Mowrer—now married to Hemingway's first wife, Hadley—had already been to Spain to report on the war, Hemingway was writing Max Perkins from Key West: "'I've *got* to go to Spain. But there's no great hurry. They'll be fighting for a long time and it's cold as hell around Madrid now!"[4]

Since Thanksgiving, the North American Newspaper Alliance had been after Hemingway to cover the Spanish Civil War, but he was trying to finish his latest novel, *To Have and Have Not*. In addition, he had encountered a fascinating blonde in a bar in Key West—Martha Gellhorn, who by that time was free of Bertrand de Jouvenel and well established in her own right as a novelist. Her collection of short stories, *The Trouble I've Seen*, based on interviews with impoverished Americans, had put her on the cover of the *Saturday Review of Literature*, and it also caught the attention of Eleanor Roosevelt, who became a good friend.

Gellhorn, a political activist who was passionately concerned with the welfare of those in need, thought that she had found a kindred soul in Hemingway. Hemingway, for his part, was a sucker for long legs and golden hair and found her irresistible. She was, for the moment, unattached, and his marriage (a second one) was already foundering. The outcome may not have been as instantaneous as legend has it, but the end result was the same: soon they were together, and by early the next year, they would be in Spain together as well.

In the middle of June, Gide at last embarked for Moscow. It was a year of big moments for him, starting with his decision in April to tell his illegitimate daughter, Catherine, who her true father was (all along, he and those around him had supported the fiction that her father was dead). Catherine, who had just turned thirteen, took it well, putting her arms around him and kissing him. Later, when the Petite Dame approached her on the subject,

Catherine's response was a broad smile "that seemed to be beyond that of a thirteen-year-old child."[5]

Gide's trip that summer to the Soviet Union was especially important for him. He had already received cautionary advice that all was not well there, especially from the Petite Dame's son-in-law, Pierre Herbart, who had just returned from Moscow. Herbart reported that everything the critics said was true, especially the situation of artists there, which was intolerable. Gide now was determined to see Stalin and complain to him in person about the regime's shortcomings, in particular its treatment of homosexuals—a plan that left the Soviet writer and propagandist Ilya Ehrenburg both appalled and amused. "I tried politely to dissuade him," Ehrenburg wrote, "but he was adamant."[6]

Everywhere in the Soviet Union, Gide was wined and dined, even carried shoulder high in triumph by airport employees when he arrived. Ensconced in luxurious quarters, he at first played the role Stalin wanted, giving a funeral oration for Maxim Gorky (who probably did not die of natural causes), complete with the deferential comments about the Soviet Union that Stalin expected. Any mention of the U.S.S.R. was to be accompanied by words like "glorious," while Stalin was to be addressed not simply as "You," but as "You, leader of the workers," or "You, master of the peoples."[7] Gide visited what his hosts wanted him to visit and continued with ardent expressions of support for the great Soviet experiment even while his brief unaccompanied walks in the streets, in stolen moments away from officials, began to diminish his former enthusiasm. Texts of his addresses had to meet with the approval of the culture police. His every move was carefully monitored. And throughout his journeys in the Soviet Union, he was met by over-the-top expressions of enthusiasm for the great Comrade Stalin.

En route, "our eyes really began to be opened," Gide later wrote, and soon after his return he told his good friend Count Kessler that "freedom of intellect seem[ed] to him to be undergoing an even more horrible suppression in Russia than in Germany; he found its harassment intolerable."[8] Nor was the oppression subtle: "In no country," wrote Pierre Herbart, who accompanied Gide, "have I seen so many barricades, barbed-wire fences, 'no entry' signs, special passes, guards, and sentry-huts." And in no nation had any of them seen such blind faith in the superiority of their leaders, and of the nation itself—one that in most cases was preposterously misplaced. When contradicted on basic facts, a typical response was, "*Pravda* gives us sufficient information on everything."[9]

Two of Gide's travel companions in fact decided that they had had enough and decided to cut short their visit, departing immediately for Paris.

They were lucky: another in their party (Eugène Dabit) caught an infection in Sebastopol and died without seeing his friends again—Soviet doctors forbade Gide and the others to visit the patient, assuring them that he would soon recover. Back in Moscow, a shaken Gide found a city obsessed with the trial of sixteen disgraced party leaders; the newspapers were filled with statements for the prosecution but none for the defense, there being no defense. On the day that Gide left Moscow, *Pravda* announced the execution of two of the leading defendants. Soon after, the rest were dead, all shot.

Although Gide was not a Marxist, nor had he ever been a Communist party member, his nine-week journey had left him with an intense feeling of betrayal and despair. "A tremendous, a dreadful confusion," he wrote in his journal on September 3. Several days later, he wrote, "Everything seems frightful. Everywhere I feel the catastrophe coming." The next day he added, "We are plunging into a tunnel of anguish, the end of which cannot yet be seen."[10]

Before his death, Eugène Dabit had urged Gide to "speak out," and soon Gide did, dedicating his book, *Retour de l'U.R.S.S.* (*Return from the U.S.S.R.*), to Dabit. Much to the fury of the Communists, both in France and in the Soviet Union, Gide quickly wrote an account of his experience, detailing his disenchantment. He published it that November, over the opposition of those who argued that it was the wrong time to attack the Soviet Union, which now was assisting Spain. Nevertheless, Gide persisted, and his little book created an uproar.

In ten months, *Retour* sold almost 150,000 copies, having been reprinted eight times and translated into fourteen languages. It was an international best seller, except in Germany and Italy, where Hitler and Mussolini wanted nothing to do with it, and of course not in the Soviet Union. Gide, as a non-party member, could not be disciplined or summoned to Moscow; yet he suffered a barrage of vilification initiated by Moscow, as well as ostracization by many of his former colleagues. No longer subject to glowing praise, he was condemned as a traitor, a fascist, and a dirty old man solely intent on making money. Suddenly Gide was a persona non grata among intellectuals.

Earlier that year, before his Soviet trip, Gide had written in his journal, "Flee! Inhabit for a time some abstract, hollow, and unfurnished region or other, in which to abstain from living, from judging, yet without betraying or deserting any cause."[11] Now he had learned that this was impossible.

That autumn, Irène and Frédéric Joliot-Curie went to Moscow to attend a scientific conference where Frédéric was to give the opening address. Earlier,

Irène had accepted a post in Blum's Popular Front government as undersecretary of state for scientific research, where she helped to lay out the basis for what would become the National Center for Scientific Research. The appointment was one she neither wanted nor enjoyed, as it kept her from her research and also required a degree of diplomacy that she neither possessed nor desired. As she wrote a good friend, "Fred and I thought I must accept [the position] as a sacrifice for the feminist cause in France, although it annoyed us very much."[12] Soon she left the post, although probably not for the reason she wanted: illness forced her once again to leave for treatment in the mountains. By autumn, though, Irène was able to accompany her husband to Moscow, where their three-week sojourn, marked by the usual rollout of wining and dining, does not seem to have annoyed them at all.

Everyone seemed to be going to Moscow that year. Jean Renoir had made the trip during the winter of 1935–1936, to show *Toni* at a film festival, and returned after a few days, having seen little but constant screenings—although, in typical fashion, he managed to slip in an all-night party celebrating the anniversary of Jewish theater, which would not have been on the approved schedule.

His propaganda film for the Communist party, *La Vie est à nous*, came out shortly after this, drawing Renoir even closer into the Communist embrace, although he continued to maintain that his political independence remained untouched and that the film was simply a way of opposing Hitler while putting him "in touch with people having a genuine love of the working class." These Communists, in his view, "were truly disinterested. They were Frenchmen . . . wholly without Russian mysticism or Latin grandiloquence. They were warm-hearted realists."[13]

Whatever Renoir's actual political affiliation was at the time, his Communist colleagues' point of view resonated with him and made a permanent impact. More than three decades later, in 1971, he wrote, "The modern world is founded on the ever increasing production of material goods. One must keep producing or die. . . . To maintain the level of production on which our daily bread depends, we must ever renew and expand our enterprises. One prefers that this process be peaceful, but events have a way of getting out of hand."[14]

Here were echoes from his far more conservative father, Pierre-Auguste, who in old age railed against mechanization rather than capitalism itself. On one occasion the elder Renoir treated young Julie Manet (Berthe Morisot's daughter) to an example of mechanization's widespread effects by conjuring up a gentleman who made his money by producing large quantities of socks.

This gentleman, he told her, had to continue producing large quantities of socks, whether needed or not, and as markets at home were not sufficient for such a profusion, "we have to sell socks to the savages, and persuade them that they have to wear socks in order to keep some gentleman's factory going." His conclusion—with which few Marxists, or even his son, would have disagreed—was that "we want to conquer in order to sell our products."[15]

Yet Jean Renoir the filmmaker was not about to be pushed around by anyone, including political parties or producers of any political stripe. Art always trumped politics with him (he was as opposed to nationalizing the film industry as he was to the practice of dubbing in foreign films), and human dignity mattered most of all. Soon after making *La Vie est à nous*, he began filming his delicately evocative *A Day in the Country*, a tale (as he put it) of "disappointed love, followed by a ruined life." Visually a delight (one critic has commented that the film was "a romantic dialogue between Renoir and nature," with at least three of Pierre-Auguste Renoir's paintings recreated in it),[16] the film ran into a barrage of difficulties and did not appear in its final version until after the war, when it was an immediate success.

After temporarily setting aside the uncompleted *A Day in the Country*, Renoir took on Gorky's *The Lower Depths*, which he turned into his own distinctly French version in *Les Bas-fonds*. As always, Renoir insisted on making the film on his own terms, even though he sent the screenplay to Gorky—who told Renoir that he was satisfied with it, despite the enormous differences between it and his own work. Renoir inserted distinct elements of humor in this otherwise bleak tale, especially in the friendship between the petty thief Pépel and the bankrupt baron, who adopts Pépel's carefree life. According to film director Claude de Givray, the film is typically Renoir in that it contains "a remarkable gallery of dissatisfied, fiercely individualistic, nicely revolutionary characters, more sociable than socialist," allowing the viewer "to experience, if not to judge, the human condition."[17] Although it starred the renowned actor and director Louis Jouvet in a slyly comic turn as the Baron, and film star Jean Gabin as the charmingly disreputable thief Pépel, *Les Bas-fonds*, like so many other Renoir films, did not appeal to the general public. Still, it did win Renoir the Louis Delluc Prize from French film critics for best film of the year, making him the prize's first recipient.

Gide, however, differed from the critics, writing in his journal that he considered the film "unworthy of Renoir."[18]

Elsa Schiaparelli also traveled to Moscow in 1936, but in the company of the young fashion photographer Cecil Beaton, and as part of a French trade exhibit of textiles, champagne, and perfumes. It was during the dead of winter, December 1936, and she found the contrast between the goods she was showing and the actualities of Russian life startling and depressing. Lamps and ashtrays in her hotel room were chained to the wall, the sheets were torn, and the hotel soap (considered a great luxury) was previously used. The women she saw were dressed in dingy dark clothes, and although she designed a practical black dress for Soviet women, complete with a red coat and small cap, the authorities turned the ensemble down on the grounds that the cap's hidden pocket would only invite theft. She survived on caviar, bread, and vodka and returned to Paris as quickly as possible.

In the meantime, Schiaparelli continued to increase the glamour and popularity of her fashions by establishing her styles on the Hollywood screen in a way that Chanel had never managed. Her styles "popped" on-screen, and starting in 1936, she designed for several Hollywood films—although her influence was already on display in the films, where actresses could be seen with padded shoulders as well as other Schiaparelli looks, including split skirts, prominent zippers, dinner dresses with matching jackets, and metallic mesh evening bags. Chanel did not think much of her rival's concepts: "You see pockets rising up like udders," she later remarked of 1930s fashions, "buttons as big as saucers, adornments in the shape of noses, mouths on the backside, swatches of fur with eyes or hands reproduced on them."[19] She didn't specifically mention Schiaparelli in her indictment, but she did not need to. The focus of her scorn was obvious.

But Schiaparelli did not care about what Chanel thought, nor did she need to. Regulars to her Place Vendôme and London salons included Marlene Dietrich, Norma Shearer, Claudette Colbert, Katharine Hepburn, Greta Garbo, and Ginger Rogers, not to mention Amelia Earhart, Gloria Swanson, Joan Crawford, Myrna Loy, Vivien Leigh, and of course Mae West, whose hourglass figure provided the unlikely model for Schiaparelli's perfume bottle, "Shocking." They were all there, and many more—so much so that by the late 1930s, Schiaparelli was too busy to have time to design specifically for the films, although she continued to use items from her collections to meet costume requests, including numerous London stage and film productions.

While Schiaparelli was managing her remarkable career, her daughter, Gogo, was managing the difficulties of growing up with a disability and without a mother. Packed off to an English boarding school, she had survived; then, under her mother's direction, she went to school in Paris, spent time in Munich, and took lessons from a Russian chef. She was already fluent in English, Italian, and French, acquainted with German, and her legs had healed thanks to constant exercise—skiing, riding, swimming, and golf. She now began to holiday with her mother, who took pride in dressing her, and learned to travel with the glamorous crowd. By her late teens—although still shy, especially around her formidable mother—Gogo, much to her mother's satisfaction, had acquired the necessary degree of sophistication to make her a star of the debutante set.

That summer, from June 11 to July 4, the Surrealists held their first international exhibit in the New Burlington Galleries in London, an exhibit displaying works by more than sixty artists from fourteen countries. André Breton, Paul Eluard, and Man Ray were the French organizers, and although Picasso (who was arm-twisted into participating) was a definite draw, and Méret Oppenheim's fur-covered cup, saucer, and spoon (titled *Breakfast in Fur*) provided giggles, it was Salvador Dalí who stole the show, especially after he gave a lecture dressed in a diving suit decorated with a Mercedes Benz radiator cap. He later complained that he had almost suffocated, but it was all in a good cause: despite some terrible reviews (one major reviewer called his paintings "vulgar trash"), Dalí had never enjoyed better sales—many of them from a one-man show that (to the irritation of the Surrealists) he held nearby.[20]

Anyone who could sell paintings as Dalí did, during the height of the Depression, could not be dismissed out of hand, and *Time* magazine placed Dalí on its cover to coincide with MoMA's New York exhibition on Surrealism and Dada that December. Man Ray's huge painting known as *The Lips* presided over the exhibition's entrance, but the star of the show unquestionably was Dalí. Sometime between Dalí's 1934–1935 trip and this second American visit, Dalí had evolved from a timid young member of a small group of avant-garde artists to an international celebrity, complete with an assured sense of how best to present and promote himself.

At the same time, Dalí was working closely with Elsa Schiaparelli, whose readiness to venture into the surreal world of Dalí imagery appealed to him. "Here [in Schiaparelli's dressmaking establishment]," he later wrote, "the tongues of fire of the Holy Ghost of Dalí were going to descend."[21] Well, perhaps not tongues of fire, but certainly arresting images of lobsters, hats that looked like upside-down high heels, and buttons of fake chocolate covered with imitation bees. As Schiaparelli put it, she sought "an absolute freedom of expression, and a daredevil approach, with no fear."[22]

By late summer, Dalí and Gala had returned to Paris, after having visited Spain just before the civil war broke out. Dalí had felt compelled to take a break from his and Gala's six-year work of "striking . . . with unwearying persistence, the hammer-blows of our personality on the red-hot anvil of the sooty Vulcan of actuality." As he less floridly put it, "It's very difficult to shock the world every twenty-four hours."[23]

In any case, Spain brought a measure of solitude plus reconciliation with a former friend, Federico García Lorca. They would never meet again: soon after, Lorca was kidnapped, captured, and shot—probably by the fascists, although no one knows for sure. Dalí reacted strangely to the news of Lorca's death, shouting "Olé!" when he heard. He tried to explain this as "what the Spanish say when a toreador executes a particularly well-performed movement before the blood-stained beast."[24] But guilt dogged him, especially that he had not insisted on bringing Lorca out of Spain with him before the civil war broke out.

When the war did erupt, Dalí—who described himself as "essentially anti-historic and a-political"—refused what he called "the hyena of public opinion . . . demanding of me with the drooling menace of its expectant teeth that I make up my mind at last, that I become Stalinist or Hitlerite. No! No! No!" he protested. "I was going to continue to be as always and until I died, Dalinian and only Dalinian!"[25]

And so Dalí did not oppose Franco. And he avoided Spain.

After the London Surrealist show, Paul Eluard invited Man Ray and Picasso to join him at a hilltop village near Cannes. That summer, Picasso was the center of the group, which included Man Ray's first real love since Lee Miller's departure, Adrienne Fidelin (known as Ady), a dancer from Guadeloupe. It was a happy moment for them both: "We were in love," Man Ray later recalled.[26]

Picasso, now separated from Olga, also had a new love interest—the young Yugoslavian photographer Dora Maar, for whom he had left his former mistress, Marie-Thérèse Walter. (Marie-Thérèse's pregnancy the year before may have contributed to Picasso's loss of interest in her. As John Richardson points out, Picasso—having already had one less-than-satisfactory son—"relished the idea rather than the fact of having children.")[27]

The news from Spain did not at first cast a cloud over the carefree group. Picasso did not immediately express concern, although he soon could be found in deep conversation with Eluard as he debated his allegiances—whether to art, or to Spain, or to both. At first Picasso decided to continue as before, avoiding all political commitment, even though only two years before this he had succumbed to the blandishments and inducements (including an expensive vacation) from the leader of the Spanish fascist Falange movement, who was interested in attracting painters, poets, and intellectuals to the fascist side.

After several days of the all-expenses-paid vacation, including some clumsy attempts at political persuasion, Picasso left in disgust, without ever explaining why he had accepted the invitation in the first place. Possibly he had been attracted by the Falange's offer to provide him with a retrospective of his work in Spain. Possibly he wanted to show off a bit before Olga and his son, who accompanied him, to demonstrate the high regard with which he was held in the land of his birth. Later, he simply credited the entire business to political naïveté. In the end, what finally convinced Picasso to leave was the Falangist announcement to the press that the Picasso meeting had been a resounding success and that "the artist had been finally won over to the right."[28]

When Picasso finally committed himself, it would be to the Republican cause, of which he became a passionate supporter. He secretly provided substantial aid to Spanish refugees, including a hospital in Toulouse; he helped a good friend print clandestinely for the Spanish Resistance; and he served as honorary director-in-exile of the Prado Museum. But Picasso's greatest public act of support for the Spanish Republic would be a deeply personal one—his magnificent painting, *Guernica*, for the 1937 Paris World's Fair.

"For God's sake," James Joyce told his brother, Stanislaus, when they met in Zurich that autumn. "I'm not interested in politics. The only thing that interests me is style." In this vein, he remarked that summer to a Danish author, "Now they're bombing Spain. Isn't it better to make a great joke [referring to his *Work in Progress*] instead, as I have done?"[29]

This was Joyce's idea of humor, but it had even more of a bitter edge than usual. Things were not going well for him. His daughter had grown much worse, until she finally had to be carried out of the house in a straitjacket and installed in a clinic, where the doctor warned that she was dangerous. At length, Joyce was able to transfer Lucia to more comfortable surroundings, but his expenses for her were mounting dramatically. Alarmed by his daughter's plight as well as by his finances, he was drinking ever more heavily, infuriating Nora, who threatened to leave him. This had happened before, and now, as always, she capitulated in the face of his dejection and his dramatic bid for sympathy, as well as his patently insincere promises to drink less. She reluctantly returned, and his drinking soon resumed, although he tried to do it on the sly.

Joyce saw Sylvia Beach only rarely now, and then only in the company of others. Beach, in turn, was keeping Shakespeare and Company afloat, but only barely, with the help of a group of staunch supporters led by André Gide. In 1936, Gide formed the Friends of Shakespeare and Company (or, Les Amis de Shakespeare and Company). Its members agreed to pay annual dues for two years, which everyone assumed would get Beach past this rough patch. Some of France's leading writers were behind the effort, including Gide and Paul Valéry, Jean Schlumberger, André Maurois, Paul Morand, and Jules Romains, each of whom agreed to give readings at Shakespeare and Company for the group's members. American and British authors such as Archibald MacLeish and Bryher were also supportive (even Helena Rubinstein pitched in, presumably on behalf of her husband, Edward Titus). Gide, Schlumberger, Maurois, and Valéry gave some of the first readings, with T. S. Eliot coming over from London to read. Eventually Hemingway and Stephen Spender gave readings as well.

Shakespeare and Company was saved for the moment, much to Beach's relief, and now she felt free to embark on her first trip back to the United States in more than twenty years. It was an intense time, with both high points and low (including an operation and subsequent recuperation). By the end, she was quite ready to return to Paris. But upon her return in October, she found that her life had been upended: not only was the franc depreciated and alarming talk about Spain swirling everywhere, but her longtime partner, Adrienne Monnier, had entered into a new relationship with a young German Jewish refugee, Gisèle Freund—a Sorbonne student, political activist, and talented photographer whom Sylvia and Adrienne had earlier befriended. Shocked and saddened, Beach immediately moved out of the apartment that she had shared with Monnier for so many years.

Freund would eventually depart, and Beach and Monnier would remain friends, but never again would it be the same between them.

That November, looking at the growing danger from Hitler, Beach confided in her sister Holly: "We're so scared you've no idea how."[30]

Lieutenant Colonel Charles de Gaulle certainly was not scared, but he was deeply concerned. Germany's remilitarization of the Rhineland appalled him, especially since it had been accomplished without even striking a blow. As he wrote in a letter to a friend, "The 'hostile act' of 7 March has shown what methods strength is going to use to carry out its aims: surprise, suddenness, speed. A nation that wishes to live must therefore not only obtain guarantees of help from others (mutual assistance) but must also organize its own strength in such a way that its reaction takes place in the same conditions as the aggressor's action." Unfortunately, though, he added, "we do not possess the means of doing so."[31]

De Gaulle was doing everything in his power to change this state of affairs, but he faced enormous resistance. As France's minister of war put it at the time of the Rhineland fiasco, "When we have devoted so much effort to the building of a fortified barrier [the Maginot Line], is it to be supposed that we should be mad enough to go outside that barrier, in pursuit of who knows what adventure?"[32]

That summer, Blum's Popular Front government—unable to ignore any longer the gravity of the danger that Hitler represented—launched a plan for rearmament that went well beyond the General Staff's requirements. Still, de Gaulle, who was not nearly as ardent a proponent of aviation as he was of grouped tanks, noted that despite an increase in the number of tanks called for, these tanks still would be under the authority of infantry commanders. Scattered among infantry units, they would be used merely as support, thus depleting their offensive value. De Gaulle responded characteristically, unhesitatingly arranging to talk directly with Prime Minister Blum about it.

Blum and the self-confident lieutenant colonel met in October 1936 (Blum especially noted de Gaulle's calmness and single-mindedness, as well as his impressive six-foot-five-inch height). By this time de Gaulle was convinced that unless something changed dramatically in the immediate future, France was on track to sit by and watch Hitler dismember Europe. Unfortunately nothing in this meeting changed his opinion, and de Gaulle came away frustrated that the government under Blum, although prepared to significantly increase France's rearmament, would continue to rely on the recommendations of the military specialists. These, in de Gaulle's opinion, were depriving France of its ability to deal in a meaningful way with Hitler.

In the meantime, de Gaulle's former mentor, Marshal Pétain, was doing his best to derail any effort to increase the number of French tanks, let alone make them autonomous divisions able to carry out rapid maneuvers. Endorsing a book in which the author—a former professor of fortification at the Ecole de Guerre—stated that "the great armored units belong to the realm of dreams," and flatly predicted that in any conceivable situation a motorized attack would "bite the dust," Pétain wrote, "There exists a mortal barrier to the passage of tanks; it consists of mines combined with the fire of anti-tank weapons." And in response to those worried about the way the Maginot Line broke off west of the Ardennes, Pétain jocularly added, "The Ardennes forest is impenetrable; and if the Germans were imprudent enough to get entangled in it, we should seize them as they came out!"[33]

It took a lot of guts to take on the entire military establishment, and the debate into which de Gaulle had so forcefully inserted himself for the past three years now almost brought his military career to a halt. That autumn of 1936, he noticed that despite his every expectation, his name was not on the promotion roster. Undaunted, he asked for intervention from his friend Paul Reynaud, who spoke to the minister of war and national defense. The minister retorted that de Gaulle's service record did not warrant a promotion. At this, de Gaulle indignantly fired off his record to the minister: three wounds, five escapes from German prisoner-of-war camps, and a series of considerable risks taken throughout his years of service, from the Great War to Poland and the Middle East.

Not long after, Charles de Gaulle's name was put on the promotion roster. He would become a full colonel the following December.

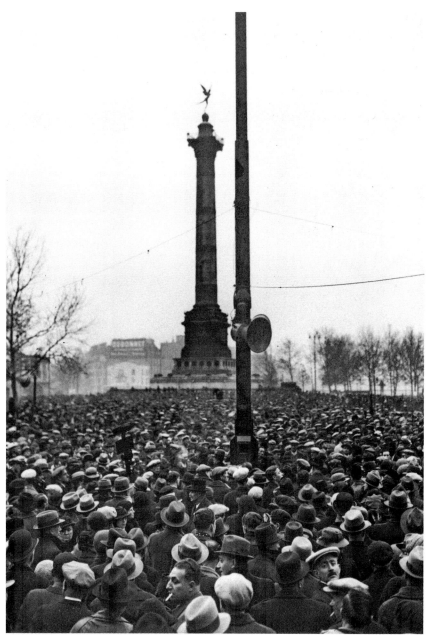

A crowd at the Place de la Bastille, Paris, listening to a speech by Léon Blum at the time of the funeral of Roger Salengro, the Popular Front's minister of the interior (November 1936). © Tallandier / Bridgeman Images

CHAPTER ELEVEN

~

End of the Dream

(1937)

Things were not going well. Not for France in general, and certainly not for Léon Blum and his Popular Front. Against a background of unrelenting economic deterioration, a poisonous atmosphere of hate had enveloped Paris—even as war continued to rage in Spain, where Stalin, Hitler, and Mussolini were flexing their muscles in what could only be understood as a preview for a far larger conflict.

The Popular Front's attempts to revive the economy by eliminating unemployment had proved a failure, with any gains in wages eaten up by higher prices, even while the necessity of rearming France—in response to its increasingly belligerent neighbors—had only added to inflationary pressures. Early in the year, Blum had attempted to appease the right with his so-called "pause" in Popular Front reforms, along with a cut in public expenditures; but even though this meant the abandonment of reforms such as retirement for older workers and national unemployment funds, it failed to gain him either time or trust with the Popular Front's foes. By June, when capital flight once again threatened the franc's stability, his government requested emergency powers to end speculation. But after the Senate—fearful of tax increases— twice blocked this bill, and with support in the Chamber of Deputies rapidly evaporating, Blum concluded that he could no longer govern effectively. On June 21, he resigned, after having been in office scarcely over a year.

Now, with the economy in increasingly desperate straits, a new and more conservative government extended the "pause" and once again devalued the franc.

⌒

Adding to the general sense of malaise was the atmosphere of animosity that was turning politics combative and making everyday life nasty. Not only had the working class soured on Blum and the Popular Front, but Blum and his entire cabinet were working under a barrage of lies and smears from the right—a barrage that in November 1936 brought Blum's minister of the interior, Roger Salengro, to suicide after an onslaught of false claims that he had deserted to the enemy in World War I. Salengro had in fact been captured by the enemy, had behaved honorably, and had been harshly treated during his German incarceration, as a military commission established. But no matter—the press that hounded him, and the readers who avidly followed, claimed the court was rigged.

At the heart of this cry for blood was the fact that Salengro, a committed Socialist, had been an important force behind the Popular Front's social reforms as well as the right-wing leagues' dissolution, and in addition he had been one of the strongest advocates for providing meaningful aid to the Spanish Republicans. This was enough to establish him as a target for whatever lies and calumny his enemies could dream up.

Goaded by resentment against the Popular Front, and against Jews, Protestants, Freemasons, and foreigners in general, an ever-larger number of French in financial free fall were finding solace in the far right's crude certainties and blistering scapegoating. When face-to-face with those they had come to hate and fear as the enemy, social explosions occurred, such as the eruption in Clichy in March 1937.

Clichy, a working-class stronghold located just over Paris's northwest border, was already at the boiling point on March 16, 1937, when the PSF, the political party of Colonel de La Rocque (formerly his far-right Croix-de-Feu), decided to hold a rally there. Despite appeals by leading political figures in Clichy, Blum's government refused to ban this rally, on the grounds that the PSF was within its rights to hold it. This may have been the case, but nonetheless, by choosing this particular location, the PSF clearly was playing provocateur, and the outcome was exactly what it wanted: the police, unable to control the resulting mayhem, fired on the mob, killing five and wounding several hundred—a disaster for which the PSF gladly blamed its leftist opponents. Blum's former allies, the centrist Radicals—anxious to retain middle-class support—were just as happy to pin responsibility on those further to their left. Blum, blamed by the Communists for being soft on fascism and, even more horribly, for being "the assassin of Clichy workers," was caught in the middle, even as he was trying to appease his opponents with his "pause" in Popular Front reforms.

Not surprisingly, he was devastated by this turn of events. Quite unexpectedly, the shooting at Clichy had "sounded the death knell of the Popular Front."[1]

～

Strikes now broke out, especially on the extensive construction site of Paris's upcoming International Exposition of Arts and Technology in Modern Life, which was scheduled to open around the Eiffel Tower on May 1, 1937. Blum and his cohorts had envisioned the exposition as a paean to the Popular Front and its vision of the future. But following the Clichy shootings, the CGT immediately called a general strike for March 18, which included about one-third of the twenty-five thousand workmen at the exposition site, plus many more in work connected with the exposition's construction. These strikes continued and even accelerated when workers learned that the Popular Front's public works program had been terminated, leaving many of them in the lurch once their current employment ended. As a result, the exposition opened three weeks late, and even then much of it was still under construction.

Three years later, Hitler would have himself photographed on the terrace of the Palais de Chaillot, posing in triumph before the Eiffel Tower. But that still lay in the future, and now, on May 24, 1937, Léon Blum stood in the same spot to inaugurate this latest of Paris's universal expositions. The Palais de Chaillot had been built specifically for the occasion, and despite discouraging news from at home and abroad, cries of "Vive Blum! Vive Lebrun!" burst from enthusiastic crowds lining the quays as Blum and President Lebrun crossed the Trocadéro Gardens and boarded riverside launches to view the pavilions, which stretched along the Seine and around the Champ de Mars and Eiffel Tower.

The exposition's theme was that of public works and technology rather than the promotion of French luxury trade, as the 1925 exposition had been. On this occasion, modernist French artists such as Robert Delaunay, Sonia Delaunay, and Raoul Dufy were commissioned to design and paint huge frescoes for the Palace of Air and Railroads, the Palace of Discoveries, and the Palace of Light and Electricity (Dufy's huge La Fée électricité is now on permanent display at the City of Paris's Museum of Modern Art).

Elsa Schiaparelli also drew considerable attention with her contribution to the pavilion of the Syndicat de la Couture, which had annoyed her with its strictures. Forced to use what she called a "hideous wooden mannequin," she laid the offending body down naked, "as the factory had delivered it," and piled flowers over it "to cheer it up." She then stretched a rope across

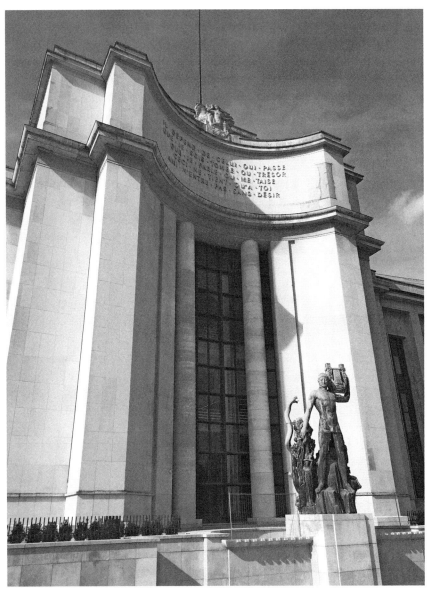

Palais de Chaillot, from the 1937 Paris International Exposition. Hitler famously posed here in 1940. © J. McAuliffe

the space above and, "as after washing-day, hung up all the clothes of a smart woman, even to panties, stockings, and shoes." Much to her satisfaction, a gendarme was required to keep back the crowds.[2]

These, and others, were attention grabbers, but historically, none was more important than Picasso's contribution to the Spanish pavilion—his legendary mural, Guernica, created in the aftermath of that historic Basque town's annihilation. This atrocity, planned by Hermann Göring, commander-in-chief of the Luftwaffe, as a birthday gift for Hitler, was also intended to test the Luftwaffe's ability to annihilate an entire city and crush its citizens' morale. Casualties and deaths (largely of women, children, and the elderly) were intentionally maximized, and both the Führer and his henchmen were thrilled by the results.

The Spanish Republican government had already commissioned Picasso to paint a mural for its pavilion at the upcoming Paris exposition when Guernica was bombed to extinction. Picasso had not yet chosen his subject, but now he began to work along the lines that the barbaric act inspired. Still a committed pacifist, he decided to omit any references to the Communist fight against Spanish fascism, such as the raised arm and fist, and focused instead on the deeply personal tragedy of the annihilated town. "I know I am going to have terrible problems with this painting," he told his current mistress, the photographer Dora Maar, "but I am determined to do it—we have to do it for the war to come." Later that year he also declared that "artists who live and work with spiritual values cannot and should not remain indifferent to a conflict in which the highest values of humanity and civilization are at stake."[3]

Uncharacteristically, Picasso now welcomed fellow artists and influential politicians into his atelier to watch him paint this particular work, on the grounds that it needed to be publicized on behalf of the antifascist cause. But its reception at the exposition itself was far from enthusiastic. The French press, even L'Humanité's Louis Aragon, virtually ignored it, while the Spanish officials in charge of the pavilion greatly preferred another far inferior painting, which they tried to substitute in its place. Le Corbusier commented that most visitors were repelled by Guernica, and Luis Buñuel even confessed to being one of these: "I can't stand Guernica," he later admitted—"[its] grandiloquent technique as well as the way it politicizes art."[4] As for the far right, it paid little attention; after all, Action Française and other rabid anti-Communists had already circulated their own version of the facts by claiming that it was retreating Communists rather than fascist planes and bombs that had destroyed the town.

Guernica would in fact sear its way into the souls of subsequent viewers and become one of the most moving and powerful paintings of this or of any century. But its first reception, at the Paris 1937 world exposition, was hardly what Picasso had hoped.

～

The two pavilions that dominated the 1937 Paris exposition were those of the Soviet Union and Nazi Germany. Perhaps these were what Fernand Léger was thinking of when he critiqued the event as being a "horrendous exhibition of the banal put on a pedestal."[5] The ultimate in kitsch, these towering stone structures, which faced one another, were capped in turn by a pair of male and female workers holding aloft a hammer and sickle (on behalf of the U.S.S.R.) and by an enormous eagle (Hitler's architectural claim to domination). The Soviet Union's outsized presence was not nearly as startling as Germany's, which was the outcome of a conscious effort on the part of the exhibition's planners to include Germany in the festivities—this, on the assumption that Germany's presence at this peaceful gathering would encourage Hitler to behave appropriately on the international stage. Since peace was understood to be the reward for mollifying Hitler, Germany managed to push the exposition's decision makers to the limit, seizing not only a prime spot for the enormous German pavilion, but also the exposition's agreement to buy a wide range of German products for a number of sites, including a German planetarium for the Parc d'Attractions. All this for Hitler, but nothing for German refugees, whose plea for a pavilion on their behalf met with an abrupt refusal.

Fewer visitors attended this world's fair than any that Paris had held before, and among those sightseers who successfully navigated the unfinished pavilions and the mud and puddles (it had been a cold and rainy spring) were more than a few who could contrast it with the extravaganza the Nazis had pulled off at their annual Nuremberg party rally only a few months before. This particular rally had celebrated Hitler's takeover of the Rhineland; but, much as the others, it had featured days of over-the-top celebration, highlighted by a rousing display of 120,000 men marching in perfect synchronization under a sea of Nazi banners. The French ambassador to Berlin reported that foreign visitors were inevitably seduced and conquered by the sheer energy and joy of the festivities, "without perceiving the sinister realities hidden behind the deceptive pomp of these prodigious parades." And Elliot Paul noted, with obvious dismay, that Hitler had quite effectively managed to convey that same spirit to the German pavilion at the 1937 Paris exposition: "As Hitler had intended," Paul wrote, "the bourgeois French were impressed and began to whisper that the Führer was, after all, looking after his own and to express quite freely the wish that France had such a man."[6]

⌒

Early in the year, Ernest Hemingway at last committed to go to Spain as a war correspondent for the North American Newspaper Alliance (NANA)—marking his first return to journalism since the early 1920s.

He was not as yet politically committed to the Spanish Republicans, being strongly in favor of keeping the United States out of the fray. "The Spanish war is a bad war, and nobody is right," he told his friend Harry Sylvester in early February. "All I care about is human beings and alleviating their suffering which is why [I] back ambulances and hospitals."[7] And so Hemingway worked that January on a documentary film, *Spain in Flames*, which graphically portrayed the plight of the Spanish people. He also joined with John Dos Passos, Archibald MacLeish, and Lillian Hellman to raise funds for a second documentary film, *The Spanish Earth*, before embarking in February for Spain, via Paris.

It was not an easy journey. Heading south from Paris, Hemingway was repeatedly stopped at the Spanish border by French border patrols. He finally resorted to taking an Air France flight to Barcelona and Valencia, where he acquired official transport to Madrid. There, he found accommodations at the grimy Hotel Florida, which would serve as headquarters for much of the press throughout the war. From this base, he was able to travel (via a succession of drivers) and write dispatches about nightmarish scenes of military struggle and civilian disaster on the city's outskirts.

Hemingway was already well established in Madrid when Martha Gellhorn showed up, having trekked across the border on foot, with rucksack and typewriter. Infuriatingly, he greeted her with, "I knew you'd get here, daughter, because I fixed it so you could."[8] In fact, he had done virtually nothing on her behalf, and she knew it. Still, despite this disastrous beginning, their affair bloomed in the erotic wartime setting of Spain and the Hotel Florida.

Madrid was under daily attack by Franco's artillery, and food and gasoline were in short supply, but Hemingway enjoyed a privileged status as a famous author and never lacked for amenities—a fact that, along with his irritating superiority, did not endear him to his companions. These by now included Dos Passos, who was there along with others who were filming *The Spanish Earth*. Despite Hemingway's ostensible concern for humanitarianism, he tangled with Dos Passos over the film's emphasis, wanting to emphasize the military side of the war, while Dos Passos wanted to stress the plight of the common people. The Soviet writer Ilya Ehrenburg, who also was on the scene as a war journalist, decided that Hemingway was "attracted by danger, death, great deeds."[9]

But forty-five days in Spain were enough for him. After visiting the war's major fronts and accompanying the filmmakers as they followed the Loyalist infantry, Hemingway returned to America via Paris. He told reporters waiting to interview him in Paris that he needed to leave in order to revise the first draft of his next novel, *To Have and Have Not.*

One of Hemingway's stops during his four-day layover in Paris was at Sylvia Beach's Shakespeare and Company, where he had agreed—under protest—to give a reading from one of his short stories. Beach had clinched the deal by talking the English poet Stephen Spender into giving the reading jointly with Hemingway, who refused to appear in front of an audience by himself. Even as it was, Hemingway was pretty drunk by the time he arrived and mumbled his way through his comments and reading. Afterward, he declared that he would never again read in public, not even for Sylvia Beach.

While Hemingway's love affair with Martha Gellhorn continued to sizzle (she accompanied him back to New York via Paris), other couples were also enjoying themselves. Picasso and Dora Maar had opted for a summer in the idyllic setting of Mougins, in southern France, where they were joined by several other couples: Man Ray and Ady, Paul Eluard and Nusch (whom Eluard had married, after his divorce from Gala), and a surprising new addition to the group—Lee Miller, who now was paired with Man Ray's good friend, the Surrealist artist, collector, and critic Roland Penrose.

Miller had just returned to Paris after an absence of five years, and Penrose, who glimpsed her at one of those over-the-top Parisian costume balls that marked the summer of 1937, was struck by her beauty and asked his good friend Man Ray for an introduction. One thing quickly led to another, and whether or not Miller was yet divorced (accounts vary), Penrose certainly was free of his first wife, and the two soon joined the other lovers in the sun of Mougins. Man Ray's deep distress over losing Lee Miller seems to have calmed after Ady entered his life, and the news that his divorce from a long-forgotten wife back in America had at last been finalized added to his well-being.

And so, only a short distance from the carnage just across the Spanish border, these four couples enjoyed their summer idyll. Though, while there, Eluard was sufficiently mindful of current events that he did compose his poem "Victory of Guernica" in honor of Picasso's painting.

〜

Le Corbusier had a secret lover—an American, Marguerite Tjader Harris—who was young, athletic, and gorgeous. She was also an heiress who had left her husband and settled, with her young son, in Switzerland. There she first fell in love with the house that Corbu had built for his parents on the shores of Lac Leman. From there, she and Corbu's mother became friends, and Marguerite soon met Corbu when he visited. Would he consider building a house for her in Switzerland? she asked, with the warning that her finances had taken a deep dive during the Depression.

Nothing came of the house project, but the two remained in touch for the next two years until Corbu arrived in New York on his 1935 U.S. tour. Marguerite, who by then was living in Connecticut, drove into the city to meet him and took him to the top of the Empire State Building, the Chrysler Building, and the RCA Building, where he could view the city from above. They rode the subway to Wall Street and to Harlem and then finished this grand day by driving to Connecticut, where they spent a blissful night in a small cabin on Long Island Sound.

It was more than a fling: for years afterward, this enchanted night would remain a treasured reminiscence for them both, and they would continue to correspond until—a decade later—they met again.

In the meantime, Corbu was depressed. He was fifty years old, and no one anywhere was building the kind of cities he advocated. Turning to Marguerite, as always, he wrote of his frustrations, including the difficulties he had encountered in trying to build his pavilion for the 1937 Paris exposition. Only when Léon Blum learned that all of Le Corbusier's proposals had previously been rejected did the architect receive some necessary funding and a spot for his pavilion.

Corbu wrote his mother that he intended to create "something strong, commanding, healthy, convincing. A battlefield, it goes without saying," and his pavilion opened to exactly the controversy that he invited. It was huge and covered in boldly colored cloth held by vertical pylons anchored with steel cables. Inside, an airplane hung from the roof, high over Corbu's latest plan for the city of Paris—one that left the city's major monuments intact but added huge skyscrapers on the periphery. His pavilion was "the boldest thing you can imagine,"[10] Corbu exulted, but this hardly endeared it to most of its visitors.

Despite the controversy, Corbu was admitted to the Legion of Honor that summer, although that, too, was mired in controversy: he had turned down the invitation on several previous occasions. Now it seemed a prudent shift, as he wanted to emphasize that he was not anti-French, as his enemies declared, especially after his recent speech at a conference held by the French Communist party.

Still uncommitted in politics, Le Corbusier was, as always, committed to himself.

Christine Renault—the much-younger wife of the wealthy auto manufacturer—had a secret lover, the writer Pierre Drieu La Rochelle, who had recently published a thinly disguised version of their relationship in the guise of a so-called Persian romance (his novel *Beloukia*).

Drieu, a decorated veteran of the Great War who once embraced communism, had by now left this well behind and—influenced by the heady spectacle of the Nazis' 1935 Nuremberg congress—was finding Hitler and fascism far more enticing. By 1937 Drieu was a stalwart member of Jacques Doriot's PPF, a supporter of Franco, and a proponent of French fascism.

Unlike Christine's elderly and notoriously crotchety husband, Drieu was tall, handsome, and (despite some who disparaged him) established as an intellectual in certain circles that counted. Christine considered herself an intellectual and was ripe for flattery. She was also rich and attractive. Their affair lasted a decade, and whether or not Louis Renault was aware of it, the connection between his wife and Drieu La Rochelle would in the end prove dangerous for him.

Jean Cocteau was never at a loss for lovers, and that autumn, the handsome young actor Jean Marais entered his life when Cocteau was testing actors for his *Oedipe-Roi*. Cocteau had recently returned from a reenactment of Jules Verne's *Around the World in Eighty Days*, which he wrote up in serial form for *Paris-Soir* (even with the modern-day advantages of air travel, he had thrillingly "just made it" within the required eighty days). Cocteau had the audacity to dedicate this lightweight travelogue to André Gide, whose chilly reception to Cocteau during the early years of his career Cocteau never forgot.[11]

At the time, Coco Chanel (who created the costumes for *Oedipe-Roi* as well as for Cocteau's 1930s *La Machine infernale* and *Les Chevaliers de la Table Ronde*) was still paying Cocteau's rent and bills, including his expensive detox cures during a time when his opium addiction was at its worst.[12] Jean Marais snagged Cocteau's admiration and a major role, in that order, and soon he would begin his ascent to stardom. But it turned out that Marais had a lot more going for him than good looks: he was also a fine actor and, in time, sufficiently strong as well as sensible to be the kind of partner that Cocteau so badly needed—in particular by insisting that Cocteau get off drugs.

But that still lay in the future, and in the meantime, Cocteau was having a bad decade, even while he was enjoying the companionship of yet one more beautiful young man.

Josephine Baker was ready for marriage. After toying with several possible husbands, she settled on a dashing twenty-seven-year-old Frenchman, Jean Lion, who flew his own plane, drove fast cars, and was reputed to be rich (he was partner in a sugar brokerage). Josephine, who by now was thirty-one, yearned for the legitimacy that she thought a white husband would give her; even more, she yearned for a baby. For his part, Jean had political ambitions and thought that Josephine's popularity could help him; in any case, Josephine's money certainly wouldn't hurt. And so, that November, they were married. The probability that Josephine was still married to Billy Baker did not seem to disturb her. "Home, children . . . those are the things I am looking forward to now," she told the press.[13]

The groom's entire village turned out for the wedding, including his parents, who were not thrilled with their son's choice of a bride but were dutifully supportive. Jean and Josephine made a handsome couple, but the marriage was a disaster from the start. Jean made the rules, spent Josephine's money, and filled her house with his relatives, especially his mother, who took charge, while he continued to see other women. Josephine tried for a time to play at contented domesticity, and even pretended to be pregnant—and then pretended to have lost the baby. But no one who knew her was fooled. There never was a baby, and Josephine's marriage was a shambles.

Soon she received her French passport, and soon after that she hit the road again, performing in London on the first portion of her so-called farewell tour and then heading for South America. But Josephine had asked that her household statements be sent to her, and when Jean visited her in Brazil, she called him a thief. While still in Brazil, she filed for divorce.

For over a year, Henry Miller's relationship with Anaïs Nin had been falling apart. He had followed Nin to New York in 1935 and stayed for several months, during which she had ended her affair with her psychiatrist and returned to Paris, via Algiers. Miller also returned to Paris, where he worked on *Tropic of Capricorn*, while Obelisk Press in 1936 published his collection of essays under the title *Black Spring*, which he dedicated to Nin. Miller told his friend Brassaï that *Black Spring* "revealed more about him than anything else he had ever written," so much so that he had even contemplated titling it *Self Portrait*.[14]

Miller increasingly focused on *Tropic of Capricorn* as his relationship with Nin deteriorated. "The differences separating Henry and myself are becoming more marked," Nin noted in her diary in the spring of 1936. "Differences in personality, habit, books, and even differences with regard to writing itself." She had grown weary of bohemian life, which she had never really enjoyed, and had wearied of the grotesquery and vulgarity with which Miller surrounded himself. Moreover, she was tired of Miller's cynicism, which she viewed as a lack of human feeling: "The Spanish Civil War, hunger, fear, misery, bombings—nothing seemed to touch him," Brassaï wrote, "so long as he could still use his typewriter." George Orwell, who spent an afternoon with Miller in Paris en route to the Spanish Civil War, was similarly struck by the totality of Miller's pacifism. Miller had a low opinion of both communism and fascism and was terrified of war. "If I am out of step with the times," he wrote a friend, "OK, I *want* to be out of step with these times. I want to be alone, if necessary, rather than with these pigs."[15]

Nin did not mind the obscenity in Miller's writing, but she did mind his absence of emotion and his obsession with sex, especially in its most depersonalized form. She had come to see Miller's depictions of women as completely exploitive and thought that "your depersonalization is leading you so far, you are disintegrating so much that it all becomes sex, and sex is a hole, and after that death. Oblivion."[16]

Soon Nin fell in love with a Peruvian newspaper critic and, with him, became entranced with Marxist politics. But that only lasted briefly, during which, as during her long relationship with Miller, she maintained her marriage. As June once remarked, Nin would never leave the wealth and security that her husband provided to marry Miller.[17]

In the meantime, a young Englishman by the name of Lawrence Durrell had appeared on the scene and immediately won Miller over by telling him what he adored about *Tropic of Cancer*. "I love its guts," he wrote Miller. "I love to see the canons of oblique and pretty emotion mopped up; to see every whim-wham and bagatelle of your contemporaries from Joyce to Eliot dunged under." Miller replied that he was the first "who's hit the nail on the head," and soon he, Durrell, and longtime Miller friend Alfred Perlès were having "the time of their lives." As Perlès later put it, "we were intoxicated with one another."[18]

Shutting out those who did not add to his enjoyment of life, Miller continued to be only minimally willing to come to the aid of his ailing parents and his destitute first wife. For the first time in his life he was making real money; but despite this, he argued that he was still an impoverished writer suffering for his art.

⌢

That autumn, Jean-Paul Sartre was at long last appointed to a teaching position in the Paris area, which finally allowed him to join Simone de Beauvoir on a permanent basis. "No more train journeys, no more hanging around on station platforms," Beauvoir later wrote. Instead, they moved into separate rooms in a quiet Montparnasse hotel that Sartre had discovered. Sartre lived one floor above Beauvoir; "thus we had all the advantages of a shared life, without any of its inconveniences," she explained.[19] Their almost-shared home was located on a back street near the cemetery, only a few blocks from the heart of Montparnasse.

By now, Sartre had received word that his novel, which would appear as *La Nausée* (*Nausea*), had at last been accepted by Gallimard for publication, after an initial rejection that the editor-in-chief later told him had been a misunderstanding. Sartre's short story "Le Mur" was also published that summer in the *NRF*, creating something of a stir. Gide called it "a masterpiece" and added, "I haven't been so pleased in a long time over anything I have read. Tell me who is this new Jean-Paul? It seems one can expect a lot from him."[20]

While *La Nausée* was the story, in journal form, of the protagonist's gradual confrontation with the essential uncertainty of his own existence, and his inescapable freedom—and responsibility—to create a meaning for his own life, "Le Mur" was a vivid description of three men facing a firing squad in the Spanish Civil War. It related directly to Sartre's own personal dilemma of whether or not to help a friend (Jacques-Laurent Bost) who wanted to fight for Republican Spain and had asked for Sartre's help, via a contact, to get into the action. Sartre realized that he should respect Bost's individual freedom of choice, but agonized over the possibility that Bost might end up wounded or killed, leaving Sartre feeling personally responsible. When Sartre finally made the contact that Bost requested, André Malraux himself jumped in and contacted Bost directly. After asking how familiar the young student was with machine guns (absolutely not), Malraux informed him bluntly that the Republic needed trained men, not raw recruits.

Bost stayed home, and Sartre's existential dilemma was solved.

Charles de Gaulle was less concerned about Spain than he was about Germany when he received temporary command of a tank regiment (the 507th) that July, with full command in September. Headquartered in Metz, a garrison town on France's border with Germany, this regiment showed its stuff that November to a group of dignitaries, including the town's military governor and—most importantly—Edouard Daladier, then France's minister of war. "I shall never forget the sight," a longtime de Gaulle friend and supporter later recalled. "Eighty tanks coming at full speed and with a thunderous roar to the Place d'Armes at Metz, headed by the tank *Austerlitz*, from which there emerged Colonel de Gaulle. The crowd, at first stupefied, burst into applause."[21]

But the dignitaries were far from pleased. A "monumental sourness" seeped from the platform, and Daladier in particular looked out of humor, with his hat pulled down over his eyes. De Gaulle had rattled off a showy challenge, but he had yet to persuade the powers like Daladier; the 507th remained under the command of the infantry.

Yet despite opposition from within and without his division, de Gaulle as always persevered, giving his regiment the characteristic motto, "Always more!" Now known as "Colonel Motor," de Gaulle led his two battalions (one each of light and medium tanks, amounting to about one hundred "fighting engines") on maneuvers and exercises to test the vulnerability of the Maginot Line. "One has to see [the tank] maneuver, fire, overwhelm and crush, among people who are on foot or on horseback or in cars," he wrote Paul Reynaud in October, "to understand that its coming is a revolution in the form and the art of war."[22]

Basic to de Gaulle's tank maneuvers was his assumption, then viewed as heretical, that the Maginot Line was indeed vulnerable. Also basic to his maneuvers was his knowledge of the astonishing progress that the Third Reich was making with its panzers, which the Nazis were taking no pains to hide.

～

That autumn, twelve writers in the *Left Review* (including Louis Aragon, W. H. Auden, Stephen Spender, Tristan Tzara, and Nancy Cunard) announced in print that it was time for all English-speaking writers and poets to declare whether they were for or against "the legal government and the people of Republican Spain." Asserting that ivory tower detachment was no longer an option and that it was "impossible any longer to take no side," they bluntly included a questionnaire with their declaration.[23]

The overwhelming majority who responded to this challenge supported the Loyalists, but James Joyce was not among them. Irritated, he testily telephoned Nancy Cunard. "No!" he told her, "I won't answer it because it is politics. Now politics are getting into everything."[24]

Joyce's life at present was divorced from politics and revolved around his *Work in Progress* [*Finnegans Wake*] and his daughter, to whom he paid weekly visits. He still was hoping to publish the book by his birthday (February 2) in 1938 and was working until late at night to meet this arbitrary but all-important deadline.[25] Nighttime was significant to him, especially for this book, which he now described as representing a third of human life—the dream life of the night portion. Moreover, he added, it represented the shifting nature of dream life, with the sounds of words. Responding to a visitor who asked if *Work in Progress* was a "blending of literature and music," Joyce replied, "No, it's pure music." Similarly, he wrote his daughter: "Lord knows what my prose means," and added, "In a word, it is pleasing to the ear."[26]

But to young Samuel Beckett (of whom Joyce grudgingly granted, "I think he has talent"), Joyce said, "I have discovered that I can do anything with language I want."[27]

⌒

Late in the year, Gertrude Stein learned that she and Alice would have to move from their longtime residence at 27 Rue de Fleurus to make way for their landlord's son. It came as a shock, especially to Gertrude, who did not like any unpleasantness; but Alice, as usual, managed to shield her from the stress and labor of the move (complete with 130 paintings). Their new apartment was on Rue Christine, a back street near the Seine, and just around the corner from the Rue des Grands-Augustins studio of Gertrude's longtime friend and sparring partner, Pablo Picasso.

Unlike Joyce, Gertrude Stein had no problem with making political pronouncements, and her pronouncements were heading ever further rightward, in tandem with her friendship with Bernard Faÿ. Although Stein never attended a fascist rally or joined a fascist organization, her opinions—which she dispensed with her customary authority—had become noticeably unfriendly to liberal democracy. Her recent time in America convinced her that Franklin D. Roosevelt had led the United States into a "real catastrophe," and a series of articles she wrote for the *Saturday Evening Post* described the New Deal as "profligate and paternalistic." She had no patience with "liberals that is intellectuals, the kind of people that believe in progress and understanding," and the Popular Front, as far as she was concerned, was simply the latest and most egregious manifestation of political and social decay. As she wrote a friend in 1937, "Disguise it to yourself as you will the majority does want a dictator, it is natural that a majority if it has come to be made up of enormous numbers do, a big mass likes to be shoved as a whole."[28]

⌒

"Gertrude was a real fascist," Picasso told the young American G.I. and future biographer James Lord, shortly after the war. "She always had a weakness for Franco. For Pétain, too. Can you imagine it?" On the other hand, Picasso had unkind words for Gertrude's no-longer friend Hemingway as well. "I never cared for him, never," Picasso told Lord dismissively. "He never had the true understanding of bullfights the way a Spaniard understands them. He was a phony, Hemingway." As for Fitzgerald, "All the rest of us always liked [him]. He was the one we all thought had the real talent."[29]

By this time, Fitzgerald had metaphorically risen from the dead and was now working in Hollywood under a lavish thousand-dollar-a-week contract for MGM.[30] That summer he met the glamorous gossip columnist Sheilah Graham, and the two soon moved in together. Writing for Hollywood may have been degrading for Fitzgerald, but it certainly paid the rent, and then some—allowing him to pay for Zelda's care and his daughter Scottie's schooling (she would soon enter Vassar) while carrying on with his own rejuvenated life. When Hemingway traveled to Hollywood that summer to raise money for the Spanish Loyalists by showing *The Spanish Earth*, the two met up—eliciting Fitzgerald's wire: "The picture was beyond praise and so was your attitude." The attitude, as Fitzgerald explained to Max Perkins, had "something almost religious about it."[31]

Hemingway had already spoken to a capacity crowd at the Second American Writers' Congress, held at Carnegie Hall in New York, and was about to participate in a showing of *The Spanish Earth* at the White House, thanks to Martha Gellhorn's friendship with Eleanor Roosevelt. He returned to New York in time to proof the galleys of *To Have and Have Not* and was preparing to return to Spain when he unfortunately encountered Max Eastman, whose "Bull in the Afternoon" review had been galling Hemingway for four years.[32] "What do you mean, accusing me of impotence?" Hemingway roared. Eastman denied it and challenged Hemingway to read what he had actually said. Infuriated, Hemingway slugged him, and the two grappled and fell, with Eastman on top. Startlingly, Hemingway regained his temper almost immediately, but lost it again when the press reported Eastman as having bested Hemingway.

Now it was Fitzgerald's role to express sympathy for Hemingway. "He is living at the present in a world so entirely his own," Fitzgerald wrote Perkins, "that it is impossible to help him, even if I felt close to him at the moment, which I don't." Still, he added, "I like him so much . . . that I wince when anything happens to him, and I feel rather personally ashamed that it has been possible for imbeciles to dig at him and hurt him."[33]

Hemingway and Gellhorn returned to Spain that autumn to find that Franco now controlled two-thirds of the country and was about to launch another assault on Madrid. There, they inspected several sectors and fronts in the war, much of it by foot and on horseback, cooking over open fires and sleeping in a truck. Winter had already arrived in the mountains when *To Have and Have Not* appeared, receiving mixed reviews, although *Time* magazine put Hemingway on its cover, including him in the front rank of American writers. Even in the midst of war, Hemingway followed the reviews and sales figures closely.

He and Martha celebrated a quiet Christmas in Catalonia, even as Pauline reached Paris unannounced, trying to save her marriage. Although she thought Martha was still in Spain with Ernest, Martha had already embarked for New York, and Ernest appeared in Paris before Pauline's visa for Spain was ready. Amid a gloomy scene of quarreling over Martha, the two left for New York, with Hemingway awash in anger and self-pity.

At the American Writers' Congress that summer, Hemingway had told the capacity crowd that "no true writer could live with fascism," and added pungently, "Fascism is a lie told by bullies."[34] Much like Nancy Cunard and other leftist writers in Paris, he had concluded that an aloof middle ground was no longer viable.

But it was a far more complicated situation than Hemingway acknowledged or perhaps yet even realized. By this time there were virtually two wars going on in Spain, one between the Loyalists and Franco's forces, which the Loyalists were losing, and the other among the Loyalists themselves, where the Moscow-directed Communists were conducting what amounted to a reign of terror against those they deemed insufficiently devoted to the party line.

In addition to the Loyalists' military setbacks and internal strife, a social tragedy was playing out as thousands of refugees seeking safety from Franco were starting to stream over the border into France. Although an international appeal went out to save the Basque children, some of whom were relocated to safety, the majority of Spanish refugees were herded into dismal

camps along the French border. In Paris, it became a point of honor for workers to agitate and strike on behalf of the Loyalists, and Parisian children of
sympathetic families saved money for milk for the Spanish children; but as
well intentioned as all of this was, it did little to help what was rapidly turning into a major social as well as military and political disaster.

⌒

Even while Parisians were flooded with bad news from abroad, they had a
growing set of worries at home. That September, bombs went off near the
Arc de Triomphe, destroying two buildings that headquartered France's
employers federations and killing two policemen standing guard. The right
was quick to blame the left, and Blum personally, for providing a climate
conducive to violence; but it turned out that the actual culprits were a group
of homegrown fascists known as the Cagoule (the "hooded ones"), who had
taken a page out of every revolutionary playbook by trying to put the blame
on the Communists, with the aim of convincing right-wingers and the military that it was time to take over. Playing provocateur did not work in this
instance (several of the Cagoulards were soon arrested, and many more in
December), but other secret far-right societies and gangs continued to work
underground, playing provocateur and spreading rumors of an incipient
Communist coup. This only added to the general edginess throughout Paris
as winter drew near.

Adding to the distress, that winter brought a return of hard times as a
new wave of economic depression hit the West, resulting in a drop in production and an increase in unemployment—everywhere, at least, except in
Germany. A surge of Paris strikes and factory sit-ins that began in autumn
accelerated that December, and when the minister of the interior, Marx Dormoy, sent in troops to break it up, the strike movement spread throughout
the Paris region, bringing it to a standstill by year's end with a general strike
of public services.

Dormoy's resulting unpopularity with the left was all the more notable
because he had been the moving force behind the breakup of the fascist Cagoule (a fact that would cost him his life a few years hence). But Dormoy, who
had taken over as minister of the interior after Salengro's suicide, had been
in charge during the Clichy shooting, with its resulting stain on his reputation. During the autumn and early winter of 1937, maintaining public safety
and rule of law in the face of an increasingly unsettled and angry public was
becoming overwhelmingly difficult. And, fearing Cagoulards as much as Communists, a small but growing group of Depression-weary French were beginning
to look beyond France's borders for an answer to their country's problems.

⌒

Jean Renoir was not among those who were wringing their hands. Although unhappy about the failure of the Popular Front, he had other things to think about. For one, his son Alain was now in his teens and was proving as unreceptive to school as Jean himself had been, having skipped enough classes at his *lycée* to be expelled. Whatever Jean thought, he did not reproach Alain—he had memories of his own school experience, which had not been a happy one—but instead sent him off to get some work experience at the Joinville studios of Pathé films. He then gave Alain his first motorcycle. For the record, Jean Renoir's idea of parenting may have been unconventional but was hardly disastrous: after more than his share of adventures, Alain would eventually receive his PhD in English literature at Harvard and become a distinguished professor of medieval English literature at the University of California at Berkeley.

But that still lay well in the future, and in the meantime Renoir—who had just been admitted to the Legion of Honor—had a multitude of plans in mind. In early 1937 he took time to write and record the French commentary for *Terre d'Espagne* (*The Spanish Earth*), which Hemingway was doing in English. And he continued his efforts to get *La Grande Illusion* into production. For several years he had been looking for someone to produce this film, largely because he was so exasperated at the way in which most war themes were treated. "Except for *All Quiet on the Western Front*," he later stated, "I had not seen a single film giving a true picture of the men who did the fighting." As a former soldier (he had fought in the trenches until he was wounded and then became a reconnaissance pilot), he wanted to avoid the usual clichés. Instead, his chief aim was the one he had been pursuing ever since he began to make films: "to express the common humanity of men."[35]

Basically an escape story, *La Grande Illusion* grew out of tales of life in prison camps, where men of entirely different social backgrounds had to live in close quarters with one another. The film took its final shape when Erich von Stroheim arrived in France, interested in resuming his acting career. Stroheim (who was no more an aristocrat than was Renoir, despite his airs) had reigned for a time in Hollywood, as both a silent film star and director. But his autocratic behavior, his insistence on total artistic freedom, and the exorbitant cost of his films had at length put an end to his career there. Renoir had always admired Stroheim as a director but understood the difficulties of working with him: "From the first," Renoir said, recapping Stroheim's early career, he "showed himself to be extravagant, dictatorial and a genius."[36] And Stroheim was no less so on the set of *La Grande Illusion*, where at first he behaved so intolerably that Renoir burst into tears. Here was Renoir's idol, who was partly responsible for his being in the film business, and Renoir was shattered by what he saw.

Stroheim in turn was so distressed by Renoir's response that he, too, had to wipe away some tears, and after that their friendship was sealed. Stroheim promised henceforth not to fight Renoir's directions, and according to Renoir, he kept his word. Renoir reestablished his direction over the film, and the outcome was everything he had hoped for. Jean Gabin once again starred, this time as a working-class officer (Renoir admired Gabin so much that he lent him his own wartime aviator's uniform to wear in the film). Pierre Fresnay played the role of an aristocratic French career officer who finds much in common with the prison camp's aristocratic commander, played to the hilt by Stroheim.

Despite the stereotypical sound of these roles, Renoir was not interested in stereotypes; he wanted to create individual human beings undergoing the experience of war. The story he chose to tell was one of prisoners and escape, each prisoner characterized by class and yet completely unique. According to Renoir's friend, the critic André Bazin, "the grand illusions are the illusion of hatred, which arbitrarily divides men," as well as "the illusion of boundaries, with the wars which result from them, [and] the illusion of races, of social classes." According to Renoir, "men are less separated by the vertical barriers of nationalism than by the horizontal cleavages of culture, race, class, profession, etc."[37] In the face of this, *La Grande Illusion* chose to show the fraternity and equality of human beings.

Germany and Italy banned *La Grande Illusion*, but the French and English-speaking public loved it, giving Renoir his first taste of truly popular success. But this scarcely marked the end of his troubles. In June, Renoir began working on *La Marseillaise*, originally titled *La Révolution Française*.

Originally this ambitious enterprise was supposed to receive significant government support, but after the "pause" and the Popular Front's subsequent demise, Renoir found that once again he had the usual lack of funds to deal with. In addition, given the subject, he faced a barrage of political opposition, which burst into print once *La Marseillaise* came out in early 1938. He had made the king too nice, the leftist critics carped, while the right complained that he made the rabble too pathetic and not sufficiently despicable. Once again, Renoir had tried to portray the complexity of human beings, whom he viewed as being inherently nuanced. Moreover, for Renoir, each person had some redeeming quality, and he wanted to discover it.

The times were not receptive to this kind of generosity.

~

That spring, Malraux returned from lecturing in America on behalf of the Spanish Republic to work at a furious pace on his next novel, the powerful *L'Espoir* (*Man's Hope*), a paean on behalf of those fighters for the Spanish Loyalist cause. *L'Espoir* takes the reader from the outset of the Spanish Civil War to the battle of Guadalajara in March 1937, a Loyalist victory, and elicited rare praise from André Gide, who told Malraux, "You have never written anything better; nor even as good."[38] At the end of the story, all hope is not lost, but by the time the book appeared in November, hope for the Loyalist cause had receded dramatically. Still, Malraux was already on to the next thing, envisioning a film version of his novel.

While Malraux's *L'Espoir* was selling well, Eve Curie's biography of her mother, also published in 1937, was en route to becoming one of the best selling biographies ever written. Published simultaneously in France, England, and the United States (with an English translation by Vincent Sheean), it was an instant hit, especially in the United States, where the American Library Association chose it as the best nonfiction book of the year and the Literary Guild made it its December 1937 selection. The American Booksellers Association bestowed its National Book Award on Eve, who received numerous other awards and forms of recognition. Criticism that she had carefully omitted any specific mention of her mother's affair with Paul Langevin would not surface for many years.[39]

Not surprisingly, Hollywood took an interest in the Marie Curie story, and Universal Studios soon bought the film rights, envisioning Irene Dunne as Marie. But then, as tales of Hollywood film rights often go, Universal sold the property to MGM, which decided to star Greta Garbo and enlisted a total of eighteen writers, including Fitzgerald and Aldous Huxley, to adapt the screenplay for her. In the end, Garbo's departure from MGM and the onset of war sent the production in yet another direction, and Greer Garson would eventually win the role, with Walter Pidgeon replacing Spencer Tracy, the studio's first choice for Pierre Curie, due to a scheduling conflict.

Throughout this saga, the entire effort to reach the big screen was hindered, if not directly undercut, by Irène Joliot-Curie, who had not been informed by her sister of the sale of film rights, and who in any case objected strenuously to Hollywood's intrusion upon what Irène viewed as sacred ground. Irène was appalled at the idea of her mother's life appearing in film and was especially opposed to the idea of Greta Garbo playing the role. Putting her foot down, she refused to cooperate with the film's researchers.

"And . . . when [Irène] refuses," wrote one of those who spent time in Paris researching the script, "it is as if the Rock of Gibraltar were to refuse."[40]

By this time, Irène and Frédéric were working separately in the frontiers of nuclear physics, with Irène at the Sorbonne and Frédéric at the Collège de France. Both, who strongly believed in the positive possibilities for artificial radioactivity, were coming close to discovering nuclear fission but did not get there in time. When three German scientists officially became the first to make this discovery in 1938, Irène and Frédéric's daughter, Hélène, remembered hearing her parents say regretfully that, if only they had worked together, they could have been the ones to make the discovery.

In the meantime, Eve was enjoying the fruits of celebrity as well as of her own remarkably good looks. Many considered her to be one of the most beautiful women in Paris, and she now found herself on the A-list for exclusive parties as well as on the December cover of French *Vogue*, wearing a dress by Schiaparelli.

It was difficult to imagine two more different sisters.

The year closed on a somber note, as death and dying pervaded the news and individual dramas were played out in private. Léon Blum, who was already having a difficult year, was in addition suffering from the decline of his critically ill second wife, whom he had married in 1933 following the death of his first wife. Thérèse Pereyra Blum was part of the group of musicians and painters with whom Blum thoroughly enjoyed associating, and he loved her dearly. But already, as the year came to a close, there was every indication that Thérèse Blum would not make it through another month, let alone another year.

That November, Count Harry Kessler, whose humanity and deep love for the arts had endeared him to friends in France even after his participation on the German side of the Great War, died after a long illness and was buried in the family tomb in Père-Lachaise. Kessler's strong opposition to Hitler had forced him to leave his home in Germany, and he had suffered an exile's fate during the last years of his life amid declining finances and health.

Although some faithful friends, including André Gide, attended the funeral service, none of the artists whom Kessler had supported throughout the years—most notably Aristide Maillol—were among them. Gide in fact was "greatly astonished not to see in the church, nor later to accompany the body to the cemetery, any of the painters and sculptors whom Kessler had so generously helped during his life."[41]

The pastor's sermon was on the "great wound in Europe," and the obituaries praised Kessler as a representative of a Europe that was already disappearing, in the face of rising hatreds and preparations for war.

⌒

Maurice Ravel remained true to his music to the end: his last known letter—typed for him, but signed by himself—was a missive to the Swiss conductor Ernest Ansermet concerning a performance of Ravel's Concerto for the Left Hand. In it, Ravel politely but firmly criticized the concert pianist Alfred Cortot for playing the concerto (commissioned by the one-armed pianist Paul Wittgenstein) with *both* hands, which Ravel found unacceptable. He gave Ansermet some suggestions for alternative soloists and then signed off in "grateful friendship."[42]

Eight weeks later, on 28 December 1937, Ravel was dead, after a delicate brain operation that failed to save his life. "I still have so much music in my head," he had told a friend with anguish just a few months before. "I have so much more to say."[43]

Several years earlier, Ravel had told an interviewer that "his dearest wish would be to be able to die gently lulled in the tender and voluptuous embrace of Claude Debussy's *Prelude to the Afternoon of a Faun*, this 'unique miracle of all music.'"[44] This did not happen, although Ravel did not die alone. Instead, he departed this life in a Paris clinic, with his beloved brother, Edouard, at his side. It was and always had been a close-knit family, and Maurice now joined his much-loved mother and father in the family tomb in Levallois-Perret, where Edouard would eventually complete the family circle.

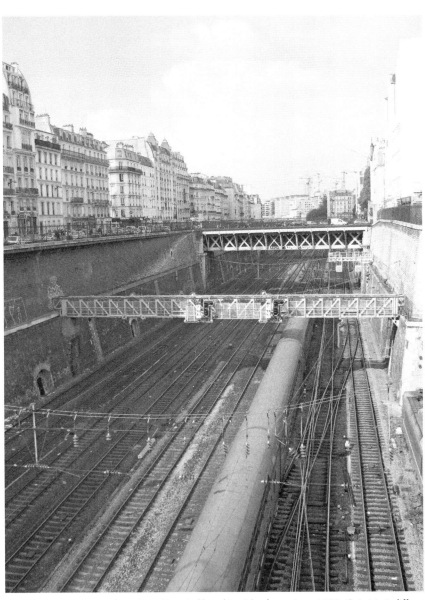

Gare Saint-Lazare, where Jean Renoir filmed La Bête humaine, *1938.* © J. McAuliffe

CHAPTER TWELVE

~

In War's Shadow

(1938)

"Everyone here wants to flee to America, away from wars and dictators," Sylvia Beach wrote her father during the waning months of 1937.[1] She was in a good position to know: Shakespeare and Company served as the nucleus of much of the English-speaking expatriate community, and Beach was privy to the gossip involving just about all of them. As she noted, many of those expats who had stuck it out so far were now leaving Paris, or thinking of leaving.

Beach was not among them. Increasingly a rarity in the expat community, she had made her permanent home in Paris and—despite rising difficulties and dangers—had no intention of departing. A few others were similarly inclined, including Samuel Beckett, who had returned to Paris in late 1937 with the firm intent to stay. Man Ray was another. Writing to his sister back in Brooklyn, Man Ray rhetorically asked, "Do you wonder why I stay in Europe?"[2] His answer was that it was there and only there that he was respected as an artist, not categorized as merely a photographer (this, despite the artistry he was demonstrating in this medium, and despite the fact that photography, and especially fashion photography, was providing him with quite a good living).

Still, despite his preferences, Man Ray was quietly putting aside some "pin money" in case he had to make a quick exit to New York, and others were giving careful attention to the same possibility.

After all, there were the increasing financial challenges of living in the City of Light, which was getting ever more expensive. Sylvia Beach in particular was feeling the financial strain. When Beckett returned to Shakespeare and Company, he immediately noticed that Beach had a "permanently worried look," as if she "had been battered against something."[3] Beckett was none too well off himself, but he was rightly concerned about Beach: despite all the readings and other measures to increase sales, she could not cover her rising costs. Shakespeare and Company had done well that autumn, but her rent and taxes were soaring. Worse yet from her perspective, many of her American and British readers had departed, and those remaining could no longer afford to buy books. The poet Bryher (who had recently inherited from her wealthy father) now set up a fund to assure monthly payments to Beach for the next several, difficult years, which provided Beach with a blessed financial cushion; but there was still much to worry about.

Among Beach's other worries, and the anxieties of those around her, was France's ongoing political instability, as well as the nation's growing social and economic unrest. As the year progressed, an even larger cause for apprehension came from abroad as the threat of war grew greater.

In January, while strikes continued to spread, France's governing coalition split into rival camps. Soon the governing coalition collapsed, although Prime Minister Chautemps managed to survive by cobbling together a new, more conservative ministry, which took virtually no action on anything as affairs on every front became steadily worse. In the midst of this inaction, the Chamber of Deputies did manage to vote itself a major increase in salary, even while unemployment was rising, production was declining, and the franc fell to new lows. The national treasury was practically empty when, on March 10, Chautemps at last resigned.

That was where matters stood when, on March 11, Hitler—taking advantage of this power vacuum to his west—marched his troops into Austria and, on March 12, declared the annexation (Anschluss) of the entire country. "The French are trembling and miserable," Sylvia Beach wrote her sister soon after, adding that she had been listening to BBC radio explain what to do during an air raid. She referred to Hitler and his ilk as "the Bullies," yet she, like so many others who had lived through the Great War, still longed for peace, even "peace at all costs."[4]

At the same time, Simone de Beauvoir was passing through what she later called "one of the most depressing periods of my whole life," in which she "refused to admit that war was even possible, let alone imminent." Even while the left was "foundering" and the fascist threat was growing, both at home and abroad, she was, in her own words, "playing the ostrich." After the

Anschluss, Sartre (again, in her words) "no longer could deceive himself: the chances of peace were now very slender indeed." But "for my own part I was still trying to delude myself."[5]

Yet Abbé Mugnier, now in his ninth decade and in frail health, was not deluded. He foresaw the future and was quietly in despair. "The German monster has swallowed Austria," he wrote in his journal on the evening of March 12. "It is a first tidbit, which will be followed by many others." And then, in a sad rhapsody to an Austria that he feared was now gone forever, he added, "Adieu! Adieu! The waltz, the music, the *café à la crème* that one drinks by the lakeside, adieu!"[6]

And where was France's government? Four days after the crisis began, Léon Blum was asked to form another government, and he met with all the leaders of the opposition, calling for unity, much as during the Great War. Blum made an emotional appeal, entreating the deputies of the opposition to join this political union to save the nation. But few were swayed by Blum's appeal to patriotism, and the great majority were contemptuous. Many were his longtime foes and were of the mind "Rather Hitler than Blum," especially since they were already contemplating a right-wing government that could avoid war by agreements with fascist Germany, Italy, and eventually Spain.

Transfixed by the Russian threat, most on the right still ignored the threat from Hitler and continued to sympathize with Mussolini, even while they continued to oppose and disparage Blum. Since early in the year, the far right had been calling for a dictatorship, or at least a strong government of national safety: "Never . . . has the necessity of a national revolution been so evident," cried the right-wing weekly *Candide*, while one of its editors, Pierre Gaxotte (a future member of the Académie Française), attacked Blum as "A Man Accursed" and fulminated that "he incarnates all that revolts our blood and makes our flesh creep. He is evil. He is death."[7] When German troops entered Austria, various figures and newspapers of the right and far right had this in mind when they called for national unity under "an incontestable national figure." This figure was not Blum, but Pétain.

Public discourse had reached new levels of nastiness, from workers to members of Parliament, and as Eugen Weber notes, "one scored and counted points, inflicted pain or, at the least, discomfort, in one long running battle" with one's fellow French. Yet despite the amplitude of animosity on all sides, it was clear that, as Weber put it, "the Right was the aggressor in this siege of hate." It had been boiling over ever since 1936, when the rise of the Popular Front had radicalized the traditional French right and galvanized a steady stream of resentment that had permeated the very atmosphere of France. More vindictive than fearful, members of this radicalized right "had been humiliated," Simone Weil observed, adding that, in "what was an unpardonable crime, [they had been] humiliated by those whom they regarded as their inferiors."[8]

In this insalubrious atmosphere, it was hardly a surprise that Blum's formation of a cabinet and attempt to govern lasted less than a month. In its place, a new government headed by Edouard Daladier soon put a definitive end to the labor and social reforms of the Popular Front. The working class was firmly reminded of its proper place—in a less bloody manner than with the Commune's demise in 1871, but nonetheless with the resolute objective of preserving the status quo.

The political right was on the move, reinforced by that spring's election of Action Française's brilliant founder and leader, the reactionary and ultra-nationalist Charles Maurras, to the Académie Française (this, after Maurras's eleven-month jail sentence in 1936 for threats against Blum and incitements to murder against the proponents of sanctions against Italy).[9] That May, the far right showed up in full force to commemorate Sainte Jeanne d'Arc with a great parade. Only a year before, the parade had been forbidden as a potentially dangerous manifestation of right-wing extremism; now, it took place with official blessing. The left, on the other hand, was as depressed as the right was newly motivated. Attendance this year at the traditional memorial services at the Mur des Fédérés was sparse, contrasting dramatically with only two years before, when attendance had crested above six hundred thousand.

That March, during the height of Hitler's Anschluss, five fully equipped panzer divisions had thundered into Austria. Three more of these divisions were being prepared in Berlin, but no single armored division was yet operational in France. Colonel de Gaulle was only too keenly aware of this disparity, and of the opposition he was receiving—especially from the French high command—to his remedy for what he saw as a dangerous imbalance between the two nations.

De Gaulle's ability to persuade the French high command was clearly limited and dwindling. Given this, and the dangers he feared for his country, he once again decided to reach out to the general public. In 1937, an opportunity to do so came his way when a publisher approached him for a book on the French army. At the time, de Gaulle was too busy with his Metz command to find time to write, but he did manage to locate an old manuscript that he thought might be of interest: it was a copy of his portion of a history of the French army, ghostwritten ten years before for Marshal Pétain, who at the time had set it aside after tangling with de Gaulle over authorship and control.[10]

The publisher, who knew nothing of the manuscript's history, was delighted, and de Gaulle signed the book contract in the spring of 1938—without informing Pétain or asking his permission to publish. In fact de Gaulle did not contact Pétain until early August, when the proofs were being corrected. Confronted with a fait accompli, Pétain exploded. De Gaulle, who seemed to have thought that Pétain could be persuaded to lift his embargo once the project had gotten this far, refused to back down, but Pétain was adamant, insisting that the work he had assigned de Gaulle was a staff study and that "this work belongs personally and exclusively to me"; therefore he "reserve[d] the right to oppose its publication now and in the future." He added that he found de Gaulle's attitude "most distressing."[11]

De Gaulle retorted that the book had been heavily revised and was his and his alone: "There no longer remains anything in these chapters of which it cannot be said with certainty 'This is by de Gaulle.'" Furthermore, de Gaulle was no longer willing to be a ghostwriter, even for Pétain: "In short, henceforward I lack both the pliability and the 'incognito' necessary for me to allow what talent I may possess in literature and history to be attributed to another." Nonetheless, de Gaulle conceded that he was willing to write a preface acknowledging Pétain's role at the book's inception. This elicited a surprisingly gracious reply from Pétain: "If, instead of confronting me with a fait accompli or what was about to be a fait accompli, you had taken the trouble to tell me about your plan, as you do today, no doubt I should not have answered your last letter with such a categoric refusal."[12] He then proposed a meeting.

The two met on August 28 at Pétain's residence. They were alone, and although in his first account (to an interviewer), de Gaulle stated that they parted in agreement, in a second version (to a subsequent interviewer), de Gaulle said that Pétain asked him to leave the proofs of the book with him, and de Gaulle refused. At this point, Pétain ordered him to hand over the proofs. De Gaulle replied, "Monsieur le Maréchal . . . you can give me orders in military matters, but not on the literary level."[13] And he left, carrying the proofs with him. It would be their last substantive meeting.

A week later, Pétain sent de Gaulle his draft for a dedication, which amounted to a list of the chapters for which he wished credit. De Gaulle ignored this and instead dedicated the book "To Monsieur le Maréchal Pétain, Who wished this book to be written, Whose advice guided the writing of the first five chapters, And thanks to whom the last two are the history of our victory." This seemed a reasonably graceful resolution, and certainly was as far as de Gaulle was willing to go. The dedication appeared in this form when the book was published in September.

La France et son armée, as the book was titled, received good reviews and sold well, although Pétain was still resentful about it. "He is an ambitious man," Pétain remarked of de Gaulle that October, "and very ill-bred. To a large extent I was the moving spirit behind his last book. He wrote it without consulting me and then did no more than send me a copy by post."[14]

While Pétain was giving this opinion of de Gaulle, de Gaulle at about the same time was sketching in his notebook his own impressions of Pétain—a series of observations culminating with, "More greatness than virtue."[15]

Despite the political turmoil and military danger, privileged members of Parisian society continued to carry on that spring and summer with their usual frothiness, occupying themselves with stylish fêtes and grand costume balls. The newspapers duly recorded that the celebrated master of the Paris Opéra Ballet, Serge Lifar, escorted Coco Chanel to a fête given by U.S. ambassador William Bullitt, who was renowned for his elaborate parties as well as for his impressive collection of French wine. Chanel also appeared in "tiers of white lace" at Elsie de Wolfe's first annual Circus Ball that July, at de Wolfe's Versailles villa.

Probably inspired by Schiaparelli's spring-summer Circus Collection, de Wolfe set up a striped canvas pavilion containing a circus ring, in which satin-clad acrobats and clowns performed to the accompaniment of several orchestras. It took three nights to install the lighting throughout the villa, the circus ring, and the garden (only nighttime would do for the installation, to properly judge its effects), and the guests—who were summoned to appear in formal wear—found the results "truly magic," as French *Vogue* enthused. "Imagine," it continued breathlessly, "a garden of indirectly-lit trees, green and white tents . . . a circus in the center of the lawn, salons trimmed with garlands of red roses and bouquets of strange flowers." Among the guests was Eve Curie, identified as a "writer and beauty," who wore pink tucked tulle.[16]

Schiaparelli had shown her Circus Collection the previous February, where it overlapped with the International Exhibition of Surrealism, which opened in Paris only a few weeks before. Schiaparelli's creations still evidenced Surrealism's heady influence, with amusing headgear in the shape of giant inkwells complete with quill pens, and brimless hats in the shape of nesting hens. There were also witty accessories such as spats worn as gloves and handbags shaped like balloons. Schiaparelli's circus theme was everywhere, from buttons shaped like prancing horses to evening jackets embroidered with elephants and acrobats. To make sure no one missed the point, a merry crew of circus performers raced up, down, and throughout the premises during her entire fashion show. It was a surefire hit, seducing the buyers from Fifth Avenue as well as Schiaparelli's own clientele, which now included the Duchess of Windsor and Helena Rubinstein as well as film stars such as Marlene Dietrich. Without question, everyone involved was trying terribly hard to show that, despite bothersome events at home and abroad, they were having a marvelous time.

Salvador Dalí unquestionably was having a marvelous time, tirelessly socializing with the elite when he wasn't painting, lecturing, or traveling. Gala was proving her worth as the "Cash Register," as Breton persisted in calling her, and the two moved that year to a larger and more elegant apartment in the upscale seventh arrondissement. He also starred in that year's Surrealist exhibition, which opened in Paris that January, with Man Ray calling it "without question" the "climax of Surrealist activity" and Simone de Beauvoir conceding that it was "the most remarkable event that winter."[17]

For the occasion, more than two hundred Surrealist works from fourteen nations graced Georges Wildenstein's usually staid gallery on the elegant Rue du Faubourg Saint-Honoré. Wildenstein had wisely stayed out of the way of this mass effort to shock, puzzle, and amuse, and Breton asked Marcel Duchamp to head up the affair. Duchamp, although never officially a Surrealist, occupied "unique prestige" among them (as Breton put it) and was happy to help design the exhibition. In turn, Duchamp looked to his longtime buddy Man Ray for technical assistance. Aiming for a Surrealistic environment, the two gleefully stripped the gallery of its red carpets and period furniture, blocked out the skylight with coal sacks (minus the coal), and lined the corridors with nude mannequins, each decorated by one of the exhibition's artists. Most of these opted for startling juxtapositions of objects and materials, but Man Ray left his mannequin unclothed, with only glass tears on her face and glass soap bubbles in her hair. Duchamp (who, typically, was absent for the opening) opted for an even more minimalist look and did not do anything to his mannequin except throw his coat and hat on it, as if it were a coatrack.

On opening night, the visitors—in evening dress, as requested—were handed flashlights as they entered the darkened gallery, trampled through mud and wet leaves brought in from Montparnasse Cemetery, and then were jolted by the sounds of hysterical laughter emitted by a hidden phonograph. Game for whatever they were about to encounter, the guests proceeded with nervous laughter until the lights once again went on to reveal treats such as Dalí's *Rain Taxi*, filled with spraying water and live snails.

Somehow, it all seemed quite fitting for this unsettling and unpredictable year.

⌣

The king and queen of England arrived in Paris that July amid a rousing welcome that belied the year's grayness: according to the *New Yorker*'s Janet Flanner, Parisians suddenly behaved "as if no one had a care in the world." Galas, fireworks, and floodlit monuments gave the city a festive look it had not had in years, and all of Paris plus a quarter of a million of out-of-towners crowded in to see the sights. "You could have walked till midnight from the Place de la Concorde to the Etoile on the tops of the immobilized taxis and cars," Flanner reported.[18]

But death and dying still hung heavy on the national consciousness. War remained on the horizon as Hitler—encouraged by the tepid response to his Austrian takeover—cast his eyes on Czechoslovakia's Sudetenland, whose pro-Nazi faction took the opportunity to demand autonomy and stir up trouble, prompting the Czech government to mobilize. Closer to home, the premature death of tennis star Suzanne Lenglen that July was regarded as "a national loss," as Flanner reported, much as if Lenglen "had been a general, or an *homme d'état*."[19] Less remarked was the death of André Gide's wife that Easter. Drawing a double black line in his journal to mark her death, Gide wrote in August, "Since Em. [Madeleine] left me I have lost the taste for life." He was devastated by her death, even though his first response was to note that his last sight of her "recalls, not her ineffable tenderness, but the severe judgment that she always felt obliged to pass on my life." Nonetheless, he wrote in his journal, "since she has ceased to exist, I have merely pretended to live."[20]

Perhaps at that point it was easier for Gide to forget that their marriage had been a complete mismatch in every way, and not only sexually: Madeleine had been a deeply devout provincial, resolutely fixed in home and place, while Gide, restless and inquiring, was quite the opposite. He was far more inclined to confide in the Petite Dame than in his wife, and after Madeleine's death, Gide told the Petite Dame that it was a blessing that Madeleine had died before him, so she would not have to undergo the "moral suffering" that the discovery of Catherine's parentage would have inflicted.

The Petite Dame knew Gide well enough that she suspected his memory of Madeleine would "grow stronger and, who knows?, she may come to occupy a larger part in his life than when she was alive."[21] And for at least a few months, she would be right.

Stravinsky's wife and daughter were both dying. His wife, Katya, had been battling tuberculosis for years, but his beloved elder daughter, Mika, had more recently taken ill with the disease and was rapidly growing worse. Katya would die in early 1939, but Mika did not make it through the year. And on top of all the death and dying, Stravinsky had mountainous doctor and sanatorium bills to deal with, which were ever more difficult to pay in the current political climate, what with concert engagements and commissions in decline.

He was not pleased with the Nazi exhibition of so-called "Degenerate Music" in Dusseldorf that May, which had followed the 1937 blockbuster Munich exhibit of "Degenerate Art" and included Stravinsky's *The Soldier's Tale* among its chief targets. Of course, Stravinsky—ever the White Russian and unapologetically anti-Bolshevist and anti-Semitic—had no problem with fascism per se, whether under the regime of Hitler, Mussolini, or Franco; but he felt unfairly victimized by what he viewed as a conspiracy by German musicians to make life difficult for him, and was especially alarmed by reports that he was still being described by the German press as Jewish.

Stravinsky performed in Berlin and Rome that year, with little evident concern for the politics of the situation, but he seemed relieved to have an American market to turn to, as with his Dumbarton Oaks concerto, which premiered in Washington, D.C., that May (with Nadia Boulanger conducting) and in Paris a month later. Critics were not pleased with the new work (Ernest Ansermet found it "desperately empty and boring"), but audiences loved it.[22] The neoclassicism of the 1930s was possibly in trouble, but listeners still preferred calm and clarity to the primitive beats of Stravinsky's prewar *The Rite of Spring*.

Nonetheless, *The Rite of Spring* still had possibilities, even in the late 1930s, although with a far broader audience than Stravinsky had ever envisioned. That autumn, Walt Disney unexpectedly contacted him about using *The Rite of Spring* for a sequence in a full-length animated cartoon—a sequence that Disney visualized as having something to do with dinosaurs.

Desperate for money, Stravinsky signed away all control over the music for six thousand dollars.

After *La Marseillaise* was released in February 1938, Jean Renoir began to move away from the Communist party. He had never been a party member, nor was his departure unfriendly. He simply stopped writing his column for the Communist *Ce soir* and turned away from political subjects for his films. It was not that he was any less antifascist, but the films he now wanted to make were not political.

That spring, while Renoir was still trying to finish *A Day in the Country*, he received a surprising offer to direct a film version of Zola's *La Bête humaine*, with Jean Gabin in the lead. Gabin was now a major star, and his love for trains had prompted the offer: as a child, he had dreamed of becoming a train engineer. In addition, Gabin looked forward to working again with Renoir. Renoir (now residing in a gated enclave in Pigalle) had previously lived in an apartment overlooking the train tracks behind the Gare Saint-Lazare, and he too had long been fascinated by steam engines. The outcome was Renoir's remarkable *La Bête humaine*, loosely based on the Zola novel, where the locomotive—named La Lison—becomes a major character. Voluptuously filmed as all curves and beauty as well as power, La Lison is irresistible, and Jean Gabin and his fireman, both of whom (after several weeks of preparation) actually drove and stoked the train, were in their element.

Receiving essential support from the SNCF (National Society of French Railroads) and the railroad union, Renoir transposed the story to 1938 and filmed the moving sequences on an unused stretch of track on the line from Paris to Le Havre, shooting from the engine at full speed or from an attached platform immediately behind. There was no trick photography for the speed, nor were there portable handheld cameras. Renoir's nephew Claude was attached to the side of the locomotive with his camera held in place by a wooden gizmo, and he almost lost his life when his camera became snagged in a tunnel and shattered.

Essentially a story of a murder on a train, a cover-up, and a woman who uses the man who loves her, Renoir turned *La Bête humaine* into a love triangle—not just between the stationmaster, his wife (played by the delectably lethal Simone Simon), and the engineer, but between the engineer, the wife, and the seductive train engine, La Lison. Now considered a precursor to film noir, Renoir began shooting *La Bête humaine* in August, and it came out just before Christmas at the Cinéma Madeleine, where it was an immediate hit.

But in the meantime, current events had embroiled the world in crisis, and Renoir by then was too preoccupied with real life to enjoy his hard-earned success.

Renoir ended shooting on *La Bête humaine* in late September, just as Hitler was massing troops on the Czech border and Czechoslovakia prepared for war. France in turn began to call up its reservists and mobilized almost one million men.

It would not have been a popular war, Janet Flanner reported, given that the political issues were too confusing. Still, she added, the French, "without enthusiasm, marched off in complete calm." A new war seemed inevitable, she concluded, but what was astonishing was the calmness of the French, "on the streets, in the churches, in the home, and even in the newspapers."[23]

Although there were reports of Parisians fleeing the capital in cars overloaded with everything their owners could pile into and on top of them,[24] others witnessed the resignation that Flanner had noted. Man Ray—who returned to Paris from vacation in the Antibes after deciding that "if worst came to worst, this is where I'd rather be"—found "no visible anxiety in Paris."[25] Instead, his friends continued to attend the usual round of parties and exhibitions. Colette, who had received a letter telling her that her auto might be requisitioned for military use, simply shrugged and told a friend that she and her husband were negotiating to write for *Paris-Soir* and that "everything would be splendid if human folly weren't hovering about our heads."[26]

But Henry Miller, although impressed with French fatalism and the way the French seemed to be accepting the possibility of war, was personally terrified of it and immediately set off for Bordeaux, intending to take a boat to America. "As long as I have two legs to run with I shall run from [war], and if necessary, I shall crawl away on all fours," he wrote at the time. As his pal Brassaï put it, "Miller thought heroism didn't mean marching straight ahead; it meant making a run for it." Convinced that Hitler would declare war at midnight on September 30 and that Paris would be bombed, Miller implored Nin to get out of the city: "I'm cured of Europe," he wrote her. (For the record, Nin went to Le Havre.) As for Miller, since there were no boats at the time leaving Bordeaux for America, he toured for a while until, after the Munich Agreement, he returned to Paris, "furious at the way in which Hitler was inconveniencing his life."[27]

Gide took a more measured approach. "Since the 22nd of September we have lived through days of anguish," he wrote in his journal, "and 'people' might be surprised not to find any echo of them here. But whoever concluded from my silence that I was indifferent to 'public affairs' would be greatly mistaken. . . . If I ceased to write anything in [this journal] during all that time, this is because [public affairs] filled my whole mind."[28]

If the threat of war prompted resignation rather than panic, the Munich Agreement of September 29 produced joy in the streets of Paris. Britain and

France had given Hitler what he wanted in return for "peace for our time," as British prime minister Neville Chamberlain put it. Hitler gained not only the German-speaking portion of Czechoslovakia but also de facto permission to help himself to the rest of the country, which the agreement had sheared of its defensible border, its fortifications, and much of its industrial capacity. Czechoslovakia was told, in effect, to put up or shut up—it could fight Germany if it wanted, but France and Britain would not come to its aid. Blind to the implications, most Parisians greeted news of the Munich Agreement with relief coupled with joy, welcoming returning Prime Minister Daladier in triumph. Léon Blum expressed this in a column he wrote shortly after the pact was signed: "War is spared us. The calamity recedes. Life can become natural again. One can resume one's work and sleep again. One can enjoy the beauty of an autumn sun."[29]

Sylvia Beach, who firmly believed that war was insanity, joined her Left Bank friends in supporting "peace at all costs," and Simone de Beauvoir was of a like mind. Jean-Paul Sartre was torn—not wanting another bloodletting like the Great War, yet worried about the consequences of appeasing Hitler. Beauvoir, however, thought that "anything, even the cruelest injustice, was better than war." The two had lived in anxiety for much of the September crisis, but then, according to Beauvoir, "the storm abruptly passed over without having broken, and the Munich Pact was signed." She was "delighted, and felt not the faintest pang of conscience at my reaction."[30]

The Communists were not among those who rejoiced, seeing this as one more victory for fascism and, quite possibly, a warning of what the Soviet Union could expect if the Western democracies and fascist Axis decided to collude at the U.S.S.R.'s expense. The Communists were the only members of the Chamber of Deputies to formally protest the Munich Agreement, although a number of progressive intellectuals, including Irène and Frédéric Joliot-Curie, were outraged. Earlier, Irène and Frédéric had written an open letter to Daladier demanding that no concessions be made to Hitler's demands, and soon after the Munich Agreement, Frédéric Joliot-Curie and Paul Langevin gathered a delegation to meet with French president Albert Lebrun on the subject. It did not go well, especially after Frédéric took the opportunity to accuse the minister for foreign affairs of "complicity verging on treason."[31] This prompted an outraged Lebrun to order the delegation from the room—although much to Frédéric's surprise, Lebrun later apologized and even conceded that Frédéric had a point.

Jean Renoir was also irate, although he expressed it with sarcasm. In his last weekly column for *Ce soir*, he asked, "Will our papers publish the pictures . . . of the nice jokes that the Nazis are certainly going to play on the Jews [in the Sudetenland]? Will we see again old men washing sidewalks with their knees in the mud? Or women forced to walk on the streets wearing ignominious signs around their necks? In short, will we again be indirect and distant witnesses to those jokes that the Nazis play so readily and with such finesse at the expense of those whom they have defeated?"[32]

Not surprisingly, Charles de Gaulle was also bitterly opposed to the Munich Agreement and what it signified. "Without a fight we are surrendering to the insolent demands of the Germans," he wrote his wife, "and we are handing our allies the Czechs over to the common enemy." Soon after, he stated, "France has ceased to be a great nation."[33]

And Prime Minister Daladier himself, in response to the crowds cheering him upon his return from Munich, turned to his aide and said, "Ah, the imbeciles! If they only knew what they are acclaiming."[34]

On Léon Blum's direction, the Socialists in the National Assembly—hitherto staunchly antifascist—abstained from a vote of confidence on the Munich Agreement, thus breaking with the Communists (who formally protested) and marking the end of any claim to a united Popular Front.

But the Popular Front had disintegrated long before this. Even prior to the Munich Agreement, Prime Minister Daladier had announced the easing of the forty-hour workweek, on the grounds that, under the current "delicate" international situation, national security required more productivity, especially in certain industries. As Elliot Paul bitterly put it, "Daladier, while the rest of the world was worrying about the Czechs, busied himself with the repeal of the labor laws and social reforms enacted under Blum and Blum-Chautemps."[35] After Munich, Daladier put France on a war footing, which increased an already-volatile situation among workers. This erupted in late November with a general strike, sparked by the official visit of Neville Chamberlain and Lord Halifax, both of whom bore the stigma of responsibility for the Munich Agreement, to which industrial workers—many of them by now Communist—strenuously objected.

Daladier acted promptly and severely, decreeing the military requisition of all principal railways and addressing the French by radio to state that he would use all means necessary to end the strike. From the standpoint of the employers, this was, as Simone Weil put it, their "battle of the Marne,"[36] and the drama surrounding the strike evoked an unmistakable aura of civil war. In one particularly tense confrontation, the workers at the extensive Renault plant in Billancourt, just outside of Paris, barricaded themselves in, leading to a battle between them and almost six thousand police and *gardes mobiles.*

Shots were fired, and workers threw bottles of sulfuric acid at the police, who used a battering ram from the back of a truck to break the factory's main door, through which they pumped tear gas. This ended the Renault strike, and the rest of the general strike fizzled away with it.

Renault was furious over his workers' latest insurrection and promptly fired more than two thousand of them, on the grounds that they were, or were suspected of being, Communists. When he got no push-back from this, he proceeded to double the dismissals, on the grounds that he was now receiving large government defense orders. Renault's nephew, François Lehideux, who had negotiated with the workers in the lead-up to the 1936 Matignon Agreements, was of quite a different mind-set: Lehideux now encouraged Renault to retire, or at least to modify the structure of his company, in the interest of doing a better job of handling problems among and with the workers. In particular, Lehideux recommended including worker participation in certain of the firm's activities, through delegates, and allowing loyal collaborators (workers as well as administrators who had been employed there for at least ten years) to become shareholders.

Louis Renault was adamantly opposed to this, as well as to Lehideux's recommendation that he associate his firm more closely, financially and technically, with one of the large American auto companies. Never, Renault emphatically told Lehideux, had he been "at the beck and call of a flock of ignorant shareholders." Nor was he about to get involved in what he viewed as "foreign entanglements."[37] Relations between Renault and his nephew now deteriorated, and Renault—in a black mood—took back complete control over the firm that he had founded three decades before.

Despite the fact that the Renault factories produced a large part of France's armaments, Louis Renault himself objected to war—had had enough of it—and was not at all enthusiastic about going back to producing tanks. What he objected to in particular was the government's role in pushing the larger industrialists into war production. In large part, his objection stemmed from the Matignon Agreements: Renault and many of his fellow industrialists feared a government that might at any moment produce another such set of agreements with labor, this time in the interest of national defense.

Léon Blum had tried to accelerate rearmament immediately following Hitler's Anschluss, but he had tied it to an economic program that included old-age pensions, family allowances, and a tax on capital. Despite an appeal to patriotism, this encountered huge opposition, barbed with crudely anti-

Semitic personal attacks on Blum himself, and led to the end of his brief second government and a shift to the right under Daladier.

But the effort to rearm continued under Daladier, with workers objecting to its potential for subjugating them, even while industrialists like Renault objected just as strenuously to its potential for government controls. At the same time, Renault and other right-wing industrialists were finding Hitler increasingly interesting, or at least worth talking to.

That March, shortly before the Anschluss, Renault traveled to Berlin to see that year's Berlin auto show and spoke with Hitler. What had drawn Renault to Berlin was not the German dictator but the new German Volkswagen, which he had come to take a close look at, hoping to pick up a few tips for his own new small car, the Juvastella. Nonetheless, while speaking with Hitler (through an interpreter), Renault remarked about his hopes for Franco-German friendship and his desire that there not be another war between their countries. To which Hitler is reported to have replied that all the talk of war was the fault of journalists, particularly French journalists: "They always have that word at the end of their pens."[38]

De Gaulle also had that word at the end of his pen and was lucky in his publication date: *La France et son armée* appeared in late September, during the height of the Czechoslovakian crisis—circumstances that certainly did not hurt sales and reviews of a book whose subject, in its author's words, "is France, suffering, fighting, and triumphing." He scarcely needed to remind his readers of the book's timeliness, "since great menaces are hanging over the mother-country once more."[39]

At the same time, James Joyce was on the final stretch of his *Work in Progress*, which had nothing whatever to do with politics or war. In part, this was a matter of defending the integrity of his own unique perspective, but it was also a hardheaded business decision: Joyce did not want *Work in Progress* to be banned in any country because of its author's supposed political bias, and Germany and Russia were already looking at him with suspicion. Still, despite Joyce's professed abstinence from politics in any form, he was no fan of Hitler or Mussolini, and he was not blind to what was going on. "I have written with the greatest sympathy about the Jews," he told one correspondent, and he was doing what he could to assist those who appealed to him for help to escape from Nazi-controlled lands. Making use of his connections in the French Foreign Office, he was able to assist several friends and relatives of friends, as well as about sixteen refugees, in their passage through France and eventual resettlement in England, Ireland, and America.

But chief on Joyce's mind during this difficult time was the necessity to complete his *Work in Progress*, whose title he kept secret up until the time the book was published (even the publisher was excluded from the secret until the last moment). That May, Joyce met for the last time with Sylvia Beach and Adrienne de Monnier at Shakespeare and Company for a publicity photo by Gisèle Freund, who was rapidly acquiring international fame (*Life* magazine was now publishing her photojournalism). Joyce detested photo shoots, and she promised never to bother him with such requests again; but the following spring, *Time* magazine asked Freund to take a color portrait of Joyce for its cover. Joyce at first resisted, but Beach recommended that Freund write him with her request, this time signing with her married name. For visa purposes, Adrienne had arranged a marriage of convenience for Gisèle with Pierre Blum, and after following Sylvia Beach's advice, Freund received an immediate acceptance as Madame Blum (Bloom): any connection to *Ulysses*, no matter how distant, always appealed to Joyce.

As late as September, Joyce remained indifferent to anything apart from his book, whether his daughter-in-law's breakdown or his own worsening health, and lay silently on the beach of Dieppe while the crisis in the Sudetenland escalated. But at last, unable to ignore the dangers any further, he and Nora hastened back to Paris to evacuate Lucia to a mental institution in La Baule in Brittany. Joyce and Nora were in La Baule awaiting Lucia when the Munich Agreement was signed, and although Joyce was more than a little scornful about the outcome—which he said amounted to giving Europe to Hitler—he was mostly relieved that he could return to Paris and finish his book without interference.

He completed it on November 13 and then collapsed in exhaustion, "as if all the blood had run out of my brain," as he told his friend Eugene Jolas. "I sat for a long while on a street bench," he added, "unable to move."[40] He had missed his earlier February 2 deadline, and then his father's birthday of July 4, but now—after some marathon proofreading (minus the usual assistance from Sylvia Beach)—he would have the manuscript in readiness for a birthday publication date of February 2, 1939. The book's title would be *Finnegans Wake*.

"They had better hurry [publication]," Joyce told a friend. "War is going to break out, and nobody will be reading my book any more."[41]

Sylvia Beach "never traded on her literary friendships," as her biographer has noted,[42] and this was as true of her friendship with James Joyce as it was of Ernest Hemingway. Despite the fact that she felt Joyce had wronged her—

something that she once confided to a close friend—Beach continued to revere Joyce's work and refused to disparage him, especially not in her memoirs (which she had begun to write, under the personal encouragement of Alfred Knopf, although she would not finish them for another twenty years).

By 1938, Beach had received honors in her own right, having been admitted to the French Legion of Honor in June. Still, business at Shakespeare and Company had dwindled to a trickle, and Beach was now dependent on the monthly charity of good friends like Bryher for survival. She was famous, and she had a wide circle of literary friends, but her lifestyle remained, of necessity, quite simple—a bicycle for transportation and an apartment that lacked even running water. That summer, she vacationed for the first time without Adrienne, living by herself in utmost simplicity at her rustic mountain retreat. There she mended from the migraine headaches that had dogged her since childhood, which only long periods of rest could cure.

Beach remained on vacation through September, but the Czech crisis finally drew her back to Paris, where the American embassy had stocked up supplies of essentials for those Americans remaining in Paris, in addition to making plans for their evacuation, should that turn out to be necessary. The Czech crisis also brought floods of refugees to Paris from France's border regions with Germany, and that autumn the City of Light began to acquire some of the characteristics of a refugee camp. Residents, meanwhile, continued to suffer from the falling franc, and hoarding began, especially of luxuries such as coffee and chocolate.

In the midst of this, Ernest Hemingway—now famous, and certainly well-off—returned that autumn to Paris and to Shakespeare and Company. There, as always, he held court, failed to return books that he borrowed, and took books without paying. Hemingway enjoyed his status as the center of attention and presumed that everything he chose to take was free. Despite this, Beach was "very fond of Hemingway," as she wrote her sister, "and accept him *tel quel* [as he is]." Unfortunately Beach's current assistant did not share in this opinion, and when she presented Hemingway with a bill for all the books he had taken, he erupted, telling Beach to "get rid of that female before you lose all of your pals." In response, Beach calmly informed her assistant, "Friends can have anything that they want. They do not have to pay." She then added, "Brentano's would *pay* for Hemingway if he would come to their shop!"[43]

She probably was right, but this generous approach was not helping her to pay the bills. Gertrude Stein was another who took advantage of Beach's kindness. Now that James Joyce was no longer a habitué of Shakespeare and Company, Gertrude and Alice now resumed their visits to the bookshop.

Gertrude, too, assumed that her lending privileges were free, but in return, she at least invited Sylvia to their new apartment on Rue Christine. Beach had the grace to accept the invitation.

Jean-Paul Sartre had emerged as a newly fledged literary success, and now he was becoming a literary critic. Simone de Beauvoir, on the other hand, was experiencing nothing but rejection for her work—although the reader who turned down her manuscript for Grasset wrote that her book "displays qualities which give reason to hope that you will one day write a successful book."[44]

In the aftermath of the Munich Agreement, Beauvoir was now sufficiently free from worry that she resumed work on a new novel, which she would publish in 1943 after what she termed "many modifications" as *She Came to Stay*—based on the complexity of the real-life ménage à trois between her and Sartre and two sisters, here combined as a single character. Her eyes "were not opened immediately after the Munich crisis," she later wrote: "far from it." In fact, after the crisis had passed, both she and Sartre found a new zest for life, and she developed an interest in fashion. Still, Beauvoir recalled, while she was "so laboriously conjuring this novel from the void . . . I became a different person. . . . Little by little I had abandoned the quasi solipsism and illusory autonomy I cherished as a girl of twenty." What happened? "History burst over me, and I dissolved into fragments. I woke to find myself scattered over the four quarters of the globe, linked by every nerve in me to each and every other individual."[45]

Others, especially Sylvia Beach's friend Bryher, were experiencing some of this same sense of history, connection, and responsibility. Bryher, who recorded 1938 as "the year of Munich, appeasement and shame," was now living in Switzerland, where she had been working since 1933 to help refugees from Nazi-dominated countries escape to safety. Although it was dangerous, she and a small group managed to smuggle out 105 persons. About sixty of these were Jewish, as she later recalled (she burned her notebook in 1940, when she expected the Nazis to invade Switzerland), and the rest "went into exile because of their moral beliefs." None of these could remain in Switzerland, which as a neutral country did not allow refugees to stay, although the Swiss authorities were "liberal about transit visas, so that many of my visitors could rest for a couple of days before going on." The Swiss also "allowed a number of students to finish their training at the Swiss universities," and these fortunate ones carried on with their studies, although under extraordinary pressures. Bryher was especially concerned about a group of medical students studying in Lausanne, whom she thought "would go crazy before their final examination because we all knew that they had no second chance."[46]

After six years of this, Bryher concluded that no one should have to work more than three years at such a task: "It is so distressing that in self-defense names have to turn into ciphers." But she had to keep working, "because we were so few." As for her fellow English, they merely turned aside. "The Right said, 'Wait and see' and the Left asked, 'What about our jobs?'"[47]

Denizens of the democracies of the West had put blinders on when it came to Hitler's Germany, and ambivalence, fear, and loathing reinforced this willful ignorance. Less than a month after Hitler stepped up his Jewish persecution with Kristallnacht (Night of the Broken Glass)—a massive pogrom that swept through Nazi Germany on the night of November 9—France signed a pact of nonaggression and mutual amity with Germany. At the same time, France was busy restricting the activities of resident aliens and aggressively hunting down illegal aliens, arresting and expelling them. The year had brought a surge of refugees into France, largely Jewish, and simultaneously had seen an explosion of anti-Semitism, precisely (in the words of Eugen Weber) "because old prejudices were stirred up by new fears."[48] Anti-Jewish demonstrations broke out in Paris and elsewhere during the Munich crisis, Jewish shop windows were smashed, and people of foreign appearance were attacked in the streets.

The closer the danger of war appeared, the higher the flames of anti-Semitism rose. Despite Pope Pius XI's September 1938 declaration that anti-Semitism was "inadmissible," many of the faithful ignored him. Gossip turned into conviction, and Frenchmen who under normal circumstances might have been cautiously skeptical now bought wholesale into the belief that—in addition to other slurs—the Jews, through their avid hatred of Hitler, were leading France into another war.

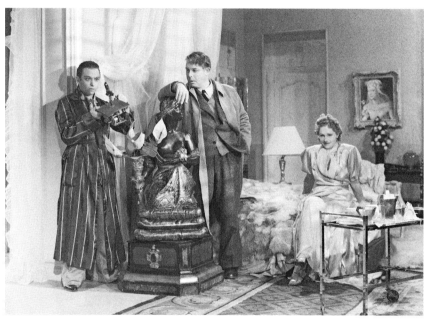

Marcel Dalio, Jean Renoir (center), and Mila Parely on the set of the film La Règle du jeu *[The Rules of the Game] by Jean Renoir, 1939. © Ministère de la Culture / Médiathèque du Patrimoine, Dist. RMN-Grand Palais / Sam Levin / Art Resource, NY*

CHAPTER THIRTEEN

~

Dancing on a Volcano

(1939)

" All the newspaper talk . . . is rot," Man Ray wrote his sister Elsie during the spring of 1939. "No one wants war here, and it's all a political game, like chess."[1]

March was beautiful that year in Paris, and Man Ray—an avid chess player—had gone back to painting, even while Hitler in his post-Munich mode was marching into Prague and helping himself to the rest of Czechoslovakia. Man Ray titled his huge work of that spring *Le beau temps* (*Fair Weather*), but the title's irony was unmistakable: the painting depicts a harlequin-like figure about to cross a bloody threshold into a dark landscape in which two savage beasts snarl and fight with one another. In his dealings with friends and family, Man Ray may have conveyed a lack of concern with current events, but all was not well in a world that he portrayed in so unsettling a fashion.

War loomed on the horizon, but virtually no one in France, and certainly not in Paris, wanted it. This led Janet Flanner to observe in early February that "the setup in Europe today is a struggle between the active and the passive"—the active being the fascist powers, the passive being France and England. This, despite the fact that Barcelona had just fallen to Franco, and its fall "has brought home to Parisians the closeness of the German flying field . . . from which Biarritz is ten minutes and Paris only three hours away by fast bomber's flight."[2]

Already, the unhappy denouement of the Spanish Civil war was changing the face of Paris, which—as Flanner had earlier informed her American readers—"is becoming more than ever a refugee camp." By early March—a month before Madrid sent up the white flag of surrender—she warned that "there has never been anything in modern history like the recent flight of the Catalonian army and civilian population into France." A multitude of roughly three hundred thousand Spanish soldiers, civilians, women, and children have fled across the border, "all hungry, exhausted, and in a panic." There, they were placed in concentration camps, whose miseries she vividly described. An international commission run by English and American Quakers, and aided by Swiss volunteers, was attempting to help refugee children, while a left-wing social relief network was sending food. But little could alleviate the suffering, in the midst of which "the discomfort and confusion for both French and Spanish have been bitter."[3]

Early in the year, André Gide confided to his journal that he was "obsessed by the thought of Spain's atrocious agony,"[4] but France's current leaders showed little signs of distress when they hurriedly recognized the Franco regime, dispatching Philippe Pétain as France's ambassador. The eighty-three-year-old hero of Verdun received an emotional send-off from his enthusiastic admirers, although Charles de Gaulle was unmoved by what he regarded as a pitiful and vain old man.

As ambassador, Pétain did succeed in his most important job, that of preventing an alliance between Franco and the Axis (Spain would remain a "nonbelligerent" throughout the war to come); but he unquestionably was aided in his mission by the trove of gold bullion that the Spanish Republic had deposited in the Banque de France, which the French now released on Franco's behalf.

Already, politicians on the right, most especially former premier Pierre Laval, began to court Pétain. Their first move was to propose that he stand for election to the presidency that spring. The very idea "horrifies me," Pétain wrote his wife,[5] but nonetheless he kept listening to those who wanted him to take power.

That March, France's Chamber of Deputies—shocked by Hitler's having broken his word, given in the Munich Agreement—voted full emergency powers to Prime Minister Daladier, including decrees that abrogated the forty-hour workweek for defense industries. This in turn caused Léon Blum to mutter, "There is nothing to be done with this Chamber. It has turned Fascist."[6] Abbé Mugnier, who was carefully following the news reports, was moved to think more and more on "Love one another" and "Thou shalt not kill." Simple enough mandates, he ruminated, but not easily achieved. And he admitted that he was becoming more and more worried.[7]

Abbé Mugnier found himself thinking in particular of the Franco-Prussian War of 1870–1871 and the Commune uprising that followed, the horrors of which had made him a quiet but earnest opponent of war. The Franco-Prussian War was especially on his mind that spring, having been the first of two military encounters between Germany and France within recent memory, and the one in which France was soundly beaten. France's victory in the Great War was all fine and good, but France had merely outlasted its enemy in a bloody slugfest, while in 1871, Bismarck had declared the formation of the German Empire from Versailles's Hall of Mirrors and had marched his troops in victory down the Champs-Elysées.

Early in March 1939, Abbé Mugnier—attending one of those elite soirées where his loveable and witty presence was much in demand—was asked by the newly minted Duke of Windsor (the former King Edward VIII of England) about his recollections of the Germans entering Paris in 1871. Mugnier, who had been a seminarian in Paris at the time, was conscious of the social niceties of speaking with royalty and simply told the duke about the Germans' uniforms and their music. He also related how the statue of Strasbourg in the Place de la Concorde was decorated with flowers; but he did not mention that, given France's loss of Alsace and Lorraine to Germany, the French would thereafter cover this statue in mourning until Armistice 1918. The subject of the Commune uprising then followed, with the former king wanting to know what Mugnier had seen of the bloody revolt. Mugnier summoned up memories of resupplying Paris following Bismarck's long siege and of the Place de la Concorde filled with police and reporters. The conversation turned to the sad destruction of the Château de Saint-Cloud on Paris's outskirts, and soon the storybook couple rose to go, after Mugnier thought he overheard the duchess mention to their hostess that they would enjoy having the delightful Abbé dine with them sometime.[8]

Emile Zola had been far more scathing about the events of 1870–1871 in his bluntly titled *La Débâcle* (published in 1892). "On the one side," he wrote, one saw "Germany with its discipline, its science, its new organization," while on the other, one saw "France, weakened, no longer keeping up with change, bound to make every mistake and making them in effect."[9] France, according to Zola, had not kept up with the modern world, had fallen into comfortable ruts, and was doomed to collapse in the face of such an enemy.

Charles de Gaulle, looking at France's army in 1939, had already come to much the same conclusion.

⌒

Elsa Schiaparelli in general avoided politics, but as an Italian, she was fierce when it came to Mussolini. "The fantastic rise of Mussolini filled me with fear," she wrote in her memoir, and during the tumultuous year of 1939, she went so far as to join the Solidarité Internationale Antifasciste. Yet Schiaparelli was far from abandoning fashion, and certainly not her role in it. Even on the eve of war, she could report with approval that "Parisian women, as if feeling it was their last chance, were particularly chic," enthusiastically following fashion crazes such as doll-sized hats and diamond fingernails.[10]

One of Schiaparelli's star clients, the heiress and socialite Daisy Fellowes, took the lead in what would be remembered as "Paris's Last Grand Season," a series of parties and balls that were given "feverishly" that summer, as Schiaparelli put it.[11] Despite—or perhaps because of—the clouds of war, these events were more lavish than ever. Elsie de Wolfe's second annual Circus Ball, held for seven hundred guests in the garden of her Versailles estate, was just as much an extravaganza as the first, featuring three elephants as well as exotic Lipizzaner horses that performed in jeweled harnesses.

An even more coveted invitation that season was to Count Etienne de Beaumont's Racine Ball, celebrating the tercentenary of Racine's birth. Beaumont asked his guests to come as characters from Racine's plays, or as one of his contemporaries, and Bettina Ballard, fashion editor of American Vogue, recalled that fortunes were spent on costumes. Maurice de Rothschild came as the Ottoman sultan Bajazet, with the Rothschild family's famous diamonds on his turban and a display of priceless Renaissance jewels on his sash. Chanel came dressed as La Belle Dame sans Merci and Schiaparelli as Prince Henri de Condé. Schiaparelli also designed the extravagant attire of the so-called Siamese Embassy, featuring several of that season's young beauties (including Eve Curie and Schiaparelli's daughter, Gogo). Bettina Ballard made the rounds of all that season's parties and remembered that she "danced until dawn, slept a few hours, made a token appearance at the office . . . stopped at the hairdresser's . . . and then I would start all over again."[12]

But Elsie de Wolfe and her cohorts were only the most extravagant manifestation of escapism that summer: July 1939 saw three million French go on holiday, whether to the mountains, the beaches, or the countryside. Many were roughing it and simply enjoying the fresh air, while others had the beach or a restful vacation of reading in mind. Those who could afford it brought with them the newly translated *Autant en emporte le vent* (*Gone with the Wind*).

⌒

While Paris was partying, Salvador Dalí was busy shocking—and making money at it. That spring, when in New York with Gala to promote his latest one-man show, he arranged to design two shop windows at Bonwit Teller on Fifth Avenue. In one, which he called "Day," a seedy-looking mannequin clad only in green feathers stood beside what Dalí called "a hairy bathtub" lined with black lamb fleece and filled with water. In the other, called "Night," an equally unappetizing mannequin slept on a black satin bed, pillowed on artificial live coals and canopied under a buffalo head with a bloody pigeon in its mouth.

Dalí believed that "this manifesto of elementary surrealist poetry right out in the street would inevitably arrest the anguished attention of passers-by with stupor,"[13] and he was certainly right. Crowds quickly gathered, and many of the passers-by were plenty anguished: Bonwit Teller was soon pummeled with complaints that Dalí's windows were "hideous" and "obscene." This prompted the management to quickly remove as much as possible from the offending displays, leading an outraged Dalí to demand that his work be restored or else his name be removed from the windows. When management refused, events quickly escalated, with Dalí managing to get inside the "Day" window, where he attempted to upset the tub of water. Unfortunately, it proved far heavier than he anticipated and, according to his account, it slipped against the window before he could stop it, crashing through the plate glass and sending shards of glass as well as cascades of water onto the sidewalk.

After an encounter with the police and several terrified hours in jail, on the charge of malicious mischief (later reduced to disorderly conduct, sentence suspended), Dalí met with a friendly judge who ruled that Dalí would have to pay for the window, but added that "every artist has a right to defend his 'work' to the limit."[14] The press had a heyday—"Through the Window to Fame" was one headline—and long lines now formed to see Dalí's gallery show.

He had gone after headlines and succeeded: he had grabbed attention and was rewarded—his paintings at the show quickly sold for large sums. It may have been difficult to shock the world every twenty-four hours, as he put it, but he was doing his best, and the rewards were great. *Life* magazine reported that Dalí, not yet even thirty-five, was now one of the richest young artists in the world.

⌒

"We are dancing on a volcano," a deeply troubled Jean Renoir observed—a view that he powerfully expressed in his 1939 masterpiece, *La Règle du jeu*

(*The Rules of the Game*). His dancers on this about-to-erupt volcano were the self-centered and capricious members of France's *haute bourgeoisie*, whose blindness and willfulness Renoir searingly portrayed, and whose responsibility for fostering the coming disaster he clearly recognized. "When I made *The Rules of the Game* I knew where I was going," he later said. "I knew the evil that gnawed at my contemporaries. My instinct guided me, my awareness of the imminent danger led me to the situations and the dialogue." And he was not alone: "My friends were like me. How worried we were!"[15]

Influenced by Beaumarchais's *The Marriage of Figaro* as well as by Musset's *Les Caprices de Marianne*, Renoir combined comedy and tragedy in an unsettling mix, in which husbands and wives, lovers and mistresses, act upon the premise that "love as it exists in society is merely the mingling of two whims and the contact of two skins," and (more famously) "Everyone has their reasons." As film historian Georges Sadoul has concluded, "*The Rules of the Game* is for the prewar era what *The Marriage of Figaro* was for the Revolution of 1789: the portrayal of a refined, oblivious, and decadent civilization."[16] Depicting a moribund age, in which love has little meaning and life can be brutally snuffed out in a moment, Renoir's dancers change partners with abandon until their world erupts with brutal suddenness—in a lengthy barrage of gunfire, as hunters gun down rabbits and death spreads across the screen.

To make this film, Renoir had formed his own production company, based on the success of *Grand Illusion* and *La Bête humaine*, and *The Rules of the Game* was both expensive and ambitious. He filmed at a château in France's hunt country, "a region of marshes," he later explained, "entirely devoted to hunting, a sport which I detest. I consider it an abominable exercise in cruelty." Complications immediately ensued, including the refusal of Jean Renoir's older brother, Pierre, to shoot on location for the length of time that Jean had in mind. This meant that, at the last moment, Jean had to take on the essential role of Octave. The length of time on location was typical of Renoir, who "works like a painter," according to one of his actors: weeks before a shooting, he would place his actors in the settings he had in mind for them, whether it was a printing factory, a locomotive, or a château in the country, so that their particular setting became natural for them. It required a large degree of commitment from his actors, but those who worked with Renoir felt it was well worth it. "What results!" this actor exclaimed.[17]

La Règle du jeu "is a war film," Renoir later observed, "and yet there is no reference to the war. Beneath its seemingly innocuous appearance the story attacks the very structure of our society." Yet despite this agenda, Renoir had hoped for a success; instead, it was quite the opposite—"a resounding flop," as he put it. The film premiered in early July to audiences that either understood nothing, or those that understood all too well and expressed their feelings vehemently. "The truth," Renoir said later, "is that they recognized themselves."[18]

On August 28, France's Ministry of Foreign Affairs blacklisted *The Rules of the Game* for giving an unfavorable picture of France. But the film was already a financial disaster, and Renoir went so far as to cut the scenes causing the most uproar (these were restored in 1959, with Renoir's approval). Today, it is recognized as a masterpiece, but at the time, Renoir was in despair, and his friends were worried about him. It was at this point that he agreed to film *Tosca* in Rome—Mussolini's Rome. But Renoir's friends, not realizing that he had no intention of glorifying Il Duce, were aghast. Even his longtime partner, Marguerite, did not understand.

But Dido Freire did. Dido Freire, who had been a virtual older sister and even mother to Jean's son, Alain, during his childhood, had quietly become close to Renoir while working as a script girl on *The Rules of the Game*. And it was Dido, not Marguerite, who accompanied Jean Renoir to Rome. Their stay was brief: on August 23, Hitler and Stalin did the unthinkable and signed a nonaggression pact. That, plus Renoir's new relationship with Dido, marked the end of his relationship with Marguerite, as with his friends in the Communist party.

Jean Renoir was not the only one who was shocked by the unimagined and unimaginable Nazi-Soviet alliance. All too many had fixed their hopes on the Soviet Union and expected that if war came, Hitler and Stalin would fight it out while the rest of Europe remained on the sidelines. Throughout the summer, the French and the British had continued their halfhearted efforts to form a triple alliance with Moscow, and then suddenly this hope disappeared. Poland's very existence—and God only knew what else—was now on the line.

"What a betrayal!" Charlotte Perriand wrote, adding, "Our world had come to an end."[19] Janet Flanner reported that, with grim fortitude, "the powerful Left labor union, C.G.T., has just declared itself against the surprising pact." Although the Communist dailies, *L'Humanité* and *Ce Soir*, clung to the Moscow line and hailed the pact (leading Daladier promptly to suppress them), "the French response in general has been summed up by the phrase, '*Nous sommes cocus* (we've been cuckolded).'"[20]

Jean-Paul Sartre and Simone de Beauvoir had just spent several "gorgeous" weeks in Juan-les-Pins when the news of the nonaggression pact reached them. They had earlier decided that the Soviet government, despite "goings-on" there, still "served the cause of world revolution" and "would line up with France and Britain" if Hitler was rash enough to go to war. Based on this assurance, and the conviction that Hitler could not possibly stand up to such an alliance, Beauvoir had blissfully hiked her way south to Marseilles, then traveled to Juan-les-Pins, where the devastating news "suddenly changed the whole balance of power in Germany's favor." The treaty, she wrote, "proved, in the most brutal way . . . that Russia had become an imperialist power like any other." As for Stalin, he "didn't give a damn for the proletariat of Europe."[21]

Sartre and Beauvoir returned to a divided Paris, where the right secretly, or not so secretly, preferred fascism to anything resembling another Popular Front, and where a substantial number of the left felt betrayed by Stalin. "The mixture of braggadocio and cowardice, hopelessness and panic, that we smelled in the air made us feel highly uneasy," Beauvoir wrote. "As we fell asleep each night our last question would be: 'What will happen tomorrow?' And when we awoke it was to the same mood of agonized anxiety."[22]

She and Sartre had already begun to gravitate from Montparnasse and the Dôme to the more chic Café de Flore in the Left Bank's Saint-Germain-des-Prés quarter, where they admired regulars such as Jacques Prévert, the poet and screenwriter, as well as others who belonged "in a vague sort of way" to the world of film or the theater. The Flore's regulars, according to Beauvoir, "were neither wholly Bohemian nor wholly bourgeois," and Prévert's "dreamy, somewhat inconsequential anarchism suited us perfectly." All that spring, as the world became more dangerous, she and Sartre frequented the Flore, although they never quite abandoned "the seedier and less predictable" regulars at the Dôme, and on Sunday evenings, they forsook the Flore's "chic, if bitter, haunts of skepticism" for "the splendid animal zest" of the Bal Nègre dance hall on the far edge of Montparnasse.[23]

All that spring and into the summer, as the world became a more perilous place, visions of the Great War kept recurring in Beauvoir's mind. "Anything is preferable to war," a friend had commented, to which Sartre replied, "No, not *anything*—not Fascism, for instance." Beauvoir hastened to explain that Sartre "was not naturally bellicose," but appeasement, he argued, "made us accessories to all of Hitler's persecutions and exterminations." At the time, Beauvoir found this line of reasoning repugnant: "What a contradiction in terms it was to condemn a million Frenchmen to death for the sake of humanity!" To this, Sartre retorted that "it was not a matter of humanitarianism or any other such moral abstraction: we ourselves were in peril, and if Hitler was not crushed, France would suffer . . . the same fate as Austria."[24]

In the end, Sartre convinced Beauvoir that war could not be avoided—largely on the grounds that if they did not take up arms against Hitler, one day they and all the French would be compelled to fight *for* him. What it came down to, she reluctantly agreed, was that there is no way to avoid political engagement, for "to abstain from politics is in itself a political attitude." Later, she found it impossible "to assign any particular day, week, or even month to the conversion that took place in me about this time." But although she still kept up hope that war would not, could not, happen, sometime during the spring of 1939, a great change took place, and she renounced her "individualistic, anti-humanist way of life."[25]

∼

The morning of September 1, Simone de Beauvoir read Hitler's demands in the newspapers and went to the Dôme, "unsettled and at loose ends." She had scarcely ordered a coffee before a waiter announced that Germany had declared war on Poland. Racing back to the hotel, Beauvoir located Sartre, who was about to make his regular visit to his mother in Passy. Beauvoir accompanied him, although she kept to a café during his visit with Maman. Passy was almost deserted, but along the *quai* she saw "an endless procession of cars crammed with luggage and children." The government had encouraged all Parisians to get out of town, and the roads leading south now were clogged with autos, piled high with belongings and (if the occupants were farsighted) containers of gasoline.

Back at their hotel in Montparnasse, she and Sartre hunted up his kit bag and army boots; the reservists had already been called up, and a general mobilization was about to go into effect—only months after the mobilization and demobilization of the previous autumn. At the Flore, people seemed cheerful enough, but in the corner, a woman was sobbing to herself. "Everywhere, underlying everything," Beauvoir wrote in the diary she began to keep that day, "a feeling of unfathomable horror."[26]

"Up and down the side streets," Elliot Paul noted, sand was being distributed for the roofs, in case of fire from German bombs, and the newspapers "contained new decrees about wearing gas masks."[27] The police stepped up their blanket policy of interning all German citizens or former citizens, despite the fact that most of these were bitter opponents of Hitler and, in the majority of cases, Nazi victims. Although people were queuing up for gas masks at various locations, Paul noted that no gas masks were available for children under two years of age or for foreigners. Everyone else, though, was required to carry one: Simone de Beauvoir noted that "tarts now wear gas masks on their beat."[28]

The next morning, September 2, Beauvoir and Sartre got up at 3 a.m. and made their way to the Gare de l'Est and Sartre's train to Nancy, where he was assigned as a meteorologist to the Seventieth Division. He kept repeating that as a meteorologist, he would not be in any danger; in any case, he was convinced that it would be a short war. And then his train pulled out, and he was gone. Beauvoir walked back to Montparnasse and noted the silence of the streets. Few cars remained in Paris.

And then came September 3. Time passed slowly for Beauvoir as news came of last-minute efforts in Berlin. "Hope is nonexistent," she recorded dismally. Walking over to see a friend, she noted that many Métro stations were shut and barricaded, and the headlights of the few cars still in Paris were painted blue. Workmen at the Dôme were blacking out its windows with thick blue curtains.

At 3:30 p.m., *Paris-Soir* announced that Britain had declared war at 11 a.m. and that France would follow at five that afternoon. "Despite everything," Beauvoir noted, "the shock is still tremendous." That evening at the Flore, people kept saying they didn't believe in the war, but "they looked pretty panic-stricken all the same."[29]

As war broke out, concierges throughout the Left Bank's Saint-Michel quarter "were working hard and arguing harder, trying to seal up their air-raid shelters and tape their windows," Elliot Paul noted. Street crossings were painted white so that pedestrians (and the rare vehicles still in Paris) could see them in a blackout, while the municipal pawnshop put out a call to those who had pledges in deposit, warning that all valuables were about to be transported to the countryside. "Every experienced Frenchman," he added, "knew that meant they would probably never be found again in any man's lifetime."[30]

The Louvre, however, had every intention of protecting its treasures; in a feat of breathtaking ingenuity and daring, it moved all of them out of Paris shortly before the war began. The museum, under the leadership of its deputy director, Jacques Jaujard, had carried out what amounted to a practice run the previous autumn during the Czech crisis, when it had moved its most precious items to châteaux in the Loire Valley and many others to the Louvre's basement (built as wine cellars for Francis I, Henri II, and Catherine de Medici, these had virtually bombproof nine-foot-thick walls). Jaujard, who had already supervised the removal of the entire art collection from the Museo del Prado in Madrid to Geneva during the Spanish Civil War, had been prepared for war with Germany as the Czech crisis escalated, and he and his curators had meticulously singled out what should be saved, in order of priority.

Among the first to be trucked away to safety that autumn of 1938 were the *Mona Lisa* and Leonardo's *Virgin and Child with Saint Anne.* Jaujard and his hundreds of staff carried out their rescue plan with split-second timing, getting the first-tier treasures packed and away in a matter of minutes, while others followed over the course of several days. It was a complex business: each item was wrapped in cloth to prevent scratching, then in wood shavings to cushion against shock, then in asbestos to protect against fire, and then in tar paper to protect against water. Then each was placed on wooden pegs in wooden cases, the pegs serving to prevent vibration.

After the Munich Agreement, everything came back again, but Jaujard—keeping an eye on Hitler—saved the protective wrappings and was ready for war when it came. Following the Nazi-Soviet Pact, Jaujard (now the Louvre's director) closed the museum, officially for repairs. When war broke out on September 3, the curators—supported by hundreds of staff and art students, as well as by skilled packers from the Samaritaine department store (whose head, Gabriel Cognacq, was a leading art collector and vice president of the Council of National Museums)—had been moving the museum's masterpieces away from Paris by night for a week.

The packers' task was daunting: the largest of the paintings (Veronese's *The Wedding Feast at Cana*), already elephantine in size and weight (two and a half tons, including frame), had accumulated considerable additional weight in dust over the centuries. Using Comédie-Française scenery trucks, the only ones big enough for the cargo, the curators got these giants out of Paris, although not without incident: *The Raft of the Medusa* got hung up en route on an electric tram line, short-circuiting the system and plunging an entire suburb into darkness. Taking due precaution with the other enormous evacuees, a squad of emergency workmen went ahead to clip telephone wires, then backtracked to restring them.

In another feat of ingenuity, the *Venus de Milo* and the *Victoire de Samothrace* (*Winged Victory*) were moved off of their pedestals via levers and pulleys, then wrapped, boxed, laid on their sides, and slid out along the corridors and down specially constructed ramps. During those few drama-infused days, more than two hundred cars, ambulances, trucks, delivery vans, and taxis were requisitioned to transport almost two thousand wooden crates to safe and dry hiding places in châteaux outside of Paris. By the time war broke out, all of the Louvre's three-thousand plus paintings, as well as its most priceless statuary, had been taken down and trucked away.

Unfortunately, many of these treasures were stashed in the Loire Valley and would have to be moved yet again as danger encroached.

⁓

After the declaration of war, Paris immediately "put on its battle dress," as Man Ray described it. There were curfews, air-raid shelters, and blackouts at night, "with dim little blue lights at the street corners to show the way home after dark." And of course the gas masks. Every schoolchild and French citizen was given one to wear, "hanging from the shoulder in its tin can." Man Ray refused to carry one and was stopped by the police, at which point he promised to do so.[31]

Three days after war was declared, Man Ray drove six hundred miles to Antibes to collect his canvases and bring them back to his St-Germain-en-Laye cottage for safekeeping. Before making the trip, he had to acquire a special pass, obtained through a friend with connections. Picasso, who had been staying in Man Ray's Antibes flat in his absence, had already abandoned it and raced back to Paris to assure the safety of his paintings. But after deciding that it was impossible to protect them all, Picasso simply threw up his hands and left for a seaside resort near Bordeaux, joining Marie-Thérèse Walter and their daughter there and bringing his current mistress, Dora Maar, with him.

Man Ray was determined to stay in Paris, motivated not only by his love for the City of Light but also by his dislike of America. Gertrude Stein's love of Paris, and of France, also benefited from her lack of enthusiasm for America, which even her successful tour and book sales there had done little to counteract. In 1939, as Europe grew increasingly unsettled, Gertrude's friends, family, and even the U.S. consulate urged her to leave, but she was unwilling to go. Presiding over a shrinking salon, she continued to maintain that, really, there could be no war. "Hitler will never really go to war," she told an interviewer. "He wants the illusion of victory and power, the glory and glamour of it, but he could not stand the blood and fighting involved in getting it." To her mind, Mussolini was the dangerous one, but until war actually broke out, she refused to believe war was possible. When it did come, she was appalled. "They shouldn't! They shouldn't!" was all she could say.[32]

Gertrude and Alice were in Bilignin when the unspeakable happened, and Gertrude swiftly secured a thirty-six-hour military pass to enable her and Alice to return briefly to Paris to pick up their winter clothes and passports, and do what they could to protect their paintings. They intended to place these on the floor to save them from falling during bombing raids, but when the two discovered that there was not nearly enough floor space for the large collection, they decided to leave them in place. Art dealer Daniel-Henry

Kahnweiler begged them to take at least some of the small Picassos with them, but they brought only Cézanne's portrait of Madame Cézanne and Picasso's portrait of Gertrude. Gertrude and Alice would not return to Paris until 1944 and would have to sell the Cézanne in the meantime simply to survive. "We ate the Cézanne," Alice later explained.[33]

～

The outbreak of war found an anguished James Joyce and Nora in La Baule, Brittany, where they had hastened from Switzerland to await Lucia, who was being evacuated from her institution in Paris. En route, they encountered massive traffic jams, further snarled by troop movements. The terrified Lucia would not arrive until mid-September, and in the meantime, Joyce agonized, envisioning his daughter left alone in a city that was about to be bombed. One evening found him, along with other refugees, in a restaurant filled with French and British soldiers who began to sing "La Marseillaise." Joyce joined in, and his clear Irish tenor caught the soldiers' attention. They hoisted him onto a table, where he sang it all over again. As someone who heard him recalled, "You never saw such an exhibition of one man dominating and thrilling a whole audience."[34]

The war's outbreak found André Gide in Pontigny, in north-central France, where he had been attending a conference on the refugee problem (he had worked on behalf of Belgian refugees during World War I and was active once again in the effort to get certain refugees, mainly German writers and intellectuals, released from the camps where they were currently interned). War brought the conference to an abrupt end, and from there, Gide attempted to get to Cabris, in southeastern France, where his daughter's mother, Elisabeth, and Elisabeth's husband lived. But getting there proved difficult: the trains were not running on schedule, and those that were functioning were crammed full. Fortunately Gide encountered a friend who offered him a lift in her car, but the resulting odyssey took them two days.

They arrived in Cabris just after midnight on the second day, where Gide found that the Petite Dame and Catherine were already there, leaving little space for him. He took a room at the village inn and spent the time reading and contemplating. By now, approaching the age of seventy, Gide had lived through three great wars with Germany, and he was overwhelmed with fear for the future—the future of culture, the future of mankind. "Yes, all that might well disappear," he wrote in his journal soon after his arrival, "that effort of culture that seemed to us so admirable (and I am speaking not only of French culture). . . . There is no acropolis that the flood of barbarism cannot reach, no ark that it cannot sink. . . . We cling to wreckage."[35]

～

Paris is "gloomy by day, sinister by six in the evening," wrote Gide's friend, Roger Martin du Gard.[36] Martin du Gard's wife had wanted to return as soon as possible from Martinique, which had involved a difficult and roundabout journey. Now he was back in Paris, and he was not happy about it.

"Paris has never been so dark," Simone de Beauvoir agreed. Worse, sirens kept going off in the middle of the night. Although it was a relief when they turned out to be false alarms, they were becoming annoying. Sirens sounded off during the day as well, when German aircraft were reported to have crossed the frontier. "You have to pay right away in the cafés now," Beauvoir recorded on September 8, "so that you can get out quickly in the event of an alert."[37] But by December, she would no longer be paying attention to the nighttime sirens and would simply put in her earplugs and sleep.

Stravinsky was not as successful in ignoring the nocturnal noise. After being discharged on September 2 from the sanatorium he had entered following his wife's death (he and much of his family had been infected with tuberculosis and required hospitalization), he had attempted to book passage for New York—having agreed to give the Charles Eliot Norton Lectures at Harvard, starting in September. But German U-boats were already active in the Atlantic, and regular shipping timetables had been suspended. Stravinsky had already vacated his Paris apartment, and he now tried to camp out in his son Theodore's apartment, since Theodore (along with his brother) had been called up for military service. But the air-raid sirens kept Stravinsky awake at night. So, after two nights of lugging his bedding down to the cellar, he took off for Nadia Boulanger's house, about thirty miles west of Paris, arriving with a carload of luggage and clutching his gas mask.

Stravinsky's redoubtable mistress, Vera, promptly went to work and found him a berth on a liner bound for New York (she could not accompany him because of visa problems of her own). He then spent much of September in terror over the drumbeat of U-boat sinkings—the Germans sank nineteen warships that month. At last, on September 22, he sailed from Bordeaux on a jam-packed ship. Even in first class there were five to a cabin, but the *Manhattan* arrived in New York Harbor without incident. As Stravinsky later put it, "the world events of 1939–40 did not bear tragically on my personal life, but they did disrupt the composition of the Symphony"—his Symphony in C.[38]

Others were also annoyed by the sirens. Colette, who had flippantly told a neighbor that "she liked spending her wars in Paris," had returned from Dieppe, much against her husband's wishes. But after two nights in the cellar below her current (and what would be permanent) address at the Palais Royal, she never went back, even during the bombing raids to come. "I never would have believed that the human race would come to this point once again," she told a friend as the war began.[39]

Coco Chanel continued to live in the Ritz and was spotted by none other than Noël Coward en route to the Ritz's air-raid shelter, followed by a servant carrying her gas mask on a cushion. Jean Cocteau was also ensconced at the Ritz, in a room that Chanel paid for. Jean Marais had been mobilized, but for now, Cocteau's immediate concern after war broke out was said to have been, "How will I get my opium?"[40]

Three weeks after France declared war, Chanel closed the House of Chanel, laying off her entire staff without notice. Schiaparelli, on the other hand, considered it a point of honor to keep her business open, although with a reduced staff and on a part-time basis. "I wonder," she later wrote, "if people fully realized the importance as propaganda for France of the dressmaking business at this time."[41]

In response to the war, Schiaparelli built a collection that was geared to patriotism and practicality. There were dresses with huge pockets, so that if a woman had to leave home in a hurry (for an air raid, or going on duty) she could do so without a bag and retain her freedom of hands for driving. Since there were few buttons or safety pins available, Schiaparelli chose dog chains to close suits and hold skirts. She introduced colors such as Maginot Line blue, Foreign Legion red, and airplane gray, and she came up with a wool boiler suit that could be kept next to one's bed to slip on in case an air raid drove one to the dark and dank cellar.

"The men were gone," she wrote. "We had no tailors." Even the hall porter, a White Russian, had joined the army. There were few customers, but "most of the time, the collection was shown as a matter of prestige." Prestige, and something else: "the *grande couture* carried on, filling the hours, the minutes, and the seconds with work and humor to prevent the soul from sinking in despair."[42]

Schiaparelli was well aware of the plight of refugees, who were pouring into the Belgian embassy next to her residence: "One gained the impression of a nightmare," she wrote.[43] She gave orders to her concierge to have hot coffee and bread and butter to be ready at any time, and she opened a bar in her cellar to British officers and American ambulance drivers, as well as to women of the French Mechanized Transport Corps, who drove between Paris and points close to the front. Gogo was now among these women, driving a six-wheeled truck, but she was so small that she had to sit on pillows to reach the steering wheel. Among the British and Americans, Gogo became known as Maginot Mitzi.

When the air-raid sirens went off, Schiaparelli herded her workers into a shelter beneath the shop. The first warning, she later recalled, occurred during lunchtime. "The airplanes flew so low that they nearly cut off Napoleon's head" (his elevated statue in the Place Vendôme), but no damage was done. Later, when Schiaparelli went to live for a time in the guest cottage on Elsie de Wolfe's estate, she recalled responding to nighttime air-raid sirens by leading one of the servants and her child to a shelter, while out of Elsie de Wolfe's house came a procession headed by Elsie's diplomat husband, Sir Charles Mendl, "in a big overcoat with a huge scarf that hid his features, an electric torch in one hand."[44]

Irène and Frédéric Joliot-Curie had always followed the example set by Marie and Pierre Curie in publishing their discoveries. But war with Hitler impelled them to place all of their documentation, including the principles behind nuclear chain reactions that they had just discovered, in a sealed envelope that they deposited in a safe at the Academy of Sciences. It would remain hidden there throughout the war.[45]

With the onset of war, Frédéric was drafted into the army. Irène pressed on at the Curie Institute in Paris, where she was adamant about protecting the laboratory and its radium; but their children remained with a nanny in Brittany, just as Marie had kept Irène and Eve in safety, in the same location, during World War I.

Both Irène and Frédéric were doing their ardent best to bring the United States into the war, but as it turned out, it was Eve Curie who would have the greater impact on American attitudes toward France, and toward involvement in the conflict. Named director of women's wartime activities for the French Ministry of Information, Eve traveled across the United States in early 1940 under the guise of promoting her biography of Marie Curie, but while doing her utmost to urge America and Americans to join the war effort. In February 1940, she even made the cover of *Time* magazine.

The Ministry of Information, the political and propaganda arm of the French government created just before war was declared, was headed throughout the early months of its existence by the respected novelist and playwright Jean Giraudoux—perhaps best known to English-speaking audiences today as the author of *The Madwoman of Chaillot*. He had served with distinction during World War I and survived wounds inflicted by the Germans as well

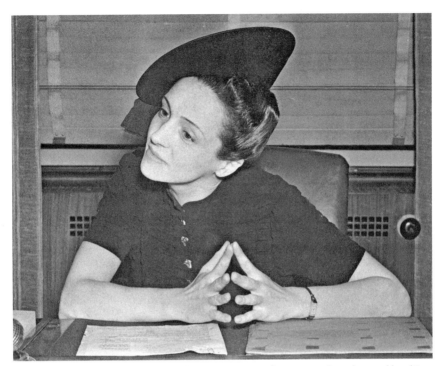

Eve Curie in New York City, 1939, during a press conference on the release of her biography of her mother, Marie Curie. © SZ Photo / Scherl / Bridgeman Images

as by clumsy surgeons; but he was left with what today would probably be diagnosed as posttraumatic stress disorder. Unsurprisingly, he came out of the experience with a deep-seated antagonism to war. Determined to defend culture from barbarism, Giraudoux had spent the decade advocating a Franco-German rapprochement based on forgetting and forgiving—a serious message that he hid behind calculated flippancy and a charming wit.

Giraudoux, like so many French, was also anti-Semitic and xenophobic, although he generally was not shrill about it. Still, in 1939 he published *Pleins pouvoirs* (*Full Powers*), in which he clearly sounded the trumpets of nativism and anti-Semitism, including his advocacy of a Ministry of Race to control immigration, which he was convinced was weakening France and the French by diluting the French racial stock.[46] Yet at the same time, there were certain restraints to be observed, including an April 1939 decree prohibiting "incitements to hatred for reasons of religion or race."[47] Drieu La Rochelle tested these that autumn with his novel *Gilles* and was outraged when Giraudoux's ministry censored some of its more virulently anti-Semitic portions (although these would be restored in time, under France's Vichy government).

As it happened, Giraudoux was also an enthusiast for urban planning, and this soon brought him into contact with Le Corbusier. Corbu, who was devastated by the outbreak of war—in large part because it meant fewer opportunities for architecture—had been excused from military service because of his age and eye problems, as well as because of a near-fatal water accident he had suffered the year before from a boat's propellers. But he was eager to make himself useful to his adopted country, and on the day war was declared, he wrote several influential contacts seeking positions in which he could be of service to his country.

Following this, he and Yvonne left Paris. When he returned that October, it was to meet with Jean Giraudoux to create a planning committee for the postwar work of urban planning, a concept that in its very loftiness thrilled Corbu. As he put it, "I felt that the way lay open and that the hour of realities was striking." After other meetings with additional government officials, he wrote, "At last, the scope of human beings is here equivalent to the scope of events."[48]

The possibility of building Corbu's ideal cities was still far distant, but employment of any sort was welcome when, in late November, the arms ministry asked him to design a large munitions factory and gave him the rank of colonel.

⁓

Jean Giraudoux seemed an odd choice for minister of information, whose purpose was to manage news and broadcast propaganda—to his mind, a vulgar mission at best. Ordinary folks had little interest in "the fine words of Monsieur Giraudoux," as Fernand Léger put it. And as one soldier wrote back from the front lines, "It's unendurable. Risk, cold, boredom, but for goodness' sake no more phrases like those of Giraudoux." As for Giraudoux himself, he was hardly the one to project optimism as war approached: "One prepares for war as one prepares for an exam," he said early on. "We shall not pass this one."[49]

Charles de Gaulle certainly was in agreement with Giraudoux's pessimism. "In 1939, it was a poverty-stricken, outmoded France that entered the conflict," he later wrote in his memoirs.[50] Yet when war came, he was ready to do his utmost to defend his country. Despite the government's determination to rely on the Maginot Line, de Gaulle unhesitatingly took up his military duties when—immediately after the declaration of war—he was appointed to the command of the tanks of the Fifth Army in Alsace. These tanks were not combined into one great unit as he had called for; instead, they were in five scattered battalions and consisted only of light tanks (Renault R35s). It was exactly what de Gaulle had been arguing against for years, but nonetheless, he was a professional soldier and took up his command.

In addition to other problems facing France's military, war production was flagging, especially from Louis Renault. Renault remained primarily interested in producing civilian vehicles and believed that World War I and its aftermath had been to blame for the interwar decline in the French auto industry. In addition to Renault's foot-dragging, relations between labor and management in Renault's factories and elsewhere continued to deteriorate. A month after war was declared, the minister of armaments, Raoul Dautry, brought the two sides together but was frustrated when the trade unions agreed, on the grounds of patriotism, to forget past differences while management did not. Interpreting labor's concessions as a sign of weakness, some industrialists even hoped to get rid of the trade unions altogether—something they would soon achieve, but under bleak circumstances.

When Dautry complained specifically of Renault's lackluster production of military vehicles, Renault laid the blame on the thousands of workers he had lost to mobilization, including some of his best technicians. "What remain," he complained, "are the older and less productive, including 4,000 women."[51] Dautry then brought Renault's nephew, François Lehideux, back from the front to help prod things along. This only increased Renault's obsession with the idea that the state had become a dictatorship and that his nephew was trying to supplant him and take over the firm. It would only be in the coming year, when Dautry sent Renault on a mission to the United States to meet with President Roosevelt and explain France's urgent need for war materiel, that Dautry would be able—for the moment—to get this recalcitrant industrialist out of his hair.

Unlike 1914, there were no chauvinist cries in 1939 as men marched off to war, nor (despite the assertions of a few) was there the expectation that the war would be short. Many were unenthusiastic as they faced the horrors to come, and the strange contrast between Paris's "battle dress," as Man Ray put it, and the eerie absence of war created an uneasy dichotomy.

As the days and weeks dragged on, people began to call it the "Phony War" and tried to proceed, as best they could, as if life were normal. By year's end, Josephine Baker was costarring with Maurice Chevalier at the Casino de Paris, after having entertained the troops at the Maginot Line. Backstage, there was considerable rivalry between them, and Chevalier complained that Baker constantly upstaged him. Yet despite their behind-the-scenes tiffs and the citywide blackouts, curfews, and rationing, the theater was always full.

By now, Josephine had begun to work for the Deuxième Bureau, the French military intelligence service, collecting information she overheard from a variety of sources as she partied and traveled. "We needed people," according to Jacques Abtey, chief of military counterespionage in Paris, "who could travel around without attracting attention, and who would be able to report what they saw." One of his colleagues soon suggested Josephine: "She is more French than the French," he told Abtey.[52] And so, while Josephine was playing at the Casino de Paris, filming (*Fausse Alerte*), doing a weekly radio show for soldiers at the front, and getting engaged to the chocolate heir Jean Menier, she was thoroughly engrossed in spying for France. Completely in character, she had an affair with Jacques Abtey.

It was a strange time, this phony war, with everything different and yet still the same. As Man Ray put it, aside from some small air raids, "nothing much changed. Although sugar, tobacco, coffee, and gas were rationed (and of course hoarded), the restaurants were full at lunchtime, at night people sat and ate behind blacked-out windows taped against concussion."[53] At the front, after a brief Saar offensive by the French, all was quiet, and boredom became more of a problem than outright warfare. "I'm waiting—I'm not sure what for," Beauvoir wrote Sartre in September. "I think I'll be waiting till the war ends." That November, as they and all the French still waited, Sartre wrote Beauvoir, "Never have I felt so forcefully that our lives have no meaning outside of our love and that nothing changes that, neither separation, nor passions, nor the war."[54]

During this odd waiting time, people marched off to war who had determined that they never again would do such a thing. The Surrealists, who despised war and had done so ever since the trauma of the First World War, nonetheless put on their uniforms. Even André Breton and Paul Eluard answered their government's mobilization call for the second war in their lifetime, Breton once again assigned to a medical post—this time at a pilots' school in Poitiers.

Sylvia Beach, who had seemed convinced right up until the war's outbreak that somehow peace would prevail, assured her friends and family that she was all right, that she could and would manage—even though, as a foreigner, she was not entitled to a government-issued gas mask, and even though business was at a standstill. Although she could only keep Shakespeare and Company open part time, she rightly considered it necessary to do so, as a kind of refuge for that dwindling number of friends who gathered there. "I will not be a quitter," she told her family.[55]

Beach had little to do with Joyce's *Finnegans Wake*, although she did sell it. The problem, as Joyce was only too well aware, was that sales were disappointing. *Finnegans Wake* had received a flood of publicity upon its May publication, but the reviews were mixed, and readers by and large were baffled. Back in Paris, Joyce morosely read the reviews, ate little, and drank a lot. The air-raid warnings upset him, especially given his bad sight, which made it difficult for him to move around at night. "What is the use of this war?" he demanded, angry that it was distracting everyone from reading *Finnegans Wake*.[56] In addition, his health, along with his eyesight, continued to deteriorate.

"We are going downhill fast," he told Samuel Beckett, who saw him just before he left Paris for the countryside that Christmas.[57]

Abbé Mugnier, who had lived through two wars with Germany and once again was watching his world fall apart, had earnestly prayed for peace. But now he took to his journal to consider the terrible choices ahead, including the necessity of resisting Hitler and the evil of Nazism by force. And then he embarked on a eulogy in praise of the things he loved: "I am for the cuckoo," he wrote, "the moss, the crocus, the wheat, the laburnum, the elder tree, the linden, the boxwood blazing in the sun." Waxing rhapsodic, he added that he was for Shakespeare's *Midsummer Night's Dream* and for Oberon, for the flowers of Balzac and the flowers from Mugnier's own childhood. "I am for the garden, the meadow, the forest," he concluded, before setting down his pen.[58]

Only two brief entries followed this, and then one on November 27—his eighty-sixth birthday. A dear friend helped him celebrate this occasion, presenting him with a cake lit with eighty-six candles. It seemed appropriate. "Enthusiasm has been the best part of my life," he wrote.[59]

It was his last sentence in the journal he had kept for more than sixty years.[60]

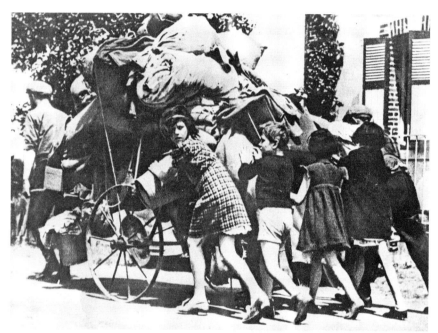

Exodus, June 1940: French civilians fleeing the German advance. © Tallandier / Bridge-man Images

CHAPTER FOURTEEN

~

Closing the Circle

(1940)

France had fought two wars with Germany during the past seventy years, although most French preferred to remember only the second conflict—the Great War, or World War I—which France had won, but at a terrible cost. Having staggered to the finish line in 1918, the French were not prepared to undertake such a sacrifice again and preferred to hunker down behind their Maginot Line in the conviction that it would protect them from any future German onslaught. As *Paris-Soir* put it on January 1, 1940, "Sheltered behind the Maginot Line, the nation is safe and working much as usual."[1]

But the Maginot Line was not France's only source of false security during that spring of 1940. Victory in 1918 had been dearly bought, with wounds more than sufficient to last a generation, but victory had also bequeathed an assurance of France's military superiority. As Man Ray recalled of that time, "There was every confidence in the army's ability to stave off the invader; the First World War slogan was taken up again: They shall not pass. There were no battles; the army sat in its nine-story Maginot Line, equipped for a long siege."[2]

Little attention was paid to Colonel de Gaulle's warnings of Germany's superb military machine, and little attention was given to the dangerous decline of morale on the front, as boredom and inaction sapped the will of those millions of mobilized Frenchmen who, after months of seeing no sign of the enemy, were simply yearning to go home. Parked at the front with all those other bored soldiers, Jean-Paul Sartre noted the marked decline in morale and observed that "there's an enormous risk in confining a nation one has unleashed for war to inglorious waiting and defensive operations."[3]

People recalled the victory of 1918, but few cared to revisit the debacle of 1870–1871, when the Prussian army under Otto von Bismarck vanquished the French, captured their emperor, and placed a hitherto-resistant Paris under a brutal winter siege. Paris endured for four desperate months, but at length France's new government capitulated. Bismarck celebrated by marching his troops down the Champs-Elysées and by holding a glittering ceremony in Versailles's treasured Hall of Mirrors, where he proclaimed Prussia's Wilhelm I as emperor over a now-unified Germany. Not insignificantly, France also had to cede Alsace and Lorraine as well as pay an enormous indemnity to its conquerors; but it was that ceremony in Louis XIV's Hall of Mirrors that seared its way into national consciousness.[4] It was no accident that the Treaty of Versailles, which ended World War I with a long-sought victory over Germany, was signed in Versailles's Hall of Mirrors.

Germany now had its own score to settle, and Hitler would make good use of symbols in his nation's yearning for revenge: among them would be the very railroad car in which the Armistice ending World War I was signed, and where he would impose a victor's armistice on the French. This still lay ahead. But had the French been paying attention, there were sufficient warnings of what was to come: Hitler's lightning-fast invasion of Denmark in April followed his mop-up of Czechoslovakia and rapid conquest of Poland. Norway soon followed. Despite what most French at the time thought, France's turn was coming.

As winter drew to a close, the first rationing began. Elsa Schiaparelli, with her usual edgy humor, printed the regulations on one of her scarves: "Monday—no meat. Tuesday—no alcohol. Wednesday—no butter. Thursday—no fish. Friday—no meat. Saturday—no alcohol." Sunday, with no restrictions, was in her words a very Parisian "toujours l'amour."[5]

Life went on, with a Gallic shrug. Simone de Beauvoir continued to keep her diary, "but without any sense of urgency." She had, in her own words, "settled down into the war; and the war had settled down in Paris." There was, of course, the absence of young men, and there were not enough street cleaners to sweep the streets after a snowstorm; but dancing had resumed at the nightclubs, restaurants (albeit with restricted menus) were full, crowds attended concerts and the theater, and the cafés—despite the nonalcohol days—continued to provide their essential dimension to Parisian life. In April, Hitler announced that he would enter Paris on June 15, but Beauvoir noted that "no one took this piece of braggadocio seriously."[6]

And then, on the morning of May 10, Beauvoir bought a newspaper on the corner of Boulevard Raspail and read the lead story: that very morning, in the early hours, Germany had invaded Holland and attacked Belgium and Luxembourg. She found a seat on one of the benches along the boulevard and began to cry.

On the morning of May 10, France did not have a government. Or to be more precise, it was between governments. As had happened with increasing frequency during the decade, the current cabinet had folded in the face of internal disagreements, and a new one had yet to be formed. Although not unexpected, the timing of this particular governmental shake-up was especially unfortunate.

From its outset in 1871, the Third Republic had survived an impressive number of crises, and by 1940 it was the longest-lasting republic in France's history.[7] But length of tenure did not equate with stability or popularity. During its early years, the greatest threat to the Third Republic's existence had come from those who sought a return to monarchy, constitutional or not, as well as from their close cousins, who yearned for the proverbial leader on a white horse, Bonaparte or not. The death of Emperor Napoleon III and his son put an end to Bonapartist dreams, but not to the threat from those who longed for strong, authoritarian leadership, who turned instead to the appealing General Georges Boulanger. In the end, Boulanger did not have the stomach for a coup d'état, and his followers floundered. But their anxiety and capacity for hatred remained, to be plumbed by astute opponents of the parliamentary Republic during scandals such as the Panama Canal imbroglio and especially during the Dreyfus Affair.

This affair rocked the nation for the better part of a decade, during which an alliance between authoritarian nationalists and the army whipped a large portion of the nation into a frenzy of anti-Semitism and hatred of the Republic, especially of the Republic's growing secularization. Dreyfus was the unfortunate scapegoat of a roiling popular movement, made up largely of conservative Catholics and those who viewed the Republic as a transitory accident in French political life, for whom the humiliation of defeat to Germany would never disappear. As a Jew, Dreyfus was considered to be a foreigner, no matter how French his birth, and his origins in the borderlands of Alsace made him even more suspect. All Jews, according to this warped point of view, were foreigners and therefore traitors—to France, and to the French (meaning in this case staunchly Catholic) way of life.

On the other hand, those who defended Dreyfus tried, in the words of Léon Blum, "to transform the coalition for review [of the Dreyfus case] into a permanent army at the service of human rights and justice. From the injustice suffered by an individual, we attempted, as Jaurès had from the very first day, to move to social injustice." But they did not succeed, certainly not in the broad sense that they envisioned. After the Dreyfus Affair had at long last simmered down, the nation—shaken to its depths—returned in large part to what it had been before, while (in Blum's words) popular imagination contorted the reviled image of Dreyfus's supporters as "'the Syndicate,' and more precisely 'the Jewish Syndicate.'" In popular imagination, the Dreyfus Affair "became a carefully organized plot paid for by the gold of the Jewish Syndicate and of Germany, the Jews wanting to save their brother Jew, and Germany wanting to save the traitor who had rendered it such precious service."[8] Even the incontrovertible proofs of Dreyfus's innocence were turned into proofs of a massive conspiracy.

Millions believed this, and continued to believe this, right down through the Popular Front, whose staunch pacifism provided proof—for those who scarcely needed it—of its ties not only to the Soviet Union but also to Germany. Hitler and Stalin, according to this view, were the puppeteers, and Léon Blum, the Jew, was the traitorous puppet. The Nazi-Soviet Pact leading to the outbreak of war only confirmed this viewpoint.

As it happened, by early 1940, Charles de Gaulle had persuaded Léon Blum of the necessity for immediate action, via a restructured and mechanized army, to defeat Hitler. In January, de Gaulle—prompted by Hitler's rapid and overwhelming conquest of Poland—had written a memo that he shared with Blum, Paul Reynaud, and many others in positions of power. Here, he stated that "the war that has begun may well be the most widespread, the most complex and the most violent of all those that have devastated the world." He then proceeded to denounce the General Staff's conduct of the war to date and openly recommended a completely different strategy. It was a dangerous and even mutinous move, but he did not hesitate. "In the present conflict," he wrote, "being inert means being beaten."[9]

De Gaulle, a staunch conservative and antifascist, was not put off either by Blum's politics or his ancestry, and he recognized a true supporter of

France when he saw one. "Only Léon Blum spoke with elevation of mind," he wrote on March 22, after hearing the words of right-wing speakers in the Assembly, who skewered their enemies under thinly veiled platitudes about the dangers facing the country and the necessity of pulling to-gether.[10] Paul Reynaud had become prime minister on March 21, and the political right was angered by his inclusion of six Socialists in his cabinet (Reynaud owed his slim majority of one vote to Léon Blum), as well as by Reynaud himself, who had deeply antagonized them with what they termed his "warmongering." But what appalled de Gaulle the most was that on this date, during full wartime, these Assembly members took the opportunity to viciously attack those among their colleagues who were determined to fight.

By March 22, Reynaud was foreign minister as well as premier, but his minister of defense, Edouard Daladier—although dead set against capitulat-ing to the Germans—had seen de Gaulle's January memo and was not im-pressed with de Gaulle or his recommendations. Reynaud had stepped in as prime minister when Daladier resigned, succumbing to a cross fire between nationalists' condemnation of his military policies and the left's anger over his virtual nullification of the forty-hour law. But in a move typical of French politics of the period—in which the same people kept appearing and reap-pearing in one role or another in any given cabinet—Daladier remained on as minister of defense (a post that he had previously occupied while prime minister). In this capacity, he opposed Reynaud, whom he disliked person-ally, especially on the question of dismissing General Maurice Gamelin as supreme commander of France's armed forces. Both Reynaud and de Gaulle viewed Gamelin as hopelessly blinkered and unfit for the job, but Daladier would have none of it. So Gamelin stayed.

It was Daladier's insistence on keeping General Gamelin that triggered the governmental crisis on May 9 that left France without a government as Hitler's offensive began. Reynaud wanted Gamelin to go, and he was just as interested in giving Daladier a push. France therefore was officially between governments on May 10, although all the government ministers had been sworn to secrecy over their resignations until a new government could be formed. As it happened, news of Hitler's offensive broke before they could make their announcement, and in response to Germany's attack, Reynaud withdrew his resignation and stayed on as prime minister. But he was not able to get rid of General Gamelin, who hung on for the moment, saved by Reynaud's difficulty in firing him just as war was breaking out.

In addition to protecting General Gamelin, Daladier had nixed de Gaulle's attempt to become secretary-general of the War Committee (ironically, the post went to a pacifist, thanks to the influence of Reynaud's profascist mistress). Still, de Gaulle remained one of Reynaud's close associates. De Gaulle also remained a colonel in the French army, and it was in this capacity that he would soon encounter the Nazis.

⌣

It was a gorgeous spring that year in Paris. "With the weather at its most perfect," recalled Man Ray, "the Nazis began to move." They "skirted around north of the Maginot Line . . . preceded by their planes," encountering little resistance. "The French army," he noted, "was never where it was most needed."[11]

"So the war, the real war, has begun," Colonel de Gaulle wrote his wife on May 10,[12] as the Germans launched their offensive in Belgium and Holland, and as panzer divisions and their motorcyclists began their sweep through the supposedly impenetrable Ardennes forest, from which they emerged in three days.

De Gaulle took up his command with only three tank battalions and less than half of his officers, and he received his assignment on May 15, even as Edouard Daladier was telephoning Prime Minister Reynaud to tell him, "All is lost. The road to Paris is open. There is nothing to prevent the Germans from reaching the capital."[13] On the following day, as de Gaulle was scouting out the countryside, he first encountered French soldiers running for their lives. The panzer divisions' motorcyclists had overtaken them and ordered them to throw away their rifles and get out of the way so as not to block the roads. "We have no time to take you prisoner," the Germans had shouted contemptuously as they stormed past. Later, de Gaulle wrote of his decision that terrible day, that "if I lived, I should fight wherever it was necessary and as long as it was necessary until the enemy was beaten and the nation's stain washed away. What I have been able to do since then was resolved upon that day."[14]

Without waiting for the reinforcements he had been promised, de Gaulle set out on his assignment of holding off the panzers until conventional forces could arrive to block the German drive toward Paris. Despite Luftwaffe attacks, the French armored units held their own against the panzer divisions, and de Gaulle received word that the operation conceived and carried out under his command had helped to "pay off the psychological mortgage of May 10."[15]

Still, German command of the air and the virtual absence of French artillery made it impossible for de Gaulle to take the initiative, and under command to withdraw, he reluctantly obeyed. Now promoted to brigadier general (temporary rank),[16] making him at the age of forty-nine one of the three youngest generals in the French army, he set off on a fresh mission for the second battle with his Fourth Armored Division. This was successful, resulting in many prisoners and a great deal of equipment taken, and General Maxime Weygand congratulated him, telling him that "you have saved our honor."[17]

De Gaulle had been vindicated, his prophecy about the role of tanks in modern warfare dramatically confirmed in battle—although by then, the German panzers had already settled the question.

The Dutch army surrendered on May 15, a day after the total destruction of Rotterdam. On May 16, with the Germans within hours of Paris, the military governor established the city in the war zone and advised top ministers of the government to evacuate. Reynaud and others were for staying, and for the moment they did—although bonfires of sensitive documents began to flare in the courtyards of the foreign ministry and friendly embassies. This only added to the nervousness of Parisians, who knew little of what was going on, thanks to government censorship, but were subject to a tsunami of rumors, much of it instigated surreptitiously by the Germans.

On May 19, Reynaud at long last removed General Gamelin from his command, but replaced him with General Weygand (another ancient relic, in de Gaulle's view). Reynaud also ousted Daladier from the ministry of defense and war, which he personally took over, and brought in Marshal Philippe Pétain (from Franco's Spain) to serve reassuringly as deputy prime minister. Pétain, revered by his countrymen, was now installed at the top levels of government.

But Charles de Gaulle was disturbed by the news. Pétain, he was sure, would favor peace with Germany. And in a letter to Paul Reynaud, de Gaulle warned, "These men of former times [Pétain and Weygand]—if they are allowed to—will lose this new war."[18]

On May 26, with Belgium about to surrender, more than three hundred thousand British, French, and Belgian troops began to board a flotilla of rescue ships from Dunkirk, under heavy fire from the Luftwaffe. After the battle of Dunkirk, the last phase of the German assault began. Having taken the major Channel ports, cutting off France from Britain, the Germans now swung south to Paris.

On June 3, German bombers launched an avalanche of bombs on the Citroën plant in southwest Paris and on the nearby Renault plant in Billancourt, both of these being major producers of military equipment. It was then that the exodus from Paris began, an exodus that, according to Man Ray, was biblical in character.[19]

A few stalwart expats hung on for a time. Even after the bombing, the American composer Virgil Thomson held his regular Friday-night open house for a group that on this occasion included André Breton and Paul Eluard (both in uniform) as well as the heiress and art collector Peggy Guggenheim (whose uncle was the founder of New York's Solomon R. Guggenheim Museum and who always described herself as belonging to the less-well-off branch of the family). Ever since war was declared, Peggy Guggenheim had been frantically buying up contemporary art to preserve it from the Nazis. But she now decided that Paris had become too dangerous, not only for her art (Hitler's antagonism to what he called "degenerate" art was well known), but especially for her children. After all, the Guggenheims were Jewish.

And so, shortly before the Germans reached Paris, Peggy Guggenheim made her exit, complete with her trove of art works—which the Louvre had refused to store, on the grounds that it was not worth saving. As she later put it, among these were "a Kandinsky, several Klees and Picabias, a Cubist Braque, a Gris, a Léger," as well as works by Mondrian, Miró, Max Ernst, Tanguy, Dalí, Magritte, and sculptures by Brancusi, Lipchitz, Giacometti, and Henry Moore.[20] After collecting her extended family in Lisbon—including her former husband, Laurence Vail; her future husband, Max Ernst; Vail's second wife, Kay Boyle; plus Peggy's two children and Vail and Boyle's three children and Boyle's son by the poet Ernest Walsh—she packed them all, plus her art collection, into a Pan American clipper to New York.

Unquestionably, she was a remarkable woman; but money helped.

Sylvia Beach did not have money, nor was she, in her own words, "a quitter." Moreover, she was worried about her friends, especially her Jewish friends. In mid-May, the military governor of Paris, General Pierre Héring, issued a decree to round up German nationals—the men at the Buffalo Stadium in Montrouge, to the south of Paris, and the women at Paris's famous (and soon to be infamous) cycling arena, the Vélodrome d'Hiver, or Vél d'Hiv, located along the Seine in Paris's fifteenth arrondissement. The idea was that these were enemy aliens; but many had left Germany because they opposed and feared Hitler. These included a large percentage of German Jews, who were especially vulnerable to Nazi persecution. Once herded into these new internment camps, the inmates slept on straw, received minimal rations, and could not communicate with the outside world. Many would be shuttled off to detention camps in central and southern France, where they would die of disease, cold, and malnutrition. "A wise measure," *Le Figaro* said approvingly.[21]

But Beach was deeply concerned. She and Adrienne Monnier had many Jewish friends, among them Walter Benjamin, the German philosopher and cultural critic. Benjamin—appalled by Hitler's rise—had left Nazi Germany in 1933, in the footsteps of his friend Bertolt Brecht, and had shuttled throughout the decade between Paris, Spain, Italy, and Denmark. With the war's outbreak, he was interned in a French detention camp for German aliens; but after his release he returned to Paris, where he dined and had long talks with Sylvia Beach and Adrienne Monnier. As the Germans approached and entered Paris, Benjamin led an increasingly precarious existence, and by summer, he decided to flee. Lacking the essential exit visa from France, he chose a difficult secret route across the Pyrenees into Spain.[22] Weak and ill when he finally reached the border, he took his own life after the Spanish border police refused him entry.

Beach and Monnier provided lodging, clothes, and food to a series of panicked persons in flight and went to the police station to get good-character certificates—anything to help. Monnier had been sharing her life (and apartment) with Gisèle Freund, a German refugee, and had arranged a marriage of convenience for her, to allow her to remain in France; but Freund's husband was also Jewish, and despite Freund's growing international reputation as a photojournalist, she was in danger. On June 10, as the Germans approached Paris, she fled—to the Dordogne and then to Argentina. Monnier also found room in her small apartment for Arthur Koestler, the Hungarian-born antifascist and anti-Soviet writer, who hid there for several days after spending four wretched months as an undesirable alien in the notorious Le Vernet internment camp. He would eventually make his way to London.

"Day and night," Beach later wrote, "people streamed through the rue de l'Odéon. People camped, and slept, in front of the railway stations in the hope of getting on a train." Some were fortunate enough to have access to cars but had to abandon them along the roadside when they ran out of gas. Most were on foot, "carrying babies and baggage, or pushing baby carriages or wheelbarrows."[23] Behind this flood of evacuating Parisians came another flood of refugees, those from the north and northeast, including the Belgians, uprooted for a second time in a generation.

But Beach and Monnier did not join the exodus. The days were sunny, with blue skies, and they went to the Boulevard Sébastapol, where "through our tears, [we] watched the refugees moving through the city." Crossing Paris along the Boulevard Saint Michel and the Luxembourg Gardens, the refugees exited to the south toward Orléans, their "cattle-drawn carts piled with household goods," and these swaying mounds topped with children, the sick, and the elderly.[24]

On June 6, Charles de Gaulle formally joined the government as undersecretary of war, having received his invitation several days earlier.[25] His mission was to organize the rear action in collaboration with those in charge of refugees and to ensure coordination with London for continuing the war. From his new position, de Gaulle argued forcefully to exclude Pétain, who was already pushing for an immediate peace and leading those who favored giving up. Reynaud replied that it was better to include than to exclude Pétain, and so Pétain—who represented at least one-third of the members of the government and half of the prime minister's close associates—stayed. But he clearly was unhappy about de Gaulle's presence in the cabinet and proceeded to do what he could to undermine it.

By now, de Gaulle had acknowledged that the war was lost in France proper, but he argued strenuously in favor of fighting on from France's colonial empire in North Africa, with Brittany as a redoubt from which France could link with Britain and the United States. The Brittany idea would soon evaporate, but the concept of fighting on did not, even as on June 10 Norway surrendered to Hitler and Italy joined the war against France and Britain. France's government promptly evacuated, heading for Tours.

What did France have with which to confront the Germans, André Gide anguished, given "the superiority of [the Germans'] arms, of their number, of their discipline, of their impetus, of their confidence in their leaders, of their unanimous faith in the Führer?" What, except "disorder, incompetence, negligence, internal divisions, decay?"[26]

Until Italy joined the war on June 10, the French government had held out hope that somehow Italy could be persuaded to remain neutral and, in Jean

Renoir's words, "was showing them every possible favor."[27] Mussolini had seen *La Grande Illusion* and wanted Renoir to come to Italy to give lectures on film directing, to which the French government promptly agreed. Renoir, now in uniform and posted to the army film service, readily obeyed. Until then, he recalled, he had done little but photograph soldiers "yawning with boredom," and Italy—despite its fascist dictator—seemed to offer interesting creative prospects.

Jean Renoir and Dido Freire left for Italy in mid-January, and in addition to his lecturing commitments, Renoir began to film his long-desired version of *Tosca*. He would never finish it. The French clearly were not welcome in Mussolini's Italy, and after being beaten up by a thug in a restaurant, Renoir—on the advice of the French ambassador—got out. Dido, a Brazilian national, remained for a few days to clear up administrative details and was still in Rome when Mussolini announced (to wildly enthusiastic crowds) his intention of fighting alongside Germany. She returned to Paris on the last train to cross the border.

There she found Jean waiting for her, anxious about her and about his son, Alain, who had been serving for some months as a noncommissioned officer in the now rapidly disintegrating French army. They finally tracked Alain down outside of Paris, where—in the absence of his officers, who had disappeared—he was trying to feed his group of fifty cavalrymen, who were dependent on one large truck. In the midst of this confusion, a staff officer appeared with orders to regroup further to the rear, and Alain disappeared with his men.

Renoir and Dido sought shelter with their friends, the Cézanne family,[28] near Fontainebleau and found them preparing to flee south. They all promptly joined forces—three of them in Renoir's three-seater Peugeot, which he drove, with the others (including Dido) following on bicycles and the Cézanne family's treasured paintings tied to the back of the small Peugeot. These would for a time decorate the interior of a rough stone barn in the Limousin where the refugees stayed for a spell, out of range of German air raids.

"Never," remembered Renoir, "had Cézanne's paintings been so appropriately hung."[29]

⌒

Simone de Beauvoir remained in Paris to supervise a baccalaureate examination on June 10, but all exams were canceled and teachers were released from duty. "My heart froze," she later wrote. "This was the end, and no mistake."

Everyone was leaving, "the stream of retreating cars never slackened." About midday she sighted about a dozen big carts coming by, "each one harnessed to four or five horses and loaded high with hay, over which a protective green tarpaulin was lashed. Bicycles and trunks were stacked against the tilt at either end, while in the middle sat motionless groups of folk."[30]

Beauvoir packed up her essentials, including all of Sartre's letters, and set out by car with friends for Chartres, crawling along behind a slow-moving column of vehicles, only stopping en route to temporarily abandon the car during air-raid alerts. From Chartres, she pressed on by train to a friend's house in Angers, with the Germans close behind. Her first encounter with German soldiers ("all very tall and blond with pink complexions") came when two approached her in a field where she was reading and spoke, in clumsy French, of their friendly feelings toward the French people. "It was the English and the Jews," they assured her, "who had brought us to this sorry pass."[31]

On June 10, as the government was preparing to evacuate Paris, Charlotte Perriand encountered chaos as she tried to get her visa to leave the country. She had parted with Le Corbusier on less than congenial terms and was headed for Japan—another war zone, like France, but a conquering rather than a conquered nation, and one that appeared to offer opportunities. Earlier in the year, she had accepted an offer to become design consultant in decorative art for the Japanese trade ministry. "I was adventurous and loved the unexpected," she later explained.[32] She had no idea what was waiting for her.

Despite her new job in the Far East and the looming Nazi threat at home, Perriand now was reluctant to leave Paris—even though, "with the blackout, it no longer looked like Paris." Before her departure, she and Pierre Jeanneret spent the night together, "lying hand in hand, listening to the city's strange sounds." Would Paris be able to defend itself, they wondered, or would it fall to the Germans?[33]

Lying there, their arms touching, "hand in hand, barely touching, my heart beating in time with the city," Perriand realized that "the wealthy have left. Only the poor remain. They won't be evacuated."[34]

On the morning of June 11, as the government departed, a vast cloud of smoke swirled through Paris and hid the sun. Ascribed variously to smoke

screens set off by the Germans or to the bombing of gasoline reserves somewhere to the north, for several hours it created a dismal setting of day turned
to night that struck many as bleakly appropriate: the City of Light was about
to become a city of darkness. As Charlotte Perriand put it, Paris was "dressed
in a heavy fog of mourning."[35]

And still the refugees came, continuing their sad march across Paris, surg-
ing southward in advance of the Germans. By this time, between seven and
eight million men, women, and children throughout France were on the
march, with almost three-quarters of the population of Paris among them.
Man Ray, who at the last possible moment decided to flee, found himself
inching his way along the highway in his Peugeot 402, accompanied by Ady
and a few possessions that he had snatched up, including his all-important
cameras. Parisians, Belgians, Luxembourgers, Poles, Dutch, and Jewish refugees from Germany were all part of this exodus of seekers of safety, and for
the moment, he had no idea where he was bound. Spain had sounded like a
good destination, but that now seemed virtually impossible, hemmed in as he
was among this mass of uprooted and desperate people.

Marie-Laure de Noailles, being half Jewish, fled at the insistence of her
good friend, the journalist and critic Paul Ristelhueber (known as Boulos).
They traveled in the style to which the wealthy were accustomed, complete
with limousine and maid, and were appalled by "the hand carts, the automobiles overloaded to bursting; . . . the poor trudging along; the shrieking horns;
the limousines, unable to move in the general confusion." Boulos was "sure
that no plague, no cataclysm, ever provoked such an exodus," and after about
ten miles of this, he decided to turn around and go back to Paris.[36]

Léon Blum, despite his resistance to leaving Paris, was also swept up in
this mass of human misery. To the last, he had refused to leave: "Wouldn't it
be a personal consecration of defeat?" he anguished. But colleagues (including Reynaud) insisted that unless he joined them, they would not go, and
so he finally capitulated. "I had never seen," he later wrote, "a spectacle as
poignant as this immense human migration."[37] But where Man Ray and so
many others saw misery, Blum saw a kind of moving Popular Front, filled
with good spirit and acts of kindness.

As Jean Cocteau and Georges Auric were smoking the last of their stash
of opium in Aix-en-Provence,[38] Coco Chanel packed up her necessities in
several huge trunks and headed south from Paris with a hastily acquired car
and driver—her own chauffeur being somewhere off among the remains of

the disintegrating army, and the newly recruited driver being wary of Chanel's Rolls Royce. Her immediate destination was the Riviera, but Italian bombings there convinced her to head toward Spain. She ended up, for the moment, at the house she had bought her nephew in the Pyrenees. Her gold dressing table followed.

Salvador Dalí and Gala, still recuperating from their eventful American tour, had just arrived for a vacation at a luxury hotel in the Pyrenees when Gala read her tarot cards and predicted the exact date of the declaration of war. Returning to Paris, Dalí studied the map with a mind to evading the Nazis while enjoying "gastronomical possibilities." He decided on Bordeaux for its proximity to the Spanish frontier and its excellence in French cooking. Bordeaux to him meant "Bordeaux wine, jugged hare, duck liver *aux raisins*, duck *aux oranges*, Arcachon claire-oysters." And that was it—Arcachon, a few kilometers from Bordeaux, where Salvador and Gala chose to spend the war.[39]

There, they met up with Coco Chanel as well as Marcel Duchamp, but their good times were interrupted by the increasingly serious nature of the war. Dalí and Gala spent a "sinister day" in Bordeaux during its first bombardment and then fled to Spain two days before the Germans occupied the bridge of Hendaye on the Spanish border. Gala left for Lisbon to make the difficult arrangements for their passage to America (which, according to Dalí, "appeared to bristle with red tape of a super-human refinement").[40] And Dalí traveled to Figueres to say good-bye to his father, whom he had not seen since their break eleven years before.

Rumors abounded: one was that the Dalís had been arrested in Spain; another, that Dalí was in Spain to paint Franco's portrait. Neither was true, but Dalí's refusal to fight or to denounce Franco had aligned many of his Surrealist colleagues against him. Max Ernst, for one, never forgave him.

On June 12, General Weygand telephoned his instructions regarding the status of Paris to the new military governor of Paris, General Henri Dentz: Paris was to be declared an open city; there was to be no defense made, including destruction of any bridges; and no fighting French troops were to enter the city. "To defend Paris would have given the city up to fire and destruction without the slightest utility," Dentz later argued. "As to having the people of Paris take up arms—and what arms?—to resist tank divisions which had just chopped up French armies—such talk would only have led to a massacre."[41]

On June 13, as the Germans approached the city's outskirts, Governor General Dentz notified Parisians of their city's open status, urging them to behave with composure and dignity and to abstain from all hostile acts. "What sinister years are coming now!" wrote one distraught woman, shortly before she killed herself. The Germans, in the meantime, basked in triumph. "Paris, unrealized dream of the First World War!" one awestruck German junior officer thought. "Starting in mid-morning, full of pride and with fast-beating hearts, we could see the city spread out before us—the outline of the delicate Eiffel Tower, the heavy white marble dome of Sacré Coeur, monuments which grew as we advanced mile by mile."[42]

Elsa Schiaparelli was one of the last to leave. A few days earlier, she had sent Gogo on to America via a liner from Genoa (the liner arrived in New York, with two thousand other refugees, the day Italy declared war on France). Now, when a friend in the cabinet called Elsa to warn that the Germans would arrive in Paris within hours, she at last threw some of her things together and set off for Biarritz—with plans to meet up there with sufficient staff to finish work on her new fall collection. With haste and good luck, she hoped to get it done and shipped out to New York before the Germans arrived. She was not the only couturier at that time in Biarritz, working against the clock: Lucien Lelong, Jeanne Lanvin, Cristóbal Balenciaga, Jacques Heim, and Jean Patou were all there, desperately putting together their last collections before their world fell apart.

The Germans entered Paris on June 14, goose-stepping through the Arc de Triomphe and down the Champs-Elysées. The journalist Paul Ristelhueber (Boulos) described their entry as Wagnerian: "ponderous and arrogant, they pass with the sound of an earthquake." Sylvia Beach recalled their arrival as "an endless procession of motorized forces: tanks and armored cars and helmeted men seated with arms folded. The men and the machines were all a cold gray, and they moved to a steady deafening roar."[43]

Soon swastikas replaced the French flag, beginning with the Hôtel de Ville, Paris's city hall, and then throughout the city—most devastatingly, on top of the Eiffel Tower and the Arc de Triomphe.

⁓

The French government in Tours was badly split. Prime Minister Reynaud and his stalwarts, among whom the most resolute was de Gaulle, strongly favored leaving for French North Africa and fighting on. The others, led by Pierre Laval and their figurehead leader, Marshall Pétain, just as strongly argued for remaining in France. According to Laval and his supporters, the battle for France—indeed the entire war—was lost, leaving France with only one option, to sue for an armistice. Given this painful truth, they contended that Pétain was the only one who could negotiate an armistice with Hitler.

At dawn on June 14, as the Germans were about to enter Paris, the French government moved further south, out of Tours and on to Bordeaux. After their arrival, amid the depressing mob of refugees and defeated military that continued to clog the roads, de Gaulle told Reynaud that he had joined the government to make war, not to submit to an armistice, and he urged Reynaud to get to Algiers as soon as possible. Reynaud in turn pressed de Gaulle to hasten to London to secure the cooperation of the British. "We shall meet again in Algiers!" Reynaud told him.[44]

De Gaulle's last encounter with Pétain came that day at dinner as Pétain sat at a nearby table with other members of the government. In silence, de Gaulle went to pay his respects. "He shook my hand without a word," de Gaulle later wrote. "I was never to see him again, never."[45]

After an overnight dash to the tip of Brittany, De Gaulle departed for Plymouth and London after warning his wife—now in seclusion in Brittany with their daughters—that he thought it was likely that "everything is about to collapse" and that she should be ready to leave at a moment's notice.[46]

By June 16, the Germans were approaching Bordeaux, and the Reynaud coalition collapsed. That evening, Prime Minister Reynaud resigned and yielded his position to Marshal Pétain (a decision he viewed at the time as inescapable but that afterward he deeply regretted). Returning from London late that night, Charles de Gaulle—now no longer a member of the government—heard of Pétain's appointment. He immediately decided to return to London the next morning.

Upon his arrival, he told a friend who asked what mission he was on, "I have not been sent on any mission, Madame. I am here to save the honor of France."[47]

A little after 12:30 p.m. on June 17, Marshal Pétain went on the radio to tell all of France that he had applied to the enemy for an armistice. Even before knowing Hitler's terms, he announced that "it is with a heavy heart that today I tell you we must stop the fighting." Headlines in that evening's British newspapers read, "France Surrenders."[48]

But the following day, General Charles de Gaulle, who saw the very soul of France in the balance, addressed an appeal on BBC radio to his countrymen to fight on: "Whatever happens," he told them, "the flame of French resistance must not and shall not go out."[49]

Pétain's supporters may have believed that the marshal (and only the marshal) had the ability to negotiate with Hitler, but from the outset, Hitler dictated the terms of France's capitulation. On June 22, Hitler humbled his adversaries by conducting the armistice talks in Compiègne, at the exact location and in the same railway car in which the November 1918 Armistice had been signed. (Until the Germans' entry into Paris, this railway car had been on exhibition at the Invalides.) Afterward, Pétain took to the radio to announce its terms.

Listening to this announcement while stopped overnight during his race to Bordeaux, Man Ray heard patriotic music, followed by Pétain's voice saying that, although every French soldier was ready to shed his last drop of blood for his country, there were other considerations, especially the priceless historic monuments of Paris that had to be saved. Emphasizing that this cease-fire was not without honor, he pointed out that a line had been agreed upon that divided France north and south into occupied and unoccupied zones. The war was over, he concluded, and exhorted the French to be dignified and do nothing to provoke the invaders, who were showing them the utmost leniency. Afterward, at the announcement's conclusion, the strains of "La Marseillaise" came over the radio, and everyone stood. Men and women were weeping.[50]

Pétain had attempted to couch it in fine words, but Léon Blum was astounded—it was "surrender, pure and simple," he later wrote. André Gide was equally horrified: "Can it be?" he asked in disbelief. "Did Pétain himself deliver it? Freely? . . . Is it not enough for France to be conquered? Must she also be dishonored?"[51]

Coco Chanel's grand-niece simply recalled that Chanel had "wept bitterly" at the news.[52]

The Third Republic ended as it had begun, in a bitter defeat to Germany. Marshal Pétain, granted full powers by the National Assembly (now meeting in non-occupied Vichy), took the position of chief of state, as a virtual monarch—much to the satisfaction of those who had yearned for such a leader.

With Parliament soon after disbanded and Pierre Laval by his side, Pétain appealed to a broad swath of authoritarian and antiparliamentary nationalists by rejecting "the false notion of the natural equality of men" and by promising that the new regime would embrace "a social hierarchy." He also denounced labor unions; promulgated laws that banned secret associations, especially the Masons; and on October 3, 1940, enacted the first anti-Jewish

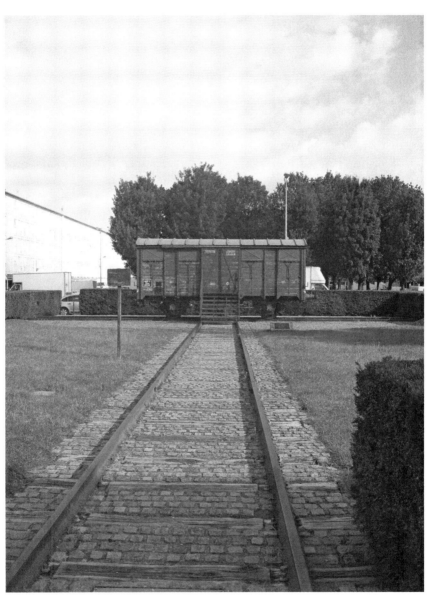

Memorial, former internment camp at Drancy, just outside of Paris. © J. McAuliffe

laws, harsh regulations constituting state-supported subjugation of France's Jews—although the exclusion of Jews had already begun. Soon the Pétain regime would begin the Nazi policy of rounding up Jews and sending them to French detention camps, including the notorious Drancy transit camp just outside of Paris, en route to death camps in the German Reich.

Tellingly, under Pétain, the new regime was called l'Etat Français, or the French State, as opposed to the French Republic, and the motto "Liberté, Egalité, Fraternité" was replaced by "Travail, Famille, Patrie" (Work, Family, Fatherland)—to the overwhelming approval of those who had always hated the Republic, as well as those who had more recently turned against it, thanks to the Popular Front. France, according to Pétain and his followers, had suffered because of its decadence and moral bankruptcy and required a thoroughgoing cleansing and redemption. As one historian has put it, Pétain's Vichy government "was launching a revolution that, eradicating the principles of 1789, aimed at transforming society from top to bottom, instilling new values and destroying the liberal, democratic, and secular heritage of the Enlightenment and the French Revolution."[53]

To this, Charles de Gaulle would offer a simple rallying cry: fight the enemy, liberate French territory, and restore France's honor along with its rightful place in the world.

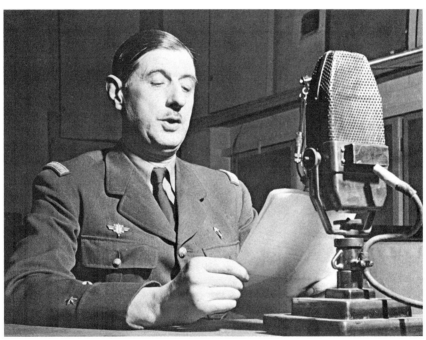

General Charles de Gaulle making a speech at the BBC in London, October 30, 1941. © Archives de Gaulle, Paris, France / Bridgeman Images

Epilogue

They scattered like the wind, with the tramp of enemy boots behind them. Those who streamed out of Paris in the panicked exodus following Occupation usually headed, via complex and hazardous routes, for Britain and, especially, for America.

Lisbon became the primary destination for those clamoring to get out, and it quickly became apparent—even before November 1942, when the Germans extended their rule to the so-called free or Unoccupied Zone—that there remained nothing "free" about France, not even in that portion governed by Pétain's Vichy government. The poet Bryher reported that her trip (by sealed bus) from Switzerland across France en route to Lisbon was a fraught one. She had been told semiofficially by the Swiss that she was on the German black list because of her refugee work and that she had better get out; but once she and her busload of forty-four passengers (representing fifteen different nationalities) entered France, she did not expect to see the patrol of German soldiers on motorcycles streaming past. "But this is the Unoccupied Zone," a man behind her exclaimed, at which everyone laughed. "The victors ride where they like," another passenger informed him.[1]

Despite German omnipresence, some Parisians chose to leave the city but remain in France. Even before the Germans entered Paris, Josephine Baker quit her job at the Casino and moved south to the Dordogne. While Maurice Chevalier was entertaining in Germany, singing over Nazi-controlled Radio Paris and enthusiastically supporting Pétain, Baker embarked in earnest on intelligence work for the Resistance, using her own inimitable methods. She began by traveling across Spain to Lisbon, with photographs pinned under her dress and pages of material, written in invisible ink, transcribed onto her sheet music. In Lisbon, she passed this along to British Intelligence, charming German and Spanish authorities as well as a bevy of journalists along the way.

Now a member of the Free French forces, Josephine continued her showbiz engagements on the road while maintaining her intelligence work, helping to set up a permanent liaison and transmission center in Casablanca, where information received from a Vichy contact was forwarded to London via Lisbon.

Back and forth she went, from the Dordogne to Morocco, and from there to Lisbon, with especially long layovers in Morocco, where she developed a network that secured passports for Eastern European Jews headed for Latin America. Only illness slowed her down, but even then she managed to pass information along to American diplomats in her hospital room. When the Allies invaded French North Africa, Josephine entertained the troops, telling the still-segregated black American soldiers, "As for getting mad because of race prejudice, wait till the war is over. I will come back to the States and join in the fight to break down segregation, but let's win the war first."[2] After the war, she kept her promise.

She came back a heroine to a liberated Paris. Awarded the Croix de Guerre for her service to her country, France also embraced her as a member of its Legion of Honor.

Unlike Josephine Baker, some French notables managed to stay quietly out of sight as they remained in France, keeping far from Paris. Henri Matisse, after a desperate run from the city just ahead of advancing German troops, remained for the duration in Nice, bedridden after a series of operations. Appalled by the fall of France—"the moral shock of this catastrophe"—and fearful for the lives of family members who were scattered across the country, he was in no position to leave and did not care to. His son Pierre made it back to New York, where he had become an established art dealer, bringing Matisse's beloved eight-year-old grandson, Claude (Marguerite's son), with him. Yet, from Matisse's point of view, leaving France at this time would have been a desertion.[3]

André Gide, too, stayed for a time in and around Nice, where he did what he could to help others escape, but he opened himself to charges of collaboration by publishing for the *NRF*, which was now under the direction of Hitler enthusiast Pierre Drieu La Rochelle (its previous editor had refused to publish under German control). When offered the necessary papers to leave the country, Gide replied that, "at present, he had no wish to leave France," although he would in fact spend much of the war in Tunis, and, according to one historian, he "never went beyond a neutral and detached attitude toward the Allies."[4] Buffeted by events, Gide was uneasy and ambivalent. "To come to terms with one's enemy of yesterday is not cowardice," he wrote on September 5; "it is wisdom, and accepting the inevitable. . . . What is the use of bruising oneself against the bars of one's cage?"[5]

Gertrude Stein and Alice B. Toklas were hardly ambivalent, and they certainly were not interested in resistance or revolt. They spent much of the war at their country home in Bilignin, where they managed well despite wartime austerity, enjoying the protection of Bernard Faÿ, who under the Pétain regime had become general administrator of the Bibliothèque Nationale de France and director of the regime's anti-Masonic purge (an effort that sent almost one thousand Freemasons to concentration camps, of whom more than half were killed). Pétain—and Faÿ—were convinced that Jews and Masons were to blame for France's troubles during the interwar years, but Faÿ nonetheless had no hesitation in using his good offices to protect Stein and Toklas, both of whom were Jewish, but also fervent Pétain supporters.

Stein's rapture for Pétain seemed unlimited. When Pétain signed the Armistice, she was certain that he had "achieved a miracle," and months later, after the nature of his government had become starkly evident, she told readers of the *Atlantic Monthly* that she was "very pleased" that France's war was over and that "a great load was lifted off France." First and foremost, Gertrude Stein required tranquility in which to live and write: "I cannot write too much upon how necessary it is to be completely conservative that is particularly traditional in order to be free," she wrote in *Paris France*, which appeared on the day that France fell to Hitler.[6] For Stein, even as a Jew in the midst of anti-Semitic terrors, Pétain provided that tranquility.

Thanks in large part to Stein's dear friend Faÿ, and possibly even to Pétain himself, she and Alice remained safe. For a year and a half, Stein even translated Pétain's speeches into English, apparently as part of a Vichy government propaganda attempt to persuade the American public that France's Vichy government was one they could trust. She continued to work on the project until after the United States had entered the war, and after the Germans had occupied all of France.

Once the war was over, when Faÿ was imprisoned as a Nazi collaborator, Alice B. Toklas seems to have aided him financially to escape to Switzerland. By this time, Gertrude Stein had died—but not before having renewed her celebrity and prestige in postwar America.

～

As the Germans closed in, those attempting to evacuate Paris and France faced a sea of obstacles. Elsa Schiaparelli, who had done the impossible by managing to acquire all the necessary visas in advance, nonetheless encountered one hurdle after another en route to Lisbon. At length she commandeered a taxi for the last two hundred kilometers, bullied her way through the police, and maneuvered her way into a luxury hotel, from where she waited out the time until departure. She arrived in New York in style, via Pan Am clipper.

By contrast, Eve Curie, who in one of her last speeches in America had told her audience, "We discovered that peace at any price is no peace at all,"[7] returned briefly to Paris to say good-bye to her family (who opted to stay) and promptly left for England on a cargo ship strafed by German aircraft.

Once in London, Eve joined de Gaulle's Free French forces, met with Churchill, and lectured in America in support of the war effort (where she received catcalls from America First and was invited to the White House). She became a special war correspondent for Allied Newspapers in London and the *New York Herald Tribune*, traveling some forty thousand miles across a series of wartime fronts. After serving with the women's medical corps of the Free French during the Italian campaign, she took part in the Provence landing with the troops in 1944, earning a Croix de Guerre. Eve Curie would eventually become a U.S. citizen, where she was nominated for the Pulitzer, and would continue her travels throughout the world with her husband, Henry Richardson Labouisse Jr., U.S. ambassador to Greece and, eventually, executive director of UNICEF (the United Nations International Children's Emergency Fund). Eve never won a Nobel, but her husband accepted one on behalf of UNICEF.

Man Ray, who like so many others made the long and hellish journey back to Paris after the Armistice, now decided to depart for good. He did not relish a return to America, but nothing remained for him now in a Paris bristling with machine guns and draped with Nazi flags; it was best for him, especially as a Jew, to get out of France. After saying good-bye to Kiki and Brancusi, he left Paris for the final time, with a small suitcase and a couple of cameras, and met up with Virgil Thomson and Thomson's fourteen trunks. These included six of musical scores—Beethoven, Mozart, Bach, and Brahms—which attracted the attention of a German border guard who commented on Thomson's good taste. Both Man Ray and Thomson were fleeing across the Spanish border toward Lisbon, with New York as their final destination.

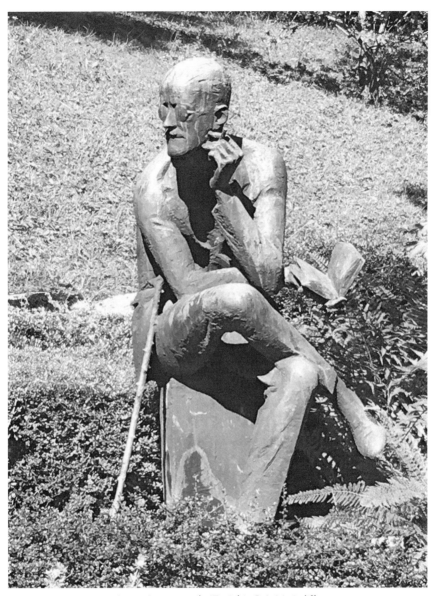

James Joyce, tomb (Zurich). © J. McAuliffe

Others followed similar flight paths, with Lisbon as the central choke point and New York the goal. In the madhouse that Lisbon quickly became, crammed with frantic refugees trying to get on steamships bound for America, Man Ray encountered Gala Dalí, who was pushing to arrange passage for herself and Dalí. There, too, was Maria Jolas, who had escorted her two daughters and Matisse's grandson through a flotsam of refugees all the way from their school in the Auvergne, via Marseilles. This, after having succored an increasingly frail and impossible James Joyce through the waning days of the war, managing at last to get him and Nora across the border to Switzerland.

Joyce would die early the following year in Zurich.

At long last, Man Ray managed to get on a liner bound for New York, along with Thomson, the Dalís, and film director René Clair and his wife (the beautiful Bronya Perlmutter, whom Cocteau's young protégée, Raymond Radiguet, had once threatened to marry).[8] Because of overcrowding, Man Ray and Thomson slept on mattresses on the floor of the ship's grand salon.

Once in New York, the Dalís traveled to Caresse Crosby's Virginia estate, where they remained for many months, wearing out their welcome, while Man Ray—depressed by New York—went to Hollywood, where he stayed for years and there befriended Henry Miller, who had arrived in California by way of Greece. Another who was Hollywood bound was Stravinsky, who married Vera soon after her arrival in the States.

Jean Renoir was yet another. Renoir had encountered all the horrors of France flooded with refugees as he endeavored to avoid German air raids and herd his small family group to safety. After the little group split up, he and Dido left for Les Collettes, his father's home on the Côte d'Azur. Fortunately, Dido—foreseeing the danger—had already made contact with an American director they knew, and by this time an offer had reached him from Hollywood. Renoir did not want to leave France, but visits he now received from agents of the Reich, urging him to make films for "the New France," galvanized him into going. By this time he clearly understood what was coming: "Better get the hell out," he told a friend. "It's going to be horrible."[9]

Despite bureaucratic obstacles and the snafus of war, by autumn Renoir and Dido were able to leave for Lisbon via Marseilles, Algeria, and Morocco. From Lisbon and New York, they went to Hollywood, where Renoir remained throughout the war, becoming an American citizen. He was also able to get his son, Alain, out of France. Alain, in turn, promptly enlisted in the U.S. Army. His father, who had fought in the trenches at the same age,

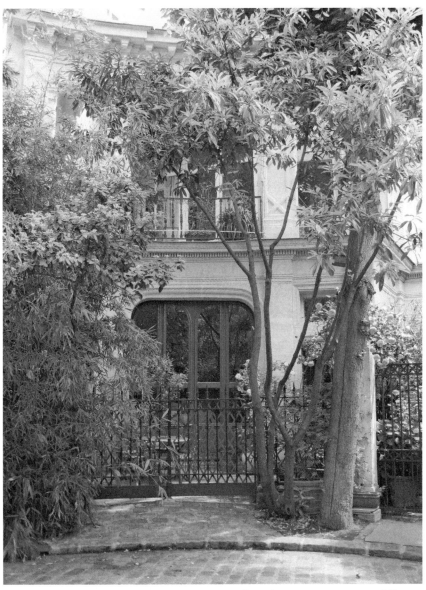

Jean Renoir's residence in Paris (Avenue Frochot), from 1937. © M. McAuliffe

completely understood. "When you're twenty years old and you're French," he wrote the French ambassador, who asked for an explanation, "if you leave the country, you enlist and you fight."[10]

Alain, who spoke virtually no English when he arrived, would serve four years in the South Pacific, including Japan. After returning to the United States as a decorated officer, he married; went to the University of California at Santa Barbara on the G.I. Bill; and, after receiving his doctorate in English and comparative literature at Harvard, taught at Ohio University before returning to the University of California at Berkeley. There he taught medieval English literature for the rest of his distinguished career.

In time, Jean Renoir and Dido (now Madame Renoir) returned to Paris, and to their rose-covered abode in the Avenue Frochot. But their ties to America would remain strong.

André Breton also ended up in the United States—thanks to help from the Emergency Rescue Committee and to Peggy Guggenheim—after the Vichy censors banned his major works and arrested and interrogated him and many of his Surrealist colleagues. Perhaps to his surprise, Breton found that life in New York was not so bad after all, especially with colleagues like Marcel Duchamp around, and he even became a regular speaker for the French broadcasts of Voice of America. Moreover, he and his friends were able to continue Surrealism in America, with exhibits and a review—again, thanks to support from Peggy Guggenheim.

The Catholic philosopher Jacques Maritain, whose wife's Jewish heritage prompted them to flee, also landed in New York, after staying for a spell at the Pontifical Institute for Medieval Studies in Canada. In America, Maritain and his wife became deeply involved in rescue activities, especially of French academics and intellectuals, and they became firm supporters of de Gaulle's Free French.

Picasso's art dealer, the famed Paul Rosenberg, was another of the lucky ones who managed to escape to New York via Lisbon. Rosenberg arrived with his wife and daughter (his son remained in France, to fight with de Gaulle's Free French) after attempting to save his renowned art collection. The Germans would find the paintings he had stashed away in a bank vault near Bordeaux. But fortunately Rosenberg had already sent a number of his works to safety in London and New York and had loaned the cream of his Picassos to New York's Museum of Modern Art, which had been planning an extensive Picasso retrospective.

Some, like Charlotte Perriand, went farther than the United States as they scattered before the Nazi storm. Yet after a year in Japan, Perriand was ready to return to France via America. But while she was on what was billed as a brief layover in Indochina, the Japanese bombed Pearl Harbor, and she found that she could no longer return to the United States or France. While exiled in Vietnam, she went to work in Hanoi, dealing in crafts, and married a Frenchman, who then was handling France's economic affairs in Indochina. It was not a happy arrangement (she described them as "two polar opposites"),[11] but they had a child before she and her husband were arrested following the Japanese conquest of Indochina. Only the war's end brought Perriand back to France, now with a daughter, where she would continue her forthright and courageous life, dedicated to creating better design—in the belief that this would encourage a more livable environment and a better society.

Others, including André Malraux, Louis Aragon, and the Surrealist poets Paul Eluard and Robert Desnos, stayed in France and joined the Resistance. Malraux, who had a way of landing on his feet, much like the cats he so admired, had been captured and imprisoned by the Germans, escaped, and eventually joined the Resistance. After the war he became one of de Gaulle's right-hand men and France's first minister of cultural affairs.

Aragon, who had been mobilized and won the Croix de Guerre for bravery, headed for the Unoccupied Zone, where he helped to organize the communist resistance to the Occupation and wrote for the underground press. Eluard, while operating with the Resistance, provided inspiration for those fighting the enemy with his poem "Liberty," which spread, underground, throughout France. Both would survive to publish their poetry about the war.

Desnos, who also joined the Resistance, was arrested by the Gestapo in Paris while trying to shield his wife, Youki, whom he feared the Germans would torture to find his whereabouts. "Go, go!" she had urged him, as she saw the black car of the Gestapo coming down the street. "Not on your life!" he exclaimed, just as the knock sounded on the door.[12] Captured and imprisoned, Desnos was deported to Auschwitz, then to Buchenwald and Terezin, where he died of typhoid.

Those in the government who tried to fight on from North Africa encountered a merciless foe. Edouard Daladier and Georges Mandel, among others, boarded a ship for Morocco, expecting the rest of their colleagues to follow. Instead, they were placed under house arrest in Casablanca and sent to their fates: Mandel and Daladier ended up in Buchenwald, where they encountered the former prime minister of France, Léon Blum.[13]

"Prison was missing from my experience of life," Blum later wrote. "Providence has provided it." Even though warned after the Occupation that he should escape from France ("If you only knew the hatred they felt for you!" a friend told him), he made no effort to leave, convinced that he was not vulnerable because he had been in retirement for two years. He was wrong. On September 15, Blum was arrested and sent to prison in Chazeron, then to Bourrassol, where he was put on trial for crimes and misdemeanors contributing to France's defeat in the war. For too many, this kind of scapegoating provided an easy answer to what had happened, one that reaffirmed what they already believed. As Charles Maurras jubilantly exclaimed, "I have verified that it is the Judeo-Masonic politicians who have thrown us into the abyss down which we are falling."[14]

The trial was political and ideological: Blum was to be tried for having been the leader of the Popular Front, in particular the 1936 factory occupation, and for the Popular Front's legislation on behalf of the working class—most notably the forty-hour law, which according to his accusers "gave the working class a taste for less effort."[15] Above all, Blum, rather than the army, was to be blamed for France's defeat.

But the trial was postponed indefinitely until, after more than a year of imprisonment, Hitler intervened. Suddenly Pétain announced that he would inflict the harshest punishment possible on those responsible for "our disaster." By these, he meant Edouard Daladier, the unfortunate General Gamelin, and Léon Blum. The indictment against Blum was that, "by compromising, through the unjustifiable weakness of his government, both the immediate results of production and the moral strength of the producers, M. Léon Blum, as Premier, betrayed the duties of his office."[16]

By this time, the Nazis had incarcerated Blum's son, Robert, in a penal colony in Germany, while they sent Blum's youngest brother, René, into internment at Drancy, from where he was sent to the death camps in Poland and never returned. After a farce of a trial, in which Blum's vigorous defense circulated underground and abroad, the trial was halted, and Blum was sentenced to life imprisonment. In March 1943, he, along with Daladier and Gamelin, were deported to Buchenwald, where they joined Georges Mandel (who would be assassinated the following year). There, Jeanne Levylier married Blum (who had been widowed since 1938) and remained with him until their release at the war's end.

During that entire time, according to Blum, he and his wife "never supposed for a single minute that we would return alive to French soil." But even while incarcerated, he was able to write, "I do not believe in fallen or damned races. I believe it no more for the Germans than for the Jews."[17]

⌒

And then there were those who remained in Paris. After the war, the stigma of collaboration hung heavy over many of these, especially over Coco Chanel and Jean Cocteau.

Chanel, whose anti-Semitism was selective and generally not on display when the Rothschilds were around,[18] notoriously slept with the enemy—a handsome German officer, Hans Günther ("Spatz") von Dincklage, who was an attaché at the German embassy in Paris and perhaps a German spy. Further stains on Chanel's reputation came from her continued residency at the Ritz, where German officers abounded, and her use of the Occupation's anti-Jewish laws to attempt to oust her Jewish business partners, the Wertheimers, when they fled France. This strategy in fact fizzled when the Wertheimers placed Les Parfums Chanel in the hands of an Aryan owner for the war's duration.

Jean Cocteau, who was far more interested in himself and his comforts than in who ran the show, was more intrigued by the novelty of the German Occupation than stirred by any sense of patriotism. The Occupation, with a Paris filled with German uniforms, offered something new and exciting; and although Cocteau tried to go to the aid of his good friend Max Jacob,[19] and on occasion could be caustic about the German occupiers, he had a fine line to tread: the Nazis were no more accommodating of homosexuals than they were of Jews. Straitlaced morality was in; decadence, as they defined it, was out. As Cocteau wrote a friend shortly before his return with Jean Marais to Paris in the autumn of 1940, "Believe it or not, those worthies [the Vichy regime] have decided that Gide and I are to blame for everything."[20]

Not only Cocteau, but any writer who wanted or needed to be published in occupied Paris had to submit to a degree of collaboration, since the Germans required licensing, or authorization, for all published writing and virtually all public activity, including theater, films, concerts, and exhibitions. Cocteau did not object, and indeed later claimed that in return for providing publicity for a Paris exhibit of Hitler's favorite sculptor, Arno Breker, French film employees subsequently were exempted from having to work in Germany. But Cocteau also had his rare moments of protest. His December 1940 article, "Adresse aux jeunes écrivains" (Address to Young Writers), ended with this rousing plea: "There is a tremendous task to be performed: to defend, against

your unworthy fellow countrymen, the domains of the spirit . . . Do not say;
'It is too hard:' . . . Say: 'I must do the impossible.'"[21]

He was, of course, calling upon others to do this, not himself.

∽

Some writers refused to submit to the Nazi censors' stamp of approval and
wrote for underground publications or did not publish at all, but Colette was
not among them. With a Jewish husband (who barely escaped deportation)
and the need to support them both, she regularly published her writings in
the pro-Vichy and pro-German press. This, even while her daughter, stepson, and close friends were working for the Resistance.

Theirs was not the only divided family. Misia Sert—whose grandmother
was Jewish, and who (as her friend Boulos noted in a diary entry for December 1940) was "beside herself about the anti-Jewish laws that turn Paris into
a prison, the exact negation of what our city is"[22]—was a fierce supporter
of the Resistance. Her former husband, the painter José-Maria Sert (who
provided the grandiose murals for 30 Rockefeller Center), was an unabashed
collaborator. Although, at Misia's instigation, Sert did intervene to prevent
Colette's husband from being deported to Germany and tried unsuccessfully
to save Max Jacob, Sert had no problem with benefiting massively from the
largesse that came his way. Technically, he and Misia were still divorced, but
by now—after the death of Sert's second wife—they were reunited, although
on less than ideal terms.

After the war, many—including Louis Renault—were anxious to put the
term "collaboration" in context. One of a number of big businessmen who
deeply feared communism and were not displeased to see an end to the laws
of the Popular Front nor to the unions, Renault saw his actions during the
Occupation as "business as usual" and as a means of continuing production
and thereby providing employment to his French workforce. "It is better to
give them [the Germans] butter, or they'll take the cows," he remarked,[23] but
others, especially after the war, did not agree: Renault went to prison as a
collaborator—not helped by his wife's long affair with the collaborator Pierre
Drieu La Rochelle.

And then there were those who capitulated wholly and happily, calling it something else. Le Corbusier, much like Cocteau, was stimulated by
Germany's invasion of France and eagerly awaited the new world that he
anticipated. "I must fight here [in France]," he wrote, "where I believe it is
necessary to put the world of construction on the right track."[24]

Corbu thought little of Hitler, but he was more than willing to work with
the Pétain regime, where he served in the Ministry of Industrial Production.

"He left for Vichy . . . to defend the cause of architecture and urban planning," Charlotte Perriand wrote. "Corbu was no politician," she added. "He would have made peace with the devil just to see his projects realized—not out of any personal interest, but because he was so convinced of the need to change life."[25]

In mid-1942, Le Corbusier left Vichy, disheartened by what he had experienced. But it was Vichy's failure to accept his ideas rather than the politics of capitulation that changed his mind.

In the meantime, Corbu's cousin and partner, Pierre Jeanneret, joined the Resistance.

Picasso navigated this war much like the previous one, submerging himself in his work and trying not to get involved. Although he found it unpleasant to continue living next door to the residence and gallery of his art dealer, Paul Rosenberg, once Rosenberg's address was taken over by the Nazis' chief looting organization (the Einsatzstab Reichsleiter Rosenberg—another Rosenberg, and not a Jewish one), Picasso managed to live comfortably in the occupied city at his studio on the Left Bank, on Rue des Grands-Augustins. This in turn raised questions as to whether, despite his status as the leading practitioner of what Hitler termed "degenerate art," Picasso was receiving special perks.

Perhaps his fame was sufficient to exempt him from Nazi abuse, but no one truly knows. Picasso remained untouched, even when bonfires of "degenerate art" went up in the courtyard outside the Jeu de Paume (after Nazi leaders like Hermann Göring first skimmed off the cream for themselves). During it all, Picasso remained mum and complied with official demands. On November 30, 1942, he signed the residence permit certifying "on my honor that I am not Jewish in terms of the law of 2 June 1941"—the law that had repeated and toughened the terms of the 1940 Jewish Statute.[26]

The challenge for those like Picasso, who chose to remain in Paris, was to stay free of the stigma of collaboration while continuing to create and, most importantly, to survive. Picasso managed this, but perhaps something more as well. Paul Eluard, writing to art historian and collector Roland Penrose soon after the liberation of Paris in 1944, wrote that Picasso "has been one of the rare painters who have behaved well and he continues to do so." Eluard referred to the manifold ways in which certain artists (among them, André Derain and Maurice de Vlaminck) had been seduced by the Germans, and "how Picasso had always been willing to help the resistance movement by sheltering anyone sent to him by his friends, whether he knew them or not."[27]

In particular, Penrose commended Picasso for appearing in public at the memorial service for Max Jacob in the spring of 1944, when Paris was still under Nazi control. Jacob was a friend, although one from a distant past, and despite the possible dangers, Picasso did not hesitate to honor him.

⁓

"I don't think I have ever felt so utterly depressed as I did during that walk back through the deserted streets, under a stormy sky," Simone de Beauvoir wrote in her diary for June 28, 1940, after she made her way back to Paris. "I shall sit here and rot for years," she added on June 30, as she desolately sat in an empty Dôme café.[28]

Sartre had been taken prisoner, although a brief note from him assured Beauvoir that he was not being badly treated. But Paris was filled with fear and confusion, and the newspapers were of little help, being "quite unspeakable," as she put it, with their "self-righteous apologies for Germany."[29] Yet despite Beauvoir's revulsion at signs reading "Out of Bounds to Jews" in shop windows, she signed a document affirming on oath that she was neither a Freemason nor a Jew. She was not proud of doing so, but she did it.

And life somehow went on, with a combination of fear, confusion, and self-interest surrounding every decision, every day. Parisians, and the French as a whole, soon adjusted to the presence of German soldiers, who behaved correctly, dispensed chocolate bars, and paid for their purchases in cash. "There'll be plenty of little Germans on the way soon," Beauvoir heard remarked again and again, with no censure whatever, as French girls flirted with the Germans.[30]

Food was minimal that summer—Beauvoir complained that she hadn't had a good square meal for days, but ration cards appeared by autumn, and theaters and cinemas reopened, although with a difference. The offerings were slim and censored, and the audiences were restricted.

And now, a new notice appeared on the stage door of the Casino de Paris: "Entrance Prohibited to Dogs and Jews."[31]

⁓

While waiting for Sartre to be released (in the spring of 1941), Beauvoir kept occupied with friends, cafés, concerts, and reading—including books in English, which she borrowed from Sylvia Beach's Shakespeare and Company, where Beauvoir was a member.

Despite efforts of the American embassy to convince Beach to leave Paris, she continued to stick it out in an increasingly hostile environment. The streets remained peaceful, but she was painfully aware of the changes that had occurred, especially those impacting Paris's Jewish population. She briefly hid one Jewish friend from the Gestapo and shared with another friend "some of the special restrictions on Jews"—though not the large yellow Star of David that her friend had to wear. "We could not enter public places such as theatres, movies, cafés, concert halls, or sit down on park [or even street] benches," Beach later recalled. Once, when they tried to picnic unobtrusively in a shady square, sitting on the ground *beside* a bench, they felt compelled to down their meager lunch in a hurry, glancing furtively around them. It was not an experience that either of them cared to repeat.[32]

Shakespeare and Company struggled as readers of English books left Paris and the Germans banned the sale of English literature published after 1870. But the end of Beach's beloved bookstore came with the United States' entry into the war. "My nationality, added to my Jewish affiliations, finished Shakespeare and Company in Nazi eyes," she later wrote.[33] One day in December 1941, soon after Pearl Harbor, a high-ranking German officer stopped by to look at a copy of *Finnegans Wake*, which Beach had put in the window. It was her last as well as her own personal copy, and she told him that it was not for sale. He was enraged and left; two weeks later he reappeared to announce that they were coming that day to confiscate all her books.

Beach promptly located her concierge, who opened unoccupied rooms over Beach's own upstairs apartment. Beach then rallied friends, who loyally carried upstairs all the shop's books and photographs, in clothesbaskets, and removed every piece of furniture—even the light fixtures. She persuaded a carpenter to quickly remove the bookshelves, and within a short space, there was nothing left of Shakespeare and Company. A housepainter even painted out the name on the front of 12 Rue de l'Odéon.

The Germans do not seem to have returned to witness the now-barren room, although in August 1942 they did come to arrest Beach, sending her to an internment camp. They never would discover the books, which remained hidden until the liberation of Paris. But Beach—released from internment after six months thanks to the efforts of a friend in Vichy headquarters who had been one of her earliest customers—had been warned by German military authorities that she could be taken back any time they chose. She promptly went into hiding on the top floor of a friend's youth hostel. Throughout this period, she secretly visited Adrienne Monnier's bookshop to hear the latest news and keep up on the latest clandestine publications, which Paul Eluard supplied and in which prominent writers of the Resistance appeared.

The liberation of Paris in August 1944 brought Ernest Hemingway to the Rue de l'Odéon. Since the outbreak of war, Hemingway had married Martha Gellhorn (who divorced him in 1945), promptly married *Time* magazine correspondent Mary Welsh, published *For Whom the Bell Tolls*, and joined up as a journalist (for *Collier's*) in the wake of the Normandy landing. He attached himself to the Twenty-Second Regiment of the Fourth American Infantry Division and then established himself as leader of a small patrol of Free French fighters outside of Paris, despite Geneva Convention prohibitions banning journalists from bearing arms.

Although Hemingway had taken the precaution of asking the commanding officer for an order to justify his assumption of command over this group of Free French, his exploits were not exactly legitimate; and although he seems to have performed capably and courageously, his deeds were not quite as glorious as he afterward made them. Most certainly, he was not the first into Paris, nor did he "liberate" his favorite bar at the Ritz. But nonetheless, Hemingway afterward won a Bronze Star for bravery, and on August 25 he appeared on the Rue de l'Odéon, where—as Beach put it—"there was still a lot of shooting going on."[34]

"It's Hemingway! It's Hemingway!" Adrienne cried, as Sylvia flew downstairs. "We met with a crash," she recalled. And then "he picked me up and swung me around and kissed me, while people on the street and in the windows cheered."[35]

~

Notes

Selected sources are listed by chapter, in the approximate order in which they informed the text.

1 End of an Era (1929)

Philippe Bernard and Henri Dubief, *The Decline of the Third Republic, 1914–1938* (New York: Cambridge University Press, 1988); Noel Riley Fitch, *Sylvia Beach and the Lost Generation: A History of Literary Paris in the Twenties and Thirties* (New York: Norton, 1983); Sylvia Beach, *Shakespeare & Company* (Lincoln: University of Nebraska Press, 1991); Michael S. Reynolds, *Hemingway: The 1930s* (New York: Norton, 1997); Carlos Baker, *Ernest Hemingway: A Life Story* (New York: Scribner, 1969); Wambly Bald, *On the Left Bank, 1929–1933* (Athens: Ohio University Press, 1987); Bryher [Annie Winifred Ellerman], *The Heart to Artemis: A Writer's Memoirs* (New York: Harcourt, Brace & World, 1962); Nancy Cunard, *These Were the Hours: Memories of My Hours Press, Réanville and Paris, 1928–1931* (Carbondale: Southern Illinois University Press, 1969); Richard Ellmann, *James Joyce* (New York: Oxford University Press, 1983); Ernest Hemingway, *Ernest Hemingway: Selected Letters, 1917–1961* (New York: Scribner, 1981); Ernest Hemingway, *A Moveable Feast* (New York: Touchstone, 1996); Julian Jackson, *The Politics of Depression in France, 1932–1936* (New York: Cambridge University Press, 1985); Jean Lacouture, *Léon Blum* (New York: Holmes & Meier, 1982); Timothy B. Smith, *Creating the Welfare State in France, 1880–1940* (Montreal: McGill-Queen's University Press, 2003); Susan Pedersen, *Family, Dependence, and the Origins of the Welfare State: Britain and France, 1914–1945* (New York: Cambridge University Press, 1993); Victoria Best,

An Introduction to Twentieth-Century French Literature (London: Duckworth, 2002); Clifford Browder, *André Breton: Arbiter of Surrealism* (Geneva, Switzerland: Librarie Droz, 1967); Meryle Secrest, *Salvador Dalí: The Surrealist Jester* (London: Weidenfeld & Nicolson, 1986); Salvador Dalí, *The Secret Life of Salvador Dalí* (New York: Dover, 1993); Salvador Dalí and André Parinaud, *Maniac Eyeball: The Unspeakable Confessions of Salvador Dalí* (New York: Creation, 2004); Luis Buñuel, *My Last Sigh* (New York: Vintage, 1984); Luis Buñuel, *An Unspeakable Betrayal: Selected Writings of Luis Buñuel* (Berkeley: University of California Press, 2000).

1. Beach, *Shakespeare & Company*, 102.
2. Bald, *On the Left Bank*, 2.
3. Bryher, *Heart of Artemis*, 214.
4. Beach, *Shakespeare & Company*, 185.
5. As Beckett explained to Nancy Cunard (*These Were the Hours*, 115).
6. Ellmann, *James Joyce*, 611; Beach, *Shakespeare & Company*, 185. Later, in 1936, Joyce told a Danish interviewer (in perfect Danish) that, "having written *Ulysses* about the day, I wanted to write this book about the night. Otherwise it has no connection with Ulysses . . . . [There is] no connection between the people in *Ulysses* and the people in *Work in Progress*. There are in a way no characters. It's like a dream" (Ellmann, *James Joyce*, 695–96).
7. Beach, *Shakespeare & Company*, 183; Ellmann, *James Joyce*, 614.
8. Beach, *Shakespeare & Company*, 138.
9. Beach, *Shakespeare & Company*, 74.
10. Hemingway to Sherwood Anderson, 9 March 1922, in *Selected Letters*, 62. See also Hemingway, *Moveable Feast*, 56, 36, and Ellmann, *James Joyce*, 529.
11. Beach, *Shakespeare & Company*, 197.
12. Fitch, *Sylvia Beach and the Lost Generation*, 294–95.
13. Beach, *Shakespeare & Company*, 189.
14. Section Française de l'Internationale Ouvrière.
15. France's 1930 social insurance legislation put into operation important legislation passed in 1928, including worker insurance (below particular wage levels) for illness, disability, and death, plus disability benefits for veterans, maternity benefits, and modest old-age pensions. It also now provided for farmers. At the heart of this vast social legislation were provisions for the wounded and dependents of the dead from World War I. See Smith, *Creating the Welfare State in France*, 93–94, and Pedersen, *Family, Dependence, and the Origins of the Welfare State*, 372n39.
16. Lacouture, *Léon Blum*, 192.
17. France's Council of State served as the nation's supreme court as well as legal advisor to the executive branch. Blum would remain here until he left for private law practice at the war's end, becoming a well-regarded (and well-reimbursed) civil lawyer.
18. Later, Blum wrote, "He [Barrès] chose nationalist instinct as a rallying point. . . . Something was broken, finished; one of the avenues of my youth was blocked" (*Souvenirs sur l'affaire*, in Lacouture, *Léon Blum*, 40).

19. As he later wrote, French Jews at first did not want to become involved, fearing that people would think that their support of Dreyfus was merely evidence of "racial solidarity." Nor did they want to provide "food for anti-Semitic feeling" (Blum, *Souvenirs sur l'affaire*, in Lacouture, *Léon Blum*, 36).

20. In 1920, the Communists would take complete control of *L'Humanité*.

21. Lacouture, *Léon Blum*, 59.

22. Blum's one child, Robert, was born in 1902, and Blum "devoted passionate attention to his education." Robert, "raised outside any religious tradition," attended the prestigious Ecole Polytechnique and became a civil aeronautics engineer (Lacouture, *Léon Blum*, 77–78).

23. Natanson was editor of *La Revue blanche*, and his wife, Misia, would become famous as an arts patron, especially of Diaghilev's Ballets Russes. By then she would be known as Misia Sert, having remarried twice after divorcing Natanson.

24. This would not go into effect until after the war.

25. Lacouture, *Léon Blum*, 180–81.

26. Dalí, *Secret Life of Salvador Dalí*, 1.

27. Dalí, *Secret Life of Salvador Dalí*, 38.

28. Secrest, *Salvador Dalí*, 58.

29. Secrest, *Salvador Dalí*, 77, 79.

30. Dalí, *Secret Life of Salvador Dalí*, 206.

31. Dalí, *Secret Life of Salvador Dalí*, 250. He would later claim, "I *was* Surrealism" (*Maniac Eyeball*, 88).

32. Buñuel, *My Last Sigh*, 104.

33. Dalí, *Secret Life of Salvador Dalí*, 243–44.

34. Dr. Roumeguère quoted in Secrest, *Salvador Dalí*, 114.

35. Dalí, *Secret Life of Salvador Dalí*, 233, 248.

36. Dalí and Parinaud, *Maniac Eyeball*, 79. "It just happened that I had written a scenario that would revolutionize contemporary cinema and that he [Buñuel] was to come at once. He came" (79). See also 80–81.

37. Dalí, *Secret Life of Salvador Dalí*, 260.

2 Rags and Riches (1929)

Elsa Schiaparelli, *Shocking Life: The Autobiography of Elsa Schiaparelli* (London: V&A Publications, 2007); Meryle Secrest, *Elsa Schiaparelli: A Biography* (New York: Knopf, 2014); John Richardson, *A Life of Picasso: The Triumphant Years, 1917–1932* (New York: Knopf, 2007); Anne Sinclair, *My Grandfather's Gallery: A Family Memoir of Art and War* (New York: Farrar, Straus & Giroux, 2014); Hilary Sperling, *Matisse, the Master: A Life of Henri Matisse; The Conquest of Colour, 1909–1954* (New York: Knopf, 2005); Stephen Walsh, *Stravinsky: A Creative Spring; Russia and France, 1882–1934* (Berkeley: University of California Press, 2002); Paul Morand, *The Allure of Chanel* (London: Pushkin Press, 2008); Rhonda K. Garelick, *Mademoiselle:*

Coco Chanel and the Pulse of History (New York: Random House, 2014); Justine Picardie, *Coco Chanel: The Legend and the Life* (New York: HarperCollins, 2010); Axel Madsen, *Chanel: A Woman of Her Own* (New York: Henry Holt, 1991); Morley Callaghan, *That Summer in Paris: Memories of Tangled Friendships with Hemingway, Fitzgerald, and Some Others* (Toronto: Macmillan of Canada, 1963); Fitch, *Sylvia Beach and the Lost Generation*; Beach, *Shakespeare & Company*; Michael S. Reynolds, *Hemingway: The 1930s*; Carlos Baker, *Ernest Hemingway*; F. Scott Fitzgerald, *A Life in Letters: F. Scott Fitzgerald* (New York: Scribner, 1994); Jeffrey Meyers, *Scott Fitzgerald: A Biography* (New York: HarperCollins, 1994); Hemingway, *Ernest Hemingway: Selected Letters*; Hemingway, *A Moveable Feast*; Mary McAuliffe, *When Paris Sizzled: The 1920s Paris of Hemingway, Chanel, Cocteau, Cole Porter, Josephine Baker, and Their Friends* (Lanham, Md.: Rowman & Littlefield, 2016); Bryher, *Heart to Artemis*; Albert J. Guerard, *André Gide* (Cambridge, Mass.: Harvard University Press, 1951); Alan Sheridan, *André Gide: A Life in the Present* (London: Hamish Hamilton, 1998); André Gide, *If It Die: An Autobiography* (New York: Modern Library, 1935); André Gide, *The Immoralist* (New York: Vintage, 1996); André Gide, *The Counterfeiters* (New York: Vintage, 1973); Tom Conner, ed., *André Gide's Politics: Rebellion and Ambivalence* (New York: Palgrave, 2000); Olivier Todd, *Malraux: A Life* (New York: Knopf, 2005); Jean Lacouture, *De Gaulle, the Rebel: 1890–1944* (New York: Norton, 1993); Jean-Claude Baker and Chris Chase, *Josephine: The Hungry Heart* (New York: Cooper Square Press, 2001); Josephine Baker and Jo Bouillon, *Josephine* (New York: Harper & Row, 1977); Simone de Beauvoir, *Memoirs of a Dutiful Daughter* (New York: World Publishing, 1959); Simone de Beauvoir, *The Prime of Life* (New York: World Publishing, 1962); Jean-Paul Sartre, *War Diaries: Notebooks from a Phoney War, November 1939–March 1940* (London: Verso, 1984); Axel Madsen, *Hearts and Minds: The Common Journey of Simone de Beauvoir and Jean-Paul Sartre* (New York: Morrow, 1977); Deirdre Bair, *Simone de Beauvoir: A Biography* (New York: Summit, 1990); John Glassco, *Memoirs of Montparnasse* (New York: Oxford University Press, 1970); Samuel Putnam, *Paris Was Our Mistress: Memoirs of a Lost and Found Generation* (New York: Viking, 1947); Janet Flanner, *Paris Was Yesterday, 1925–1975* (New York: Viking, 1972); Hugh Ford, *Four Lives in Paris* (San Francisco, Calif.: North Point Press, 1987); Linda Hamalian, *The Cramoisy Queen: A Life of Caresse Crosby* (Carbondale: Southern Illinois University Press, 2005); Caresse Crosby, *The Passionate Years* (New York: Dial Press, 1953); Jean Hugo, *Le Regard de la Memoire* (Arles et Paris: Actes Sud, 1983); Judith M. Hughes, *To the Maginot Line: The Politics of French Military Preparation in the 1920s* (Cambridge, Mass.: Harvard University Press, 1971).

1. Richardson, *Picasso: The Triumphant Years*, 384.

2. Sinclair, *My Grandfather's Gallery*, 104.

3. Rosenberg's granddaughter, Anne Sinclair, notes that "during the Great Depression, Paul returned to the nineteenth century, which was easier to sell than modern painting during those difficult economic times" (Sinclair, *My Grandfather's Gallery*, 101).

4. They had no children and eventually divorced.

5. Morand, *Allure of Chanel*, 165, 169.

6. Morand, *Allure of Chanel*, 165.

7. Callaghan, *That Summer in Paris*, 128.

8. Hemingway gave similar instructions to Morley Callaghan, who had just had dinner with Fitzgerald (*That Summer in Paris*, 167–68).

9. Callaghan, *That Summer in Paris*, 125–26.

10. Callaghan, *That Summer in Paris*, 213–14.

11. Callaghan, *That Summer in Paris*, 214–15.

12. Callaghan, *That Summer in Paris*, 241–50; Hemingway to Callaghan, 4 January 1930, in *Selected Letters*, 318–19.

13. Hemingway to Fitzgerald, 4 and 13 September; 24 or 31 October 1929, in *Selected Letters*, 305, 307, 309–10.

14. See McAuliffe, *When Paris Sizzled*, 209–10.

15. Hemingway to Fitzgerald, 24 or 31 October 1929, in *Selected Letters*, 309, 310.

16. Michael S. Reynolds, *Hemingway: The 1930s*, 10–11.

17. Bryher, *Heart to Artemis*, 215.

18. Guerard, *André Gide*, 5.

19. Gide, *If It Die*, 285–86.

20. One of the arguments that the Petite Dame used with Gide on behalf of this apartment arrangement was that it would be "the best solution for Beth and Catherine, the best way of giving them continuing, but discreet contact with Gide without restricting his freedom" (Sheridan, *André Gide*, 415).

21. Guerard, *André Gide*, 25.

22. Todd, *Malraux*, 17 and 484n7.

23. Todd, *Malraux*, 11.

24. Todd, *Malraux*, 39.

25. The case files would eventually be "forgotten" (Todd, *Malraux*, 62).

26. Todd, *Malraux*, 41.

27. See McAuliffe, *When Paris Sizzled*, 235.

28. Lacouture, *De Gaulle, the Rebel*, 93.

29. Jean-Claude Baker, *Josephine*, 165, 167.

30. Beauvoir, *Prime of Life*, 21. "When we met again in Paris we found a name for our relationship before we had decided just what that relationship was to be. 'It's a morganatic marriage,' we said" (*Prime of Life*, 21).

31. "Over and above the books I read with Sartre," she wrote of this time, "I went through Whitman, Blake, Yeats, Synge, Sean O'Casey, all of Virginia Woolf, a vast quantity of Henry James, George Moore, Swinburne, Frank Swinnerton, Rebecca West, Sinclair Lewis, Theodore Dreiser, Sherwood Anderson," and more. Much more (Beauvoir, *Prime of Life*, 46).

32. Madsen, *Hearts and Minds*, 48.

33. Beauvoir, *Prime of Life*, 93.

34. Sartre, *War Diaries*, 28 February 1940, 266.

35. Sartre thought a lot about his own unattractiveness and the fact that it did not prevent his many sexual conquests: "I'm not so sure I didn't seek out women's company, at one time," he wrote in 1940, "in order to get rid of the burden of my ugliness. By looking at them, speaking to them and exerting myself to bring an animated, joyful look to their faces, I'd lose myself in them and forget myself" (29 February 1940, *War Diaries*, 282).

36. Madsen, *Hearts and Minds*, 43.

37. Beauvoir, *Prime of Life*, 24. Beauvoir added, "There was no question of our actually taking advantage, during our 'lease,' of those 'freedoms' which in theory we had the right to enjoy" (*Prime of Life*, 24). This assumption would prove less than accurate.

38. Glassco, *Memoirs of Montparnasse*, 211.

39. Putnam, *Paris Was Our Mistress*, 241.

40. Fitch, *Sylvia Beach and the Lost Generation*, 300.

41. Ford, *Four Lives in Paris*, 225.

42. Putnam, *Paris Was Our Mistress*, 239. Harry Crosby, age thirty-one, killed himself on December 10, with his mistress, in the Hotel des Artistes in New York—in either a murder-suicide or a suicide pact. According to the writer Kay Boyle, who knew the Crosbys well, "In his complicated sun-worshipping system [Crosby] had found his refuge and a shield that protected him from 'his Boston environment, his position in the bank, his education, and above all, against people, against all kinds of people. . . . People were the enemy'" (Ford, *Four Lives in Paris*, 199). Crosby's suicide reminded Hemingway of his own father's suicide the previous December (Carlos Baker, *Ernest Hemingway*, 206).

43. Putnam, *Paris Was Our Mistress*, 239.

44. Putnam, *Paris Was Our Mistress*, 241.

45. Flanner, *Paris Was Yesterday*, 61–62.

46. Hugo, *Le Regard de la Memoire*, 295.

3 It Could Never Happen Here (1930)

Youki Desnos, *Les Confidences de Youki* (Paris: Librairie Arthème Fayard, 1957); Eugen Weber, *The Hollow Years: France in the 1930s* (New York: Norton, 1994); Flanner, *Paris Was Yesterday*; Charlie Schelps, *Elsie de Wolfe's Paris: Frivolity before the Storm* (New York: Abrams, 2014); Valérie Bougault, *Montparnasse: The Heyday of Modern Art, 1910–1940* (Paris: Editions Pierre Terrail, 1997); Man Ray, *Self Portrait* (Boston: Little, Brown, 1988); Neil Baldwin, *Man Ray, American Artist* (New York: Da Capo Press, 2001); Herbert R. Lottman, *Man Ray's Montparnasse* (New York: Harry N. Abrams, 2001); Secrest, *Elsa Schiaparelli*; Madsen, *Chanel*; Morand, *Allure of Chanel*; Paul Poiret, *King of Fashion: The Autobiography of Paul Poiret* (Philadelphia: J. B. Lippincott, 1931); Yvonne Deslandres, *Poiret: Paul Poiret, 1879–1944* (Paris: Editions du Regard, 1986); Nicholas Fox Weber, *Le Corbusier: A Life* (New York:

Knopf, 2008); Tim Benton, *The Villas of Le Corbusier, 1920–1930* (New Haven, Conn.: Yale University Press, 1987); Deborah Gans, *The Le Corbusier Guide* (New York: Princeton Architectural Press, 2006); Charlotte Perriand, *A Life of Creation: An Autobiography* (New York: Monacelli Press, 2003); Jackie Wullschläger, *Chagall: A Biography* (New York: Knopf, 2008); Richardson, *Life of Picasso: The Triumphant Years*; Judith Thurman, *Secrets of the Flesh: A Life of Colette* (New York: Ballantine, 1999); Flanner, *Paris Was Yesterday*; Ruth Brandon, *Ugly Beauty: Helena Rubinstein, L'Oréal, and the Blemished History of Looking Good* (New York: Harper, 2011); Herbert R. Lottman, *The Michelin Men: Driving an Empire* (New York: I. B. Taurus, 2003); John Reynolds, *André Citroën: The Man and the Motor Cars* (Thrupp, Stroud, UK: Sutton, 1996); Anthony Rhodes, *Louis Renault: A Biography* (New York: Harcourt, Brace & World, 1970); Alain Frerejean, *André Citroën, Louis Renault: Un duel sans merci* (Paris: Albin Michel, 1998); McAuliffe, *When Paris Sizzled*; Fitch, *Sylvia Beach and the Lost Generation*; Billy Klüver and Julie Martin, *Kiki's Paris: Artists and Lovers, 1900–1930* (New York: Abrams, 1989); Kiki, *Kiki's Memoirs* (Hopewell, N.J.: Ecco Press, 1996); Herbert R. Lottman, *The Left Bank: Writers, Artists, and Politics from the Popular Front to the Cold War* (Boston: Houghton Mifflin, 1982); Bald, *On the Left Bank*; Alfred Perlès, *My Friend Henry Miller: An Intimate Biography* (London: Neville Spearman, 1955); Samuel Putnam, *Paris Was Our Mistress: Memoirs of a Lost and Found Generation* (New York: Viking, 1947); Ellmann, *James Joyce*; John Malcolm Brinnin, *The Third Rose: Gertrude Stein and Her World* (Reading, Mass.: Addison-Wesley, 1987); Sisley Huddleston, *Back to Montparnasse: Glimpses of Broadway in Bohemia* (Philadelphia: J. B. Lippincott, 1931); Hamalian, *Cramoisy Queen*; Crosby, *Passionate Years*; Nancy Cunard, *These Were the Hours*; Morrill Cody, *The Women of Montparnasse* (New York: Cornwall Books, 1983); Adam Gopnik, *Paris to the Moon* (New York: Random House, 2000); Robert McAlmon, *Being Geniuses Together, 1920–1930* (San Francisco, Calif.: North Point Press, 1984); Sandra Whipple Spanier, *Kay Boyle, Artist and Activist* (Carbondale: Southern Illinois University Press, 1986); Hemingway, *Moveable Feast*; Michael S. Reynolds, *Hemingway: The American Homecoming* (Cambridge, Mass.: Blackwell, 1992).

1. Youki Desnos, *Confidences de Youki*, 154.

2. Charles Mestorino, a Paris jewelry designer and former World War I fighter pilot (for Italy), had been tried for the grisly murder of a diamond merchant and, after a sensational trial, sentenced to life imprisonment on Devil's Island. The crime's solution greatly burnished the reputation of police commissioner Marcel Guillaume, whom Georges Simenon would use as a model for Inspector Maigret in his acclaimed series of Maigret mysteries.

3. Youki Desnos, *Confidences de Youki*, 155–56.

4. Youki Desnos, *Confidences de Youki*, 157.

5. Eugen Weber, *Hollow Years*, 30.

6. Morand, *Allure of Chanel*, 155.

7. Morand, *Allure of Chanel*, 147–48.

8. Poiret, *King of Fashion*, 78.

9. Deslandres, *Poiret*, 78.

10. There is some difference of opinion on whether the Villa Savoye was completed in 1930 or 1931.

11. Nicholas Fox Weber, *Le Corbusier*, 4.

12. Perriand, *Life of Creation*, 28.

13. Frank Lloyd Wright quoted in Nicholas Fox Weber, *Le Corbusier*, 288.

14. Nicholas Fox Weber, *Le Corbusier*, 291.

15. The Cité de Refuge, located at 12 Rue Cantagrel (13th), has recently been extensively renovated and reopened. The Asile Flottant, a humble barge of reinforced concrete named the *Louise-Catherine*, is currently moored on the Seine just below the Gare d'Austerlitz (13th) and is undergoing complete reconstruction.

16. Perriand, *Life of Creation*, 22.

17. Perriand, *Life of Creation*, 24, 25.

18. Perriand, *Life of Creation*, 28.

19. Nicholas Fox Weber, *Le Corbusier*, 291.

20. Thurman, *Secrets of the Flesh*, 362.

21. Flanner, *Paris Was Yesterday*, 70.

22. Brandon, *Ugly Beauty*, 35, 37.

23. Lottman, *Michelin Men*, 160.

24. This extended factory has since been demolished and replaced in part by Parc André-Citroën (15th).

25. It would remain there, in letters one hundred feet high, until 1934. See McAuliffe, *When Paris Sizzled*, 178 and 194.

26. John Reynolds, *André Citroën*, 168.

27. Beach told Lawrence that she was too busy, but privately she did not care for the book, which she called a "kind of sermon-on-the-mount—of Venus" (Fitch, *Sylvia Beach and the Lost Generation*, 280).

28. Billy Klüver, introduction to *Kiki's Memoirs*, 29.

29. Bald, *On the Left Bank*, 9 September 1930, 28.

30. Putnam, translator's note in *Kiki's Memoirs*, 60–61.

31. Putnam, *Paris Was Our Mistress*, 68–69.

32. Ellmann, *James Joyce*, 588, 584.

33. Huddleston, *Back to Montparnasse*, 108.

34. Bald, *On the Left Bank*, 4 November 1930, 39–40.

35. From introduction by Hugh Ford to Cunard, *These Were the Hours*, xi.

36. Cody, *Women of Montparnasse*, 89; Hugh Ford, introduction to Cunard, *These Were the Hours*, xi.

37. Cunard, *These Were the Hours*, 8.

38. Cunard, *These Were the Hours*, 5, 17.

39. Much to Cunard's amazement, Beckett had composed this "intricate" and "intense" poem in just a few hours, having only heard of the contest the afternoon on the final day (Cunard, *These Were the Hours*, 111).

40. Cunard, *These Were the Hours*, 26–27.

41. Putnam, *Paris Was Our Mistress*, 71.

42. Boyle in McAlmon, *Being Geniuses Together*, 337.

43. Spanier, *Kay Boyle*, 31, 24.

44. For more on this episode, see McAuliffe, *When Paris Sizzled*, 206–10.

45. Hemingway, *Moveable Feast*, 118; Michael S. Reynolds, *Hemingway: The American Homecoming*, 84.

46. Brinnin, *Third Rose*, 259.

47. Baldwin, *Man Ray*, 162–63; Man Ray, *Self Portrait*, 147.

48. See Richardson, *Life of Picasso: The Triumphant Years*, 426–27.

49. Putnam, *Paris Was Our Mistress*, 138. Samuel Putnam and Wambly Bald were present.

50. Hemingway, *Moveable Feast*, 28; Beach, *Shakespeare & Company*, 32.

51. Boyle in McAlmon, *Being Geniuses Together*, 241; Spanier, *Kay Boyle*, 24; Ellmann, *James Joyce*, 529. On a later occasion, when scolded by the wife of a longtime friend, Joyce muttered, "I hate women who know anything" (634).

4 The Ooh La La Factor (1930)

Jean-Claude Baker, *Josephine*; Flanner, *Paris Was Yesterday*; Jennifer Anne Boittin, *Colonial Metropolis: The Urban Grounds of Anti-Imperialism and Feminism in Interwar Paris* (Lincoln: University of Nebraska Press, 2010); Eve Curie, *Madame Curie: A Biography by Eve Curie* (Garden City, N.Y.: Garden City Publishing, 1940); Susan Quinn, *Marie Curie: A Life* (New York: Simon & Schuster, 1995); Shelley Emling, *Marie Curie and Her Daughters: The Private Lives of Science's First Family* (New York: Palgrave Macmillan, 2012); Mary McAuliffe, *Twilight of the Belle Epoque: The Paris of Picasso, Stravinsky, Proust, Renault, Marie Curie, Gertrude Stein, and Their Friends through the Great War* (Lanham, Md.: Rowman & Littlefield, 2014); Spanier, *Kay Boyle*; McAlmon, *Being Geniuses Together*; Kay Boyle, *My Next Bride* (New York: Harcourt, Brace, 1934); Hamalian, *Cramoisy Queen*; Crosby, *Passionate Years*; Peggy Guggenheim, *Out of This Century: Confessions of an Art Addict* (New York: Universe Books, 1979); Pedersen, *Family, Dependence, and the Origins of the Welfare State*; Bernard and Dubief, *Decline of the Third Republic*; Smith, *Creating the Welfare State in France*; André Gide, *The Journals of André Gide*, vol. 3, *1928–1939* (London: Secker & Warburg, 1949); Ellmann, *James Joyce*; Fitch, *Sylvia Beach and the Lost Generation*; Beach, *Shakespeare & Company*; Janet Flanner, *Janet Flanner's World: Uncollected Writings, 1932–1975* (New York: Harcourt Brace Jovanovich, 1979); Robert Ferguson, *Henry Miller: A Life* (New York: Norton, 1991); Perlès, *My Friend Henry Miller*; Brassaï, *Henry Miller: The Paris Years* (New York: Arcade, 2011); Henry Miller, *Tropic of Cancer* (New York: Grove Weidenfeld, 1961); Meyers, *Scott Fitzgerald*; Fitzgerald, *A Life in Letters*; Nancy Mitford, *Zelda: A Biography* (New York: Harper & Row, 1970); Carlos Baker, *Ernest Hemingway*; Michael S. Reynolds, *Hemingway: The*

1930s; Richardson, *Life of Picasso: The Triumphant Years*; Brinnin, *Third Rose*; Linda Simon, *The Biography of Alice B. Toklas* (Garden City, N.Y.: Doubleday, 1977); Barbara Will, *Unlikely Collaboration: Gertrude Stein, Bernard Faÿ, and the Vichy Dilemma* (New York: Columbia University Press, 2011); Gertrude Stein, *The Autobiography of Alice B. Toklas* (New York: Vintage, 1990); Secrest, *Salvador Dalí*; Jean Hugo, *Avant d'oublier: 1918–1931* (Paris: Fayard, 1976); Francis Steegmuller, *Cocteau: A Biography* (Boston: Little, Brown, 1970); Jean Cocteau, *The Journals of Jean Cocteau* (New York: Criterion Books, 1956); Barry J. Eichengreen, *Golden Fetters: The Gold Standard and the Great Depression, 1919–1939* (New York: Oxford University Press, 1992); Kenneth Mouré, *The Gold Standard Illusion: France, the Bank of France, and the International Gold Standard, 1914–1939* (New York: Oxford University Press, 2002); Eugen Weber, *The Hollow Years*; Browder, *André Breton*; Abbé (Arthur) Mugnier, *Journal de l'Abbé Mugnier: 1879–1939* (Paris: Mercure de France, 1985); Count Harry Kessler, *The Diaries of a Cosmopolitan: Count Harry Kessler, 1918–1937* (London: Weidenfeld & Nicolson, 1971); McAuliffe, *When Paris Sizzled*; Eugen Weber, *Action Française: Royalism and Reaction in Twentieth-Century France* (Stanford, Calif.: Stanford University Press, 1962); Walsh, *Stravinsky: A Creative Spring*; Bryher, *Heart to Artemis*; Julien Green, *Journal, 1928–1949*, vol. 1 (Paris: Plon, 1961).

1. Jean-Claude Baker, *Josephine*, 171.

2. Flanner, *Paris Was Yesterday*, 72.

3. Jean-Claude Baker, *Josephine*, 172.

4. Eve Curie, *Madame Curie*, 372, 373.

5. On the story of Marie Curie's affair with Paul Langevin, which occurred several years after Pierre Curie's death, see Susan Quinn's carefully researched biography, *Marie Curie*. Pierre Curie was Paul Langevin's doctoral professor.

6. Quinn, *Marie Curie*, 425.

7. Spanier, *Kay Boyle*, 26–27.

8. Boyle, *My Next Bride*, 64.

9. Spanier, *Kay Boyle*, 27. Boyle dedicated *My Next Bride*, her autobiographical novel dealing with these events, to Caresse Crosby.

10. Guggenheim, *Out of This Century*, 111, 94.

11. According to Pedersen, "unemployment insurance was not introduced until 1958, and family benefits remained a central feature of the French welfare state" (*Family, Dependence, and the Origins of the Welfare State*, 414).

12. Pedersen, *Family, Dependence, and the Origins of the Welfare State*, 407.

13. Gide, 2 September 1928, in *Journals*, 3:20.

14. Ellmann, *James Joyce*, 629.

15. After a six-month residence in England, James and Nora were wed there on July 4, 1931 (see Ellmann, *James Joyce*, 637).

16. Flanner, *Janet Flanner's World*, 313.

17. A copy of the document, dated 9 December 1930, is shown in Beach, *Shakespeare & Company*, 203, and Fitch, *Sylvia Beach and the Lost Generation*, 308.

18. Perlès, *My Friend Henry Miller*, 4–5.

19. Perlès, *My Friend Henry Miller*, 5.

20. See especially Salman Rushdie's 1984 *Outside the Whale*, where Rushdie (in response to George Orwell's 1939 defense of Miller, *Inside the Whale*) wrote that Miller "now looks to be very little more than the happy pornographer beneath whose scatological surface Orwell saw such improbable depths" (Ferguson, *Henry Miller*, xv).

21. Ferguson, *Henry Miller*, 1.

22. Perlès, *My Friend Henry Miller*, 33.

23. Miller, *Tropic of Cancer*, 1.

24. Simon, *Biography of Alice B. Toklas*, 140.

25. Gertrude Stein, *Autobiography of Alice B. Toklas*, 248.

26. Brinnin, *Third Rose*, 270.

27. In *La Revue Européanne*, as "*le plus puissant écrivain américan d'aujourd'hui*" (Simon, *Biography of Alice B. Toklas*, 145).

28. Gertrude Stein, *Autobiography of Alice B. Toklas*, 245–46. Later, Faÿ conceded this point (246).

29. Richardson, *Life of Picasso: The Triumphant Years*, 399.

30. Steegmuller, *Cocteau*, 400 (see Hugo, *Avant d'oublier*, 280, for the original account).

31. "*Jean est enchanté. Il a eu son scandale*" (Valentine writing to her former husband, Jean Hugo, in Hugo, *Avant d'oublier*, 280).

32. Steegmuller, *Cocteau*, 407.

33. There is some disagreement over whether Charles de Noailles was actually kicked out. According to an editorial note in the journal of Abbé Mugnier, who was close to the Noailles, Charles never was kicked out, although some wanted it; he remained a member until his death (Mugnier, *Journal de l'Abbé Mugnier*, 606n196).

34. Kessler, 15 September 1930, in *Diaries of a Cosmopolitan*, 396–97.

35. See the events leading to Daudet's sentence, in McAuliffe, *When Paris Sizzled*, 131, 152, 233.

36. Eugen Weber, *The Hollow Years*, 102.

37. Walsh, *Stravinsky: A Creative Spring*, 493. Walsh also mentions Bartók's *Cantata profana* (1930) and Hindemith's oratorio, *Das Unaufhörliche* (1931), 498.

38. Bryher, *Heart to Artemis*, 259.

39. Green, 16 and 22 October 1930, in *Journal*, 1:24–25 (my translation).

5 Navigating a Dangerous World (1931–1932)

Perriand, *A Life of Creation*; Todd, *Malraux*; Quinn, *Marie Curie*; Eve Curie, *Madame Curie*; Emling, *Marie Curie and Her Daughters*; Boittin, *Colonial Metropolis*; Jean-Claude Baker, *Josephine*; Lacouture, *De Gaulle, the Rebel*; Julian Jackson, *Charles de Gaulle* (London: Haus, 2003); John Reynolds, *André Citroën*; Madsen, *Chanel*; Picardie, *Coco Chanel*; Garelick, *Mademoiselle*; Baldwin, *Man Ray*; Bald, *On the Left Bank*; René Clair, *A nous la liberté* (New York: Criterion Collection, 2002); René Clair, *Le Million* (New York: Criterion Collection, 2000); André Bazin, *Jean Renoir* (New York: De Capo Press, 1992); Sheridan, *André Gide*; Célia Bertin, *Jean Renoir: A Life in Pictures* (Baltimore, Md.: Johns Hopkins University Press, 1991); Jean Renoir, *My Life and My Films* (New York: Da Capo Press, 2000); Jean Renoir, *Boudu Saved from Drowning* (U.S.: Home Vision Entertainment, 2005); Georges Simenon, *Night at the Crossroads* (New York: Penguin, 2014); Bernard and Dubief, *Decline of the Third Republic*; Eugen Weber, *Hollow Years*; Hughes, *To the Maginot Line*; Pedersen, *Family, Dependence, and the Origins of the Welfare State*; Jackson, *Politics of Depression in France*; Lacouture, *Léon Blum*; Eichengreen, *Golden Fetters*; Rhodes, *Louis Renault*; Madsen, *Chanel*; Morand, *Allure of Chanel*; Flanner, *Paris Was Yesterday*; Frederick Brown, *The Embrace of Unreason: France, 1914–1940* (New York: Knopf, 2014); Eugen Weber, *Action Française*; Herbert R. Lottman, *Return of the Rothschilds: The Great Banking Dynasty through Two Turbulent Centuries* (London: Taurus, 1995); McAuliffe, *When Paris Sizzled*; Nicholas Fox Weber, *Le Corbusier*; Norma Evenson, *Paris: A Century of Change, 1878–1978* (New Haven, Conn.: Yale University Press, 1979); Mary McAuliffe, *Twilight of the Belle Epoque*; Luc Sante, *The Other Paris* (New York: Farrar, Straus & Giroux, 2015); Miller, *Tropic of Cancer*; Brassaï, *Henry Miller*; Perlès, *My Friend Henry Miller*; Ferguson, *Henry Miller*; Beach, *Shakespeare & Company*; Fitch, *Sylvia Beach and the Lost Generation*; Ellmann, *James Joyce*.

1. Perriand, *Life of Creation*, 37, 39, 40, 45.

2. Todd, *Malraux*, 97.

3. Todd, *Malraux*, 97.

4. According to the writer Maurice Martin du Gard, who reported his conversation with Valéry in his memoirs (Todd, *Malraux*, 101).

5. Quinn, *Marie Curie*, 424.

6. Eve Curie, *Madame Curie*, 356.

7. Eve Curie, *Madame Curie*, 356–57.

8. Eve Curie, *Madame Curie*, 357.

9. The pagoda representing Togo and Cameroon has been preserved and is now an active Buddhist temple. Nearby is a small Tibetan Buddhist temple, and another small temple on the same grounds is being renovated.

10. Jean-Claude Baker, *Josephine*, 176.

11. Jean-Claude Baker, *Josephine*, 175.

12. Lacouture, *De Gaulle, the Rebel*, 118.

13. Lacouture, *De Gaulle, the Rebel*, 118.

14. Lacouture, *De Gaulle, the Rebel*, 101.

15. Instead of bolting the car body onto a separate chassis frame, this completely eliminated the chassis frame—allowing the body to hold engine, transmission, and suspension together, and reducing the car's weight, center of gravity, and height of ride (John Reynolds, *André Citroën*, 172).

16. Madsen, *Chanel*, 186.

17. Garelick, *Mademoiselle*, 228.

18. Baldwin, *Man Ray*, 168.

19. Bald, 9 September 1931, in *On the Left Bank*, 75. Sergei Eisenstein was the foremost Soviet filmmaker at the time.

20. Pierre-Auguste Renoir, according to Jean, "had no use for callings in which the hands played no part. He mistrusted intellectuals. 'They poison the world,'" he said. "'They don't know how to see or hear or touch'" (Renoir, *My Life and My Films*, 48).

21. With the stage name Catherine Hessling.

22. Jean Renoir, *My Life and My Films*, 50.

23. Truffaut in Bazin, *Jean Renoir*, 217.

24. Bazin, *Jean Renoir*, 22.

25. Bernard and Dubief, *Decline of the Third Republic*, 280.

26. Renoir quoted in Bazin, *Jean Renoir*, 156.

27. Renoir, *My Life and My Films*, 108. Their legal separation would not take place until 1935.

28. Renoir, *My Life and My Films*, 104, 105; Bertin, *Jean Renoir*, 89.

29. Renoir, "Memories," in Bazin, *Jean Renoir*, 156–57.

30. According to Georges Simenon, quoted in Bertin, *Jean Renoir*, 93.

31. Renoir quoted in Bertin, *Jean Renoir*, 94.

32. Bazin, *Jean Renoir*, 231.

33. Eugen Weber, *Hollow Years*, 17.

34. The Socialists, however, advocated "reflation," a mild version of inflation meant to curb the effects of deflation.

35. Rhodes, *Louis Renault*, 123. After a year's preparation, one-third of the entire Quai de Javel works were torn down and reconstructed between April and July 1933 (John Reynolds, *André Citroën*, 177).

36. Madsen, *Chanel*, 183.

37. Morand, *Allure of Chanel*, 121.

38. Flanner, *Paris Was Yesterday*, 87.

39. Eugen Weber, *Action Française*, 299.

40. The origins of this myth seem to refer to the two hundred largest shareholders in the Bank of France (Lottman, *Return of the Rothschilds*, 202–3).

41. See McAuliffe, *When Paris Sizzled*, 203, 229, 231, 245–46, 265.

42. Nicholas Fox Weber, *Le Corbusier*, 346–47.

43. For more on the history of the Thiers fortification, dating from the 1840s, as well as Paris's long history of walls, see "The Walls of Paris," in Mary McAuliffe, *Paris Discovered: Explorations in the City of Light* (Hightstown, N.J.: Princeton Book Company, 2006), 68–77.

44. See especially the work of Eugène Hénard (Evenson, *Paris*, 272–73 and McAuliffe, *Twilight of the Belle Epoque*, 170–72).

45. Evenson, *Paris*, 275.

46. See chapter 3 note 15.

47. Perlès, *My Friend Henry Miller*, 71.

48. The Cité de la Muette was completed after the war, and people now actually live there. It surrounds a Holocaust Memorial, which includes an old railroad boxcar typical of those used to transport the tens of thousands of French Jews to the death camps. A museum dedicated to these victims of the Holocaust is located nearby.

49. Miller, *Tropic of Cancer*, 182.

50. Brassaï, *Henry Miller*, 46. He is citing Miller's description of the Rue de Lourmel (15th) that Alfred Perlès excerpted as an early sketch in *My Friend Henry Miller*, 25–28.

51. Ferguson, *Henry Miller*, 189.

52. Miller seems to have been "puzzled by the rumors that Proust was a homosexual who had disguised his lover as a female character" but then decided that the actual sex of the real-life Albertine made no difference: "What we are enthralled by is the vast panorama of deceit, treachery, lying, jealousy," he wrote Nin (Ferguson, *Henry Miller*, 197).

53. Brassaï, *Henry Miller*, 123.

54. Brassaï, *Henry Miller*, 174.

55. Perlès, *My Friend Henry Miller*, 93.

56. Brassaï quoting Miller, in *Henry Miller*, 90.

57. Ferguson, *Henry Miller*, 205.

58. Ferguson, *Henry Miller*, 206.

59. Beach, *Shakespeare & Company*, 207.

60. Fitch, *Sylvia Beach and the Lost Generation*, 313.

61. Ellmann, *James Joyce*, 651–52.

62. A friend reported that he showed the letter to her and was "deeply wounded" (Fitch, *Sylvia Beach and the Lost Generation*, 316; Ellmann, *James Joyce*, 651).

63. Fitch, *Sylvia Beach and the Lost Generation*, 317–18; Beach, *Shakespeare & Company*, 202.

64. Beach, *Shakespeare & Company*, 202.

65. Fitch, *Sylvia Beach and the Lost Generation*, 322–23; Beach, *Shakespeare & Company*, 204.

66. See McAuliffe, *When Paris Sizzled*, 111–12.

67. Beach, *Shakespeare & Company*, 201. "I knew how desperately he needed the money," she later wrote, and "I felt an immense joy over his good fortune. . . . As for my personal feelings, well, one is not at all proud of them, and they should be promptly dumped" (*Shakespeare & Company*, 205).

6 Taking Sides (1933)

Brown, *Embrace of Unreason*; Bernard and Dubief, *Decline of the Third Republic*; Bryher, *Heart to Artemis*; Kessler, *Diaries of a Cosmopolitan*; Laird McLeod Easton, *The Red Count: The Life and Times of Harry Kessler* (Berkeley: University of California

Press, 2002); Lacouture, *Léon Blum*; Raymond Spiteri and Donald LaCoss, eds., *Surrealism, Politics and Culture* (Burlington, Vt.: Ashgate, 2003); Gide, *Journals*, vol. 3; Sheridan, *André Gide*; Weber, *Hollow Years*; Roger Shattuck, "Having Congress: The Shame of the Thirties," in Tom Conner, ed., *André Gide's Politics: Rebellion and Ambivalence* (New York: Palgrave, 2000); Browder, *André Breton*; Todd, *Malraux*; Perriand, *A Life of Creation*; Beauvoir, *Prime of Life*; Madsen, *Hearts and Minds*; Bair, *Simone de Beauvoir*; Heinrich August Winkler, *Germany: The Long Road West* (New York: Oxford University Press, 2006); Kenneth Silver, *Chaos and Classicism: Art in France, Italy, and Germany, 1918–1936* (New York: Guggenheim Museum, 2010); Nicholas Fox Weber, *Le Corbusier*; McAuliffe, *When Paris Sizzled*; Garelick, *Mademoiselle*; Picardie, *Coco Chanel*; Madsen, *Chanel*; Morand, *Allure of Chanel*; Thurman, *Secrets of the Flesh*; Secrest, *Salvador Dalí*; Ferguson, *Henry Miller*; Hamalian, *Cramoisy Queen*; Crosby, *Passionate Years*; Hemingway, *Ernest Hemingway: Selected Letters, 1917–1961*; Michael S. Reynolds, *Hemingway: The 1930s*; Carlos Baker, *Ernest Hemingway*; Meyers, *Scott Fitzgerald*; Stein, *Autobiography of Alice B. Toklas*; Simon, *Biography of Alice B. Toklas*; Brinnin, *Third Rose*; Will, *Unlikely Collaboration*; Gertrude Stein, *Everybody's Autobiography* (New York: Random House, 1937); Bald, *On the Left Bank*; Richardson, *Picasso: The Triumphant Years*; Morrill Cody, with Hugh Ford, *The Women of Montparnasse* (New York: Cornwall Books, 1983); Jimmie Charters, *This Must Be the Place: Memoirs of Montparnasse* (New York: Collier Macmillan, 1989); Fitch, *Sylvia Beach and the Lost Generation*; Beach, *Shakespeare & Company*; Jackson, *Politics of Depression in France*; Roulhac B. Toledano and Elizabeth Z. Coty, *François Coty: Fragrance, Power, Money* (Gretna, La.: Pelican, 2009); Robert Soucy, *French Fascism: The First Wave, 1924–1933* (New Haven, Conn.: Yale University Press, 1995); Kevin Birmingham, *The Most Dangerous Book: The Battle for James Joyce's "Ulysses"* (New York: Penguin, 2014); Ellmann, *James Joyce*; Renoir, *My Life and My Films*; Bertin, *Jean Renoir*; Bazin, *Jean Renoir*; Lacouture, *De Gaulle, the Rebel*; Jackson, *De Gaulle*.

1. Brown, *Embrace of Unreason*, 179.

2. A week before the Reichstag fire, Count Harry Kessler received word from "reliable sources" that "the Nazis plan a fake attempt on Hitler's life which is to be the signal for a general massacre." When the Reichstag burned, Kessler noted in his diary, "The planned [fake] assault has taken place, though not on Hitler but the Reichstag building" (20 and 27 February 1933, in *Diaries of a Cosmopolitan*, 446, 448).

3. Bryher, *Heart to Artemis*, 260, 261. She would not return to Berlin for twenty-eight years.

4. Bryher, *Heart to Artemis*, 260, 261.

5. Kessler, 1 April, 5 and 24 May, 1933, in *Diaries of a Cosmopolitan*, 451, 454, 456.

6. Kessler, 28 February and 8 April 1933, in *Diaries of a Cosmopolitan*, 449, 452.

7. Easton, *Red Count*, 397.

8. Kessler, 19 October 1933, in *Diaries of a Cosmopolitan*, 463.

9. See Eugen Weber, *Hollow Years*, 104, for these statistics.

10. Lacouture, *Léon Blum*, 201.

11. Lacouture, *Léon Blum*, 201.

12. Spiteri and LaCoss, *Surrealism, Politics and Culture*, 93.

13. Gide, 20 May 1933 and 13 May 1931, in *Journals*, 3:270, 160.

14. Gide, 27 July 1931, 13 December 1932, and 30 January 1932, in *Journals*, 3:179, 180, 250, 219.

15. Gide, 24 July 1931, 8 January 1932, in *Journals*, 3:179, 210, 211.

16. Gide, 13 December 1932 and 6 June 1933, in *Journals*, 3:250, 273.

17. Sheridan, *André Gide*, 460.

18. Gide, 14 April 1933, in *Journals*, 3:268.

19. Gide, June 1933, in *Journals*, 3:275, 276.

20. Todd, *Malraux*, 104, 105.

21. Eugen Weber, *Hollow Years*, 227.

22. Perriand, *A Life of Creation*, 71.

23. Beauvoir, *Prime of Life*, 112, 111.

24. Madsen, *Hearts and Minds*, 61.

25. Beauvoir, *Prime of Life*, 120, 146.

26. Beauvoir, *Prime of Life*, 146.

27. Winkler, *Germany*, 411.

28. Madsen, *Hearts and Minds*, 61.

29. Nicholas Fox Weber, *Le Corbusier*, 358, 344. See also McAuliffe, *When Paris Sizzled*, 246–47.

30. Garelick, *Mademoiselle*, 236.

31. Thurman, *Secrets of the Flesh*, 401.

32. See McAuliffe, *When Paris Sizzled*, on Chanel's agreement with the Wertheimer brothers to form the Société des Parfums Chanel, 161.

33. Morand, *Allure of Chanel*, 109, 111. Morand was another in Chanel's inner circle with strong anti-Semitic views, who would actively collaborate with Pétain's Vichy government.

34. Secrest, *Salvador Dalí*, 135.

35. Dalí and Gala lived at 101 bis Rue de la Tombe-Issoire (14th), at the corner of Villa Seurat, from July 1934 until January 1938; Miller lived several houses away, at 18 Villa Seurat, from September 1934 to 1939.

36. Secrest, *Salvador*, 179.

37. Hemingway to Fitzgerald, 12 April 1931, in *Ernest Hemingway: Selected Letters*, 339.

38. Carlos Baker, *Ernest Hemingway*, 246; Michael S. Reynolds, *Hemingway: The 1930s*, 139.

39. Hemingway to Perkins, 13 June 1933, in *Ernest Hemingway, Selected Letters*, 393–94.

40. Bald, *On the Left Bank*, 142–43.

41. Brinnin, *Third Rose*, 309; Stein, *Everybody's Autobiography*, 4, 40.

42. Brinnin, *Third Rose*, 316, 311.

43. Stein, *Autobiography of Alice B. Toklas*, 216, 217.

44. Hemingway to Arnold Gingrich, 3 April 1933; Hemingway to Janet Flanner, 8 April 1933; Hemingway to Maxwell Perkins, 26 July 1933, all in *Ernest Hemingway, Selected Letters*, 384, 387, 395.

45. Cody, *Women of Montparnasse*, 84.

46. Hemingway introduction to Charters, *This Must Be the Place*, 2.

47. See McAuliffe, *When Paris Sizzled*, especially 206–7, 208–10.

48. Coty had changed the name of *Le Figaro* to *Figaro* when he bought it in 1922; it reverted to *Le Figaro* (and to its former moderately conservative leanings) after he lost control.

49. Gertrude Stein, *Autobiography of Alice B. Toklas*, 195; Fitch, *Sylvia Beach and the Lost Generation*, 333, 341.

50. See McAuliffe, *When Paris Sizzled*, 102–3, 111–12.

51. The U.S. Circuit Court of Appeals would uphold the decision in August 1934.

52. And in fact she contracted with Albatross Press to sell her Continental rights to publish *Ulysses* (Fitch, *Sylvia Beach and the Lost Generation*, 335).

53. Fitch, *Sylvia Beach and the Lost Generation*, 328, 329.

54. Renoir, *My Life and My Films*, 97, 98.

55. Renoir, *My Life and My Films*, 96.

56. Renoir, *My Life and My Films*, 96.

57. Lacouture, *De Gaulle, the Rebel*, 131.

58. Lacouture, *De Gaulle, the Rebel*, 129.

59. Jackson, *De Gaulle*, 8.

60. Flanner, *Paris Was Yesterday*, 109.

61. Kessler, New Year's Eve, 1933, in *Diaries of a Cosmopolitan*, 464.

7 Bloody Tuesday (1934)

Eugen Weber, *Hollow Years*; Jackson, *Politics of Depression in France*; Bernard and Dubief, *Decline of the Third Republic*; Eugen Weber, *Action Française*; Julian Jackson, *The Popular Front in France: Defending Democracy, 1934–38* (New York: Cambridge University Press, 1988); Brown, *Embrace of Unreason*; Robert Soucy, *French Fascism: The Second Wave, 1933–1939* (New Haven, Conn.: Yale University Press, 1995); Lacouture, *Léon Blum*; Flanner, *Paris Was Yesterday*; Elliot Paul, *The Last Time I Saw Paris* (New York: Random House, 1942); Fitch, *Sylvia Beach and the Lost Generation*; Will, *Unlikely Collaboration*; Browder, *André Breton*; Perriand, *Life of Creation*; Eve Curie, *Madame Curie*; Quinn, *Marie Curie*; Emling, *Marie Curie and Her Daughters*; Sheridan, *André Gide*; Gide, *Journals*, vol. 3; Stephen Walsh, *Stravinsky: The Second Exile; France and America, 1934–1971* (New York: Knopf, 2006); Walsh, *Stravinsky: A Creative Spring*; Igor Stravinsky and Robert Craft, *Memories and Commentaries* (New York: Faber & Faber, 2002); Igor Stravinsky, *An Autobiography* (New York: Norton, 1998); Arthur Gold and Robert Fizdale, *Misia: The Life of Misia Sert* (New

York: Morrow, 1981); Beauvoir, *Prime of Life*; Brinnin, *Third Rose*; Simon, *Biography of Alice B. Toklas*; Crosby, *The Passionate Years*; Ferguson, *Henry Miller*; Brassaï, *Henry Miller*; Perlès, *My Friend Henry Miller*; Bertin, *Jean Renoir*; Renoir, *My Life and My Films*; Madsen, *Chanel*; Picardie, *Coco Chanel*; Secrest, *Elsa Schiaparelli*; Schiaparelli, *Shocking Life*; Secrest, *Salvador Dalí*; Dalí, *Secret Life of Salvador Dalí*; Baldwin, *Man Ray*; Lottman, *Man Ray's Montparnasse*; Man Ray, *Self Portrait*; John Reynolds, *André Citroën*; Rhodes, *Louis Renault*; Lottman, *Michelin Men*; Maurice Ravel, *A Ravel Reader: Correspondence, Articles, Interviews* (Mineola, N.Y.: Dover, 2003); Lacouture, *De Gaulle, the Rebel*; Jackson, *De Gaulle*; Easton, *The Red Count*.

1. See especially Eugen Weber, *Hollow Years*, Jackson, *Politics of Depression in France*, and Bernard and Dubief, *Decline of the Third Republic*.

2. A detailed 1936 American review of Paris newspapers (Weber, *Hollow Years*, 130).

3. Eugen Weber gives this figure in *Action Française*, 319, while Lacouture (*Léon Blum*, 205) writes that "the decline in [French] living standards between 1930 and 1934 has been evaluated at 20 percent (although Alfred Sauvy [historian of the French economy] is more cautious about the figure)."

4. Eugen Weber, *Action Française*, 321–22.

5. Eugen Weber, *Action Française*, 327.

6. Paul, *Last Time I Saw Paris*, 264, 263, 267.

7. Flanner, *Paris Was Yesterday*, 112, 114.

8. Lacouture, *Léon Blum*, 214, 213.

9. Lacouture, *Léon Blum*, 214.

10. Perriand, *Life of Creation*, 79.

11. Emling, *Marie Curie and Her Daughters*, 131.

12. Eve Curie, *Madame Curie*, 376, 385.

13. Gide, 6 February 1934, 4 July 1933, in *Journals*, 3:291–92, 277; Sheridan, *André Gide*, 465.

14. Walsh, *Stravinsky: A Creative Spring*, 533–34.

15. Stravinsky and Craft, *Memories and Commentaries*, 180, 176.

16. Gold and Fizdale, *Misia*, 230.

17. Walsh, *Stravinsky: A Creative Spring*, 521.

18. Beauvoir, *Prime of Life*, 128.

19. Will, *Unlikely Collaboration*, 227n26.

20. James Laughlin, founder of the publishing house New Directions, quoted in Will, *Unlikely Collaboration*, 69.

21. Will, *Unlikely Collaboration*, 70.

22. Will, *Unlikely Collaboration*, 69.

23. Will, *Unlikely Collaborators*, 91, 94.

24. Brinnin, *Third Rose*, 348.

25. Ferguson, *Henry Miller*, 235, 231–32.

26. See Ferguson, *Henry Miller*, 231–32, 234.

27. Ferguson, *Henry Miller*, 246, 262. The titles, *Tropic of Cancer* and *Tropic of Capricorn*, were Miller's pet names for June's breasts (262).

28. Bertin, *Jean Renoir*, 103.

29. Renoir, *My Life and My Films*, 136. Renoir cited this remark about himself, because "it greatly pleased me."

30. Bertin, *Jean Renoir*, 106; Renoir, *My Life and My Films*, 155, 154.

31. Renoir, *My Life and My Films*, 157, 154, 155.

32. Bertin, *Jean Renoir*, 108; Renoir, *My Life and My Films*, 155.

33. Eugen Weber, *Hollow Years*, 136.

34. Crosby, *Passionate Years*, 298–99.

35. Flanner, *Paris Was Yesterday*, 114.

36. Schiaparelli, *Shocking Life*, 48.

37. Dalí had numerous one-man exhibits that year, including two in Paris, one in London, one in Barcelona, and an earlier one in New York, in addition to these two exhibits—an extraordinary number for any artist, but especially for one as young as he was (thirty years old).

38. Crosby, *Passionate Years*, 319.

39. Dalí, *Secret Life of Salvador Dalí*, 329, 330.

40. *The Bride Stripped Bare by Her Bachelors, Even (The Large Glass)* is now a proud possession of the Philadelphia Museum of Art—as is Duchamp's *Nude Descending a Staircase* and other stars of the 1913 Armory Show. When Duchamp completed *The Green Box*, he began the six-year process of constructing another box, *The Box in a Valise*, which was a kind of portable museum and tiny retrospective of his most important efforts. For more on *The Large Glass*, see McAuliffe, *When Paris Sizzled*, 94.

41. Baldwin, *Man Ray*, 183.

42. Man Ray, *Self Portrait*, 206–7.

43. Baldwin, *Man Ray*, 178, 179.

44. Baldwin, *Man Ray*, 188.

45. John Reynolds, *André Citroën*, 184.

46. Rhodes, *Louis Renault*, 124.

47. Ravel, to Manuel de Falla, 6 January 1933, in *Ravel Reader*, 314 and 314n1.

48. Unsigned interview in the *Evening Standard*, 24 February 1932; Nino Frank, "Maurice Ravel Between Two Trains," in *Candide*, 5 May 1932, both in *Ravel Reader*, 490, 497.

49. Flanner, *Paris Was Yesterday*, 81.

50. *Ravel Reader*, 495n6.

51. In *Ravel Reader*, 497. He reiterated this on other occasions: see his interview, 16 October 1931, in *Ravel Reader*, 482.

52. *De Telegraaf*, 31 March 1931; unsigned interview in the *Evening Standard*, 24 February 1932, both in *Ravel Reader*, 474, 490. According to Ravel, a bolero is not "a

short, bright jacket worn for fancy dress" but "a long, black crepe cape with a train the length of a hall carpet, worn exclusively when walking to funerals" (Flanner, *Paris Was Yesterday*, 81).

53. C. B. L., *Neue Freie Presse*, 3 February 1932, in *Ravel Reader*, 489. "I find this upsetting, as you realize," he wrote to the Italian critic and musicologist Guido Gatti on 5 January 1933, following the Madeleine Grey incident (*Ravel Reader*, 313–14).

54. *Ravel Reader*, 317n1.

55. Ravel to Marie Gaudin, 12 March [1934], in *Ravel Reader*, 321.

56. Jean-Claude Baker, *Josephine*, 185.

57. Jean-Claude Baker, *Josephine*, 185.

58. Jean-Claude Baker, *Josephine*, 184.

59. Lacouture, *De Gaulle, the Rebel*, 108.

60. Lacouture, *De Gaulle, the Rebel*, 132.

61. Lacouture, *De Gaulle, the Rebel*, 135.

62. Easton, *Red Count*, 406. Kessler died on November 30, 1937.

8 Sailing, Sailing (1935)

John Malcolm Brinnin, *The Sway of the Grand Saloon: A Social History of the North Atlantic* (New York: Delacorte Press, 1971); John Maxtone-Graham, *Crossing and Cruising: From the Golden Era of Ocean Liners to the Luxury Cruise Ships of Today* (New York: Scribner, 1992); Paul, *Last Time I Saw Paris*; Thurman, *Secrets of the Flesh*; Caroline Moorehead, *Martha Gellhorn: A Life* (London: Chatto & Windus, 2003); Daniel J. Mahoney, *Bertrand de Jouvenel: The Conservative Liberal and the Illusions of Modernity* (Wilmington, Del.: ISI Books, 2005); Jean-Claude Baker, *Josephine*; Nicolas Fox Weber, *Le Corbusier*; Le Corbusier, *When the Cathedrals Were White* (New York: McGraw-Hill, 1964); Perriand, *Life of Creation*; Crosby, *Passionate Years*; Dalí, *Secret Life of Salvador Dalí*; Secrest, *Salvador Dalí*; Buñuel, *My Last Sigh*; Garelick, *Mademoiselle*; Madsen, *Chanel*; Picardie, *Coco Chanel*; Steegmuller, *Cocteau*; Gold and Fizdale, *Misia*; McAuliffe, *When Paris Sizzled*; Secrest, *Elsa Schiaparelli*; Schiaparelli, *Shocking Life*; Suzanne F. Cordelier, *Femmes au travail: etudes pratique sur dix-sept carriers féminines* (Paris: Plon, 1935); Eugen Weber, *Hollow Years*; Bernard and Dubief, *Decline of the Third Republic*; Jackson, *Politics of Depression in France*; Jackson, *Popular Front in France*; Jean-Denis Bredin, *The Affair: The Case of Alfred Dreyfus* (New York: George Braziller, 1986); Mary McAuliffe, *Dawn of the Belle Epoque: The Paris of Monet, Zola, Bernhardt, Eiffel, Debussy, Clemenceau, and Their Friends* (Lanham, Md.: Rowman & Littlefield, 2011); Lacouture, *De Gaulle, the Rebel*; Flanner, *Paris Was Yesterday*; Lacouture, *Léon Blum*; Conner, ed., *André Gide's Politics*; Sheridan, *André Gide*; Brown, *Embrace of Unreason*; Todd, *Malraux*; Eugen Weber, *Action Française*; Browder, *André Breton*; Emling, *Marie Curie and Her Daughters*; Bertin, *Jean Renoir*; Bazin, *Jean Renoir*; Renoir, *My Life and My Films*; Jean Renoir, *The Crime of Monsieur Lange* (New York: Interama Video Classics,

1935); John Reynolds, *André Citroën*; Rhodes, *Louis Renault*; Lottman, *Michelin Men*; McAuliffe, *Twilight of the Belle Epoque*; Spanier, *Kay Boyle, Artist and Activist*; Meyers, *Scott Fitzgerald*; Fitzgerald, *A Life in Letters*; F. Scott Fitzgerald, *Tender Is the Night* (Hertfordshire, UK: Cumberland House, 1993); Hemingway, *Selected Letters*; Carlos Baker, *Ernest Hemingway*; Michael S. Reynolds, *Hemingway: The 1930s*; Madsen, *Hearts and Minds*; Fitch, *Sylvia Beach and the Lost Generation*; Beach, *Shakespeare & Company*; Ellmann, *James Joyce*.

1. Brinnin, *Sway of the Grand Saloon*, 475, 477.

2. War abruptly ended the *Normandie*'s brief career: when the United States entered the war, the U.S. government took possession of the *Normandie* in New York Harbor, refitting it as a troop transport ship and renaming it the U.S.S. *Lafayette*. Unhappily, a fire started during the refitting and devoured the unfortunate liner, which capsized. Eventually, she was cut up and sold as scrap (Brinnin, *Sway of the Grand Saloon*, 474–75). Even the *Normandie*'s brief career was interrupted for six months, during which modifications were made to reduce vibrations at speed. Elliot Paul, presumably on a lower deck, experienced this during his 1936 crossing, which he said had been dreadful "because of the frightful vibration caused by her powerful engines." But he did not have the heart to tell his French friends this, because "the *Normandie* was the pride, not only of the French marine, but of all the French" (Paul, *Last Time I Saw Paris*, 304).

3. Maxtone-Graham, *Crossing and Cruising*, 153.

4. Thurman, *Secrets of the Flesh*, 411.

5. Jean-Claude Baker, *Josephine*, 188, 190.

6. This was according to Fayard Nicolas (Jean-Claude Baker, *Josephine*, 198). See also *Josephine*, 195.

7. Jean-Claude Baker, *Josephine*, 202–3.

8. Jean-Claude Baker, *Josephine*, 215.

9. Nicolas Fox Weber, *Le Corbusier*, 368, 362; Le Corbusier, *When the Cathedrals Were White*, 55, 58, 36.

10. Le Corbusier, *When the Cathedrals Were White*, 38, xxii, 40, 43.

11. Perriand, *Life of Creation*, 87.

12. Le Corbusier, *When the Cathedrals Were White*, 168.

13. Nicolas Fox Weber, *Le Corbusier*, 380; Le Corbusier, *When the Cathedrals Were White*, 213.

14. Le Corbusier, *When the Cathedrals Were White*, 114.

15. Perriand, *Life of Creation*, 89–90.

16. Le Corbusier, *When the Cathedrals Were White*, 178; Nicolas Fox Weber, *Le Corbusier*, 375.

17. Dalí, *Secret Life of Salvador Dalí*, 337.

18. Dalí, *Secret Life of Salvador Dalí*, 337–38.

19. Secrest, *Salvador Dalí*, 152.

20. Dalí, *Secret Life of Salvador Dalí*, 338.

21. Crosby, *Passionate Years*, 323.

22. Secrest, *Salvador Dalí*, 153.

23. Secrest, *Salvador Dalí*, 153. See also Buñuel, *My Last Sigh*, 183.

24. See McAuliffe, *When Paris Sizzled*, 220, 259.

25. Gold and Fizdale, *Misia*; Picardie, *Coco Chanel*, 327.

26. Madsen, *Chanel*, 198.

27. Schiaparelli, *Shocking Life*, 65.

28. Crosby, *Passionate Years*, 299.

29. Cordelier, *Femmes au travail*, vi; Eugen Weber, *Hollow Years*, 83.

30. Eugen Weber, *Hollow Years*, 85; Bernard and Dubief, *Decline of the Third Republic*, 190.

31. Bredin, *The Affair*, 489. See also McAuliffe, *Dawn of the Belle Epoque*, especially chapters 22, 25, and 27.

32. Jackson, *Popular Front*, 3.

33. Lacouture, *De Gaulle, the Rebel*, 128.

34. Flanner, *Paris Was Yesterday*, 145.

35. Eugen Weber, *Hollow Years*, 240.

36. Paul, *Last Time I Saw Paris*, 291, 292. The newspaper was *Le Petit Journal*.

37. Todd, *Malraux*, 146–47.

38. Eugen Weber, *Action Française*, 355.

39. Eugen Weber, *Action Française*, 286.

40. Eugen Weber, *Action Française*, 361.

41. Emling, *Marie Curie and Her Daughters*, 145–46.

42. Renoir would continue to support Catherine as well as her mother and sister (Bertin, *Jean Renoir*, 86).

43. Bertin, *Jean Renoir*, 118.

44. Bazin, *Jean Renoir*, 242.

45. Renoir, *My Life and My Films*, 125, 127.

46. See McAuliffe, *Twilight of the Belle Epoque*, 289, 328, for more on Citroën's management style.

47. Spanier, *Kay Boyle*, 124.

48. Fitzgerald to Hemingway, 10 May 1934, in Fitzgerald, *A Life in Letters*, 261; Hemingway to Fitzgerald, 28 May 1934, in Hemingway, *Selected Letters*, 407–8.

49. Fitzgerald to Sara Murphy, 30 March 1936, in Fitzgerald, *A Life in Letters*, 298; Meyers, *Scott Fitzgerald*, 264, 265.

50. Hemingway to Fitzgerald, 21 and 16 December 1935, in Hemingway, *Selected Letters*, 428 and 425.

51. Hemingway to John Dos Passos, 17 December 1935, in Hemingway, *Selected Letters*, 427; Meyers, *Scott Fitzgerald*, 272.

52. Fitzgerald, *A Life in Letters*, 302n1.

53. Fitzgerald to Hemingway, 16 July 1936, in Fitzgerald, *A Life in Letters*, 302. Fitzgerald reported that Hemingway "answered with such unpleasantness that it is hard to think he has any friendly feeling to me any more" (Fitzgerald to Maxwell

Perkins, c. 19 March 1937, in Fitzgerald, A *Life in Letters*, 318). Hemingway, at Perkins's urging, did substitute the name "Julian" for Fitzgerald (Fitzgerald, A *Life in Letters*, 302n2).

54. Carlos Baker, *Ernest Hemingway*, 290–91; Meyers, *Scott Fitzgerald*, 270.

55. Madsen, *Hearts and Minds*, 71.

56. Fitch, *Sylvia Beach and the Lost Generation*, 350, 351.

57. Ellmann, *James Joyce*, 679 and note. Ellmann believes that Jung was mistaken about Joyce in "insisting that he was a latent schizoid who used drinking to control his schizoidal tendencies" (680).

58. Lacouture, *De Gaulle, the Rebel*, 140.

59. Paul, *Last Time I Saw Paris*, 294–95.

60. Eugen Weber, *Hollow Years*, 252.

61. Brinnin, *Sway of the Grand Saloon*, 505. The *Graf Zeppelin* operated a regularly scheduled transatlantic service from 1932 to 1937. When Le Corbusier took the *Graf Zeppelin* to return to Brazil in July 1936 to help develop plans for government buildings there, it took four days (Nicolas Fox Weber, *Le Corbusier*, 386).

9 Coming Apart (1936)

Lacouture, *Léon Blum*; Eugen Weber, *Action Française*; Brown, *Embrace of Unreason*; Jackson, *Popular Front in France*; Bernard and Dubief, *Decline of the Third Republic*; Clair, *A nous la liberté*; Michel Coste et al., *Villes ouvrières: 1900–1950* (Paris: L'Harmattan, 1989); Pedersen, *Family, Dependence, and the Origins of the Welfare State*; Paul, *Last Time I Saw Paris*; Danielle Tartakowsky, *Le Front Populaire: La Vie est à nous* (Paris: Gallimard, 1996); Jean Vigreux, *Le front populaire, 1934–1938* (Paris: Presses Universitaires de France, 2011); Perriand, *A Life of Creation*; Rhodes, *Louis Renault*; Mugnier, *Journal de l'Abbé Mugnier*; Garelick, *Mademoiselle*; Madsen, *Chanel*; Picardie, *Coco Chanel*; Morand, *Allure of Chanel*; Secrest, *Elsa Schiaparelli*; Lottman, *Michelin Men*; Leni Riefenstahl, *Olympia* (U.S.: Pathfinder Home Entertainment, 2006); Mike O'Mahony, *Olympic Visions: Images of the Games through History* (London: Reaktion Books, 2012); Patricia Kapferer and Tristan Gaston-Breton, *Lacoste the Legend* (Paris: Cherche midi, 2002); Silver, *Chaos and Classicism*.

1. Lacouture, *Léon Blum*, 225; Eugen Weber, *Action Française*, 363; Brown, *Embrace of Unreason*, 229–30.

2. Lacouture, *Léon Blum*, 226.

3. On April 4, the Conseil d'Etat rejected Action Française's appeal of the decree of dissolution. In addition, in March, Maurras was sentenced to four months in jail for incitements to murder against the proponents of sanctions against Italy. While making his appeal, Maurras made new threats against Blum, which cost him eight more months in jail—although the total would be cut down to eleven months rather than twelve (Eugen Weber, *Action Française*, 370).

4. Jean-Pierre Maxence quoted in Jackson, *Popular Front in France*, 252.

5. Eugen Weber, *Action Française*, 364.

6. See Lacouture, *Léon Blum*, 232–33, 547n49.

7. Françoise Cribier, "Le logement d'une génération de jeunes parisiens à l'epoque du Front Populaire," in Michel Coste et al., *Villes ouvrières*, 113, 119.

8. Eugen Weber, *Action Française*, 293.

9. Eugen Weber, *Action Française*, 375. Blum's father came from Alsace, and his mother was born in Paris. Léon Blum was born on Rue Saint-Denis in Paris in 1872.

10. Paul, *Last Time I Saw Paris*, 315, 322.

11. Eugen Weber, *Action Française*, 291. Blum's biographer, Jean Lacouture, notes that this summer, after spending several weeks in France, the Portuguese minister of foreign affairs expressed his concern that France might be shattered, because "the hatreds within the country were greater than the hatred of some Frenchmen for the foreign enemy" (Lacouture, *Léon Blum*, 334).

12. Lacouture, *Léon Blum*, 251.

13. Brown, *Embrace of Unreason*, 230–31.

14. Perriand, *Life of Creation*, 79.

15. Rhodes, *Louis Renault*, 143.

16. Rhodes, *Louis Renault*, 144; Mugnier, 6 and 8 June, 20 November 1936, in *Journal de l'Abbé Mugnier*, 559, 560, 562.

17. Rhodes, *Louis Renault*, 145.

18. Morand, *Allure of Chanel*, 125.

19. Secrest, *Elsa Schiaparelli*, 210.

20. Perriand, *Life of Creation*, 80.

21. Perriand, *Life of Creation*, 80.

22. Lacouture, *Léon Blum*, 281.

10 War in Spain (1936)

Lacouture, *Léon Blum*; Jackson, *Popular Front in France*; Bernard and Dubief, *Decline of the Third Republic*; Eugen Weber, *Hollow Years*; Eichengreen, *Golden Fetters*; Todd, *Malraux*; Carlos Baker, *Ernest Hemingway*; Hemingway, *Selected Letters*; Michael S. Reynolds, *Hemingway: The 1930s*; Moorehead, *Martha Gellhorn*; Sheridan, *André Gide*; Gide, *Journals*, vol. 3; André Gide, *Return from the U.S.S.R.* (New York: Knopf, 1937); Kessler, *Diaries of a Cosmopolitan*; Emling, *Marie Curie and Her Daughters*; Bertin, *Jean Renoir*; Renoir, *My Life and My Films*; Bazin, *Jean Renoir*; Julie Manet, *Growing Up with the Impressionists: The Diary of Julie Manet* (London: Sotheby's, 1987); Jean Renoir, *A Day in the Country* (New York: Criterion Collection, 2015); Renoir, *Les Bas-fonds* (U.S.: Criterion Collection, 2004); Secrest, *Elsa Schiaparelli*; Schiaparelli, *Shocking Life*; Morand, *Allure of Chanel*; Secrest, *Salvador Dalí*; Dalí, *Secret Life of Salvador Dalí*; Baldwin, *Man Ray*; Man Ray, *Self Portrait*; Richardson, *Picasso: The Triumphant Years*; Ellmann, *James Joyce*; Fitch, *Sylvia Beach and the Lost*

Generation; Beach, *Shakespeare & Company*; Lacouture, *De Gaulle, the Rebel*; Williams, *Last Great Frenchman*; Hughes, *To the Maginot Line*.

1. Jackson, *Popular Front in France*, 10.
2. See Bernard and Dubief, *Decline of the Third Republic*, 313–14, for a discussion of this problem.
3. Eugen Weber, *Hollow Years*, 19.
4. Carlos Baker, *Ernest Hemingway*, 292–93; Hemingway to Perkins, 15 December 1936, in *Selected Letters*, 455.
5. Sheridan, *André Gide*, 488.
6. Sheridan, *André Gide*, 488. Gide had already asked to take with him whomever he wanted, requiring a special dispensation, which was granted. He brought Pierre Herbart, Jacques Schiffrin (founder and editor of Editions de la Pléiade, now published by Gallimard), and two left-wing novelists of working-class origin, Eugène Dabit and Louis Guilloux, plus his Dutch friend Jef Last (Sheridan, *André Gide*, 489; Gide, *Journals*, 3:344n16).
7. Gide, *Return from the U.S.S.R.*, 45.
8. Sheridan, *André Gide*, 499; Kessler, 30 October 1936, in *Diaries of a Cosmopolitan*, 477.
9. Sheridan, *André Gide*, 500; Gide, *Return from the U.S.S.R.*, 32.
10. Gide, 3, 6, and 7 September 1936, in *Journals*, 3:344, 347.
11. Gide, 12 February 1936, in *Journals*, 3:336.
12. Emling, *Marie Curie and Her Daughters*, 153.
13. Renoir, *My Life and My Films*, 125.
14. Jean Renoir in Bazin, *Jean Renoir*, 11.
15. Pierre-Auguste Renoir quoted in Julie Manet, *Diary*, 28 September 1897, 112.
16. Renoir, *My Life and My Films*, 129; the critic and film director Jacques Doniol-Valcroze, in Bazin, *Jean Renoir*, 245. The three Renoir paintings Doniol-Valcroze mentions are *La Grenouillère*, *La Balançoire*, and *Le Déjeuner des canotiers*.
17. Bazin, *Jean Renoir*, 247. Gorky did not live to see the film: he died a month after seeing the screenplay, with speculation still surrounding the cause of his death.
18. Gide, 8 May 1937, in *Journals*, 3:353.
19. Morand, *Allure of Chanel*, 115.
20. The reviewer was Clive Bell in the *New Statesman and Nation* (Secrest, *Salvador Dalí*, 164).
21. Dalí, *Secret Life of Salvador Dalí*, 340.
22. Schiaparelli, *Shocking Life*, 66.
23. Dalí, *Secret Life of Salvador Dalí*, 345–46; Secrest, *Salvador Dalí*, 166.
24. Secrest, *Salvador Dalí*, 157.
25. Dalí, *Secret Life of Salvador Dalí*, 357, 360.
26. Man Ray, *Self Portrait*, 237.
27. Richardson, *Picasso: The Triumphant Years*, 469.
28. Richardson, *Picasso: The Triumphant Years*, 498.

29. Ellmann, *James Joyce*, 697, 693.
30. Fitch, *Sylvia Beach and the Lost Generation*, 368.
31. Lacouture, *De Gaulle, the Rebel*, 143.
32. Lacouture, *De Gaulle, the Rebel*, 142. See also Hughes, *To the Maginot Line*, 4.
33. Lacouture, *De Gaulle, the Rebel*, 147.

11 End of the Dream (1937)

Jackson, *Popular Front in France*; Bernard and Dubief, *Decline of the Third Republic*; Lacouture, *Léon Blum*; Brown, *Embrace of Unreason*; Eugen Weber, *Hollow Years*; Schiaparelli, *Shocking Life*; Xabier Irujo, *Gernika, 1937: The Market Day Massacre* (Reno: University of Nevada Press, 2015); John Richardson, "A Different Guernica," *New York Review of Books*, 12 May 2016; Karen Fiss, *Grand Illusion: The Third Reich, the Paris Exposition, and the Cultural Seduction of France* (Chicago: University of Chicago Press, 2009); Perriand, *Life of Creation*; Paul, *Last Time I Saw Paris*; Hemingway, *Selected Letters*; Carlos Baker, *Ernest Hemingway*; Michael S. Reynolds, *Hemingway: The 1930s*; Fitch, *Sylvia Beach and the Lost Generation*; Beach, *Shakespeare & Company*; Baldwin, *Man Ray*; Lottman, *Man Ray's Montparnasse*; Nicholas Fox Weber, *Le Corbusier*; Rhodes, *Louis Renault*; Steegmuller, *Cocteau*; Madsen, *Chanel*; McAuliffe, *Twilight of the Belle Epoque*; Jean-Claude Baker, *Josephine*; Ferguson, *Henry Miller*; Brassaï, *Henry Miller*; Perlès, *My Friend Henry Miller*; Best, *Introduction to Twentieth-Century French Literature*; Madsen, *Hearts and Minds*; Beauvoir, *Prime of Life*; Lacouture, *De Gaulle, the Rebel*; Williams, *Last Great Frenchman*; Ellmann, *James Joyce*; McAuliffe, *When Paris Sizzled*; Brinnin, *Third Rose*; Simon, *Biography of Alice B. Toklas*; Will, *Unlikely Collaboration*; James Lord, *Six Exceptional Women: Further Memoirs* (New York: Farrar, Straus & Giroux, 1994); Fitzgerald, *A Life in Letters*; Eugen Weber, *Action Française*; Bertin, *Jean Renoir*; Renoir, *My Life and My Films*; Bazin, *Jean Renoir*; Renoir, *Grand Illusion* (New York: Criterion Collection, 2008); Todd, *Malraux*; Emling, *Marie Curie and Her Daughters*; Quinn, *Marie Curie*; Kessler, *Diaries of a Cosmopolitan*; Easton, *Red Count*; Gide, *Journals*, vol. 3; Ravel, *Ravel Reader*.

1. Lacouture, *Léon Blum*, 377.
2. Schiaparelli, *Shocking Life*, 74–75.
3. Richardson, "A Different Guernica," 5.
4. Richardson, "A Different Guernica," 6.
5. Perriand, *Life of Creation*, 91.
6. Brown, *Embrace of Unreason*, 262; Paul, *Last Time I Saw Paris*, 328.
7. Hemingway to Harry Sylvester, 5 February 1937, in *Selected Letters*, 456.
8. Carlos Baker, *Ernest Hemingway*, 304. Baker notes that the source for this quote wished to remain anonymous.
9. Carlos Baker, *Ernest Hemingway*, 307.
10. Nicholas Fox Weber, *Le Corbusier*, 391.
11. See McAuliffe, *Twilight of the Belle Epoque*, 234.

12. Steegmuller, *Cocteau*, 434.

13. Jean-Claude Baker, *Josephine* 221.

14. Brassaï, *Henry Miller*, 122.

15. Brassaï, *Henry Miller*, 191, 193; Ferguson, *Henry Miller*, 312.

16. Brassaï, *Henry Miller*, 194.

17. Ferguson, *Henry Miller*, 258.

18. Ferguson, *Henry Miller*, 251; Brassaï, *Henry Miller*, 200–201; Perlès, *My Friend Henry Miller*, 167.

19. Beauvoir, *Prime of Life*, 251.

20. Madsen, *Hearts and Minds*, 77. "Le Mur" would also appear in book form, in early 1939, as the title story in a collection of Sartre's short stories.

21. Lacouture, *De Gaulle, the Rebel*, 149.

22. Lacouture, *De Gaulle, the Rebel*, 152, 151.

23. Fitch, *Sylvia Beach and the Lost Generation*, 376.

24. Ellmann, *James Joyce*, 704.

25. *Ulysses* was also published on his birthday, in 1922. See McAuliffe, *When Paris Sizzled*, 111–13.

26. Ellmann, *James Joyce*, 703, 702.

27. Ellmann, *James Joyce*, 701, 702.

28. Will, *Unlikely Collaboration*, 9, 96–97.

29. Lord, *Six Exceptional Women*, 15.

30. Things went well for Fitzgerald for a while, but he once again was on the downslide when he died of a heart attack in December 1940 at the age of 44.

31. Fitzgerald to Hemingway, 13 July 1937, in Fitzgerald, *A Life in Letters*, 328; Meyers, *Scott Fitzgerald*, 287.

32. See chapter 6.

33. Fitzgerald to Perkins, 3 September 1937, in *Life in Letters*, 335.

34. Michael S. Reynolds, *Hemingway: The 1930s*, 270.

35. Renoir, *My Life and My Films*, 145, 147, 148.

36. Renoir, *My Life and My Films*, 167.

37. Bazin, *Jean Renoir*, 65.

38. Todd, *Malraux*, 219.

39. For more on this affair, see Susan Quinn's biography, *Marie Curie*.

40. Emling, *Marie Curie and Her Daughters*, 164.

41. Gide, 8 December 1937, in *Journals*, 3:364.

42. Ravel to Ernest Ansermet, 29 October 1937, in *Ravel Reader*, 327 and 327n3.

43. Arbie Orenstein, introduction to *Ravel Reader*, 12.

44. Interview with Ravel in *Excelsior*, 30 October 1931, in *Ravel Reader*, 486.

12 In War's Shadow (1938)

Fitch, *Sylvia Beach and the Lost Generation*; Beach, *Shakespeare & Company*; Baldwin, *Man Ray*; Lacouture, *Léon Blum*; Jackson, *Popular Front in France*; Bernard and Dubief,

Decline of the Third Republic; Eugen Weber, *Action Française*; Beauvoir, *Prime of Life*; Madsen, *Hearts and Minds*; Mugnier, *Journal de l'Abbé Mugnier*; Paul, *Last Time I Saw Paris*; Brown, *Embrace of Unreason*; Lacouture, *De Gaulle, the Rebel*; Herbert R. Lottman, *Pétain, Hero or Traitor: The Untold Story* (New York: Morrow, 1985); McAuliffe, *When Paris Sizzled*; Williams, *Last Great Frenchman*; Schiaparelli, *Shocking Life*; Madsen, *Chanel*; Schelps, *Elsie de Wolfe's Paris*; Secrest, *Elsa Schiaparelli*; Secrest, *Salvador Dalí*; Man Ray, *Self Portrait*; Baldwin, *Man Ray*; Lottman, *Man Ray's Montparnasse*; Flanner, *Paris Was Yesterday*; Gide, *Journals*, vol. 3; Sheridan, *André Gide*; Walsh, *Stravinsky: The Second Exile*; Eugen Weber, *Hollow Years*; Bertin, *Jean Renoir*; Renoir, *My Life and My Films*; Bazin, *Jean Renoir*; Renoir, *La Bête humaine* (New York: Criterion Collection, 2006); Thurman, *Secrets of the Flesh*; Ferguson, *Henry Miller*; Brassaï, *Henry Miller*; Emling, *Marie Curie and Her Daughters*; Rhodes, *Louis Renault*; Ellmann, *James Joyce*; Bryher, *Heart to Artemis*.

1. Fitch, *Sylvia Beach and the Lost Generation*, 374.
2. Baldwin, *Man Ray*, 194.
3. Fitch, *Sylvia Beach and the Lost Generation*, 374.
4. Fitch, *Sylvia Beach and the Lost Generation*, 379.
5. Beauvoir, *Prime of Life*, 254, 256.
6. "Adieu! Adieu! La valse, la musique, le café à la crème qu'on buvait au bord des lacs, adieu!" (Mugnier, in *Journal*, 12 March 1938, 570).
7. Eugen Weber, *Action Française*, 411.
8. Eugen Weber, *Action Française*, 410–11.
9. See chapter 9, note 3.
10. See McAuliffe, *When Paris Sizzled*, especially p. 235.
11. Lacouture, *De Gaulle, the Rebel*, 159; Lottman, *Pétain*, 145.
12. Lacouture, *De Gaulle, the Rebel*, 159, 160.
13. Lacouture, *De Gaulle, the Rebel*, 161.
14. Lacouture, *De Gaulle, the Rebel*, 165.
15. Lacouture, *De Gaulle, the Rebel*, 165.
16. Schelps, *Elsie de Wolfe's Paris*, 77, 69.
17. Man Ray, *Self Portrait*, 232; Beauvoir, *Prime of Life*, 258–59.
18. Flanner, *Paris Was Yesterday*, 183, 184.
19. Flanner, *Paris Was Yesterday*, 186.
20. Gide, 21 August 1938, in *Journals*, 3:393, 394; Sheridan, *André Gide*, 522–23.
21. Sheridan, *André Gide*, 523.
22. Walsh, *Stravinsky: The Second Exile*, 79.
23. Flanner, *Paris Was Yesterday*, 191.
24. Eugen Weber, *Hollow Years*, 176.
25. Man Ray, *Self Portrait*, 238.
26. Thurman, *Secrets of the Flesh*, 427.
27. Ferguson, *Henry Miller*, 260–61; Brassaï, *Henry Miller*, 217; Eugen Weber, *Hollow Years*, 176.

28. Gide, 7 October 1938, in *Journals*, 3:405.

29. Brown, *Embrace of Unreason*, 273.

30. Beauvoir, *Prime of Life*, 267, 268.

31. Emling, *Marie Curie and Her Daughters*, 158.

32. Bertin, *Jean Renoir*, 154–55.

33. Lacouture, *De Gaulle, the Rebel*, 154.

34. Brown, *Embrace of Unreason*, 270.

35. Paul, *Last Time I Saw Paris*, 346.

36. Jackson, *Popular Front in France*, 105.

37. Rhodes, *Louis Renault*, 158.

38. Rhodes, *Louis Renault*, 155.

39. Lacouture, *De Gaulle, the Rebel*, 164. This is taken from de Gaulle's short description of the book, written for publicity purposes.

40. Ellmann, *James Joyce*, 713.

41. Ellmann, *James Joyce*, 721. Despite Joyce's expectations, *Finnegans Wake* was not officially published until May 4, 1939.

42. Fitch, *Sylvia Beach and the Lost Generation*, 383.

43. Fitch, *Sylvia Beach and the Lost Generation*, 383, 384, 389.

44. Beauvoir, *Prime of Life*, 261. Beauvoir says that the reader was Henry Miller, but there is no evidence that this was the same Henry Miller as *Tropic of Cancer*.

45. Beauvoir, *Prime of Life*, 268, 295.

46. Bryher, *Heart to Artemis*, 282–83, 277–78.

47. Bryher, *Heart to Artemis*, 278.

48. Eugen Weber, *Hollow Years*, 108.

13 Dancing on a Volcano (1939)

Baldwin, *Man Ray*; Man Ray, *Self Portrait*; Lottman, *Man Ray's Montparnasse*; Flanner, *Paris Was Yesterday*; Gide, *Journals*, vol. 3; Lottman, *Pétain*; Brown, *Embrace of Unreason*; Eugen Weber, *Action Française*; Mugnier, *Journal*; Ghislain de Diesbach, *l'Abbé Mugnier: le confesseur du tout-Paris* (Paris: Perrin, 2003); Eugen Weber, *Hollow Years*; Schiaparelli, *Shocking Life*; Secrest, *Elsa Schiaparelli*; Madsen, *Chanel*; Garelick, *Mademoiselle*; Picardie, *Coco Chanel*; Schelps, *Elsie de Wolfe's Paris*; Secrest, *Salvador Dalí*; Dalí, *Secret Life of Salvador Dalí*; Bazin, *Jean Renoir*; Jean Renoir, *The Rules of the Game* (Criterion Collection, 2011); Renoir, *My Life and My Films*; Bertin, *Jean Renoir*; Perriand, *Life of Creation*; Beauvoir, *Prime of Life*; Madsen, *Hearts and Minds*; Paul, *Last Time I Saw Paris*; Flanner, *Janet Flanner's World*; Michel Rayssac, *L'Exode des musées: l'histoire des oeuvres d'art sous l'Occupation* (Paris: Payot & Rivages, 2007); Hélène Badinter and Laura Barraud, *Illustre et Inconnu: Comment Jacques Jaujard à sauvé le Louvre* (Paris: Ladybirds Films, 2014); Will, *Unlikely Collaboration*; Brinnin, *Third Rose*; Simon, *Biography of Alice B. Toklas*; Ellmann, *James Joyce*; Sheridan, *André Gide*; Walsh, *Stravinsky: The Second Exile*; Stravinsky and Craft, *Memories and Commentaries*;

Thurman, *Secrets of the Flesh*; Steegmuller, *Cocteau*; Madsen, *Chanel*; Emling, *Marie Curie and Her Daughters*; Soucy, *French Fascism: The Second Wave*; Nicolas Fox Weber, *Le Corbusier*; Lacouture, *De Gaulle, the Rebel*; Rhodes, *Louis Renault*; Lottman, *Michelin Men*; Jean-Claude Baker, *Josephine*; Simone de Beauvoir, *Letters to Sartre* (London: Radius, 1991); Jean-Paul Sartre, *Witness to My Life: The Letters of Jean-Paul Sartre to Simone de Beauvoir, 1926–1939* (New York: Scribner, 1992); Browder, *André Breton*; Fitch, *Sylvia Beach and the Lost Generation*.

1. Baldwin, *Man Ray*, 222.
2. Flanner, *Paris Was Yesterday*, 199–200.
3. Flanner, *Paris Was Yesterday*, 197, 201.
4. Gide, 26 January 1939, in *Journals*, 3:413.
5. Lottman, *Pétain*, 151.
6. Eugen Weber, *Action Française*, 415.
7. Mugnier, 21 March 1939, in *Journal*, 574.
8. Mugnier, 4 March 1939, in *Journal*, 573–74. There is no indication that this invitation was ever followed up. As for the Château de Saint-Cloud, it was burned during cross fire between the Communards and government troops.
9. Zola quoted in Eugen Weber, *Hollow Years*, 256.
10. Secrest, *Elsa Schiaparelli*, 215; Schiaparelli, *Shocking Life*, 100.
11. Schiaparelli, *Shocking Life*, 101.
12. Schelps, *Elsie de Wolfe's Paris*, 79.
13. Dalí, *Secret Life of Salvador Dalí*, 372.
14. Dalí, *Secret Life of Salvador Dalí*, 375.
15. Bazin, *Jean Renoir*, 72; Bertin, *Jean Renoir*, 159.
16. Jean Renoir, *The Rules of the Game*; Bazin, *Jean Renoir*, 73; Renoir, *My Life and My Films*, 169–72.
17. Jean Renoir, *My Life and My Films*, 170; Bertin, *Jean Renoir*, 160.
18. Renoir, *My Life and My Films*, 171, 172.
19. Perriand, *Life of Creation*, 119–20.
20. Flanner, *Paris Was Yesterday*, 223.
21. Beauvoir, *Prime of Life*, 297, 298, 299–300.
22. Beauvoir, *Prime of Life*, 301.
23. Beauvoir, *Prime of Life*, 278–80.
24. Beauvoir, *Prime of Life*, 284–85.
25. Beauvoir, *Prime of Life*, 285.
26. Beauvoir, *Prime of Life*, 303.
27. Paul, *Last Time I Saw Paris*, 384.
28. Beauvoir, *Prime of Life*, 307.
29. Beauvoir, *Prime of Life*, 305.
30. Paul, *Last Time I Saw Paris*, 389–90, 397.
31. Man Ray, *Self Portrait*, 239.
32. Brinnin, *Third Rose*, 365.

33. Simon, *Biography of Alice B. Toklas*, 182.

34. Ellmann, *James Joyce*, 727.

35. Sheridan, *André Gide*, 538.

36. Sheridan, *André Gide*, 540.

37. Beauvoir, *Prime of Life*, 306, 309.

38. Stravinsky and Craft, *Memories and Commentaries*, 189.

39. Thurman, *Secrets of the Flesh*, 430, 429.

40. Steegmuller, *Cocteau*, 436.

41. Schiaparelli, *Shocking Life*, 104.

42. Schiaparelli, *Shocking Life*, 105, 106.

43. Schiaparelli, *Shocking Life*, 103.

44. Schiaparelli, *Shocking Life*, 107.

45. Soon after the Curies' discovery, Enrico Fermi and Leo Szilard in the United States made a similar discovery, leading to the United States' atomic bomb project.

46. Nicolas Fox Weber, *Le Corbusier*, 407. See also Brown, *Embrace of Unreason*, 239 note.

47. Eugen Weber, *Hollow Years*, 109, 305n65.

48. Nicolas Fox Weber, *Le Corbusier*, 406.

49. Eugen Weber, *Hollow Years*, 326n33; 267.

50. De Gaulle's *Memoirs*, vol. 3, quoted in Rhodes, *Louis Renault*, 158.

51. Rhodes, *Louis Renault*, 161.

52. Jean-Claude Baker, *Josephine*, 226.

53. Man Ray, *Self Portrait*, 239, 240–41.

54. Beauvoir to Sartre, 12 September 1939, in *Letters to Sartre*, 57; Sartre to Beauvoir, 15 November 1939, in *Witness to My Life*, 345.

55. Fitch, *Sylvia Beach and the Lost Generation*, 397.

56. Ellmann, *James Joyce*, 728.

57. Ellmann, *James Joyce*, 729.

58. Mugnier, 1 September 1939, in *Journal*, 577.

59. Mugnier, 27 November 1939, in *Journal*, 578.

60. Mugnier lived until 1944 but was frail and virtually blind during his last years. Still, he continued to hear confessions, to say mass daily, and to embrace his many friends and a love for life. On his ninetieth birthday, not long before his death, he told a friend that he loved humanity, whatever its condition, and would like to live another hundred years (see Diesbach, *L'Abbé Mugnier*, 315).

14 Closing the Circle (1940)

Eugen Weber, *Hollow Years*; Herbert R. Lottman, *The Fall of Paris: June 1940* (New York: HarperCollins, 1992); Julian Jackson, *The Fall of France: The Nazi Invasion of 1940* (New York: Oxford University Press, 2003); Man Ray, *Self Portrait*; Sartre, *War Diaries*; McAuliffe, *Dawn of the Belle Epoque*; McAuliffe, *Twilight of the Belle*

Epoque; McAuliffe, *When Paris Sizzled*; Schiaparelli, *Shocking Life*; Beauvoir, *Prime of Life*; Lacouture, *Léon Blum*; Jackson, *De Gaulle*; Lacouture, *De Gaulle, the Rebel*; Hughes, *To the Maginot Line*; Baldwin, *Man Ray*; Cody, *Women of Montparnasse*; Guggenheim, *Out of This Century*; Fitch, *Sylvia Beach and the Lost Generation*; Beach, *Shakespeare & Company*; Andy Marino, *A Quiet American: The Secret War of Varian Fry* (New York: St. Martin's Griffin, 1999); André Gide, *The Journals of André Gide, 1889–1949* (New York: Vintage, 1956); Sheridan, *André Gide*; Renoir, *My Life and My Films*; Bertin, *Jean Renoir*; Bazin, *Jean Renoir*; Beauvoir, *Prime of Life*; Perriand, *Life of Creation*; Gold and Fizdale, *Misia*; Steegmuller, *Cocteau*; Madsen, *Chanel*; Picardie, *Coco Chanel*; Dalí, *Secret Life of Salvador Dalí*; Secrest, *Salvador Dalí*; Secrest, *Elsa Schiaparelli*; Emling, *Marie Curie and Her Daughters*; Lottman, *Pétain*; Brown, *Embrace of Unreason*; Eugen Weber, *Action Française*; Zeev Sternhell, *Neither Right nor Left: Fascist Ideology in France* (Princeton, N.J.: Princeton University Press, 1995); Christine Levisse-Touzé, *Paris libéré, Paris retrouvée* (Paris: Gallimard, 1994); Henry Rousso, *The Vichy Syndrome: History and Memory in France since 1944* (Cambridge, Mass.: Harvard University Press, 1991).

1. Eugen Weber, *Hollow Years*, 266.
2. Man Ray, *Self Portrait*, 242.
3. From Sartre's *War Diaries*, 20 February 1940, 223–24. On February 18, 1940, Sartre wrote, "Two months ago, they [two *chasseurs*, or light infantry] were complaining about a pretty foolish taste for heroics among their comrades. . . . Today, they say the morale of the troops is very low. It's what I've had occasion to observe everywhere, lately" (204). And on February 20, he added, "It's been six months now that our army has been on a war footing. The men are being held far away from their homes and their jobs, and are subject to military discipline. A dictatorship is exercised over the press, over speech, and over thought. Our whole life has the external aspect of war. But the war machine is running in neutral" (224).
4. For more background on these events, see Mary McAuliffe, *Dawn of the Belle Epoque*.
5. Schiaparelli, *Shocking Life*, 106.
6. Beauvoir, *Prime of Life*, 336, 344.
7. The Fifth Republic, founded in 1958, is now a close second.
8. Lacouture, *Léon Blum*, 51, 39.
9. Lacouture, *De Gaulle, the Rebel*, 173, 172.
10. Lacouture, *De Gaulle, the Rebel*, 175.
11. Man Ray, *Self Portrait*, 242–43.
12. Lacouture, *De Gaulle, the Rebel*, 179.
13. Lottman, *Fall of Paris*, 46.
14. Lacouture, *De Gaulle, the Rebel*, 181.
15. Lacouture, *De Gaulle, the Rebel*, 182.
16. The most junior of the general officer ranks. This was a battlefield promotion.
17. Lacouture, *De Gaulle, the Rebel*, 187.

18. Lacouture, *De Gaulle, the Rebel*, 188. This letter was dated 3 June 1940, as de Gaulle prepared to enter the government as undersecretary of war.

19. Man Ray, *Self Portrait*, 243.

20. Guggenheim, *Out of This Century*, 219.

21. Lottman, *Fall of Paris*, 40.

22. For more on the underground movement that took refugees across the Pyrenees, see Marino, *Quiet American*.

23. Beach, *Shakespeare & Company*, 213.

24. Beach, *Shakespeare & Company*, 214.

25. Lacouture, *De Gaulle, the Rebel*, 187. It was as de Gaulle prepared to join the government that General Weygand told him that he had saved the nation's honor.

26. Gide, 19 July 1940, in *Journals, 1889–1949*, 2:260. But Jean-Paul Sartre was slow to condemn his fellow soldiers. "The men have had a very tough time of it from the first," he wrote in his war diaries, and they've borne everything without complaining, or even thinking they had any right to complain. They weren't sustained by any patriotic or ideological ideal. They didn't like Hitlerism, but they weren't wild about democracy, either—and they didn't give a bugger about Poland. Into the bargain, they had the vague impression of having been tricked. Yet they endured everything with a kind of undemonstrative dignity" (*War Diaries*, 20 February 1940, 225).

27. Renoir, *My Life and My Films*, 175.

28. Jean Renoir and Paul Cézanne, the son of the painter, had been good friends for years.

29. Renoir, *My Life and My Films*, 181.

30. Beauvoir, *Prime of Life*, 349, 350.

31. Beauvoir, *Prime of Life*, 353–54.

32. Perriand, *Life of Creation*, 121.

33. Perriand, *Life of Creation*, 123, 125.

34. Perriand, *Life of Creation*, 127.

35. Perriand, *Life of Creation*, 127. It would turn out to be fires from the ignition of French oil reserves, by French command, to prevent them from falling into German hands.

36. Gold and Fizdale, *Misia*, 284–85.

37. Lacouture, *Léon Blum*, 408, 409.

38. Cocteau's biographer notes that "Cocteau's slavery to opium continued now to be at its worst," affecting the quality of his literary output (Steegmuller, *Cocteau*, 434).

39. Dalí, *Secret Life of Salvador Dalí*, 381.

40. Dalí, *Secret Life of Salvador Dalí*, 384.

41. Lottman, *Fall of Paris*, 298.

42. Lottman, *Fall of Paris*, 331, 312.

43. Gold and Fizdale, *Misia*, 285; Beach, *Shakespeare & Company*, 214.

44. Lacouture, *De Gaulle, the Rebel*, 201.

45. Lacouture, *De Gaulle, the Rebel*, 201.

46. Lacouture, *De Gaulle, the Rebel*, 201. En route, de Gaulle stopped briefly to see his mother, who was dying. It would be the last time he saw her.

47. Lacouture, *De Gaulle, the Rebel*, 208.

48. Lacouture, *De Gaulle, the Rebel*, 219, 222.

49. Lacouture, *De Gaulle, the Rebel*, 225.

50. Man Ray, *Self Portrait*, 246–47.

51. Lacouture, *Léon Blum*, 411–12; Gide, 24 June 1940, in *Journals, 1889–1949*, 254.

52. Picardie, *Coco Chanel*, 251.

53. Sternhell, *Neither Right nor Left*, xix.

Epilogue

Bryher, *Heart to Artemis*; Jean-Claude Baker, *Josephine*; Thurman, *Secrets of the Flesh*; Sperling, *Matisse, the Master*; Sheridan, *André Gide*; Brown, *Embrace of Unreason*; Conner, *André Gide's Politics*; Guerard, *André Gide*; Gide, *Journals, 1889–1949*; Gertrude Stein, *Paris France* (New York: Liveright, 2013); Will, *Unlikely Collaboration*; Brinnin, *Third Rose*; Simon, *Biography of Alice B. Toklas*; Secrest, *Elsa Schiaparelli*; Emling, *Marie Curie and Her Daughters*; Man Ray, *Self Portrait*; Baldwin, *Man Ray*; Secrest, *Salvador Dalí*; Ellmann, *James Joyce*; McAuliffe, *When Paris Sizzled*; Lottman, *Left Bank*; Ferguson, *Henry Miller*; Bertin, *Jean Renoir*; Renoir, *My Life and My Films*; Browder, *André Breton*; Sinclair, *My Grandfather's Gallery*; Marino, *A Quiet American*; Perriand, *Life of Creation*; Todd, *Malraux*; Youki Desnos, *Les Confidences de Youki*; Lacouture, *Léon Blum*; Rousso, *Vichy Syndrome*; Garelick, *Mademoiselle*; Madsen, *Chanel*; Picardie, *Coco Chanel*; Gold and Fizdale, *Misia*; Steegmuller, *Cocteau*; Max Jacob and Jean Cocteau, *Correspondance, 1917–1944* (Paris: Paris-Méditerranée, 2000); Thurman, *Secrets of the Flesh*; Rhodes, *Louis Renault*; Nicholas Fox Weber, *Le Corbusier*; Roland Penrose, *Picasso: His Life and Work* (Berkeley: University of California Press, 1981); Beauvoir, *Prime of Life*; Madsen, *Hearts and Minds*; Eugen Weber, *Hollow Years*; Fitch, *Sylvia Beach and the Lost Generation*; Beach, *Shakespeare & Company*; Carlos Baker, *Hemingway*.

1. Bryher, *Heart to Artemis*, 299.

2. Jean-Claude Baker, *Josephine*, 252.

3. Sperling, *Matisse the Master*, 393, 395–96.

4. Sheridan, *André Gide*, 543–44; Conner, *André Gide's Politics*, 9–10.

5. Gide, 5 September 1940, in *Journals, 1889–1949*, 264. See also Guerard, *André Gide*, 29.

6. Stein, *Paris France*, 36. See also Will, *Unlikely Collaboration*, 7, 119.

7. Emling, *Marie Curie and Her Daughters*, 169.

8. See McAuliffe, *When Paris Sizzled*, 143.

9. Bertin, *Jean Renoir*, 180.

10. Bertin, *Jean Renoir*, 204.

11. Perriand, *Life of Creation*, 182.

12. Youki Desnos, *Les Confidences de Youki*, 206. Youki had left Foujita for Desnos several years before this.

13. Daladier survived, as did Paul Reynaud, who was sent to a series of German concentration camps. Mandel was returned to Paris, where he was executed by Vichy's Milice.

14. Lacouture, *Léon Blum*, 417, 418.

15. Lacouture, *Léon Blum*, 419.

16. Lacouture, *Léon Blum*, 424.

17. Lacouture, *Léon Blum*, 458, 457.

18. Although, on one notable occasion in December 1940, Chanel went "into a long tirade against the Jews" in the presence of the husband of a Rothschild. Boulos, who recorded the incident, noted that "fortunately, she was sidetracked" (Gold and Fizdale, *Misia*, 288).

19. Despite Jacob's much earlier conversion to Catholicism, he was arrested by the Gestapo and interned at Drancy, where he died shortly before he was scheduled to be shipped out to Auschwitz.

20. Steegmuller, *Cocteau*, 441.

21. Steegmuller, *Cocteau*, 441.

22. Gold and Fizdale, *Misia*, 287.

23. Rhodes, *Louis Renault*, 174.

24. Nicholas Fox Weber, *Le Corbusier*, 413.

25. Perriand, *Life of Creation*, 203–4.

26. Sinclair, *My Grandfather's Gallery*, 192.

27. Penrose, *Picasso*, 347–48. See Steegmuller, *Cocteau*, for reference to André Derain, Maurice de Vlaminck, and Charles Despiau, who accepted invitations to tour Germany during the Occupation (443).

28. Beauvoir, *Prime of Life*, 359, 360.

29. Beauvoir, *Prime of Life*, 362, 365.

30. Beauvoir, *Prime of Life*, 361.

31. Eugen Weber, *Hollow Years*, 279.

32. Beach, *Shakespeare & Company*, 215.

33. Beach, *Shakespeare & Company*, 415.

34. Beach, *Shakespeare & Company*, 219.

35. Beach, *Shakespeare & Company*, 220.

Bibliography

Badinter, Hélène, and Laura Barraud. *Illustre et Inconnu: Comment Jacques Jaujard à sauvé le Louvre*. Paris: Ladybirds Films, 2014.

Bair, Deirdre. *Simone de Beauvoir: A Biography*. New York: Summit, 1990.

Baker, Carlos. *Ernest Hemingway: A Life Story*. New York: Scribner, 1969.

Baker, Jean-Claude, and Chris Chase. *Josephine: The Hungry Heart*. New York: Cooper Square Press, 2001. First published 1993.

Baker, Josephine, and Jo Bouillon. *Josephine*. Translated by Mariana Fitzpatrick. New York: Harper & Row, 1977.

Bald, Wambly. *On the Left Bank, 1929–1933*. Edited by Benjamin Franklin V. Athens: Ohio University Press, 1987.

Baldwin, Neil. *Man Ray, American Artist*. New York: Da Capo Press, 2001. First published 1988.

Bazin, André. *Jean Renoir*. Translated by W. W. Halsey II and William H. Simon. Edited with introduction by François Truffaut. New York: De Capo Press, 1992. First published 1973.

Beach, Sylvia. *Shakespeare & Company*. Lincoln: University of Nebraska Press, 1991. First published 1959.

Beauvoir, Simone de. *Letters to Sartre*. Translated and edited by Quintin Hoarre. London: Radius, 1991.

———. *Memoirs of a Dutiful Daughter*. Translated by James Kirkup. New York: World Publishing, 1959.

———. *The Prime of Life*. Translated by Peter Green. New York: World Publishing, 1962.

Benton, Tim. *The Villas of Le Corbusier, 1920–1930*. With photographs in the Lucien Hervé collection. New Haven, Conn.: Yale University Press, 1987.

Bernard, Philippe, and Henri Dubief. *The Decline of the Third Republic, 1914–1938.* Translated by Anthony Forster. New York: Cambridge University Press, 1988. First published in English, 1985.

Bertin, Célia. *Jean Renoir: A Life in Pictures.* Translated by Mireille Muellner and Leonard Muellner. Baltimore, Md.: Johns Hopkins University Press, 1991. First published 1986.

Best, Victoria. *An Introduction to Twentieth-Century French Literature.* London: Duckworth, 2002.

Birmingham, Kevin. *The Most Dangerous Book: The Battle for James Joyce's "Ulysses."* New York: Penguin, 2014.

Boittin, Jennifer Anne. *Colonial Metropolis: The Urban Grounds of Anti-Imperialism and Feminism in Interwar Paris.* Lincoln: University of Nebraska Press, 2010.

Bougault, Valérie. *Montparnasse: The Heyday of Modern Art, 1910–1940.* Paris: Editions Pierre Terrail, 1997.

Boyle, Kay. *My Next Bride.* New York: Harcourt, Brace, 1934.

Brandon, Ruth. *Ugly Beauty: Helena Rubinstein, L'Oréal, and the Blemished History of Looking Good.* New York: Harper, 2011.

Brassaï [Gyula Halász]. *Henry Miller: The Paris Years.* Translated by Timothy Bent. New York: Arcade, 2011. First published 1975.

Bredin, Jean-Denis. *The Affair: The Case of Alfred Dreyfus.* Translated by Jeffrey Mahlman. New York: George Braziller, 1986.

Brinnin, John Malcolm. *The Sway of the Grand Saloon: A Social History of the North Atlantic.* New York: Delacorte Press, 1971.

———. *The Third Rose: Gertrude Stein and Her World.* Reading, Mass.: Addison-Wesley, 1987. First published 1959.

Browder, Clifford. *André Breton: Arbiter of Surrealism.* Geneva, Switzerland: Librarie Droz, 1967.

Brown, Frederick. *The Embrace of Unreason: France, 1914–1940.* New York: Knopf, 2014.

Bryher [Annie Winifred Ellerman]. *The Heart to Artemis: A Writer's Memoirs.* New York: Harcourt, Brace & World, 1962.

Buñuel, Luis. *L'Age d'Or,* DVD. New York: Kino on Video, 2004. Original release, 1930.

———. *My Last Sigh.* Translated by Abigail Israel. New York: Vintage, 1984.

———. *An Unspeakable Betrayal: Selected Writings of Luis Buñuel.* Translated by Garrett White. Berkeley: University of California Press, 2000.

Callaghan, Morley. *That Summer in Paris: Memories of Tangled Friendships with Hemingway, Fitzgerald, and Some Others.* Toronto: Macmillan of Canada, 1963.

Charters, Jimmie, as told to Morrill Cody. *This Must Be the Place: Memoirs of Montparnasse.* Edited and with a preface by Hugh Ford. Introduction by Ernest Hemingway. New York: Collier Macmillan, 1989. First published 1934.

Clair, René. *A nous la liberté,* DVD. New York: Criterion Collection, 2002. Original release, 1931.

———. *Le Million*, DVD. New York: Criterion Collection, 2000. Original release, 1931.

Cocteau, Jean. *The Journals of Jean Cocteau*. Edited and translated with an introduction by Wallace Fowlie. New York: Criterion Books, 1956.

Cody, Morrill, with Hugh Ford. *The Women of Montparnasse*. New York: Cornwall Books, 1983.

Conner, Tom, ed. *André Gide's Politics: Rebellion and Ambivalence*. New York: Palgrave, 2000.

Cordelier, Suzanne F. *Femmes au travail; études pratique sur dix-sept carrières féminines*. Paris: Plon, 1935.

Coste, Michel, et al. *Villes ouvrières: 1900–1950*. Paris: L'Harmattan, 1989.

Crosby, Caresse. *The Passionate Years*. New York: Dial Press, 1953.

Cunard, Nancy. *These Were the Hours: Memories of My Hours Press, Réanville and Paris, 1928–1931*. Edited with foreword by Hugh Ford. Carbondale: Southern Illinois University Press, 1969.

Curie, Eve. *Madame Curie: A Biography by Eve Curie*. Translated by Vincent Sheean. Garden City, N.Y.: Garden City Publishing, 1940. First published 1937.

Dalí, Salvador. *The Secret Life of Salvador Dalí*. Translated by Haakon M. Chevalier. New York: Dover, 1993. First published 1942.

Dalí, Salvador, and André Parinaud. *Maniac Eyeball: The Unspeakable Confessions of Salvador Dalí*. New York: Creation, 2004.

Deslandres, Yvonee, assisted by Dorothée Lalanne. *Poiret: Paul Poiret, 1879–1944*. Paris: Editions du Regard, 1986.

Desnos, Youki. *Les Confidences de Youki*. Dessins originaux de Foujita et Robert Desnos. Paris: Librairie Arthème Fayard, 1957.

Diesbach, Ghislain de. *L'Abbé Mugnier: le confesseur du tout-Paris*. Paris: Perrin, 2003.

Easton, Laird McLeod. *The Red Count: The Life and Times of Harry Kessler*. Berkeley: University of California Press, 2002.

Eichengreen, Barry J. *Golden Fetters: The Gold Standard and the Great Depression, 1919–1939*. New York: Oxford University Press, 1992.

Ellmann, Richard. *James Joyce*. New York: Oxford University Press, 1983. First published 1959.

Emling, Shelley. *Marie Curie and Her Daughters: The Private Lives of Science's First Family*. New York: Palgrave Macmillan, 2012.

Evenson, Norma. *Paris: A Century of Change, 1878–1978*. New Haven, Conn.: Yale University Press, 1979.

Ferguson, Robert. *Henry Miller: A Life*. New York: Norton, 1991.

Fiss, Karen. *Grand Illusion: The Third Reich, the Paris Exposition, and the Cultural Seduction of France*. Chicago: University of Chicago Press, 2009.

Fitch, Noel Riley. *Sylvia Beach and the Lost Generation: A History of Literary Paris in the Twenties and Thirties*. New York: Norton, 1983.

Fitzgerald, F. Scott. *A Life in Letters: F. Scott Fitzgerald*. Edited by Matthew J. Bruccoli, with the assistance of Judith S. Baughman. New York: Scribner, 1994.

———. *Tender Is the Night*. Hertfordshire, U.K.: Cumberland House, 1993. First published 1934.

Flanner, Janet. *Janet Flanner's World: Uncollected Writings, 1932–1975*. Edited by Irving Drutman. New York: Harcourt Brace Jovanovich, 1979.

———. *Paris Was Yesterday, 1925–1939*. Edited by Irving Drutman. New York: Viking, 1972.

Ford, Hugh. *Four Lives in Paris*. San Francisco, Calif.: North Point Press, 1987.

Frerejean, Alain. *André Citroën, Louis Renault: Un duel sans merci*. Paris: Albin Michel, 1998.

Gans, Deborah. *The Le Corbusier Guide*. New York: Princeton Architectural Press, 2006. First published 1987.

Garelick, Rhonda K. *Mademoiselle: Coco Chanel and the Pulse of History*. New York: Random House, 2014.

Gide, André. *The Counterfeiters*. Translated by Dorothy Bussy. New York: Vintage, 1973. First published 1927.

———. *If It Die: An Autobiography*. New York: Modern Library, 1935. First published 1924.

———. *The Immoralist*. Translation by Richard Howard. New York: Vintage, 1996. First published 1902.

———. *The Journals of André Gide*. Vol. 3, *1928–1939*. Translated by Justin O'Brien. London: Secker & Warburg, 1949.

———. *The Journals of André Gide, 1889–1949*. Vol. 2, *1924–1949*. Edited and translated by Justin O'Brien. New York: Vintage, 1956.

———. *Return from the U.S.S.R.* Translated by Dorothy Bussy. New York: Knopf, 1937.

Glassco, John. *Memoirs of Montparnasse*. New York: Oxford University Press, 1970.

Gold, Arthur, and Robert Fizdale. *Misia: The Life of Misia Sert*. New York: Morrow, 1981.

Gopnik, Adam. *Paris to the Moon*. New York: Random House, 2000.

Green, Julien. *Journal*. Vol. 1, *1928–1949*. Paris: Plon, 1961.

Guerard, Albert J. *André Gide*. Cambridge, Mass.: Harvard University Press, 1951.

Guggenheim, Peggy. *Out of This Century: Confessions of an Art Addict*. New York: Universe Books, 1979.

Hamalian, Linda. *The Cramoisy Queen: A Life of Caresse Crosby*. Carbondale: Southern Illinois University Press, 2005.

Hemingway, Ernest. *Ernest Hemingway: Selected Letters, 1917–1961*. Edited by Carlos Baker. New York: Scribner, 1981.

———. *A Farewell to Arms*. New York: Scribner, 1957. First published 1929.

———. *For Whom the Bell Tolls*. New York: Scribner, 1995. First published 1940.

———. *A Moveable Feast*. New York: Touchstone, 1996. First published 1964.

Huddleston, Sisley. *Back to Montparnasse: Glimpses of Broadway in Bohemia*. Philadelphia: J. B. Lippincott, 1931.

Hughes, Judith M. *To the Maginot Line: The Politics of French Military Preparation in the 1920s*. Cambridge, Mass.: Harvard University Press, 1971.

Hugo, Jean. *Avant d'oublier: 1918–1931*. Paris: Fayard, 1976.

———. *Le Regard de la Memoire*. Arles and Paris: Actes Sud, 1983.

Irujo, Xabier. *Gernika, 1937: The Market Day Massacre*. Reno: University of Nevada Press, 2015.

Jackson, Julian. *Charles de Gaulle*. London: Haus, 2003.

———. *The Fall of France: The Nazi Invasion of 1940*. New York: Oxford University Press, 2003.

———. *The Politics of Depression in France, 1932–1936*. New York: Cambridge University Press, 1985.

———. *The Popular Front in France: Defending Democracy, 1934–38*. New York: Cambridge University Press, 1988.

Jacob, Max, and Jean Cocteau. *Correspondance, 1917–1944*. Edited and with an introduction by Anne Kimball. Paris: Paris-Méditerranée, 2000.

Joyce, James. *Finnegans Wake*. New York: Penguin Classics, 1999. First published 1939.

Kapferer, Patricia, and Tristan Gaston-Breton. *Lacoste the Legend*. Paris: Cherche midi, 2002.

Kessler, Count Harry. *The Diaries of a Cosmopolitan: Count Harry Kessler, 1918–1937*. Translated and edited by Charles Kessler. London: Weidenfeld & Nicolson, 1971.

Kiki. *Kiki's Memoirs*. Introductions by Ernest Hemingway and Tsuguharu Foujita. Photography by Man Ray. Edited and with a foreword by Billy Klüver and Julie Martin. Translated by Samuel Putnam. Hopewell, N.J.: Ecco Press, 1996.

Klüver, Billy, and Julie Martin. *Kiki's Paris: Artists and Lovers, 1900–1930*. New York: Abrams, 1989.

Lacouture, Jean. *De Gaulle, the Rebel: 1890–1944*. Translated by Patrick O'Brian. New York: Norton, 1993. First published in English, 1990.

———. *Léon Blum*. Translated by George Holoch. New York: Holmes & Meier, 1982.

Le Corbusier. *When the Cathedrals Were White*. Translated by Francis E. Hyslop Jr. New York: McGraw-Hill, 1964. First published in French, 1937.

Levisse-Touzé, Christine. *Paris libéré, Paris retrouvée*. Paris: Gallimard, 1994.

Lord, James. *Six Exceptional Women: Further Memoirs*. New York: Farrar, Straus & Giroux, 1994.

Lottman, Herbert R. *The Fall of Paris: June 1940*. New York: HarperCollins, 1992.

———. *The Left Bank: Writers, Artists, and Politics from the Popular Front to the Cold War*. Boston: Houghton Mifflin, 1982.

———. *Man Ray's Montparnasse*. New York: Harry N. Abrams, 2001.

———. *The Michelin Men: Driving an Empire*. New York: I. B. Tauris, 2003.

———. *Pétain, Hero or Traitor: The Untold Story*. New York: Morrow, 1985.

———. *Return of the Rothschilds: The Great Banking Dynasty through Two Turbulent Centuries*. London: Tauris, 1995.

Madsen, Axel. *Chanel: A Woman of Her Own*. New York: Henry Holt, 1991.

———. *Hearts and Minds: The Common Journey of Simone de Beauvoir and Jean-Paul Sartre*. New York: Morrow, 1977.

Mahoney, Daniel J. *Bertrand De Jouvenel: The Conservative Liberal and the Illusions of Modernity*. Wilmington, Del.: ISI Books, 2005.

Man Ray. *Self Portrait*. Boston: Little, Brown, 1988. First published 1963.

Manet, Julie. *Growing Up with the Impressionists: The Diary of Julie Manet*. Translated and edited by Rosalind de Boland Roberts and Jane Roberts. London: Sotheby's, 1987.

Marino, Andy. *A Quiet American: The Secret War of Varian Fry*. New York: St. Martin's Griffin, 1999.

Maxtone-Graham, John. *Crossing and Cruising: From the Golden Era of Ocean Liners to the Luxury Cruise Ships of Today*. New York: Scribner, 1992.

McAlmon, Robert. *Being Geniuses Together, 1920–1930*. Revised with supplementary chapters and an afterword by Kay Boyle. San Francisco, Calif.: North Point Press, 1984.

McAuliffe, Mary. *Dawn of the Belle Epoque: The Paris of Monet, Zola, Bernhardt, Eiffel, Debussy, Clemenceau, and Their Friends*. Lanham, Md.: Rowman & Littlefield, 2011.

———. *Twilight of the Belle Epoque: The Paris of Picasso, Stravinsky, Proust, Renault, Marie Curie, Gertrude Stein, and Their Friends through the Great War*. Lanham, Md.: Rowman & Littlefield, 2014.

———. *When Paris Sizzled: The 1920s Paris of Hemingway, Chanel, Cocteau, Cole Porter, Josephine Baker, and Their Friends*. Lanham, Md.: Rowman & Littlefield, 2016.

Meyers, Jeffrey. *Scott Fitzgerald: A Biography*. New York: HarperCollins, 1994.

Miller, Henry. *Tropic of Cancer*. New York: Grove Weidenfeld, 1961.

Mitford, Nancy. *Zelda: A Biography*. New York: Harper & Row, 1970.

Moorehead, Caroline. *Martha Gellhorn: A Life*. London: Chatto & Windus, 2003.

Morand, Paul. *The Allure of Chanel*. Translated by Euan Cameron. London: Pushkin Press, 2008. First published 1976.

Mouré, Kenneth. *The Gold Standard Illusion: France, the Bank of France, and the International Gold Standard, 1914–1939*. New York: Oxford University Press, 2002.

Mugnier, Abbé (Arthur). *Journal de l'Abbé Mugnier: 1879–1939*. Paris: Mercure de France, 1985.

O'Mahony, Mike. *Olympic Visions: Images of the Games through History*. London: Reaktion Books, 2012.

Paul, Elliot. *The Last Time I Saw Paris*. New York: Random House, 1942.

Pedersen, Susan. *Family, Dependence, and the Origins of the Welfare State: Britain and France, 1914–1945*. New York: Cambridge University Press, 1993.

Penrose, Roland. *Picasso: His Life and Work*. 3rd ed. Berkeley: University of California Press, 1981.

Perlès, Alfred. *My Friend Henry Miller: An Intimate Biography*. London: Neville Spearman, 1955.

Perriand, Charlotte. *A Life of Creation: An Autobiography*. Translated by Odile Jacob. New York: Monacelli Press, 2003.

Picardie, Justine. *Coco Chanel: The Legend and the Life*. New York: HarperCollins, 2010.

Poiret, Paul. *King of Fashion: The Autobiography of Paul Poiret*. Translated by Stephen Haden Guest. Philadelphia: J. B. Lippincott, 1931.

Putnam, Samuel. *Paris Was Our Mistress: Memoirs of a Lost and Found Generation*. New York: Viking, 1947.

Quinn, Susan. *Marie Curie: A Life*. New York: Simon & Schuster, 1995.

Ravel, Maurice. *A Ravel Reader: Correspondence, Articles, Interviews*. Edited by Arbie Orenstein. Mineola, N.Y.: Dover, 2003. First published 1990.

Rayssac, Michel. *L'Exode des musées: l'histoire des oeuvres d'art sous l'Occupation*. Paris: Payot & Rivages, 2007.

Renoir, Jean. *Boudu Saved from Drowning [Boudu Sauvé des Eaux]*, DVD. U.S.: Home Vision Entertainment, 2005. Original release, 1932.

———. *The Crime of Monsieur Lange [Le Crime de Monsieur Lange]*, DVD. New York: Interama Video Classics, 1935.

———. *A Day in the Country [Une Partie de Campagne]*, DVD. New York: Criterion Collection, 2015. Original release, 1936.

———. *The Grand Illusion [La Grande Illusion]*, DVD. New York: Criterion Collection, 2008. Original release, 1937.

———. *La Bête humaine*, DVD. Irvington, N.Y.: Criterion Collection, 2006. Original release, 1938.

———. *La Chienne*, DVD. New York: Criterion Collection, 2016. Original release, 1931.

———. *Les Bas-fonds*, DVD. U.S.: Criterion Collection, 2004. Original release, 1936.

———. *My Life and My Films*. Translated by Norman Denny. New York: Da Capo Press, 2000. First published 1974.

———. *On purge bébé*, DVD. New York: Criterion Collection, 2016. Original release, 1931.

———. *The Rules of the Game [La Règle du jeu]*, DVD. Irvington, N.Y.: Criterion collection, 2011. Reconstruction (1959, with Renoir's approval) of 1939 film.

Reynolds, John. *André Citroën: The Man and the Motor Cars*. Thrupp, Stroud, UK: Sutton, 1996.

Reynolds, Michael S. *Hemingway: The 1930s*. New York: Norton, 1997.

———. *Hemingway: The American Homecoming*. Cambridge, Mass.: Blackwell, 1992.

Rhodes, Anthony. *Louis Renault: A Biography*. New York: Harcourt, Brace & World, 1970.

Richardson, John. "A Different Guernica." *New York Review of Books* 63, no. 8 (12 May 2016): 4–6.

———. *A Life of Picasso: The Triumphant Years, 1917–1932*. New York: Knopf, 2007.

Riefenstahl, Leni. *Olympia*, DVD. U.S.: Pathfinder Home Entertainment, 2006.

Rousso, Henry. *The Vichy Syndrome: History and Memory in France since 1944*. Translated by Arthur Goldhammer. Cambridge, Mass.: Harvard University Press, 1991.

Sante, Luc. *The Other Paris*. New York: Farrar, Straus & Giroux, 2015.

Sartre, Jean-Paul. *War Diaries: Notebooks from a Phoney War, November 1939–March 1940*. Translated by Quintin Hoare. London: Verso, 1984.

———. *Witness to My Life: The Letters of Jean-Paul Sartre to Simone de Beauvoir, 1926–1939.* Edited by Simone de Beauvoir. Translated by Lee Fahnestock and Norman McAfee. New York: Scribner, 1992.

Schelps, Charlie. *Elsie de Wolfe's Paris: Frivolity before the Storm.* New York: Abrams, 2014.

Schiaparelli, Elsa. *Shocking Life: The Autobiography of Elsa Schiaparelli.* London: V&A Publications, 2007.

Secrest, Meryle. *Elsa Schiaparelli: A Biography.* New York: Knopf, 2014.

———. *Salvador Dalí: The Surrealist Jester.* London: Weidenfeld & Nicolson, 1986.

Shattuck, Roger. "Having Congress: The Shame of the Thirties." In Tom Conner, ed., *André Gide's Politics: Rebellion and Ambivalence.* New York: Palgrave, 2000.

Sheridan, Alan. *André Gide: A Life in the Present.* London: Hamish Hamilton, 1998.

Silver, Kenneth. *Chaos and Classicism: Art in France, Italy, and Germany, 1918–1936.* New York: Guggenheim Museum, 2010.

Simenon, Georges. *Night at the Crossroads.* Translated by Linda Coverdale. New York: Penguin, 2014. First published 1931.

Simon, Linda. *The Biography of Alice B. Toklas.* Garden City, N.Y.: Doubleday, 1977.

Sinclair, Anne. *My Grandfather's Gallery: A Family Memoir of Art and War.* Translated by Shaun Whiteside. New York: Farrar, Straus & Giroux, 2014.

Smith, Timothy B. *Creating the Welfare State in France, 1880–1940.* Montreal: McGill-Queen's University Press, 2003.

Soucy, Robert. *French Fascism: The First Wave, 1924–1933.* New Haven, Conn.: Yale University Press, 1986.

———. *French Fascism: The Second Wave, 1933–1939.* New Haven, Conn.: Yale University Press, 1995.

Spanier, Sandra Whipple. *Kay Boyle, Artist and Activist.* Carbondale: Southern Illinois University Press, 1986.

Sperling, Hilary. *Matisse, the Master: A Life of Henri Matisse; The Conquest of Colour, 1909–1954.* New York: Knopf, 2005.

Spiteri, Raymond, and Donald LaCoss, eds. *Surrealism, Politics and Culture.* Burlington, Vt.: Ashgate, 2003.

Steegmuller, Francis. *Cocteau: A Biography.* Boston: Little, Brown, 1970.

Stein, Gertrude. *The Autobiography of Alice B. Toklas.* New York: Vintage, 1990. First published 1933.

———. *Everybody's Autobiography.* New York: Random House, 1937.

———. *Paris France.* New York: Liveright, 2013. First published 1940.

Sternhell, Zeev. *Neither Right nor Left: Fascist Ideology in France.* Translated by David Maisel. Princeton, N.J.: Princeton University Press, 1995.

Stravinsky, Igor. *An Autobiography.* New York: Norton, 1998. First published 1936.

Stravinsky, Igor, and Robert Craft. *Memories and Commentaries.* New York: Faber & Faber, 2002.

Tartakowsky, Danielle. *Le Front Populaire: La Vie est à nous.* Paris: Gallimard, 1996.

Thurman, Judith. *Secrets of the Flesh: A Life of Colette.* New York: Ballantine, 1999.

Todd, Olivier. *Malraux: A Life*. Translated by Joseph West. New York: Knopf, 2005.

Toledano, Roulhac B., and Elizabeth Z. Coty. *François Coty: Fragrance, Power, Money*. Gretna, La.: Pelican, 2009.

Vigreux, Jean. *Le front populaire, 1934–1938*. Paris: Presses Universitaires de France, 2011.

Walsh, Stephen. *Stravinsky: A Creative Spring; Russia and France, 1882–1934*. Berkeley: University of California Press, 2002.

———. *Stravinsky: The Second Exile; France and America, 1934–1971*. New York: Knopf, 2006.

Weber, Eugen. *Action Française: Royalism and Reaction in Twentieth-Century France*. Stanford, Calif.: Stanford University Press, 1962.

———. *The Hollow Years: France in the 1930s*. New York: Norton, 1994.

Weber, Nicholas Fox. *Le Corbusier: A Life*. New York: Knopf, 2008.

Will, Barbara. *Unlikely Collaboration: Gertrude Stein, Bernard Faÿ, and the Vichy Dilemma*. New York: Columbia University Press, 2011.

Williams, Charles. *The Last Great Frenchman: A Life of General de Gaulle*. New York: Wiley, 1993.

Winkler, Heinrich August. *Germany: The Long Road West*. Translated by Alexander J. Sager. New York: Oxford University Press, 2006.

Wullschläger, Jackie. *Chagall: A Biography*. New York: Knopf, 2008.

Index

Page references for illustrations are italicized.

Action Française, 58, 78, 95, 96, 107,
    121, 129, 130, 158, 161, 169, 224;
    dissolution of, 170, 178, 321n3
Action Française, 58, 96, 124, 128, 170,
    173, 201
Allégret, Marc, 40; as filmmaker, 33,
    88; and Gide, 29–30, 32, 33
Anderson, Sherwood, 29, 36, 59,
    120–21
anti-Semitism, 1, 2, 58, 78–79, 95–96,
    109–10, 116, 131, 172, 173, 198,
    234–35, 239, 257, 265–66, 285.
    See also Chanel; Stravinsky; Vichy
    France government
Aragon, Louis, 35, 55, 78, 111, 112,
    201, 210, 291
Association of Revolutionary Writers
    and Artists, 111, 112, 114, 132
Auric, Georges, 40, 179, 275
Austin, A. Everett, Jr., 140

Baker, Josephine, 36, 62, 84; and
    America, 145, 153; at Casino de
    Paris, 63–64; and Maurice Chevalier,
    259; in *La Créole*, 145; honors, 284;
and Le Corbusier, 36; and marriage,
    207; and Mistinguett, 64; and
    Pepito, 63, 64; as spy, 260, 283–84;
    and war, 259–60; and Ziegfield
    Follies, 151–53
Bald, Wambly, 6, 53, 54, 73, 88, 101,
    119
Bal Nègre, 248
Barney, Natalie Clifford, 58
Barr, Alfred, 140
Barrès, Maurice, 11, 32, 300n18
Barthou, Louis, 138, 158
Bauhaus, 115–16
Beach, Sylvia, 39, 40, 52, 221,
    306n27; arrest and internment
    of, 297; and Austrian Anschluss,
    222; background of, 6; and Bloody
    Tuesday, 130; and Bryher, 6, 193,
    222, 237; and Czech crisis, 237;
    and exodus from Paris, 271–72;
    and Gisèle Freund, 4, 193, 236,
    271; hard times, 104, 121, 221–22;
    and Hemingway, 5, 27, 104,
    121,193, 204, 236, 237, 297–98;
    and Hitler, 123, 193; Jewish friends,

271, 297; and James Joyce, 6–8,
70, 103–5, 122–23, 166–67, 193,
236–37, 308n17, 312n62, 312n67,
315n52; Legion of Honor, 237; and
liberation of Paris, 298; and Henry
Miller, 103; and Adrienne Monnier,
6, 40, 103–4, 123, 130, 193, 236,
271–72, 297, 298, 312n62; and
Munich Agreement, 232; during
Occupation, 296–97; Paris, remains
in, 221, 272, 296–97; and Ezra
Pound, 123; and refugees, 270–72;
and Shakespeare and Company,
4, 5–6, 8, 36, 60, 72, 104, 122,
166, 193, 204, 221, 222, 237, 260,
296, 297; and Gertrude Stein,
60–61, 122, 237–38; and *Ulysses*, 6,
60–61, 70, 103–5, 122–23, 308n17,
312n67, 315nn51–52; and Wall
Street collapse, 8; and war, 260,
270–71
Beaumont, Etienne de, 44, 244
Beauvoir, Simone de, 38, 56, 227;
and Austrian Anschluss, 222–23;
background of, 36–37, 39; and
Bloody Tuesday, 134–35; books
read, 36, 303n31; exodus from Paris,
273–74; literary rejection, 238; and
Munich Agreement, 232, 238; and
Nazi-Soviet pact, 247–48; during
Occupation, 296; and politics,
114–15; and Sartre, 36–37, 39, 115,
166, 209, 260, 303n30, 304n37;
and Shakespeare and Company, 36,
296; *She Came to Stay*, 238; and war,
248–50, 254, 260, 264–65, 296
Beckett, Samuel, 7, 54, 56, 211, 221–
22, 261, 306n39
Benjamin, Walter, 271
Berenson, Bernard, 40–41
Bloody Tuesday (February 6, 1934),
129–30; aftermath, 130–31, 132,
133, 134, 135, 139

Blum, Léon, 1, 9, *10*, *126*, *196*, 242; and
Armistice (1940), 279; background
of, 9, 11–12, 300n17, 301n22;
Jeanne Levylier Blum, 292–93;
Robert Blum, 11, 292, 301n22;
Thérèse Blum, 218; in Buchenwald,
292; and Clichy riots, 198–99; and
coalition governments, 12–13,
93, 110, 173; and de Gaulle, 194,
266–67; and Dreyfus Affair, 11, 158,
266, 300n18, 301n19; the economy,
197; and Gide, 32; gold standard,
182; hatred of, 12, 169–70, 173,
198, 223, 224, 266, 292, 321n3;
and Le Corbusier, 205; and Munich
Agreement, 232, 233; and Neo-
Socialists, 110; origins myth, 172;
and pacifism, 110; flees Paris, 275;
and Paris Exposition of Arts and
Technology, 199; and Popular Front,
173, 182, 197, 198, 199; as prime
minister, 173–75, 197, 223, 224; and
rearmament, 194, 234–35; and Paul
Reynaud, 267; as SFIO leader, 12,
110, 170, 233; on trial, 292
Boyle, Kay, 39, 58–59, 61, 67–68, 164,
270, 304n42, 308n9
Brancusi, Constantin, 55, 67, 141, 286
Braque, Georges, 24, 34, 120, 270
Brassaï, 72, 100, 102, 208, 231
Brecht, Bertolt, 137, 160, 271
Breker, Arno, 176, 293
Breton, André, 13, 76, 77–78, 190,
227; and anti-Communist efforts,
111, 131–32, 160–61; and Bloody
Tuesday, 131; and Salvador Dalí, 16,
76, 117, 156; escape from Paris and
France, 290; and war, 260, 270
Bryher (Annie Winifred Ellerman), 79,
108; and Sylvia Beach, 6, 193, 222,
237; and escape, 283; and Gide, 29–
30; and James Joyce, 6; and refugees,
238–39

Buñuel, Luis, 87–88; and *L'Age d'Or*, 16, 18, 77, 96; and *Un Chien Andalou*, 16, 18, 77; and Salvador Dalí, 14, 16, 17, 18, 156, 301n36; and *Guernica*, 201

Café Les Deux Magots, 56, 57, 58
Café du Dôme, 248, 249, 250, 296
Café de Flore, 56, 58, 248, 249, 250
Cagoule, 78, 130, 214
Callaghan, Morley, 26–28, 303n8
Camelots du Roi, 16, 78, 95, 96, 128, 170
Camus, Albert, 56
Cercle Fustel de Coulanges, 95
CGT (General Confederation of Labor), 131, 176, 199
CGTU (United General Confederation of Labor), 131, 176
Chagall, Marc, 49
Chanel, Coco, 24, 44, 45, 87; anti-Semitism of, 94, 116, 293, 333n18; and Armistice, 279; and Bloody Tuesday, 139; *Les Chevaliers de la Table Ronde*, 206; and Cocteau, 26, 94, 206; and collaboration, 293; and De Beers, 94–95; Depression, impact of, 156; and drug use, 156; flees Paris, 275–76; glamour of, 157, 226, 244; and Hollywood, 86; and Paul Iribe, 94–95, 116–17, 140, 156; *La Machine infernale*, 206; and Paul Morand, 26, 95, 117, 175, 314n33; *Oedipe-Roi*, 206; right-wing sympathies of, 94, 95; and Schiaparelli, 24, 139–40, 156–57, 189; and Misia Sert, 86; and Wall Street Crash, 24, 25; and war, 255, 275–76, 279; and the Duke of Westminster, 25–26, 94, 303n4; and her workers, 157, 175
Chautemps, Camille, 129, 222, 233
Chevalier, Maurice, 259, 283

Chiappe, Jean, 77, 108, 129
Cité Internationale Universitaire de Paris, 96–97, 98, 99
Citroën, André, 50–52, 85–86, 93, 270, 306nn24–25, 311n25; bankruptcy and death, 143, 163; and Michelin, 50, 51, 143, 163–64; and Renault, 50–51, 52, 94, 143, 164; Traction Avant, 52, 85, 94, 142–43, 163–64, 310n15; tribute to, 163–64
Clair, René, 88, 90, 171, 288
Clemenceau, Georges, 11, 157
Cocteau, Jean, 40–41, 175; and Chanel, 26, 94, 206; *Les Chevaliers de la Table Ronde*, 206; and Jean Desbordes, 40, 76; and Gide, 206; and Max Jacob, 293; *La Machine infernale*, 206; and Jean Marais, 206–7, 255, 293; during Occupation, 293–94; *Oedipe-Roi*, 206; and opium addiction, 40–41, 156, 206–7, 255, 275, 331n38; and Raymond Radiguet, 288; and Elsa Schiaparelli, 21, 157; *Le Sang d'un poète*, 77, 87, 309n33; and Surrealists, 76; *La Voix humaine*, 76–77; and war, 255, 275
Cody, Morrill, 55, 120, 121
Colette, 49, 116, 150–51, 231, 254–55, 294
Communist party (PCF), 12, 36–37, 78, 93, 111, 114, 118, *126*, 301n20; and Bloody Tuesday, 129–30, 131–32, 137; and Clichy riots, 198; fear of, 214, 294; and intellectuals, 13, 55, 78, 112–14, 118, 131–32, 160–61, 162–63, 186, 187, 206, 229, 247; and Munich Agreement, 232; and Nazi-Soviet Pact, 247; opposition to, 95; and Popular Front, 160, 161, 173; and Socialist party, 11–12, 93, 233; and Surrealists, 13, 78, 111. *See also* Association of Revolutionary

Writers and Artists; CGTU;
    Spanish Civil War; workers
Cortot, Alfred, 11, 219
Coty, François, 78, 95, 121–22, 128,
    315n48
Croix-de-Feu, 95, 96, 122, 129, 130,
    158, 170, 178, 198
Crosby, Caresse, 40, 54, 67, 68, 118,
    139, 140–41, 155–56, 157, 288,
    308n9
Crosby, Harry, 40, 54, 67, 68, 304n42
Cunard, Nancy, 23, 54–56, 210–11,
    213, 306n39
Curie, Eve, 65, 66, 83, 217–18, 226,
    256, 257, 286
Curie, Irène. See Joliot-Curie, Irène
Curie, Marie, 64–66, 82–83, 132–33,
    217–18, 308n5

Dada, 13, 14, 22, 35, 190
Daladier, Edouard, 9, 210, 224, 233,
    235, 242, 267, 268, 269, 291–92,
    333n13
Dalí, Gala Eluard: background of, 17;
    and Salvador Dalí, 17–18, 76, 155–
    56, 190–91, 227, 276, 288; in New
    York, 155–56
Dalí, Salvador, 19; and L'Age d'Or, 16,
    18, 77, 96; background of, 13–18;
    break with his father, 18, 19; and
    André Breton, 16, 76, 117, 156;
    and Luis Buñuel, 14, 16, 17, 18,
    156, 301n36; Un Chien Andalou,
    16, 18, 77; and Gala Dalí, 17–18,
    76, 155–56, 190–91, 227, 276, 288;
    and exhibits, 117, 140–41, 190, 227,
    317n37; flees Paris and France, 276,
    288; and Hitler, 117; and Federico
    García Lorca, 14, 191; and Henry
    Miller, 118, 314n35; and Joan
    Miró, 15, 16; in New York, 141,
    155–56, 190, 245; and Anaïs Nin,
    118; and Charles and Marie-Laure

de Noailles, 16, 76; and "paranoiac-
    critical method," 117; and Picasso,
    15–16, 76; and Elsa Schiaparelli,
    21, 157, 190; and Spanish Civil
    War, 191; and Surrealism, 16, 76,
    156, 190, 227, 301n31; wealth and
    success of, 76, 227, 245; and Zodiac
    group, 117
Daudet, Léon, 78, 169
de Gaulle, Charles: in Beirut, 35–36;
    and Léon Blum, 194, 266–67; family
    of, 145–46, 332n46; Le Fil de l'épée,
    85; flees to London, 278; France,
    devotion to, 124, 146, 224, 278; La
    France et son armée, 224–26, 235;
    Free French forces of, 281, 282,
    284, 286; German panzers, 224,
    263, 268–69; on Hitler's Germany,
    124, 159, 167, 193–94, 210; joins
    government, 272; Maginot Line,
    views on, 41, 84–85, 167, 194,
    210; on military preparedness, 224,
    243, 258; and Munich Agreement,
    233; and Pétain, 36, 84, 85, 146,
    147, 194–95, 224–26, 242, 269,
    272, 278; on professional army,
    124; promotions of, 195, 210, 269,
    330n16; and Paul Reynaud, 195,
    210, 266–68; on Soviet Union, 159;
    Spanish Civil War, 210; at Supreme
    National Defense Council (SGDN),
    84–85, 124; and tanks, 124, 146,
    167, 210, 258–59, 268–69; Towards
    an Army of the Future, 146–47; and
    war, 258–59, 268–69, 272, 277–78,
    281, 331n25
Delaunay, Robert, 199
Delaunay, Sonia, 199
Depression, 1–2, 8, 39–40, 51, 92, 93,
    107, 110, 128, 156, 157, 158, 161,
    197, 214. See also economy
Derain, André, 34, 295, 333n27
Desnos, Robert, 291, 333n12

Desnos, Youki Foujita, 43–44, 291, 333n12
Doriot, Jacques, 170, 206
Dormoy, Marx, 214
Dos Passos, John, 40, 133, 164, 165, 203
Drancy, 100, 280, 281, 292, 312n48, 333n19
Dreyfus, Alfred, 11, 32, 96, 158, 265–66
Dreyfus Affair, 11, 32, 58, 78, 96, 158, 162, 265–66, 301n19
Drieu La Rochelle, Pierre, 107, 111, 206, 257, 284, 294
Duchamp, Marcel, 76, 141–42, 227, 276, 290, 317n40
Dufy, Raoul, 199
Duncan, Raymond, 67–68

Eastman, Max, 119, 121, 212
economy, 2; deflationary measures, 158, 172; family allowances, 68–69; franc, devaluation of, 182, 197; French, 2, 8–9, 44, 77, 92, 121–22, 156, 197, 222; French war debt, 96; global, 8–9, 93; gold standard, 77, 93, 182; inequality (economic), 171; inflation, fear of, 77, 93, 311n34; pay cuts, 121, 128, 316n3; during Popular Front, 182, 197; reparations payments, 77, 93; surplus, 8; tariff walls, 93; taxes, 121, 197; unemployment, 78, 92, 93, 171, 308n11. See also Depression; strikes
education, 9, 178
Ehrenburg, Ilya, 185, 203–204
Einstein, Albert, 109
Eliot, T. S., 136, 193
Eluard, Paul, 17, 76–77, 111, 117, 141, 161, 190, 191, 204, 260, 270, 291, 295, 297
Ernst, Max, 17, 76, 270, 276
expatriates, 5–6, 39, 54, 58, 221, 270

fascism, 110, 136, 144, 151, 155, 208, 210, 229, 232, 248, 281; resistance against, 113, 114, 124, 160, 179, 213, 248; support for, 111, 164, 206, 248. See also Germany; Hitler, Mussolini; Spanish Civil War
Fauré, Gabriel, 11
Faÿ, Bernard, 75, 135, 211, 285, 309n28
Fellowes, Daisy, 23, 44, 244
Fitzgerald, F. Scott, 26, 40, 72, 119; breakdown, 165–66; and Hemingway, 27–29, 73, 165–66, 212–13, 320n53; and Hollywood, 212, 217, 325n30; and Gertrude Stein, 29; Tender Is the Night, 27, 164–65
Fitzgerald, Zelda, 27, 29, 40, 73, 165, 212
Flanner, Janet, 40, 49, 64, 70, 95, 125, 130, 139, 228; on Czech crisis, 231; on Nazi-Soviet pact, 247; on Spanish refugees, 241–42
Ford, Ford Madox, 26–27, 29, 58
Ford, Hugh, 55
foreign affairs: Britain, visit of king and queen, 228; Czech crisis, 230–32, 241, 250–51; French nonaggression pact with Germany, 239; Italy (Mussolini), 138, 158, 272–73; Nazi-Soviet pact, 247; Rhineland (Hitler), 78–79, 172; Saar, 138–39, 158; Soviet Union (Stalin), 2, 92, 138, 158–59, 161, 182, 184. See also Germany; Hitler; Soviet Union; Spanish Civil War; war (World War II)
France: internal divisiveness, 172, 197, 198, 214, 223–24, 322n11; political instability, 93; population, 78–79, 171; surrender to Germany, 278–79; on war footing, 233. See also economy; foreign affairs
Franco-Prussian War, 243, 264, 328n8

Free French forces, 281, *282*, 284, 286, 290, 298

Freemasons: hostility toward, 96, 131, 170, 198; Vichy's anti-Masonic purge, 279, 285, 296

French Popular Party (PPF), 170, 206

French Social Party (PSF), 170, 178, 198–99

Freund, Gisèle, *4*, *106*, 193, 236, 271

Gabin, Jean, 188, 216, 230

Gallimard, Gaston, 32, 35, 81, 82, 137

Gamelin, Maurice, 267, 269, 292

Gellhorn, Martha, 151, 184, 203–4, 212, 213, 297

Germany, 2, 78, 110–11, 159; and Austrian Anschluss, 222, 224; Axis, 182; and Czechoslovakia, 228, 230–31, 241; French visitors to, 79, 108, 115, 123–24; *Graf Zeppelin*, 167, 321n61; Munich Agreement, 231–32, 242, 251; Nazism, 78, 108–9, 113–14, 115, 131, 261; Nazi-Soviet pact, 247; nonaggression pact with France, 239; Olympics (1936), 176–77; and Paris exposition, 202; rearmament of, 158; Rhineland, 78, 79, 172, 193–94, 202; Saar, 138–39, 158; and Spanish Civil War, 181, 197, 201; Sudetenland, 228; and World War II, 249, 256, 264, 266, 268–70, 272, 278–79. *See also* fascism; Hitler; Occupation (German)

Gide, André, 9, *31*, 56, 58, 75, 107, 109, 188; and Marc Allégret, 29–30, 32, 33; and Armistice (1940), 279; and Association of Revolutionary Writers and Artists, 114, 132; background of, 30, 32–33; and Bloody Tuesday, 133; and Léon Blum, 32; *Les Caves du Vatican*, 33, 112–13; and Communist party, 112–13, 160; and Czech crisis, 231; *Les Faux-Monnayeurs* (*The Counterfeiters*), 33; and Catherine Gide, 32–33, 184–85, 303n20; and Madeleine Gide, 30, 133, 228; *L'Immoraliste* (*The Immoralist*), 32; and James Joyce, 103; and Count Kessler, 218; and Malraux, 34, 114, 217; *Les Nouritures terrestres* (*Fruits of the Earth*), 32, 33; and Occupation, 284–85; and refugees, 109, 253; *Return from the U.S.S.R.*, 186; and Maria van Rysselberghe (the Petite Dame), 32, 184–85, 228, 303n20; and Shakespeare and Company, 193; *Si le grain ne meurt* (*If It Die*), 30, 32; and Soviet Union (U.S.S.R.), 111–12, 184–86, 323n6; and Stravinsky, 133–34; and war, 253, 272, 279; and Oscar Wilde, 32; and women, 69–70

Giraudoux, Jean, 256–58

Gorky, Maxim, 160, 185, 188, 323n17

Goudeket, Maurice, 49, 150

Great War. *See* World War I

Green, Julien, 79

Guggenheim, Peggy, 68, 270, 290

Hemingway, Ernest, 40, 53, 54, 55, 58, 72, 304n42; and Sherwood Anderson, 29, 59, 120–21; and Sylvia Beach, 5, 27, 104, 121, 193, 204, 236, 237, 297–98; and boxing, 27–28; and Communist party, 118; and John Dos Passos, 203; and Max Eastman, 119, 121, 212; *A Farewell to Arms*, 5, 27, 29, 73, 118; and fascism, 213; and Fitzgerald, 27–29, 73, 165–66, 212–13, 303n8, 320n53; and Martha Gellhorn, 151, 184, 203–4, 213, 297; and Pauline Hemingway, 27, 29, 40, 74, 121, 165, 213; and James Joyce, 60; and liberation of Paris, 297–98; and Archibald MacLeish, 119, 203; and

Robert McAlmon, 26; and Maxwell Perkins, 27, 28, 119, 120, 166, 184, 212; and Picasso, 212; and Gertrude Stein, 29, 59, 60, 120–21; and Spanish Civil War, 164, 184, 203–4, 212, 213; his style, 29; and success, 118–19; and Alice B. Toklas, 29, 59; his wives, 74

Hemingway, Hadley. *See* Mowrer, Hadley Richardson Hemingway

Hitler, 2, 92, 107, 108, 112, 125, 151, 161, 186; Armistice (1940), 278–79; Austrian Anschluss, 222, 224; Axis, 182; and Czechoslovakia, 228, 230–31, 241; Dollfuss assassination, 138; French views on, 81, 84–85, 93, 110–11, 115, 117, 123–24, 127, 135, 161, 202–3, 214, 223, 252; and Guernica, 201; Kristallnacht, 239; Munich Agreement, 232, 242, 251; Nazi-Soviet pact, 247; Night of the Long Knives, 138; Nuremberg rallies, 2, 115, 158, 202, 206; and Paris, 199, 200, 202–3; rearms Germany, 158; Reichstag fire, 107, 313n2; Sudetenland, 228; and symbols, 264; and World War II, 264, 265, 266, 278–79. *See also* Germany; Occupation (German); peace movement

Huddleston, Sisley, 40, 54

Hugo, Jean, 40–41

Hugo, Valentine, 77

L'Humanité, 12, 112, 301n20

Huxley, Aldous, 55, 217

Iribe, Paul, 94–95, 116–17, 139, 140, 156

Italy. *See* Mussolini

Jacob, Max, 34, 293, 294, 296, 333n19

Japan, 107, 108, 182, 274, 291

Jaurès, Jean, 11, 12, 179, 266

Jeanne d'Arc, Sainte, 224

Jeanneret, Pierre, 47, 48, 274, 295

Jeunesses Patriotes, 16, 95, 96, 129, 130, 161

Jolas, Eugene, 53–54, 67, 120, 236

Jolas, Maria, 288

Joliot-Curie, Frédéric, 66–67, 83, 132, 162, 186, 218, 232, 256, 329n45

Joliot-Curie, Irène, 65–67, 83, 131–32, 162, 186–87, 217–18, 232, 256, 329n45

Jouvenel, Bertrand de, 151, 184

Joyce, James, 40, 72, 321n57; and Sylvia Beach, 6–8, 70, 103–5, 122–23, 166–67, 193, 236–37, 308n17, 312n62, 312n67, 315n52; and Samuel Beckett, 211; and Czech crisis, 236; death of, 287, 288; his drinking, 192; escape to Switzerland, 288; eyesight problems, 6–7; *Finnegans Wake* (*Work in Progress*), 6–8, 53–54, 104, 211, 235–36, 260–61, 300n6; and Gisèle Freund, 236; and Gide, 103; Lucia Joyce, 166–67, 192, 211, 236, 253; living beyond his means, 7–8, 103, 105; marriage of, 70, 103, 308n15; and Munich Agreement, 236; and Ezra Pound, 123; and refugees, 235; and Spanish Civil War, 190, 211; and Gertrude Stein, 59, 60, 61, 103, 237; *Ulysses*, 6, 70, 103–5, 122–23, 166, 300n6, 308n17, 312n67, 315n51, 325n25; and war, 253, 260–61, 288; and Harriet Weaver, 70; and women, 70, 306n51

Joyce, Nora, 70, 103, 192–93, 253, 308n15

Kahane, Jack, 102, 103, 136

Kessler, Count Harry, 78, 108–9, 125, 147, 185, 218–19, 313n2

Kiki, 39, 52–53, 286

Lacoste, René, 177–78
Langevin, Paul, 66, 131, 132, 232, 308n5
La Rocque, François de, 95, 122, 130, 198–99
Laval, Pierre, 96, 159–60; background of, 159; and the economy, 158; and extreme-right leagues, 159; and Germany, 159; and Mussolini, 138, 158, 159; opposition to, 160; and Pétain, 242, 277–78, 279; and the Soviet Union, 158–59; and Vichy government, 279, 280, 281
Lawrence, D. H., 52, 54, 101, 306n27
Le Corbusier (Corbu): and the Académie des Beaux Arts, 116; American tour, 153–55; and Josephine Baker, 36; and Léon Blum, 205; and Cité de Refuge, 47–48, 100, 306n15; Depression, impact of, 47, 48–49; and Jean Giraudoux, 258; and Guernica, 201; and Marguerite Tjader Harris, 205; Legion of Honor, 205–6; and Mur des Fédérés, 176; and Paris city planning attempts, 99, 100; and Paris Exposition of Arts and Technology, 154–55, 205; and Charlotte Perriand, 48, 81, 97, 100, 154, 155, 274; and Soviet Union, 47, 116, 155; and Swiss Pavilion, 97, 98; and Vichy France, 294–95; and Villa Savoye, 46, 47, 306n10
Léger, Fernand, 75, 176, 202, 258, 270
Lenglen, Suzanne, 177, 228
Lifar, Sergei, 226
Louvre, Musée du, 15, 60, 250–52, 270

MacLeish, Archibald, 39, 119, 193, 203
Maginot Line, 2, 41, 85, 167, 194, 210, 258, 259, 263, 268
Maillol, Aristide, 75, 218
Mallet-Stevens, Robert, 46, 154

Malraux, André, 56, *106*, 107; and antiquities, 34–35, 81–82, 303n25; and Association of Revolutionary Writers and Artists, 132; background of, 33–35; and Communist party, 112–13, 132, 160; *La Condition humaine* (*Man's Fate*), 113; *Les Conquérants* (*The Conquerors*), 35; and de Gaulle, 291; *L'Espoir* (*Man's Hope*), 217; and Gide, 34, 114, 217; Goncourt Prize, 35, 113; joins Resistance, 291; marriage, 34, 114, 183; and Soviet Union, 160, 183–84; and Spanish Civil War, 183, 217; *Le Temps du mépris* (*Days of Wrath*), 160; *La Tentation de l'Occident* (*The Temptation of the West*), 35; travels, 34–35, 81–82; *La Voie royale* (*The Royal Way*), 35
Mandel, Georges, 291–92, 333n13
Man Ray, 23, 55, 142, 221; and Armistice, 279; *Le beau temps* (*Fair Weather*), 241; and Czech crisis, 231; and Marcel Duchamp, 141; and Ady Fidelin, 191, 204, 275; flees Paris and France, 275, 286, 288; in Hollywood, 288; *The Lips*, 142, 190; and Lee Miller, 87, 142, 191, 204; and Gertrude Stein, 59; and Surrealist exhibitions, 190, 227; and war, 241, 252, 260, 268, 275; on World War I, 263
Marais, Jean, 206–7, 255, 293
Martin du Gard, Roger, 182–83, 254
Matignon Agreements, 176, 178, 234
Matisse, Henri, 24, 120, 284, 288
Matisse, Pierre, 155–56, 284
Maurois, André, 193
Maurras, Charles, 12, 58, 78, 169, 170, 224, 292, 321n3
Maxwell, Elsa, 44
McAlmon, Robert, 26, 54, 67
Michelin, 50–51, 143, 163–64

Miller, Henry, 53, 101; background of, 70–73; and Wambly Bald, 73, 101; and Sylvia Beach, 103; *Black Spring*, 208; and Bloody Tuesday, 136; and Brassaï, 72, 100, 102, 208, 231; in California, 288; and Czech crisis, 231; and Dalí, 118, 314n35; and Lawrence Durrell, 208; and his family, 209; and Michael Fraenkel, 73, 101, 136; and June Miller, 71–73, 101–3, 136, 137, 309n20, 317n27; and Anaïs Nin, 101–2, 103, 136–37, 207–8, 231; and Richard Osborn, 73, 100–101; and Paris, 100, 312n50; and Alfred Perlès, 71, 72, 73, 101, 102, 136, 208; and Proust, 73, 101, 312n52; *Tropic of Cancer*, 73, 101, 102, 103, 136, 317n27; *Tropic of Capricorn*, 72, 137, 208, 317n27

Miller, Lee, 87, 142, 191, 204

Miró, Joan, 15, 16, 270

Mistinguett, 64

Monnier, Adrienne. *See* Beach, Sylvia

Montherlant, Henry de, 69

Moore, George, 55, 56

Morand, Paul, 26, 44, 45, 95, 117, 193, 314n33

Mowrer, Hadley Richardson Hemingway, 5, 27, 29, 74, 184

Mowrer, Paul, 184

Mugnier, Abbé (Arthur), 175, 223, 242–43, 261, 328n8, 329n60

Munich Agreement, 231–33, 236, 238, 239, 241, 242, 251

Mur des Fédérés, 175–76, 224

Murphy, Gerald and Sara, 40, 165

Mussolini, 2, 138, 172, 186, 244; Axis, 182; Ethiopian invasion, 158, 159, 161; French enthusiasm for, 129, 134, 152, 158, 159, 161, 223; Italy under, 2, 95, 115; joins Germany in war, 272; Spanish Civil War, 181, 182, 197

Natanson, Misia. *See* Sert, Misia Godebska Natanson Edwards

Natanson, Thadée, 11, 32, 301n23

nativism, 78, 257

Nazism. *See* fascism; Germany; Hitler

Nazi-Soviet Pact, 247, 251, 266

Nin, Anaïs, 101–2, 103, 118, 136–37, 207–8, 231

Noailles, Charles de, 40, 44, 76; *L'Age d'Or*, 16, 18, 77; *Un Chien Andalou*, 16, 18; *Le Sang d'un poète*, 77, 309n33

Noailles, Marie-Laure de, 40–41, 44, 76, 77; *L'Age d'Or*, 16, 18, 77; *Un Chien Andalou*, 16, 18; fleeing Paris, 275; *Le Sang d'un poète*, 77

S.S. *Normandie*, 148, 149–50, 151, 153, 319n2

La Nouvelle Revue Française (NRF), 32, 34, 35, 81, 209, 284–85

Occupation (German), 276–78, 283–97. *See also* Resistance

Olivier, Fernande, 59–60

Olympics (1936), 176–77, 178

Paris: bombing of, 270; city planning failure, 99, 100; cost of living in, 221; exodus from, 262, 271–77, 283–84, 286, 288, 290–91; and Jews, 270–71; liberation of, 297–98; population of, 99, 100; press, 127–28; riots, 198–99; round-up of German nationals, 270–71; and war, 252, 254, 259–60, 269; as working-class center, 171. *See also* Bloody Tuesday; Occupation (German); Paris Colonial Exposition; Paris Exposition of Arts and Technology in Modern Life; parties and balls; refugees

Paris Colonial Exposition, 63, 80, 83–84, 310n9

Paris Exposition of Arts and
Technology in Modern Life, 154–55,
199, *200*, 201–2
parties and balls, 44–45, 139, 204,
226–27, 244
Patou, Jean, 45, 87, 177, 277
Paul, Elliot, 130, 159, 167, 172, 202–3,
233, 249, 250
PCF (Parti Communiste Français). *See*
Communist party
peace movement (and pacifism),
92–93, 108, 125, 132, 161, 162,
172; assaults upon, 96. *See also* Cité
Internationale Universitaire de Paris
Perkins, Maxwell, 27, 28, 119, 120, 166,
184, 212
Perlès, Alfred, 71, 72, 73, 100, 101, 102,
136, 208
Perriand, Charlotte, 48, 81, 97, 100,
114, 154, 155, 174, 176, 247, 274,
275, 291, 295
Pétain, Philippe, 159–60, 212, 223,
269; as ambassador to Spain, 242;
and Armistice, 277–79; after
Austrian Anschluss, 223; after
Bloody Tuesday, 130; and trial of
Léon Blum, 292; and de Gaulle, 36,
84, 85, 146, 147, 194–95, 224–26,
242, 269, 272, 278; and Laval, 242,
277–78, 279; and Maginot Line, 85,
194–95; as prime minister, 278; and
Vichy France, 279, 280, 281, 283,
285, 292, 314n33
Picabia, Francis, 22, 23, 76, 270
Picabia, Gabrielle, 22–23
Picasso, Pablo, 75, 116, 190; and
Salvador Dalí, 15–16, 76; and fascism,
191–92; finances of, 24–25, 75; and
Fitzgerald, 212; *Guernica*, 192, 201–2,
204; and Hemingway, 212; and Dora
Maar, 191, 201, 204, 252; and the
Occupation, 295–96; and Fernande
Olivier, 59–60; and Olga Picasso, 60,
74, 192; and Popular Front, 179; and

Spanish Civil War, 191–92, 201–2;
and Gertrude Stein, 75, 211, 212; and
the Wall Street Crash, 24–25; and
Marie-Thérèse Walter, 74, 191, 252;
and war, 252
Poiret, Paul, 23, 45–46, 94
Polignac, Princesse Edmond de, 48, 100
Popular Front, 1, 158, 161, 163,
172; 1936 victories of, 172–73;
attacks on, 198; Catholic support
of, 174; and Clichy riots, 198–99;
economic woes during, 182, 197; and
education, 178; end of, 224, 233;
high point of, 178, 179; "pause," 182,
197; and rearmament, 194, 197, 198;
and Spanish Civil War, 182; and
strikes, 173–75, 199. *See also* Blum;
Matignon Agreements
Pound, Ezra, 54, 55, 56, 123, 164
PPF (Parti Populaire Français). *See*
French Popular party; Doriot, Jacques
PSF (Parti Social Français). *See* French
Social Party
Putnam, Samuel, 39–40, 53, 54, 101

Radical party, 9, 93, 127, 130, 173, 181,
198
Ravel, Maurice, 75, 143–45, 219,
318n53
refugees, 2, 108, 202, 235, 238–39, 253;
exodus from Paris, 262, 271–78;
fleeing France, 286, 288, 331n22;
German nationals, 249, 270–71;
Jewish, 108, 109, 131, 239, 270–71;
in Paris, 109, 237, 249, 255; Spanish,
180, 192, 213–14, 241–42
Renault, Louis, 164, 206; and André
Citroën, 50–51, 94, 143; and Hitler,
235; and postwar imprisonment, 294;
and strikes, *168*, 174, 175, 233–34;
and war, 234, 259, 270
Renault, Christine, 206, 294
Renoir, Jean: and his actors, 137,
317n29; background of, 88, 90,

311n20; *Les Bas-fonds*, 188; *La Bête humaine*, 220, 230, 246; and Bloody Tuesday, 137; *Boudu Saved from Drowning*, 91; *Madame Bovary*, 137; and Cézanne family, 273, 331n28; *La Chienne*, 89, 90–91; and Communist party, 137–38, 162–63, 187, 229–30, 247; *Le Crime de Monsieur Lange*, 163; *A Day in the Country*, 188, 323n16; exiting Paris and France, 273, 288; Jean Gabin, 188, 216, 230; and Germany, 123, 162–63; *La Grande Illusion*, 215, 246; in Hollywood, 288; and Marguerite Houllé, 92, 162, 247; in Italy, 247, 273; Legion of Honor, 215; *La Marseillaise*, 163, 216, 229; and Munich Agreement, 232–33; and Nazi-Soviet pact, 247; *La Nuit du carrefour*, 91; and Popular Front, 163, 215; *On purge bébé*, 90; and Alain Renoir, 215, 247, 273, 288, 290; and Andrée Heuschling Renoir (Catherine Hessling), 88, 90, 162, 311n27, 320n42; and Dido Freire Renoir, 247, 273, 288, 290; return to Paris, 289, 290; *The Rules of the Game*, 240, 245–47; and Michel Simon, 88, 90, 91; and Soviet Union, 163, 187; and Spanish Civil War, 215; and Erich von Stroheim, 215–16; *Toni*, 137–38, 139, 162–63, 187; and François Truffaut, 88, 90, 163; U.S. citizenship, 288; *La Vie est à nous*, 163, 187

Renoir, Pierre-Auguste, 88, 92, 187–88, 311n20, 323n16

Resistance, 283, 291–92, 294, 295, 297

La Revue blanche, 9, 32, 301n23

Reynaud, Paul, 167, 195, 210, 266–68, 269, 272, 275, 277–78, 333n13

Riefenstahl, Leni, 176–77, 178

Rosenberg, Paul, 24–25, 290, 295, 302n3

Rothschild family, 44, 244, 293, 333n18

Rubinstein, Helena, 49–50, 52, 193, 227

Rysselberghe, Maria van (the Petite Dame), 32, 184–85, 228, 253, 303n20

Salengro, Roger, 196, 198, 214

Sartre, Jean-Paul, 56, 166; and Austrian Anschluss, 222–23; background of, 36–37; and Simone de Beauvoir, 36–37, 39, 115, 166, 209, 260, 303n30, 304n37; in Berlin, 115; and literary success, 209, 238; and Munich Agreement, 232; *La Nausée*, 209; and Nazi-Soviet pact, 247–48; and politics, 114–15; and Spanish Civil war, 209; taken prisoner, 296; and war, 247–50, 260, 263–64, 296, 330n3, 331n26; and women, 304n35

Schiaparelli, Elsa, 20, 87, 177; background of, 21–24; and Chanel, 139–140, 156–57, 189; Circus Collection, 226–27; and Jean Cocteau, 21, 157; and Salvador Dalí, 21, 157, 190; flees Paris and France, 277, 286; and Hollywood, 86, 189; in Moscow, 188–89; and Mussolini, 244; and Paris exposition, 199, 201; and Paris's Last Grand Season, 244; success of, 139–140; and Surrealism, 24, 226; and war, 255–56, 264, 277; and her workers, 175

Schiaparelli, Maria Luisa (Gogo), 22, 23, 140, 189–90, 244, 255–56, 277

Sert, José-Maria, 156, 294

Sert, Misia Godebska Natanson Edwards, 11, 86, 94, 134, 147, 156, 294, 301n23

SFIO (Section Française de l'Internationale Ouvrière). *See* Socialist party

Shakespeare and Company. *See* Beach, Sylvia

Simenon, Georges, 91, 305n2
Sitwell, Edith, 55, 103
social insurance, 9, 69, 300n15, 308n11
Socialist party (SFIO), *126*; background of, 11–12; and Bloody Tuesday, 131; and coalition governments, 9, 12–13, 93, 110, 173; and Communist party, 11–12, 93, 173, 233; and Munich Agreement, 233; and pacifism, 93, 125; and Popular Front, 160, 173; splits within, 12, 110; and World War I, 12. *See also* Blum, Léon
Solidarité Française, 95, 122, 129, 130, 161
Soviet Union (U.S.S.R.), 2, 111, 158, 172, 214, 223, 232; Franco-Soviet pact, 138, 158–59, 161; French visitors to, 81, 87–88, 111, 160, 185–89; and intellectuals, 111–14, 116, 132, 160–61, 248; Nazi-Soviet pact, 247–48, 266; and Paris exposition, 202. *See also* Stalin
Spain, 242. *See also* Spanish Civil War
Spanish Civil War, 2, 179, 250; background of, 181–82; Blum and, 181, 182; Britain and, 182; Franco and, 181–82, 203; 213, 241; French response to, 181, 210–11; Germany and, 181, 197, 201; Guernica, 201; Hemingway and, 164, 184, 203–4, 212, 213; Italy and, 181, 182, 197; Loyalists, division among, 213; Malraux and, 183, 217; outcome of, 241–42; Picasso and, 191–92, 201–2; refugees, *180*, 192, 213–14, 241–42; Soviet Union and, 182, 197, 213
Spender, Stephen, 193, 204, 210
Stalin, 2, 92, 111, 116, 158–59, 160, 161, 182, 184, 185, 197, 247, 248. *See also* Soviet Union
Stavisky Affair, 114, 125, 127–30, 132, 135, 136, 137, 139. *See also* Bloody Tuesday

Stein, Gertrude, 54; and America, 135, 211, 252, 285; and Sherwood Anderson, 29, 59, 120–21; and Armistice, 285; *Autobiography of Alice B. Toklas*, 60, 75, 119–20, 122, 135; and Sylvia Beach, 60–61, 122, 237–38; Bilignin residence, 74–75, 285; and Bloody Tuesday, 135; and Bernard Faÿ, 75, 135, 211, 285, 309n28; finances of, 75; and Fitzgerald, 29; *Four Saints in Three Acts*, 75, 135; and Hemingway, 29, 59, 60, 120–21; and Hitler, 135, 252; and James Joyce, 59, 60–61, 237; and Man Ray, 59; move from 27 Rue de Fleurus, 211; and Occupation, 285; and Fernande Olivier, 59–60; and Pétain, 212, 285; and Picasso, 75, 211, 212; politics of, 211–212, 285; her salon, 29, 58–59, 72; and self-publication, 75; and Edith Sitwell, 103; and Virgil Thomson, 75, 135; and Alice B. Toklas, 28–29, 58, 59, 61, 74, 103, 211, 237, 252–53, 285; and war, 252–53
Stein, Leo, 120
Stravinsky, Igor: and anti-Semitism, 134, 229; and Bloody Tuesday, 134; and Chanel, 134; deaths in family, 229; and Disney, 229; and Germany, 134, 229; and Gide, 133–34; in Hollywood, 288; income of, 25, 75, 134, 229; and Mussolini, 134, 229; *Symphony of Psalms*, 79; and war, 254
strikes. *See* Bloody Tuesday; Matignon Agreements; Popular Front; workers
Surrealism and Surrealists, 2, 13; Louis Aragon, 35, 78, 111; André Breton, 13, 16, 35, 76, 77–78, 111, 156, 190, 227, 290; and Communist party, 13, 78, 111; Salvador Dalí, 16, 76, 156, 190, 227, 301n31; London exhibition, 190; New York

exhibition, 190; Paris exhibition, 227; and Schiaparelli, 24, 226

Taittinger, Pierre, 95
Tardieu, André, 8, 9
Tate, Allen, 29, 54
Third Republic, 93, 129, 265–66, 279, 281, 330n7
Thomson, Virgil, 75, 135, 270, 286, 288
Titus, Edward, 49, 52–53, 54, 193; and *This Quarter*, 53, 54, 87
Toklas, Alice B., 28–29, 58–59, 61, 74, 103, 211, 237, 252–53, 285
transition, 8, 53–54, 58, 61, 67, 120, 130
Tzara, Tristan, 23, 210

Vail, Laurence, 68, 270
Valéry, Paul, 9, 58, 82, 133, 160, 193
Vichy France government, 279, 280, 281, 283, 285, 290, 293, 294, 295, 297; abolition of labor unions, 110, 279; anti-Jewish laws, 257, 279, 281, 295, 296, 297, 314n33; bans Freemasons, 279; internment camps, 280; trial and imprisonment of Léon Blum, 292–93. *See also* Laval; Pétain
Vlaminck, Maurice de, 295, 333n27

Wall Street Crash, 5, 8, 25, 47, 65; impact on art market, 24, 40, 49; impact on France, 8, 24, 39–40; impact on world of fashion, 24. *See also* economy
war (World War II): declaration of, 249, 250–61; exodus from Paris, 262, 271–77, 283–84, 286, 288, 290–91; fall of France and Armistice, 278–79; German invasion, 268, 269, 270; military service, 161; phony war, 259–60, 263–64; portents of, 79, 84–85,

146, 159, 161, 172, 197, 201, 221, 223, 228, 230–31, 233, 236, 241, 249. *See also* Occupation (German)
Weil, Simone, 224, 233
Williams, William Carlos, 55, 67
Wolfe, Elsie de (Lady Charles Mendl), 45, 226, 244, 256
women: and abortion, 68, 69; during the Depression, 157–58; and family allowances, 68–69, 234; French feminist movement, 69, 92, 162, 187; misogyny, 69, 71; and social insurance, 9, 69, 300n15; and the vote, 37, 69, 157–58; in the workplace, 2, 92, 157–58
workers: foreign-born, 2, 78; forty-hour week, 176, 178, 233, 242, 267; housing conditions, 171; mass production, 51–52, 85, 171; mortality and illness of, 171; paramilitary leagues, dissolution of, 178, 198; in Paris, 171; and pay cuts, 121; protests, 121; reforms suppressed, 224; and social insurance, 9, 68–69, 182, 197, 300n15, 308n11; strikes, 51, 108, 126, 129–30, 131, 139, 158, 168, 173–75, 176, 182, 199, 214, 222, 233–34; unemployment, 9, 78, 92, 93, 111, 157, 171, 214, 222, 308n11; vacations, 176, 178, 244. *See also* Matignon Agreements; Popular Front; women
World War I (Great War), 5, 9, 11–12, 13, 88, 92, 124, 222, 223, 232, 248, 253, 256; and French population, 2, 9, 68, 78; French victory, 2, 243, 263, 264
World War II. *See* war (World War II)

Zola, Emile, 11, 230, 243

~

About the Author

Mary McAuliffe holds a PhD in history from the University of Maryland, has taught at several universities, and has lectured at the Smithsonian Institution. She has traveled extensively in France, and for many years she was a regular contributor to *Paris Notes*. Her books include *Paris Discovered, Dawn of the Belle Epoque, Twilight of the Belle Epoque, When Paris Sizzled*, and *Clash of Crowns*. She lives in New York City with her husband, and she shares insights on Paris on her weekly photo blog (see www.ParisMSM.com).